INDIA AND THE UNITED STATES

INDIA AND THE UNITED STATES

From Estrangement to Engagement

NAROTTAM GAAN

PUBLICATIONS

KALPAZ PUBLICATIONS

DELHI-110052

India and the United States : From Estrangement to Engagement

Rs. 790

ISBN: 81-7835-595-7

Published in 2007 in India by
Kalpaz Publications
C-30, Satyawati Nagar,
Delhi-110052
Phone : 9112729499
E-mail: kalpaz@hotmail.com

Lasser Type Setting by: Rudra Computer Graphics, Delhi
Printed at : Salasar Imaging System, Delhi

Dedicated To:

The Memory of My Beloved Gurudev
on His Birth Centenary

A Divine Dew Drop Shining Radiantly in every page
by the Light of Thy Wisdom

Contents

Foreword

This book addresses one of the favourite themes in India's foreign policy: the nature of the relations between India and the USA and their likely evolution in the coming years.

Ever since 1947, when India became independent, many statesmen and public figures in both nations have advocated and hoped for a partnership of the "world's largest democracy with the oldest" but so far they have had reasons to be disappointed by the generally lukewarm attitudes that their political establishments have shown towards each other, despite occasional expressions of mutual sympathy and moments of official cordiality. A historical analysis of the circumstances that account for the persistent tendency to diverge or take opposite sides on a variety of issues is hence in order and Professor Gaan undertakes to locate the bones of contention that lie at the heart of the long-standing disagreement.

American foreign policy-makers and scholars rarely fail to point out that the disproportion between the wealth, military power and political influence of the two countries is such that an equal relationship is impossible. Since the second world war the USA has not needed nor really been able to maintain a rapport based on equality with any other country, diplomatic protocol notwithstanding, since Washington's imperial preponderance resulted in it treating all other states as vassals or rebels that it could brand as outlaws. Even the lone exception, the Soviet Union was regarded as geopolitical anomaly which had to be eventually brought to heel or destroyed. The USSR's downfall in 1989 left the US with no credible rival and only in the last few years has the rise of China forced the increasingly dysfunctional superpower to grudgingly show some respect to that emerging colossus which it helped build up.

India is not yet in China's league in terms of industrial and economic clout but its fast growth and increasing self-confidence has led to a considerable change in the American attitude toward a state that it can no longer afford to ignore and which it finds more difficult to patronize. The desire to find a potential match for China impels Washington to flatter the country by acknowledging its legitimate aspirations to be recognized as one of the world's largest, most ancient and now most powerful nations. If, according to projections from Goldman Sachs quoted by James Wolfensohn, the former Chairman of the World Bank (AFP, November 26th, 2006) China's GDP is expected to exceed 48 trillion in US Dollar value by 2050, well over the USA's anticipated 37 trillion USD GDP, India's economy is likely to rise to 27 trillion on that same year, putting it in third place worldwide. Thus, while Asia rises, the USA is on the decline and the inequalities are thus gradually decreasing.

The self-centered interest of the United States towards India is proving to be both a motive of satisfaction and a cause of worry for the rulers and for many of the citizens of the South Asian giant. The main reason for this ambivalence is that that any political favours from the "only superpower" come with strings attached while many profound and essential disagreements remain unresolved. Narottam Gaan warns that the new honeymoon between Washington and New Delhi is likely to be ephemeral. The US, he notes, remains committed to its long-standing policy of containing India strategically with the help of Pakistan, Bangladesh and possibly China, even while it seeks to make the most out of the rapid expansion of the Indian economy for the benefit of its own business interests. A well known example of this policy of "engagement for gaining control" is provided by the Indo-US nuclear treaty being negotiated between the two countries, whereby Washington intends to bring the independent Indian dual civil-military atomic research programme under some sort of supervision as a part of the "strategic alliance" it seeks to form with New Delhi.

Superficial observations based on received wisdom tend to prove misleading. Thus the oft repeated assertion that India and the USA are brought together by their common commitment to democracy is belied by an analysis of the many differences between their respective notions of democracy.. The American republican form of government is rooted in Locke's liberal utilitarianism which in its day served the causes of Anglo-Saxon imperial conquest and exploitation by providing economic and moral justifications for the colonisation of India and of other lands, just it was lately invoked to rationalize the occupation of Afghanistan and Iraq. On the other hand India's practice of democracy needs to accommodate a millenary, multi-communal, diverse and deeply religious civilization which can only survive through compromise between several heterogeneous traditions and ways of life. For one, while officially denouncing it without always moderating its harmful effects, the modern Indian political dispensation in fact has assimilated and adapted to many features of the caste system whose social compartmentalization actually makes more room for diversity than the more uniform social models found in the West, as various social scientists have acknowledged.

The age-old South Asian socio-political construct stands poles apart - just as India and the USA are at the geographic antipodes - from the essentially mono-cultural, aggressively uniformizing and "domesticising" model promoted in the USA and based on the "American Creed", which Samuel Huntington defines as secular "Christianity without Christ". Indeed America aims to evangelize the world and thus remake it into its own image. There is an unmistakable streak of messianic monotheism in American democracy, despite its superficial claims about universalism and pluralism. The puritanical worship of the Torah's "Jealous and Vengeful Lord of the Hosts" commands its votaries to save mankind or at least make it more free and prosperous, by force if necessary. As a result, the USA constantly waves the banner of democracy - equated with the Stars and Stripes - in order to penetrate and dominate other countries and cultures. For more than a century, America has defined democracy according to its own historical experience and it has largely succeeded in setting the rules for the rest of mankind just as it has imposed the US Dollar as the global reserve currency, based solely on its government's "full faith and credit" even though the Federal Reserve Bank is in fact a private corporation.

The French journalist Jacques Sapir has, in a recent article on the daily "Le Figaro" well described the American national character as the collective attitude of individualistic, uprooted and isolated newcomers moving across a seemingly boundless continent whose resources and promises appeared never-ending. The resulting philosophy of life and government inherited by most Americans is mostly unrelated and unsuited to the management of problems in a crowded, ancient and poor country such as India and furthermore, it is quite inappropriate for a shrinking, over-exploited and overpopulated planet facing ecological collapse.

One consequence of the widening "disconnect" between the US socio-economic and political regime and the real, concrete survival requirements of mankind at large is the increasingly visible and tragic estrangement of America's leadership from the large majority of the world's citizens. As Prof. Jan Pieterse from the University of (World Affairs, Vol. 8, No. 2, April-June 2004) puts it the USA, far from being a beacon of freedom, has turned into a "global warlord" spending in fiscal year 2007 more than seven hundred billion Dollars a year (i.e. 60% of the world's total) on its defence budget and on its various military adventures and imperial endeavours. He wryly notes "war is not the answer to the world's problems, but five per cent of the world population that spends (so much) of world military spending probably has no other answers to give" (ibid. p. 143).

The relevance and the sustainability of the American way of life and political system must therefore be severely questioned because the "drone of the world's wealthiest, richest, most powerful country in fact refers to the world's and history's largest debtor nation with unsustainable levels of debt" (ibid. p. 143). The implications of that ominous situation is that any close ally or partner is likely to be contaminated by the terminally ill superpower, especially if it is an emerging country such as India whose economy is undergoing the pressures of globalisation while its social fabric is strained by its traumatic transformation. Thus there is a good reason to be suspicious of Washington's desire to forge close ties at a time when the eclipse of US economic dominance is leading to the loss of its political influence.

The American writer Dan Elpenor writes in "Father Richard's Choice": 'America withers in the new Imperium; debt, usury, materialism, pornography and drug addiction, soaring rates of divorce and abortion, violence, perpetual war, mass media that beggars description for its vulgarity and inanity, corporate and political corruption and crime, burgeoning privatized prisons, dumbed down schools, a cynical youth culture and epidemic isolation and anomie" and he concludes with the withering observation that "with the recent military commissions act, the American Republic founded to secure rights and prohibit arbitrary power and violence has ended with barely a whimper".

Many facts lead an objective observer to the conclusion that the USA has reached a stage of terminal decay as a country and as a society and that it may sooner or later be going through a violent catharsis like its nineteenth century Civil War if it is to renew itself in order to survive.

If that is indeed the shape of things to come, there is little that India can gain from edging closer to the ailing colossus especially if it is at the cost of compromising with its traditional domestic and foreign policy principles, in many ways quite contrary to America's Manichean instincts. The fact that both countries tend to behave as 'apostles of righteousness" and are exceptionist powers does not lead to a natural convergence between India's traditional preference for non-alignment and peaceful resolution of disputes through negotiations and the USA's proclivity for the use of threats and overwhelming force. As a nation that was colonised for centuries, India is naturally suspicious of imperial powers and the transformation of the American Republic from a rebel colony, then chastised as such by Samuel Johnson, the "conscience" of the XVIIIth British elite, into the very bastion of a global system founded on Western supremacy makes any real, long-term association with it problematic. That political incompatibility does not necessarily affect the fruitful exchanges that are taking place between the respective civil societies, through the large and affluent Indian diaspora in America on the one hand and though the influence of Indian spiritual and scientific traditions on what is now described in the US as "Karma Capitalism".

Whether the raw dynamism, the famed "can do" attitude of the Americans can combine well with the values and the age-old knowledge disciplines of South Asia to build a new, prosperous and well managed India remains to be seen because the brash aggressiveness and the uninhibited consumerism inherent to the American way of life do not necessarily make a good match with the South Asian fatalistic, tradition-oriented philosophy of "live and let live". A skeptic might see more potential for confusion than for fusion in that marriage of East and West but an optimist would hope that India can teach America the virtue of the hoary Hindu and Buddhist middle path, the "Madhyama Pratipad", for both private life and public policy. In any case, by tradition and by instinct India wishes for and feels at home in a diverse, multi-polar open world in which it can be one of the independent great powers. The United States could learn from India to live in such a new global system by shedding its pretensions to planetary hegemony and abandoning its attempts to define an "American century" by its own rules. If the US establishment does not steer the country towards a "New Deal", for peaceful coexistence with other countries and planetary ecological restoration, there is a strong possibility that it will be remembered by the late American essayist Hunter Thompson's scathing indictment: "We have become a Nazi monster in the eyes of the whole world - a nation of bullies...who would rather kill than live peacefully. We are not just whores for power and oil, but killer whores with hate and fear in our hearts. We are human scum, and that is how history will judge us".

Come Carpentier de Gourdon
Secretary General of the Tissot Economic Foundation in Switzerland; Member of the Global Commission to finance the United Nations;
Advisor of the Nuclear Disarmament Forum,
Zug, Switzerland, Convener, World Affairs,
Kapur Surya Foundation, New Delhi

Preface

" We who are free- and who prize our freedom above all other gifts of God and nature- must know each other better; trust each other more; support each other." These sonorous words uttered by Dwight Eisenhower in Delhi in1959 with profound implications to dent into the estranged Indo-U.S. relations, could not be able to penetrate into the cold war miasma, which shrouded their vision and outlook, nearly took forty five years to find renewed resonance in their relations when the present American President Bush calls India a natural partner of the United States. It was a historical baffling and irksome to hold that the two countries being the largest democracies, could not become firmer friends. The phase of Indo-US relation during the cold war is as flummoxing as foggy while confining it to the intricate yet proverbial syndrome whether "egg is first or hen is first." The question stays whether it was Nehru's Fabian upbringing in England during his college days and impeccable socialistic credentials and inclination to Soviet Union" socialistic and state controlled economy as the key to resolving India's premier problems of poverty, which remained important causal considerations in American policy making to sideline India. From American point of view, Nehru's defining India's foreign policy in terms of its greatness of civilization, independence and sovereignty and non-alignment, and seeking a major status at par with great powers in the international realm but in disproportionate to its military and economic power appeared to be too ambitious, unaccommodating and vast to fit into American strategic Procrustean bed. At other end of the spectrum, America's seeing India and comprehending its conflict with Pakistan through British imperialistic eyes stands equally important to India to lean toward

Soviet Union. There is also sense in American allegation that most of the members of NAM including India being former colonies under British imperialism and moved by the socialistic and state owned economy as a panacea, were naturally inclined to put the blame for their socio-economic ills on their western colonial masters. What agonized U.S. is the vitriolic lecture of these NAM countries under India to it about cold war while turning a blind eye to Russian and Chinese imperial activities, both at home and abroad. Equally sensitive India was to the lukewarm military support America extended to India with some mere spare parts in its war with China. Sparing India from the humiliation it suffered from China in 1962 war could have stalled India's slide into the Communist camp. When Nehru and Mahatma Gandhi were castigated as imperialistic lackeys, Washington did nothing to woo India into its orbit of friendship. The age old proverbial puzzle "egg is first or hen is first" remains unresolved as yet the unanswered question whether India's preference for socialistic pattern of development, Nehru's Fabian credentials and non-aligned foreign policy and its unwillingness to go hammer and tongs with America or America's primacy to cold war strategy over all other objective considerations, domestic imperatives and problem of fitting a vast and independent India always harping on a major status in world forum along with great powers on the basis of its glorified civilization, is the cause. But the fact remains that their relationship was strained, acrimonious and estranged full of distrust and misperception during the cold war. The battle line was clearly drawn when Pakistan joined the American camp for its own reasons of settling its scores with its adversary India, and India slipped gradually into Soviet camp.

The holistic path chiseled by visionary Nehru, was ultimately cemented by his successor and daughter Indira Gandhi when all her moves were susceptible to leading to Russia. Nowhere this battle line was so clearly visible than in 1971 Bangladesh war when American militarily and economically strengthened Pakistan stood against India militarily propped up by Soviet Union. The last opportunity to settle Kashmir imbroglio by invading West Pakistan and releasing Pak occupied Kashmir from Pakistan hands was lost by her in 1971 when she declared unilateral ceasefire and conceded more than what is due to Pakistan's Bhutto in Shimla agreement.. The question whether it was America's seventh fleet or Soviet pressure that halted India's move intrigues many but what inexcusably rankles the mind of the Indian people exacerbating the crisis is the very fact that India ineptly exhibited its incapability again as Nehru did in 1948 by calling ceasefire to its war with Pakistan at the behest of U.S. dominated United Nations. Freeing herself from the visionary and idealistic moorings of her father, she strived to define India's foreign policy in terms of tangible power, which ultimately led her to detonate nuclear explosion for peaceful purposes in 1974. During these periods as found from American policy toward India, U.S. was trying to clip the wings of India so that it would not fly high detrimental to American interests and that of Pakistan as well.

When Rajiv Gandhi assumed leadership in 1984, America could hear the first fluttering of a new fledgling in India's foreign policy and economic development. In economic front, Rajiv Gandhi attempted some liberalization measures, aimed mainly at increasing efficiency in the private sector, and rectifying the bloated public sector. In foreign policy, during the mid-1980s India was virtually stuck in diplomatic isolation. Russia had become bogged down in Afghanistan and could no longer be counted on for economic and military support. Starting in 1985 under Gorbachev, the Soviets eased tensions with the Chinese. In as much as the Soviets had supported India principally to irritate China, Soviet interest in India was fading fast. Rajiv attempted to rejuvenate Delhi's relationship with the U.S., making his official trip to the US in 1985 and another in 1987. In the 1991 elections, a new, but minority, Congress party coalition came to power under the leadership of Prime Minister P.V. Narsimha Rao. The collapse of Soviet Union and a decade of success in China under its market reforms were not lost on this Rao government. In the 1990s, India-US relations witnessed a sea change with the demise of Soviet Union- India's main trading partner and most reliable source of economic and military assistance for most of the cold war-and New Delhi's resulting imperative to diversify its international relationships. Also significant were India's adoption of ramifying economic policy reforms beginning in1991, an exacerbating bitterness between India and Pakistan over Kashmir, and signs of a growing Indian preoccupation with China as a potential long term strategic rival. With the fading of cold war constraints, the United

States and India began exploring the possibilities for a more normalized relationship between the world's two largest democracies. However, the end of cold war unburdened India-U.S. relations from the constraints of infested global bipolarity, but interactions continued for a decade to be affected by the distrust of history, most notably the long standing India- Pakistan rivalry and nuclear weapons proliferation in the region.

During this period what was an irritant in Indo-U.S. relations was American calculated reticence on China's clandestine help to Pakistan to become a nuclear power, where as Washington was very much pronounced in its criticisms of India for its nuclear programme even for peaceful purposes. American double standard in nuclear proliferation in South Asia, and its dubbing Pakistan's sponsored terrorism in Kashmir as independence movement, and not accepting Kashmir, as part of India in tune with Pakistan's diplomatic note could not help improve their relations rather bedevil their bilateral relations. A perusal of the following chapters would certainly unearth many of the hidden underpinnings behind Indo-U.S. relations.

In May 1998, both India and Pakistan conducted nuclear tests inviting proliferation related restrictions and sanctions from U.S. later on lifted through congressional-executive cooperation from 1998 to 2000. These nuclear tests were an unwelcome surprise and seen to be a policy failure in Washington. America's militarily and economically strengthening Pakistan on the plea that this would reinforce its leverage in Pakistan did not deter it from producing nuclear weapons clandestinely with the active connivance of China, a signatory to NPT, and treating both India and Pakistan, the victim and the culprit respectively on parity were not lost on Indian leadership. Washington failure to be sensitive to New Delhi's perception of security threats emanating from both nuclear China and Pakistan estranged them from each other.

In the wake of this nuclear crisis, the engagement of the then Deputy Secretary of State Strobe Talbott with Indian foreign Minister Jaswant Singh fourteen times in seven different countries over a two-year period on a broader scope of Indo-U.S relations could be considered the most extensive engagement to bring New Delhi in line with U.S. arms control and non proliferation goals, and enabled circumstances in which the United States could play a key role in defusing the 1999 Kargil crisis, as well as laying the groundwork for a land mark US presidential visit in 2000.

President Clinton's March 2000 visit to South Asia seemed a major U.S. initiative to improve relations with India. A US – India Joint Working group on Counterterrorism was established in 2000 and continues to meet regularly. Later that year Indian Prime Minister Atal Bihari Vajpayee paid a visit to America and addressed a joint session of Congress and issued a joint statement with President Clinton agreeing to cooperate on arms control, terrorism and HIV/AIDS. The September 2001 terrorist attacks on the United States marked a change in American approach to terrorism. America recognized India's line of argument that Pakistan sponsored terrorism in Kashmir is a part of the entire web of global terrorism and cannot be treated in isolation or in the context of American cold war understanding of Indo-Pak conflict. But in practice, both India and America differed on Pakistan's role in countering terrorism. While Pakistan continues terrorist attacks in various places of India through its agents and terrorist groups, American is feigning ignorance and patting on the back of President Musharraf for his commendable support to America in countering terrorism. The very hope that US will fight Pakistan sponsored terrorism in Kashmir was belied and strikes a dissordant note in their relations. In the wake of this September 11 /2001 incident, India took the immediate and unprecedented step of offering to the United States full cooperation and the use of India's bases for counterterrorism operations. Engagement was accelerated after a November 2001 meeting between President Bush ; and Indian Prime Minister Vajpayee, when the two leaders agreed to greatly expand U.S.- India cooperation on a wide range of issues, including regional security, space and scientific collaboration, civilian nuclear safety, and broadened economic ties. Remarkable progress reached in the area of security cooperation, with an increasing focus on counterterrorism, joint military exercises, and arms sales. In late 2001 U.S.- India Defense Policy Group met in New Delhi for the first time since India's 1998 nuclear tests and outlined a defense partnership based on regular and high-level policy dialogue. President Bush's 2002 National Security Strategy of the United States stated, "US interests require a strong partnership with India." Bush administration's major first term diplomatic achievements culminated in Next Steps in Strategic partnership (NSSP), which was announced in January 2004 after months of negotiation drawing its inspiration from the Bush-Vajpayee joint statement of November 2001. In pursuant to this, Prime Minister Manmohan Singh paid a landmark visit to Washington in July 2005 reciprocated by President Bush in March 2006. The result of this path breaking diplomatic activity was signing of an agreement on full civilian nuclear energy cooperation between the two countries with Bush avowing to help India become a major world power in the 21st century. As a reversal of three decades of U.S. non-proliferation policy, such proposed cooperation is controversial and requires changes in both U.S. law and international guidelines. There has been a spurt of debates over the nuclear issue in India and abroad exacting divergent views from a host of sources starting from the nuclear scientists, and politicians to statesmen and the journalists this has been vividly analyzed in this book. The considered and dominant view doing the round is that nuclear cooperation between India and U.S. would clip the wings of India. For many in India, "non-alignment" is a synonym for independence, and should not be sacrificed however enticing the prize may be. Closing the Indian option of nuclear testing in case Pakistan and China test nuclear weapons would be another U.S. attempt at containing Indian power by further sucking it in the quagmire of new conditionalities. The bills in the House of Representatives and in the Senate finally enacted into a law recently incorporating new conditionalities not envisaged in the nuclear agreement stand a witness to the contour and content of the dialogue that will bind the two countries in their efforts to define their partnership.

Narottam Gaan

Acknowledgements

Another long intellectual journey commenced from the day I conceived of inking a book on Indo- US relation taking not only my own ideas but also ideas and facts from various conferences and seminars abroad and in India I attended, imbibing new thinking, approaches and views from scholars I met, and from books I rummaged through, getting articles, and papers published in various journals of international repute, and reached its logical conclusion when all these variant strands of ideas seeped through my in-depth analytical acumen and rigour of scientific scrutiny to be blended nicely into a synthesized and pithy tapestry. But for the help and cooperation from others it could not have been possible to bring out this book in the present form. My unbounded thanks and gratitude flow from the core of my heart to a galaxy of scholars to name a few like Come Carpentier De Gourdon, Dr. Arthur H. Westing, Dr. Thomas F Homer Dixon of Toronto University, Dr. Richard A Matthew of California University, George Perkovich, Ashley J.Tellis, Sumit Ganguly, Johan Galtung, John Perkins, Mohan Raja , and Stephen Cohen who have played a key role in shaping my views and vision about the multidimensional aspects of Indo- US relations from different perspectives. From the abyss of my heart I always convey my sense of gratification to a host of erudite scholars for the materials, articles and books they have provided me without exhibiting even a shred of evidence of their being hesitant. I will fail in my duty if I do not give my heart rendering thanks to the authorities of European University Center for Peace Studies, (EPU), Stadtschlaining, Austria and the Austrian Government for having privileged me with a much coveted scholarship to go to Austria and Hungary and to have higher studies on International Relation. This helped me a lot come in contact with a number of great scholars like Arthur H. Westing, Gunther Bachler and Galtung whom I consider as yet the very prominent authorities to have provided me different perspectives to my work. I also thank the authorities of Jawaharlal Nehru University Library, Indian Council of World Affairs, Teenmurti Library, United Nations Library and American Centre for having allowed me to work and collect materials.

My words are inadequate to express my humble gratitude and indebtedness to Prof. Mahendra Prasad Lama, Chair person, South Asian Studies, School of International Studies, Jawaharlal Nehru University, Prof, Annpurna Nautiyal of HNB University, Garhwal, Srinagar, my teachers Dr. Benudhar Pradhan, Director, Gandhian Institute for Peace Research and Action, and Dr. Asha Hans, former Professor in Political Science, Utkal University, Vanivihar, and S. N. Girish, I.A.S, a man of honesty, exemplary probity and humanist, and my friend Kailash for their inspiration, kind help and choicest good wishes kept in store for me . My joys knew no bounds to proffer my humble indebtedness to Come Corpentier De Gourdon who without a smack of hesitance acquiesced in my request to write a foreword to my book.

I always feel a paucity of words to express my deepest sense of gratitude to my affectionate Mahesh and Sitakanta, two prominent alumni of JNU, New Delhi who have played a very significant role in providing me materials ungrudgingly as and when I needed. Dr. Amarendra Mishra, a very promising scholar in international politics, a product of JNU who always keeps me in high esteem and inspires me in my work deserves my thankfulness and gratitude from the inner realm of my heart. Over and above, I always keep my ardent critics in high esteem, for it is they who through their stridency of attack, inspire me to ascend to the higher altitudes of learning.

I am extremely grateful to my parents, my life partner Reena in our eternal journey, and my two loving beautiful flowers Tattwamasi and Yogeswar who have always spurred me inspiringly to the ethos of trailblazing and emerging shining, and withstand difficulties in the preparation of the book. My eldest son Tattwamasi deserves all credit and exacts my love and blessings for having computerized the entire work to my utmost satisfaction. Behind all these and the sole doer, but for who it is not possible to write such a book is Paramhamsa

Prajnanananda and my Gurudev Paramhamsa Hariharananda. I deem it a God given privilege to sing in paeans of their Beatific Bliss and Glory in this humble work, which I consecrate at their Lotus Feet.

1

Foundation of Indian and American Foreign Policy: Divergent Paradigms

The irony is at its grandeur when one thinks that two countries India and the United States being the largest democracies in both East and West respectively, could not be able to find in that democracy, a commonality and connectivity to weave together all divergent and similar strands into a nice tapestry of enduring friendship and goodwill during all these years. While India was an inchoate, and nascent democracy just starting from a scratch on a western paradigm leaving aside all its crusted cultural specificity and significance formed by centuries of experience and achievement amidst a pluralistic society, America was by then a fully matured, consummate and quite experienced democracy built on its home spun political, liberal and market economy, and was on a missionary crusade quite emblematic of effete colonial days to externalize its domestic imperatives of providing an inordinate consumption and extravagant life style to its people on exorbitant production of wealth at the cost of both nature and other countries in South, as to be the foundation of other people's political and economic edifice both differed in what fundamentally defines democracy in its rhetoric, content and contour. Just arising afresh from the tumultuous travail and tribulation of an independence struggle against British imperialism on Gandhian principles of non-violence, truth, rights, and unencumbered self rule- nonpareil and inspiringly showing beacon to all other freedom struggle elsewhere in the world- India was not oblivious of the intrinsic human values outsourced partly to its inherited, enriched and glorious past and the other to the configuration of these values by the mentors of freedom struggle in their experiences in the context of a different and changing world quite different from their world view. To a country believing in non-violent means of protestations, speeches derived from their ardent adherence to these intrinsic human and saintly values personified in Mahatma Gandhi and Indian spiritual history, became important arsenals in their struggle to ignite all scattered sparks of discontent into mass volcanic movement. Similarly, it is not surprising to find that a country long habituated to speeches and saintly maxims during freedom struggle, would ultimately be guided by this while behaving in its international relations, and world politics. The reputation that India found heaped on it from all over the world for its showing a different and unique path of freedom, Nehru tried to use it as source and strength of his foreign policy after his investiture as first Prime Minister of India. If a mighty British empire could be crumbled to shreds by an unarmed India believing impeccably in its values and moral strength, why modern India under Nehru would not occupy the same position as with the world powers, and cast judgment on world issues objectively and freely? Thus, aware that moral words secreted from its enriched culture are mightier than sword, Nehru chiselled Indian foreign policy on this, and started to carve out a niche for itself in world politics by simply casting judgments on issues afflicting nations and humanity on principles of justice, rights and democracy. He said, "I just do not see why the possession of great armed might or great financial power should necessarily lead to right decisions or a right mental outlook... I am not prepared... to give up my right of independent judgment to anybody else in other countries."[1] Initially, India reaped rich diplomatic dividends but later on when faced with a different world and mindset, India faced its waterloo from the China in 1962 war. An excerpt from one of Nehru's speech would enlighten on what constitutes the bedrock of Indian foreign policy:

> "India is a country with a tremendous vitality which it has shown through its history. It has often imposed enough of its own cultural pattern on other countries, not by the force of its arms but by the strength of its vitality, culture and civilization. There is no reason why we should give up our way of doing things, our way of considering things, simply because of some particular ideology, which emanates from Europe.... We should be flexible in mind and we should be receptive, but I have also no doubt at all that we should not allow ourselves... to be swept off our feet by any wind from anywhere. We should approach these problems, whether domestic or international problems, in our own way."[2]

In other words, a country adopting western democracy from its very birth as a nascent nation state went by the rulebook of what democracy is. So strict adherence to the nomenclatural exactitude of democracy is what marked the difference between India and America. On the other hand, Washington understood democracy as a rhetoric and euphemism to spread its domestic imperatives built on the edifice of Hobbes and Locke's possessive individualism and Newtonian and Cartesian view of world to all parts of the globe as it has at present culminated in globalization. Very honestly speaking, it earnestly wanted in pursuance of the above objective that all the nations of the world put on American political and economic straightjacket irrespective of their divergent culture and civilization. When this assumed the character of a cultural hegemony pontificating to all nations of the world to acquiesce in American political economy with a religious awe, it is bound to come in clash with communism, the stranglehold of Soviet Union, preaching a different path. None would disagree with the very fact that American cultural hegemony is what explains the thesis behind Huntington's clash of civilization and rise of Islamic terrorism on a global scale against it. In pursuant to this, America put a premium on containment of communism in its foreign policy as a part of its domestic imperatives over adherence to democratic and intrinsic human values. Though it was eloquent on preaching these values, in practice it preferred to show them short shrift.

With the eclipse of cold war and disintegration of Soviet Union, the prediction of Fukuyama about an apocalypse of new world order and "end of history" did not come true and proved all euphoria built around it as evanescent. How it is to be explained? It is as platitudinous to hold that end of cold war would automatically usher in a new world order based on democratization of existing western dominated political and economic institutions, equity, justice, objectivity in analyzing issues, and multilateralism as ramifying to underestimate or gloss over the domestic imperatives behind American foreign policy. As said above, guided by Newtonian metaphor, America tends to see the universe or entire planet earth as not a living subject like itself but a mere lifeless, and compendium of raw materials to be exploited to satisfy its domestic imperatives of providing its people an inordinate life style, exorbitant consumption and production of limitless wealth. Thus, US main policy is to domesticise the universe for the uncontested attainment of the above goals in the name of export of democracy or establishing global village reminiscent of colonial masters justifying their rule for civilizing the people in Asia and Africa. On the other hand, Soviet Union wanted to universalize its Bolshevik party engineered militancy in the name of establishing a socialistic society in all parts of the globe. The cold war was nothing but a clash between US strategy of domesticisation and Soviet Union's strategy of universalization. The end of cold war witnessed the demise of Soviet Union's universalization doctrine and the ascendancy of US domesticisation doctrine[3]. Unless one rightly understands the underpinnings of this domesticisation doctrine of US, the visibility of unipolar moment in American foreign policy cannot be explained. All predictions about a new world order after the demise of cold war were hypothetical not based on the domestic imperatives of the United States. Given the trends and tendencies of unipolarism in American foreign policy, Indian euphoria over a new partnership with US is likely to be short lived, if India ever sticks to its long cherished non-aligned culture. While striking deals with Washington on defense, and nuclear issues, New Delhi is likely to be wary of its moves, which would not compromise its values it holds so close to its heart.

On this ground, India unflinchingly believing in and going by the rulebook of democracy, freedom, rights and independence of action and sovereignty differs from America, which tends to give priority to containment of communism. The fundamental differences between Washington and New Delhi in explaining the content and contour of democracy continues persistently in all their talks even on the issues of nuclear or any deal that America wants to strike with India. Whether it is Indo- Pak 1965 or 1971 war, the American weapons, which were purported to be used against Soviet Union, were used by Pakistan against India contrary to Washington's assurances to New Delhi. A perusal of the ensemble of records of Washington's support to dictatorial, military and totalitarian regimes in the world during and after cold war comes as a testament to American preferential values. This is also one of the reasons to explain its unequivocally military and economic support to Pakistan against India, as the former was a frontline and client state to work as a bulwark against Soviet Communism. It was well nigh known to American that an independent, freedom loving and large democratic India would not be cajoled into its global strategic orbit. Throughout the United States made it a point in its foreign policy toward India to contain the latter by clipping its wing of freedom of choice and action President Bush's pledges to enable India to ascend to a major power status by signing a historic nuclear deal fly in the face of American Congress drafts to incorporate extraneous clauses into the July 18 agreement, which are indicative of the hackneyed American strategy of containment of India. To a plain, truthful, and straightforward Gandhian state, moral uprightness and its universal applicability is abhorrent of American double standard in foreign policy. High eloquence in words and rhetoric, but invidious and diplomatic in deeds, America considered the actions of Pakistan in its secret pursuant to acquisition of nuclear weapons in connivance with China as morally worth doing, but the Indian indigenous explosion In 1974 and 1998 at Pokharan was castigated as unethical and morally obnoxious. China a main accomplice in missile and nuclear programme of Pakistan and a signatory to NPT could survive American good relation with rewards in terms of economy and trade, but India, a non signatory to NPT yet abides by the nuances of nuclear non-proliferation and adheres to its unilateral moratorium on further nuclear testing, could not survive American relation. This constitutes the backdrop in which the entire gamut of Indo-US relation is to be understood and analyzed throughout from the cold war period to the present.

There is no gainsaying the fact that both India and America share innumerable similarities in terms of sustaining religious strongholds in the country, exhibiting a commitment to political and economic freedom with assimilative and integrative characteristics in the society. On a cultural plane, adherence to values for deep-rooted multi-ethnic diversity and respect for religion are the common thread that runs in their relation. After the cold war thrown into scrap heap, India adopted American scripted liberal market economy and opened its doors to globalization, thus binding itself into a new ontological tie with America, which marks a shift in paradigm from its much-valued path of socialism. This paved the way for the transition from the national consensus on building a "socialist society" to building a "modern capitalist" one. The word "socialism" in India is embedded in a curio of national ethos for ushering in of a society free from hunger, poverty and basic human needs. The constitutional architects put into the Indian constitution all that is meant by socialism without inscribing the word socialism. Indira Gandhi made it more explicit by putting the word socialism into the preamble of the constitution by 42nd amendment. She nationalized the banks, took away right to property of individuals by simply bringing amendments and declared emergency, and ultimately dethroned from power. It once played a key role in enthroning her in power, and making her most popular and powerful leader of the country. In the external realm she cemented India's leaning toward Soviet Union to the discomfiture of the United States. America then failed to understand the ground realities of a poverty stricken country urgently needing attention from a strong state. Thus, acceptance of American dictated market economy means to put into backburner all that India stood for all these years. No longer the fulfillment of the basic human needs of the majority poor people in India occupied primacy in Indian policy. The domestic imperatives of America through its agents, Trans National Corporations (TNCs) crept into the mainstream of Indian foreign policy as a state within a state. Deification of liberal market economy means subjecting India permanently to the dictates of these TNCs and ultimately to their mentor America. A country solely depending on TNCs and MNCs for higher economic growth is bound to remain captive to American dictates thereby facing economic and political challenges to its independence and sovereignty. Once Nehru said,

"Countries should be independent... The first thing... is to have this process of the independence of countries extended until it covers the whole world".[4] The greatest political and economic challenges to Indian policy making lie in whether distancing away from Nehruvian vision and values once forming the core of Indian foreign policy, is conducive to Indian national interest. With the collapse of Soviet Union, the anti western verbiage in Indian foreign policy begins to be discarded. Once India casts its lot with American dictated political economy, it stops being a "free rider" in international issues as it was enjoying in the past. India's muting response in case of American war against Iraq and India's support to American resolution against Iran on nuclear issue at Washington's behest are indicative of considerable shrinking of freedom once enjoyed by non-aligned India.

As explicated above, India relied on the power of argument derived from its cultural and civilizational strength to play a major role in world politics, equal to the role played by super powers. Gradual militarization of the world, India's China debacle and Pakistan's attack on India brought home to New Delhi that cultural strength is likely to play an emasculated role in absence of sufficient military and economic power. This would explain the reasons for which India went for nuclear tests, adopted liberal market economy and decided to forge ties with America on civilian nuclear energy. Thus, a shift from reliance on "power of argument" to "argument of power" has already taken place in Indian foreign policy[5]. The fundamental question remains whether discarding Indian value structure to get ascension to major power status purely on military and economic strength with American support is worth pursuing for greater national interest.

Some glaring instabilities and differences exist between the two. Dissimilar economic and military capabilities of the two countries and the fluctuating Indo-American political relationships are major factors. Politically, India and the US have rarely been on an even keel. Misperceptions complicated by Indo- American political relationships following the Non-aligned Movement and the cold war, and divergent national and foreign policy priorities have almost indelible effects on both countries. The perceived inclination of India toward the Soviet Union in the post-war period that inflamed America and the cold war actions of the United States that ignited

New Delhi have wrought a deep chasm in the interactions between the two countries. The remnants of the past still pervade the present. To minimize the range of dissimilitude between the countries and the imperatives on America to bury ever the ingrained misperception and distrust about India would be the key to a responsive environment for interaction between the undisputed superpower and the emerging one.

Geopolitically, both evince a greater interest in combating terrorism to create a stable Asia, though from different perspectives. Indian perception of and stand on terrorism does not converge with that of America. America's war on terrorism does not point toward Pakistan for its terrorism in Kashmir. Rather than take any action against Pakistan, President Bush has patted on President Musharraf for his actions to the great chagrin of India. Past record of Pakistan as reliable friend, always standing in good stead to America, and the current Afghanistan crisis weighed heavily against taking any stringent action against terrorism in Kashmir and other parts of India. Besides, United States has not yet steered its mind clear of all misperception and understanding of Kashmir issue. Despite all shreds of evidences in American hands proving Pakistani indulgence in acts of terrorism or bomb blasts in parts of India, America feigns ignorance and pats on Pakistan. This attitudinal incongruity between the two in combating terrorism in Asia would remain a challenging task to be tackled in their relations. This American policy is in continuation of its past habit of glossing over Pakistan when it was busy producing nuclear weapons and missiles with China's support, instead, it was very critical of India's position. This preferential treatment to Pakistan, which has in the past-bedeviled Indo- US relation, is likely to remain a factor in their efforts to put their relations on an even keel. A view doing the round all over the diplomatic and intellectual circles that the collapse of the cold war would plummet the significance of Pakistan in the strategic calculation of America, seems to be overrated. So long as America wants to keep its economic and political stakes harnessed to the brim without any opposition in Middle East, Central Asia, and Afghanistan with an eye over the emergent Russia, Pakistan remains important as it was in the past. Given the Kashmir imbroglio afflicting both India and Pakistan, Indo – US relation is likely to pass through the miasma of a crossroad at which America stands keeping eyes on both Pakistan and India. Cracking the Gordian knot of Kashmir issue and impetus to cementing new strategic partnership with US are dialectically correlated. Thus, Kashmir predicament has a great bearing on the Indo-US relation.

The cooperation of two democracies would also mean a more in-depth interaction on the basis of shared values and building on the existing coalition. India and the US have always shared a mutual awe for other's vision of pluralism, tolerance and equal opportunity. Despite all the disparity, India and America share a strong bond- a bond of "unity in diversity" which is celebrated as an integral part of their national identities. India has been a land of mystery and enchantment that eludes any attempt by America to deny, define or resist. Similarly America has been a role model of development and a source of intense curiosity and interest in India. In the positive light at present, Indian art, literature social sciences, history and several languages are taught in American universities, exhibiting a wide representation of Indian civilization and culture in the US, Establishment of many yoga centers, ashrams, dance and music centers in America stands a witness to the beseeching and mellowing impression, India has left on busy and buzz of modern American life. Thus, the myriad diversities and pluralism of India have begun to get represented in America as a unique form of "unity in diversity" enabling Americans to have a realistic appreciation of Indian society and culture in the United States. Besides, America recognizes the role of Indian immigrants and Indian Diaspora in transforming American economic life as entrepreneurs, researchers, academicians, lawyers, engineers, managers and administrators. America greatly benefits from the "brain gain". The intrinsic value of "unity in diversity" in their respective cultural pluralistic society can be brought to focus in their interactions to root out disharmony, differences, misunderstanding and misperceptions in their political relations.

Despite the cultural affinity and recognition of "unity in diversity" between the two countries, substantial differences in value systems exist to become a preponderant factor in their bilateral relations. In the domestic field, the emphasis put on self-reliance, the liberal social pattern, laissez faire economy and belief in upholding civil rights of citizens with minimal governmental interference has worked well in America. But in India, a country afflicted by poverty, social and economic inequality cannot afford to remain as a police state, simply distancing away from the compulsions of meeting the essentials of life such as food, education, housing, and social security. It cannot survive on constitutional rights guaranteed to its citizens, and on acceptance of American dictated liberal market economy. Indian policy makers while opening its door to American liberal market economy cannot stonewall the imperatives of a welfare and socialistic state. The cascading implications of globalization in economic and social life of Indian people are bound to create political and social cleavages, discontentment and polarization in India with a great bearing in their bilateral relations.

A differential value structure existing between the two in the international realm would affect their new partnership. Historically, India's age old hallowed tradition of openness, accommodation, coexistence, tolerance, compromise, democratization of international institutions, and pluralism remains an appropriate model for a stable and fair order nationally and internationally. When Nehru defined non-alignment as an independent policy, he used the expression independent in a deep and comprehensive sense and not merely as avoidance of military alliances in a tactical sense. He was insistent upon India making its contribution to world politics not merely in proportion to its material power as enjoined by the western conception of international relations but also in consonance with India's civilizational values and norms. India, given its tradition of coexistence, plurality, non-violence, and freedom is in a unique position to vouchsafe for independence, diversity, support for universal organization, a liberal and comprehensive definition of security and a negotiated settlement of disputes in the international realm, and complete disarmament without discrimination. Nowhere the chasm between what is preached in home front and practiced in the international arena is seen than in American policy. The use of "double standard" value pattern by America in its international relations clashes with India's much vaunted universal value structure. The point is how India is going to adjust its age old value structure with those of America, which believes in intricacies, diplomatic dexterity, political tactics, dirty skills, manipulation and machination quite appropriate to a business and economic man always concerned with immediacy and temporal gains. The current

American policy of unilateralism and preemption and the trans-boundary nature of the contemporary problems like environmental degradation, terrorist violence, human rights abuses, spread of human killing diseases and decimation of millions of children, women, and poor people because of malnutrition, impoverishment and human disturbance of nature, only reinforce the significance India attaches to its long pronounced values for urgent attention for solution. It is not Samuel Huntington's clash of civilization to be used as a euphemism for reinforcement of American unipolarism and pre-emption strike, but a clash of value pattern between the two countries that is going to define Indo-US relation in this new millennium. Asking all nations of the world to religiously conform to American political and economic Procrustean bed is what is called cultural hegemony. It means decimation of all other cultures and civilizations. It is not unnatural to insist that US climb down from the apex of hegemony in order to harmonize its relation with India. American dominance of the entire globe in political and economic realm is closely connected with its domestic imperatives of providing an inordinate life style, exorbitant consumption and abundant production of wealth at the expense of both nature and the developing world. Climbing down means compromising the domestic imperatives on the basis of which the legitimacy to political system has been exacted. This was the reason propelling President Bush to withdraw from the Kyoto obligations on the ground that America cannot compromise with the existing life style of its people. Unless a slice of the life style of its people is parted with the poor people inhabiting the developing world, the Indian vision of a new international economic order based on equity and justice cannot be fostered. Given the non-aligned nations pronouncement for a new world order based on India's long professed value structure, and the United States' intransigence to compromise with its domestic imperatives, there is likely to be an incongruence between the value structure of the two countries, which augurs ill for their bilateral relations. What will exact unqualified support and respect to America from all nations is not its military prowess and hegemony but a determined political will of America to take exemplary steps in building a new world well informed by justice, equity and human rights by way of subscribing to the universal value structure much longed for by all the nations of the world. It appears far-fetched and ramifying-a distant goal not easily attainable at so heavy a price, which America is not in a position to pay. A country long subscribed to realistic understanding of the Hobbesian nature of the anarchical world, and Newtonian view of universe and life, cannot so soon be expected to harbinger a transfiguration of their established mindset into a different view rethinking their political and economic paradigm, and inordinate life style. In order to command the respect and obeisance from others for its policy based on universal values not on egotistic domestic imperatives, US has to play the role of a primus inter pares not like an emperor sitting on a high pedestal with a moist heart and determined will for the cause of humanity as a whole without any distinction. This prescriptive path suggested to America for ushering in a new world is no doubt revolutionary, and requires the genius of a Gandhi, who in the words of Schopenhauer, was a genius in the world of will, and with his strongest and sanctified will shook the mighty British empire to its roots. The atavism of this tremendous will and attitudinal revolution in American leadership blended with strands of wisdom, dynamism and sensitivity to scourging humanity would certainly build a bridge, a strong and lasting one between India and US, thus facilitating a smooth transition from aspiration to achievement, a transformation of a dream to a reality. On this pedestal will begin a joint venture between America, an apostle of materialism and India, a scion of enriched spiritual value system to change the world for the better. This is not a wishful thinking. What 2330 years ago, the Great King Alexander did exemplarily at Opis remains significant today to American leadership as a shining emblem of wisdom. About 150 km north of Babylon Opis was an ancient city on the banks of the Tigris River. One day the great king Alexander decided to dismiss the old guards of his Greek Army, who served with him for a longest period and needed to return their homes in Greece. In their places when Persians, Bactrians, Medeans, Parthians, Phhrygians and other men of all races and cultures from the new empire were appointed, the old guards rose in revolt, remonstrating that the barbarians could not be possibly allowed to replace them in the ranks of Alexander's army, and declined to step down. Alexander alighted from his throne and ordered the twelve of them to be put in jail. Then, he retired to his tent for two days and remained silent not talking to any body.

The rebels soon were in deep contrition over what they did and desired to surrender, which they did after three days crying at the feet of Alexander. Then, Alexander ordered a great dinner on the plains of Opis where more than nine thousand men including Greeks, nobles and commoners from Persia, Phrygia, Medea, Bactria, Armenia, Parthia, Egypt and Mesopotamia, and from the other provinces of his vast empire were invited to dine with him. Then he delivered his speech, which is historically known as the Oath of Alexander to his subjects. An excerpt from his oath at Opis deserves mentioning:

> "It is my wish, now that wars are coming to an end, that you should all be happy in peace. From now on let all mortals live as one people, in fellowship, for the good of all. See the whole world as your homeland, with laws common to all, where the best will govern regardless of their race. Unlike the narrow- minded, I make no distinction between Greeks and barbarians. The origin of citizens, or the race into which they were born, is of no concern to me. I have only one criterion by which to distinguish them- virtue. For me, any good foreigner is a Greek and any bad Greek is worse than a barbarian. If disputes ever occur among you, you will not resort to weapons but will solve them in peace. If need be, I shall arbitrate between you. See God not as an autocratic despot, but as the common father of all and thus your conduct will be like the lives of brothers within the same family. I, on my part, see you all as equal, whether you are white or dark-skinned. And I should like you not simply to be subjects of my commonwealth, but members of it, partners of it. To the best of my ability, I shall strive to do what I have promised. Keep as a symbol of love this oath, which we have taken tonight with our libations."[6]

Whether the present American political leadership has shown the necessary signs of being readied to imbibe the gracious spirit of this great man, on whose demise, Montesquieu, the French political philosopher observed that, "when Alexander was gone, nations became orphans."[7] Like Alexander's oath reflecting his gracious spirit, American leadership's will to mete out equal treatment to all nations as not subjects but partner brothers will define the course of international order and its relationship with all other nations.

References

1. Jawaharlal Nehru, India's Foreign Policy, Selected Speeches, September 1946-April 1961 (New Delhi: The Publication Division, Ministry of Information and Broadcasting, Government of India, 1961), p. 80.
2. *Ibid.* p.39.
3. N.Gaan, "Post-Iraq War World Order: American Script, Pax Romana or Pax Brittanica", BIISS JOURNAL, Vol. 25, No. 3, July 2004, pp.207-36.
4. *Ibid.*
5. C. Raja Mohan, "India's New Foreign Policy Strategy", Draft paper presented at a seminar in Beijing by China Reform Forum and the Carnegie Endowment for International Peace, Beijing, May 26,2006, visited website www.foreignaffairs.org/ 2006070/faessa of 85402/c.rajamohan/ India-and-the- balance of- power.html
6. Nicholas S Papanicolaou, "The Ideals of Greek Culture", World Affairs, Vol.7, no. 4, October- December 2003, pp.23-24.
7. *Ibid.* p. 24.

2

Indo- US Relation During the Cold War: Pakistan Factor

No nation in the present world can live in total isolation. In pursuit of one's own interest for survival and welfare, an interaction takes place among and between states which marks the characteristics of the present international system and other subordinate state system. The international system is dominated by the super powers whose major aim is to increase their 'sphere of influence' in all parts of the globe. The subordinate state systems such as South Asia, South-East Asia, Middle East, Africa and Latin America are rife with regional conflicts largely rooted in their historic territorial claims. Though both international and subordinate state systems are affected by each other, the super power global strategy largely sets the context and direction of regional conflicts in subordinate state systems. As J. David Singer observes "the international system itself is the key element in explaining why and how nations attempt to influence the behaviour of one another". [1]

The behaviour of a nation in a crisis situation of its own or other nations goes as an 'input' into the international system or subordinate state system, which is further reinforced by the actors in the system. The 'output' policy of these actors reinforces the 'output' policy of the responding nation.[2] Since India is geographically and historically linked to a number of subordinate state systems, any crisis in the international environment affecting any subordinate state system has its impact on India's decision making. One of Nehru's speeches reveals this:

> Look at the map. If you have to consider any question affecting the Middle East, India inevitably comes into the picture. If you have to consider any question concerning South-East Asia, you cannot do so without India. So also with the Far East. While the Middle East may not be directly connected with South East Asia, both are connected with India. Even if you think in terms of regional organizations in Asia, you have to keep in touch with the other regions. And whatever regions you may have in mind, the importance of India cannot be ignored. [3]

Since India is situated in South Asia- a subordinate state system, the impact of super power global strategy on its decision-making is undeniable. Thus, the international environment acts as a constraint on the decision- making process of India.

The existence of two dominant powers like India and China in South Asia further affects the decision -making of India in foreign policy in view of China acting as an active co-participant with the United States in the super power global strategy. Further, as Cantori has remarked, this subordinate state system gives rise to an 'intrusive system' which ensures the active participation of external powers in the foreign policy behaviour of the subordinate state system.[4]

Interaction with the United States

The substructure of Indian foreign policy shaped by both domestic and international environment, perceives its national interest in terms of autonomy, international peace, independent decision-making and aversion to any super power military alignment. As Nehru observed:

> I think that not only in the long run, but also in the short run, independence of opinion and independence of action will count ... Purely from the point of view of opportunism, if you like, a straight forward honest policy, an independent policy is the best. [5]

Keeping this in view, India has always apportioned blame on both super powers for their scramble for increasing their sphere of influence by interfering in the national sovereignty and independence of countries of Asia and Africa. In consonance with this, it has put emphasis on a solution to crisis in Asia, Africa and Latin America, by super power withdrawal from these strategic areas. Thus, Nehru devised non-alignment as one of the anchor-sheets of India's foreign policy in the cold war phase, which was thought to have reaped multi-pronged dividends to India.

1. It would guarantee freedom of judgment and action without any interference from super powers and freeing the constraint to toe a super power line always on all events. [6]
2. It would facilitate India's envisaged desire to play a vital role for the cause of world peace because of its aversion to any super power military bloc. [7]
3. Advocacy of non-alignment was not meant to be oblivious of India's national interests for the cause of world peace. Nehru observed that " whatever policy we may lay down, the art of conducting the foreign affairs of a country lies in finding out what is most advantageous to the country." [8]

4) It would help India build its security arrangements. As Nehru said that " the normal idea is that security is protected by armies. That is only partly true; it is equally true that security is protected by policies. A deliberate policy of friendship with ether countries goes further in gaining security than almost anything else"[9].
5) From India's long-term interests it would enable India to get economic assistance from both blocs of the cold war without injuring its self-respect.[10] As Nehru said that "Even in accepting economic help or in getting political help it is not a wise policy to put all our eggs in one basket. Nor should we get help at the cost of our self respect". [11]

To this end India's size, population, strategic location and cultural heritage played an important role. Since independence through its policy of non-alignment, India was determined not to be an object of super power manipulation and not to play second fiddles to them. Nehru pointed out in one of his speeches: "For too long have we of Asia been petitioners in Western courts and chancelleries. That story must now belong to the past. We propose to stand on our own legs and cooperate with all others who are prepared to cooperate with us. We do not intend to be the plaything of others". [2] Thus, a divergence in strategic perception of both the United States and India began to emerge. The lack of identity in strategic perception was rooted as much in historical experiences, and geographical location as in their ideological differences. It was India's perception that the interference of super powers in suppressing national movements in the Third World would be a grave threat to international peace. This was reflected in one of Indira Gandhi's speeches:

> Our objection to military blocs is that the military presence of any one nation or group automatically attracts a counter presence, and therefore adds to the tension. We stand for the unqualified right of nations to choose their own form of Government and for total non-interference with this right. We stand for the withdrawal of all outside military forces and we reiterate this not only in relation to the two conflicts which are so obvious today, i.e., in South-East Asia and in the Middle East, but to all parts of the world. [13]

The United States on the other hand has detected in all national movements and uprisings in Asia and Africa, the presence of communism. After the Sino-Soviet rift and Sino-American thaw, this has been confined to only Soviet communism. Hence the containment of communism has become the mainspring of the United States global strategy[14]. To this policy India has not adhered. In Europe, the United States carried out its policy of containment of communism in the initial phase the Marshall Plan and since then the North Atlantic Treaty. [15] It succeeded relatively in this area. But the establishment of Communist Government in China in the late 1949 harbingered a shift of balance of power against the United States.[16] The close relationship between Soviet Union and China and their policy to spread the tentacles of communism in South East Asia was perceived by the United-States as a menace to its security.[17] Thus the policy of containment of communism in South East Asia occupied a peremptory place in the United States foreign policy objectives.[18]

The United States in order to prevent the spread of Sino-Soviet communism resorted to a policy of military alliances like SEATO (South East Asia Treaty Organization) and CENTO (Central

Treaty Organization) in which Pakistan became a member. India's policy of non-alignment, which admonishes against membership in a military bloc, came in direct clash with America's policy. Thus, India was to disapprove of United States Policy of containment of communism and opposition to the rise of nationalist movements in Asia and Africa. [19] Thus, a clash of perception of both the United States and India occurred in world forums over the issue of independence of colonial countries, the cessation of apartheid in South Africa, to which India appeared to have provided the leadership. [20] India's advocacy of anti-colonialism, anti-racialism and independent attitude free from super power influence widened the cleavages between India and the United-States. [21]

India's approach to the Korean crisis in the fifties differed from that of the United States. India's stand on it created a flutter of resentment in the United States. India's opposition to sending of UN forces to Korea was perceived as an attempt to undermine the effectiveness of UN and India was regarded as a "neutral on the communist side". [22]

The conflict between India and Pakistan over the issue of Kashmir strained the relationship between India and the United States. The United States' support to Pakistan on this issue was perceived by India as damage to India's national interests. [23] In the Indian view, "the initiative in debate was taken over by the United States from the day the (present) sittings began". [24] In a similar tone Nehru retorted, " now the same distinguished representative tells us what to do about Kashmir not realizing that Kashmir is flesh of our flesh and bone of our bone". [25] That's why India asked all the American personnel in Kashmir to be withdrawn. Nehru speaking in the Lok Sabha said: "American military officers serving as United Nations observers in Kashmir could no longer be treated by India as neutrals... and their presence there appears to be improper".[26] This tendency to impose on Indian decision makers their own perspective continued, and the pressure applied during the Chinese attack on India was with a view not to strain its relationship with Pakistan. [27] This act of the United States resulted in Pakistan raising the question again in the Security Council on 9 October 1963. [28] It was seen from the United States' delegate's speech in the Security Council that the United States stood solidly behind Pakistan on the question of plebiscite in Kashmir. [29]

India's military intervention to liberate Goa and make it an integral part of Indian Union in 1961 was heavily criticized by the United States in the Security Council. Kennedy himself was very critical of Nehru's "blatant seizure" of the Portuguese colony of Goa. [30] Nehru wrote a letter to Kennedy "Why is it," he asked, "that something that thrills our people should be condemned in the strongest language in the United States"? He had been "deeply hurt, he remarked, by the extraordinary and bitter attitude of Adlai Stevenson". [31] Thus, Indo-US relations plummeted back to low ebb after India's liberation of Goa militarily in December 1961. [32]

The issue of the cessation of nuclear tests constantly cropped up in the United Nation and in the Disarmament Commission from 1954 to 1958, When the Soviets after agreeing to a moratorium on resumed testing, Nehru pronounced that nothing was served by "condemning this country or that". [33] This statement and the conduct of the Indian delegate at the United Nation on the issue of nuclear testing acerbated resentment in the United States towards India. [34] Throughout the debate the United States remained persistent in its refusal to isolate the test suspension from a test ban treaty. [35] On the other hand, India preferred to isolate test suspension from a test ban treaty. [36] Thus, a clash of approach to this vexed nuclear issue continued to hamper Indo-US relations. In the view of the United States delegate, Dean Acheson, the United States was more harshly criticized than the Soviet Union by India though it was the Soviet Union which violated the moratorium on nuclear tests first." [37]

Thus, on issues such as Vietnam and Middle -East, the stand of both the United States and India has been different. Bound by history, geographic proximity, trade and commerce and Arab and Asian nationalism, India has always supported the cause of Arabs against Israel. India's support to the United Nations resolution against Israel would explain the widening of gap between the United States and India.

China Factor

Indo- U.S. relations can also be studied from the perspective of India's relation with China. In the initial phase of the Cold War, the United States was trying to contain Chinese communism. This was expressed during Nehru's visit to America in October 1949. [38] But the 1962 Chinese war opened the possibility of a better understanding between India and the United States. India's approach for military aid was immediately responded to by the United States, though attempts were made that Pakistan did not suffer. So Kennedy tried " to balance off" what was one of Washington's more difficult problems".[39] To achieve this, the U.S. gave up its idea of a joint air defense pact, which could have achieved for it a major breakthrough in relationship.[40] Rather it went all out to encourage an India-Pakistan dialogue.[41] To crown success it agreed with the Prime Minister of Great Britain at Nassau, a Joint military assistance programme in mid December 1962. T.N.Kaul in his analysis of this phase perceives that:

> His (John Kennedy) attitude to the Sino- Indian war of 1962 was sympathetic to India. But some of his advisers tried to use it as a lever to put pressure on India; they failed. It was an opportunity America could have utilized to bring India closer to herself, but she missed it. The US administration tried to tie down in a joint defence pact with Pakistan, which went directly against India's potential value and strategic importance. US experts treated us as if we were a client state and wanted us to make impossible concessions to Pakistan on Kashmir. [42]

But with the eruption of Sino-Soviet rift, a reconsideration of America's relationship with China retained its importance in the decision- making of the United States foreign policy. Nixon's Guam doctrine would reveal this. China was no longer considered as adventurous and revolutionary and thus a Sino-American thaw set in.[43]

By 1971 thus, the pendulum had swung in the favour of China and against India. US attempted at balancing the three regional powers, which became an important factor in Indo-US relation. American tendency was to support Pakistan against all odds and would under no circumstance attempt to disrupt its detente with China.

The Soviet Factor

American policy towards India is part of its global policy, where the major factor is its relationship with the Soviet Union.

That India is of secondary or even of less importance is proved by the fact that, even in the initial years of India's independence when the Soviets refused to recognize its emergence as an independent unit, the Americans made no attempt to attract it.[44] Again at the next stage in 1965 during the Indo-Pak crisis when it could have tried again, the Americans preferred to remain neutral leaving the door open to the Soviet Union which used the opportunity to increase its power in the region. The reason obviously as pointed out earlier was the presence of the Pakistan factor in the fulfillment of its national interest.

Pakistan Factor

The application of British strategy in the colonial days of building up Pakistan against India constituted one of the cornerstones of American foreign policy towards the Indian subcontinent. The United States looked "at India through British eyes". [45] Pakistan's geographic location being situated as it is in the northern tip of the subcontinent suited the United States' strategic outlook of containing communism (both Soviet Union and China in the sixties). To execute this policy, in 1954, Pakistan was not only provided with direct military aid but also invited to join CENTO and SEATO of which the United States is a member. Consequently, Pakistan provided the United States with intelligence and military bases until 1968. Later Pakistan became the main channel of communication between China and the United States, when they reopened relations. It also had close links with oil producing Persian Gulf States. Thus, Pakistan seemed to have participated as subordinate ally in the United States global strategy. In the strategic evaluation and calculation Pakistan appeared more peremptorily important than India. "In practice however, US strategic imperatives placed Pakistan in the category of an ally in a global confrontation and India in the low priority bracket of a potential regional power". [46] According to Lloyd and Susanne Hoeber Rudolf, America seemed to have given prominence to short-term global consideration over regional imperatives around India. [47] Despite Pakistan's conclusion of a series of agreements with Soviet Union for assistance for Pakistan's 4th and 5th Five Year Plans, Ayub Khan's proclamation of foreign policy with non-aligned flavour and its close friendship with China in an era of

Sino-US rivalry, the United States did not reconsider Pakistan's strategic importance to it, and both countries remained close allies.

In view of the strategic importance of Pakistan to the United States, it was inevitable that in any conflict between India and Pakistan, the United States' diplomatic and military help would be forthcoming In favour of Pakistan. Indian decision makers could not wholly rule out even the possibility of the United States' involvement in the imbroglio, because the only exception to American support of Pakistan was the 1965 Indo-Pak war. But there was no surety that the American policy would be repeated in an all out Indo-Pak war, for America's moral and material support to Pakistan continued. Even in 1965 the United States had reacted mildly to Pakistan's attack across the cease-fire line in Kashmir in September 1965 and sharply to India's counter attack in Punjab. In addition to this, suspension of military and economic aid to both Pakistan and India by the United States in the 1965 war was buttressed India's earlier misgivings that the weapons provided by the United States would be used against India. Eisenhower's written pledges to Nehru that American weapons would not be used by Pakistan in its war with India were thus meaningless as B. K. Nehru. India's ambassador pointed out to Secretary of State Dean Rusk. [48] For, if, "the suspension of the US aid to Pakistan was specific without taking similar action against India, the United States, in one sense, would have honoured the Eisenhower pledge. But unfortunately this was not done". [49]

The conclusion drawn from this can be that the United States policy was less than neutral. " While the US and India have differed on this central theme of United States foreign policy, the United States and Pakistan have mainly agreed. This has been the primary reason for American approval of Pakistan and displeasure with India". [50] Towards the close of the sixties when the Bangladesh crisis erupted, the international political scene was showing some far-reaching changes. Sino-Soviet rivalry was at its height during the Ussuri river border clashes. The United States was trying to disengage itself from the Vietnam War, and a Sino-American thaw was in the offing with Pakistan's mediation. The Indian decision kept in mind this changed political scenario in international relations where the United States involvement in an Indo-Pak conflict would not be ruled out and the decision makers in India thus had to opt for a policy to overcome this United States constraint.

Military Aid

The question of military aid to Pakistan has always been resented in India and a major irritant in the relationship between India and the United States. [51] Despite India's protestations and consternation, the United States has not withdrawn itself from its policy of supplying military weapons and aid to Pakistan. All US assurances that its weapons to Pakistan would not be used against India have been infringed by Pakistan. The Indo-Pak war of 1965 would add credence to this. During the phase of its crusade against communism (both Soviet Union and China) when the Sino-Indian border war occurred in 1962, Nehru's approach for supply of modern supersonic Jet fighters which were made available to Pakistan and helped set up its own defence industry for production of such sophisticated weaponry, was turned down by US to frustrate India's aspiration to become self-sufficient in military strength. All requests for military assistance to the United States were tied with strings like dialogue with Pakistan on Kashmır, lowering its ceiling on rupee and foreign exchange for defence expenses, delaying its decision on purchase and manufacture of fighter air craft and acquiescing in the supervisory role of the United States personnel[52]. In lieu of this, India was hopeful of getting from the United States supplies continuously for a period of five years and was hopeful of becoming autonomous in taking decisions on deployment of specific equipment provided by the United States and getting an assurance from the United States that its officials would not offset the restrictions imposed by the Indian Government on its own military and civilian officials. To the utter dismay of India it was found that Johnson considered himself not to be bound by any financial obligation, which lasted longer than one year. No part of India's activity would remain without the presence of the United States. All equipment supplied by the United States would not be used against any adversary except China.[53] According to Chester Bowles' confidential cables to the White House, this attachment of one-sided conditions prompted "the Indians to conclude that we attribute to the People's Republic of China lion like qualities in South East Asia and sheep like qualities along India's 2,200 mile border".[54]

President Kennedy's plan to evolve a long-term military understanding between India and United States in order to lessen the former's dependence on Soviet Union for defence military purpose could not be implemented due to his incumbent's disinterestedness. The upshot of this was India's dependence on Soviet Union for military equipment.

Economic Aid

In economic matters also there was divergence of approach between the United States and India. The extent to which India depended on the United States in regard to trade can nowhere be compared to US need of India which is non existent. While the United States accounted for about 2.8 billion out of India's total turnover of about 8 billion dollar,[55] India constituted an insignificant fraction of the United States' total trade turnover of about 240 billion dollar. From the economic point of view this argument may be convincing.[56] But in US foreign policy economic aid has been used to satisfy allies and punish detractors. In this regard perhaps as its use as a political weapon, economic aid holds some meaning in American foreign policy. This can be seen from the fact that on a per capita basis India was the recipient of half of the total aid given to Pakistan.

Fifty percent of American economic aid to India consisted of agricultural commodities, " of the remaining half relatively little was given for industrial investment, and the United States refused to have anything to do with building heavy industry, which Indians deemed essential for their economic independence, military security and political sovereignty".[57] The United States aid policy was thus largely responsible for Indian dependence on Soviet Union for heavy industry. The United States economic aid to India tied with many strings annoyed the Indian leadership. "Nehru was greatly annoyed. He resented any suggestion that the Government of India should try to conciliate public opinion in America by readjusting some aspects of his foreign policy in emphasis, if not in substance. He was the last man to accept dictation from any quarter".[58] As another Indian diplomat reveals: "Nehru was not a man who would sell his country or policies to any other country, however great and powerful".[59] Economic aid which would compromise India's independence, autonomy and sovereignty would naturally be averse to decision makers. This was clearly revealed from Indira Gandhi's talks with Johnson during her visit to America in 1966 at the height of the food crisis in India, where " the President was advised to strike a bargain with Prime Minister covering three areas - South East Asia, Pakistan and economic reform in India". [60]

No bargain was struck, as mounting criticism in India of a sell-out to American pressure and compromise on national sovereignty to solve the food crisis, prompted the Indians to write to Johnson that national pride cannot be the price to be paid for foreign aid. [61] Though during this period Indira Gandhi was less critical of the United States bombing raids in Vietnam than several European leaders, and understood to have pressed Hanoi to grant unilateral concession, if the United States stopped bombing, soon after the policy was reversed.

It was perceived in the United States that to support India in its policy for autonomy and independence through non-alignment would be prejudicial to America's national interest. Beginning with a denial of support to any military bloc Indian policies clashed with those of the United States. Their dissimilarity of views on issues such as Kashmir, Goa, Soviet Union as well as general policies on each other's national interest constituted mutual suspicion, which could not be overlooked in any policy formulation. To sum up in the words of an American author, H. R. Issacs: "If one could venture any kind of generalization at all, it might be to say that both the Indians and Americans tend to be in some measure apostles of righteousness, and when two apostles of righteousness meet, it is not the beginning of a beautiful friendship". [62]

Constraints on Decision Making

The United States Factor

1. The foreign policy of the United States towards India, since independence has been one of indifference and antipathy. In the fifties, though India supported the United-States on many issues, the latter opposed India on critical issues such as Kashmir, Goa and criticized policy of non-alignment. At its best it maintained a stance of neutrality in the Indo-Pak war fought in 1965. Here as has been discussed its neutrality was inclined in the favour of Pakistan. Besides, the United States could not prevent Pakistan from using the United States military weapons against India.

Thus, in any issue involving both Pakistan and India, the American perception of a crisis differed from that of India and identified itself with that of Pakistan. The United States' involvement in Vietnam and Pakistan's policy of keeping good relationship even with the Soviet Union did not result in the United States' favour of India. Keeping this perspective, India would be hamstrung by America's policy of antipathy and indifference or its non-identification with India's stand.

2. India's decision makers were confronted with a possibly new development in US foreign policy if the Soviet's preponderant role in South Asia amplified in the Tashkent agreement between India and Pakistan after 1965 Indo-Pak war continued. To compensate for its lessening influence and presence in South East Asia, because of its policy of withdrawal from Vietnam, the United States could not relish the idea of leaving the field to the dominance of Soviet Union. To buttress its hold it was interested in Asia.

3. US policy of withdrawing from South East Asia would result in a greater Chinese role In South East Asia. Thus, Sino-American cooperation in containing Soviet communism could be perceived and could be an important factor in any crisis involving India and Pakistan. It was obvious that any such alliance would work against Indian interest.

Despite the irritants present in Indo-US policy and clash of interest, it would be fair to conclude that as seen in 1970, perhaps a close relationship did not exist, but neither was there the possibility of the United States exercising a policy which would be completely anti-Indian.

Interaction wIth Soviet Union

Before India attained independence, the leaders of the Indian National Congress had not only perceived the value of friendship of the Soviet Union but also evinced greater interests in cultivating this. Jawaharlal Nehru as head of the Interim Government sent his greetings to the Soviet Union:

> To that other great nation of the modern world, the Soviet Union, which also carries a vast responsibility for shaping world events, we send our greetings. They are our neighbours in Asia and

inevitably we shall have to undertake many common tasks and have much to do with each other.[63]

A historical factor would explain the reasons for having established cordial relationship between the two countries, despite disagreements between the two over certain aspects of their ideologies. The Bolshevik Revolution in the Soviet Union was a source of inspiration to Indians for their struggle against British imperialism. As the Montague Chelmsford Report stated, "The Revolution in Russia in its beginning was regarded in India as a triumph over despotism it has given an impetus to Indian political aspirations".[64] Thus the crusade against imperialism struck a common cord between the two countries.[65]

The second factor was the similarity of economic backwardness in both countries in their pre-independence days. Soviet Union's communism was stated to have raised a ray of hope in Nehru that "if Russia finds a satisfactory solution for these, our task in India is made easier".[66] As he further said before the 49th Session of the Indian National Congress: "Much has happened there which had pained me greatly and with which I disagree but I look upon that great and fascinating unfolding [of new order and new civilization as the most promising feature of our dismal age. If the future is full of hope, it is largely because of Soviet Russia and what it has done, and I am convinced that if some world catastrophe does not intervene, this new civilization will spread to other lands".[67]

The third factor was the geographical proximity that makes one the neighbour of another. Hence the situation of a very powerful country like the Soviet Union adjacent to India and this fact has been magnified both for geographical and security considerations.[68] For this reason the British bogey of Soviet invasion on India has always been discounted by Indian leaders.[69] But sometime Jawaharlal Nehru pointed out "Russia cannot be ignored by us, because she is our neighbour, which may be friendly to us or may be a thorn in our side".[70]

From the above account it can be deduced that Indian leaders specifically Nehru, the architect of India's foreign policy, had a keen interest in establishing a cordial relationship with the Soviet Union prior to independence. As he stated in the Constituent Assembly: "... The Soviet Union being our neighbour, we shall inevitably develop closer relations with it. We can not afford to antagonize Russia".[71]

In his keenness to befriend the Soviet Union after India became independence, Nehru reached an agreement with the Soviet Union to establish diplomatic relations between the two countries.[72] The appointment of Vijayalaxmi Pandit, sister of Nehru as ambassador of India to Soviet Union on 25 June 1947[73] demonstrated Nehru's eagerness to establish diplomatic relations with Soviet Union.

The same keenness was not expressed by the Soviet Union.[74] The reasons for Soviet Union's being lukewarm in reciprocating India's overtures may "be found in Soviet Union's lack of proper under standing of India's leaders and its sovereign status after it got independence in 1947. As Zhdanov declared in September 1947 that the imperialists were keeping China and India in "obedience and enslavement".[75] This was indicative of Soviet Union's thinking that India was even after independence resembling China under Ching Kai-shek. The British Act of Independence had in no way changed India's status in the British Empire, an article commented.[76]

Besides this misperception of India's sovereign and independent status, a wrong appraisal was made of Mahatma Gandhi and Nehru.[77] India's policy of non-alignment was not viewed in its correct perspective by the Soviet Union nor its international policy was properly understood.[78] Thus, even India's progressive policies as condemnation of South Africa were termed as "a coincidence" the result of "close discussion and collaboration"[79] "Nehru's initiative to convene a conference of 18 Afro-Asian nations in January 1949 in New Delhi was seen as suspect by the Soviet Union.[80] In the same vein, in the United Nation India's stand was divergent from that of Soviet Union.[81]

On the Kashmir issue, the Soviet Union in the initial stage saw it very differently than it was to do so a decade later. At this point it felt that "the people of Kashmir today face two enemies: the forces of intervention who have invaded their territory and the Indian reactionaries, who are out to restore the rule of the Maharajah".[82]

India's membership of the Commonwealth added to Soviet Union's suspicion of influence of western countries on India.[83] In the face Soviet Union's cold and indifferent attitude, India leaned to west for economic and political reasons. [84] It also compelled Nehru to make statements critical of the Soviets. As he said: " World Communism in its expansionist aspect, just as any other expansionist movement, is considered a danger to peace and freedom". [85]

He allegedly saw the Soviet hand in fomenting communist revolt in South India. [86] Finally, it may be said that in the initial phase the potential of India's friendship was not clearly perceptible to the leaders of the Soviet Union in view of closer alliance between them and China. [87]

Korean crisis brought a change in Indo-Soviet relationship. India's mediating role as a non-aligned country was highly commended in Soviet capital. Nehru sent appeals to Stalin and Dean Acheson during the beginning of the crisis: "The aim of India is to localize the conflict and assist a speedy peaceful settlement through the elimination of the present impasse in the Security Council". [88] Nehru's proposal was accepted by Stalin[89] and jettisoned by Acheson. The signing of the Korean armistice agreement in July 1953 on the basis of the original unchanged Indian formula helped in clearing the misunderstanding between India and Soviet Union to the extent that the Soviets declared: " From the political and practical point of view there should be included not only the Soviet Union but also such states as India, which had made a considerable contribution to the cessation of hostilities". [90]

Stalin's death hastened the process and the Soviet clarified that " relations between India and the USSR will grow stronger and develop in a spirit of friendly cooperation". [91] The Soviet Union took an appreciative note of India's non-aligned posture. [92] From 1954 onwards as a sign of gesture of friendship, the Soviet Union worked for the inclusion of India in all international forums. It pleaded for the inclusion of Communist China, Czechoslovakia and India in the UN's Disarmament Commission[93].

The signing of the Pakistan-US military pact in May 1954 strengthened Indo-Soviet amity. Nehru's criticism of these pacts harbingered a new thaw between India and the Soviet Union. [94] Thus, a convergence of interests took place between India and the Soviet Union, though for different reasons. Both countries' perception of each other as upholders of peace strengthened the move for friendship and ultimately coordinated their attempts at reducing "world tensions".[95] Removal of political misunderstandings gave way to increased diplomatic access to each other.[96]

Visits of dignitaries, from both countries further strengthened the relationship between the two countries. Nehru visited the Soviet Union in June 1955. The reception that Nehru got was unparallel before or since.[97] The Joint communiqué issued at the end of Nehru's visit on 23 June 1955 marked a watershed in Indo-Soviet relationship. Both countries affirmed expression of faith in the Panchasheela principles of conduct in international relations. Common points were reached on the representation of Red China in the United Nations, peaceful settlement of the Formosa dispute and appreciation of Bandung Conference.[98] The Joint statement was entirely Indian in style and substance.[99]

Nehru's visit was reciprocated by the visit of Soviet Prime Minister Bulganin and Khrushchev. Their visits appended new significance to India. The Soviet support to India on Kashmir and Goa issue was assured by both the leaders.[100] India's newly found independence through its non-aligned policy compelled Nehru to explain that: "We are happy that India and the Soviet Union have come closer... But this friendship and cooperation is not aimed against any nation of people. I have often said we do not propose to join any camp or alliance. This is our basic policy"[101].

The most important outcome of this phase of Indo-Soviet relations was economic in nature. It produced a new era in economic cooperation,[102] and provided a deep base on which future policy could be built. This friendship would no way be a colossal with clay feet. The Suez and Hungarian crisis were to prove this. India's support of the Soviets "caused much misunderstanding regarding India's foreign policy".[103] Its criticism of the Suez crisis was immediate.[104] It asked for United Nations troops under the UN Emergency Force to be stationed in Egypt.[105]

But in regard to Hungarian crisis, the reaction of Nehru was cautious and mild,[106] and voted against a resolution, which demanded not only immediate withdrawal of Soviet troops but also an early election to be held under the aegis of the United Nation.[107] In all other resolutions sponsoring Soviet withdrawal and other related moves India abstained.[108] From all these it can be gleaned that India though espoused national independence, non-interference into the internal affairs of another state, it did not condemn Soviet Union for its action in Hungary.[09]

India's differential attitude in both Suez and Hungary crises was explained by the growing relationship between India and Soviet Union.[110] But in the context of Cold war, military alliances, and its own national interests India's role can be understood. As Nehru stated: "... because we felt this (election) was contrary to the charter and would reduce Hungary to less than a sovereign state. Any acceptance of intervention of this type and foreign supervised elections seemed to us to set a bad precedent which might be utilized in future for intervention in other countries".[111]

The Kashmir issue became the catalyst in Indo-Soviet relation because of Indian need of Soviet veto. Coordination of views on bilateral issues led to a new perception on international issues, which projected similarity of opinion. Thus, Nehru along with the Soviet Union criticized the Eisenhower doctrine for the Middle East enunciated on 5 January 1957.[112] When the crisis culminated in the intrusion of American and British forces into Lebanon and Jordan in July 1958, Khrushchev sought the participation of India in any Summit Conference even in the Security Council for solution of the crisis.[113] Similarly, on the issues of disarmament for world peace and easing tensions, the Soviet Union's views were in agreement with that of India. The Soviet Union raised the participation of India in London Conference fourteen times as revealed by the Soviet delegate to the UN Disarmament Subcommittee.[114]

From the above analysis, it may be averred that the friendship between the two countries was growing, though it was not free of irritants. Nehru was critical of Soviet Union's pressure tactics on Yugoslavia to which Khrushchev replied: "I hope, you will let us solve our ideological disputes in our own way".[115] Nehru also supported the stand of West Germany, which was contrary to the Soviet position. But despite the occasional irritants, no decline in the friendship between the two countries was seen.

When India intervened in Goa in 1961 to liberate it from Portugal, Soviet Union unlike the United States supported India's action.[116] Later when the matter was raised in the Security Council on 18 December, the Soviet Union opposed it and exercised its veto on the ground that it was within the domestic jurisdiction of India. [117]

China Factor

While analyzing Indo-Soviet relations the China factor has to be considered. For no, "Indian statesman can ignore the compelling fact that two great powers of the communist world stand at the gates of the Indian subcontinent".[118] One must also not overlook the fact that China was at the same time very important for the Soviets. Thus, any policy of befriending India would be misunderstood in Chinese circles. Especially the fact that China did "not want India to be non-aligned and it was one of the reasons why the Chinese had fallen out with the Soviet Union".[119]

Though the different paths chosen by the both communist countries, envisaged the disintegration of the monolithic communist structure and created a reason for Soviet continuation of friendly relations with India. At that stage the Sino-Indian worsening relations only preempted Soviet policy for which they were not yet prepared. Though Nehru was to have remarked during his visit to the United States: " Khrushchev sees India as a future bulwark against China and it is in the Soviet interest to help restrain Peking".[120] The fissures in the Sino-Soviet relations were neither too deep nor too obvious for a clear-cut break.

Thus, in mid 1959 when border clashes took place between India and China, the Soviet Union maintained a neutral stand by appealing both countries to settle dispute amicably.[121] On December 22,1959 the Soviet Press published the Indian allegation without waiting for the Chinese reaction.[122] This neutralist stand was highly appreciated by the Indian leaders. As Nehru stated: "Considering everything, the statement was a fair one and unusual one for the Soviet Government to sponsor".[123]

The three years preceding the Chinese attack on India must have prepared the Soviets for what was to come. Thus, though in the initial stages its tilt in favour of China was perceptible as it held Chinese stand on the McMahon line as correct, and held as constructive the Chinese proposals, and asked India to accept these proposals without conditions.[124] But with the Cuban missile crisis and Chinese criticism of Soviet handling the balance tilted completely in the favour of India. Without any reference to McMahon line or Chinese proposal or taking any offence at India's insistence, it called for Chinese withdrawal before negotiation and simultaneously for a ceasefire.[125] The vacillation in Soviet Union's stand for a short period did not bring any deterioration in Indo-Soviet relationship. As Nehru stated: "not that we are anxious to see other countries falling out among themselves, but still something that affects us, something that increases our good relations with other countries, is welcome".[126] The predicament of the Soviet Union was well understood by the Indian leadership. As stated by Nehru:

> The Soviet Union has been, as the House knows, consistently friendly to us. It has been put in a very difficult position in this matter because they (the Soviets) have been and are allies of China, and hence the embarrassment to them as between a country with which they are friendly and a country which is their ally. We have realized that and we do not expect them to do anything, which would definitely mean a breach over there. It is not for us to suggest to any country. But we have had their good will and good wishes all along, even very recently, and that is a consolation to us and we certainly hope to have that in the future. [127]

This Indian understanding of the Soviet Union must have helped strengthen their friendship. Despite the phase of understanding in the inter-regional scene, the Pakistan factor, much closer to India remained obtuse.

Pakistan Factor

In the Indo-Pak war of 1965 the Soviet Union was a major influence, which resolved the conflict. The main purpose of the Soviet Union was to wean away Turkey, Iran and Pakistan, its southern neighbours from the United States' military pacts like CENTO. [128] The unreserved support given by the Soviet Union to India earlier seemed to be diluted. Nehru's death and Khrushchev's removal from power saw the initiation of a new Soviet policy. [129]

In pursuance of its policy to retain its influence, in Pakistan the Soviet Union decided to supply military hardware to Pakistan, which was a matter of great concern to Indian decision makers. In reply to Indira Gandhi's letter expressing concern Kosygin stated that if military hardware was supplied to Pakistan, it was in the larger interests of promoting peace in the region.[130] On President Zakir Hussain' s visit soon after, the Soviet Union asked India and Pakistan to settle all their disputes amicably and establish "good neighbourly relations".[131]

Despite strong reactions against the policy of the Soviet Union in India, [132] the Indian leadership led by Indira Gandhi showed a sign of restraint and adroitness, and diplomatic efforts were made by her to modify the stand of Soviet Union. She said, "friendship is not exclusive. If you are friends with one, you can not prevent that person from having other friends".[133] The Soviet Union's shift in foreign policy during this period was certainly "to exercise Indian Government's mind for sometime".[134] But, despite the efforts by the Indian Government, no change was found in Soviet policy. On 9 April 1969, Swaran Singh, the Defence Minister stated in the Parliament: "We have ... to admit that we have not been able to convince USSR of the greater danger implicit in the supply of arms to Pakistan".[135]

It was only towards the end of 1970 that a change in Soviet policy was seen. This came to be highlighted following President Giri's visit to Moscow in October 1970,[136] and Foreign Secretary T. N. Kaul's trip to Moscow.[137] The Indian Government was satisfied that the Soviet Union did not intend to supply any military hardware to Pakistan in addition to that already supplied in the past.[138]

Another irritant, which stayed, was the showing of large chunks of Indian territory as belonging to China. Against all public outrage at this, the Government of India played cool and said that this was not significant for any wrong description in Soviet Encyclopedia about India's territory which did not "in any way affect or reflect the Soviet government's understanding of and respect for India's frontiers." [139]

India repeated its stand in Czechoslovakia crisis in 1968 as it had done in Hungary crisis. It refrained from all attempts at UN to condemn Soviet action. The Soviet leaning in Indian foreign policy was a preponderant factor explaining America's indifference toward India.

Military and Economic Aids

United States' aversion to India becoming economically and militarily independent and strong prompted India to turn to the Soviet Union. From a negligible figure of Rs. 8.1 million, the rise of trade turnover was 719,7 million in 1961, Rs.1, 753.6 million in 1965,[140] Rs.2, 269.5 million in 1966-67[141] and Rs.4, 970 million at the end of 1968[142]. India's primacy to public sector economy got not only accolades but also economic assistance from USSR in establishing steel plants, military factories, and oil refineries, heavy engineering and electric plants flowed to India.

Though the total aid of USSR to India was less than what the US had given to India, its aid towards public sector and heavy industry contributed to India's economic self-reliance. After the visits of Indian Planning and Food Minister to Soviet Union, Indira Gandhi paid her visit in July 1966. Her visit confirmed Soviet aid totaling 970 million roubles (830 crores) to India's Fourth Five-year plan. Between 1954-67 Moscow invested nearly 800 crores in economic assistance to India and the trade between India and the Soviet Union jumped (1970-76) from about 300 crores to some 800 crores.[143]

Initially the Soviet offer of military hardware in 1954 was not accepted by India, but in the late fifties, the IAF received a squadron of IL-14/ transport aircraft. In the first week of August 1962, the MIG deal was finalized. In August 1964 India negotiated with the Soviet Union for three squadrons of MIG-21 interceptors, plant and machinery for the proposed MIG plant, P7-76 amphibious and 130 medium guns. In order to modernize its navy, India signed an agreement in 1965 with USSR under which 4 submarines and 5 Deta-class patrol boats were to be built by Soviet Union for India. The installation of MIG manufacturing plant by Moscow in India strengthened the relationship between two countries. [144] According to a Washington report of January 25 1966, India had to obtain 100 SU-7 supersonic jet fighter bombers from the Soviet Union. Initially India had requested the US for F-104 and later for F-105s. The Soviet Union offered India MIG-21s and SU-7s to strengthen India's air defense. When the United States and other western countries expressed their unwillingness to meet India's defense needs, the Soviet Union came forward to help India with advanced fighter-bomber aircraft. [145]

Reemergence of the China Factor before the Bangladesh Crisis

In 1969 the entrance of China as a nuclear power into the international realm, marked a tough competition for the Soviet Union, This antipathy between the two giants finally culminated in border conflicts and recurrent clashes. Along with this the secret minute between US and China in 1969[146] prompted the Soviets to reconsider their relationship. It heightened their need to cultivate India as a countervailing force against China.

India was not unprepared diplomatically as it had faced the same problem with China in 1962. Its foreign Minister thus pointed out that "Judging by our own experience with China we are not surprised that the Chinese government is adopting similar postures towards the Soviet Union. The tactics of provoking border incidents in order to reopen the whole boundary question ... Our position is quite clear. We are not in favour of altering historically established borders". [147] Despite this firm commitment and policy the Soviet Union has not unequivocally accepted India's definition of its northern borders, which the great Soviet Encyclopedia of 1969 expressed in its erroneous maps to the discomfiture of India. Soviet Union explained this aberration as of little significance in view of their overall relationship. [148] The increment of animosity between Soviet Union and China and Nixon's indifference to India and equipping Pakistan with modern advanced weapons, a revoking of arms embargo after 1965, occasioned a convergence of interests of both India and USSR.

When the presence of China and America in the Indian subcontinent became preponderant, the Soviets seemed to have offered a treaty of friendship to India in 1969. [149] India's response to the Soviet initiative was not instantaneous. A treaty of friendship with a super power like Soviet Union seemed to have waned India's much vaunted non-aligned posture. That's why India's response to Soviet initiative was one of hesitation and reluctance. The option was kept open to India to sign it when the proper time would come.[150]

Indira Gandhi's securing absolute majority of seats in the Lok Sabha in 1971 general election marked the elimination of rightist forces. TASS praised her 1971 election victory as " a great success for the supporters of the policy of peace and social progress". [151] Similar was the reaction of a Soviet academician when he said that the defeat of " rightist parties" was a "positive change" with which India had "entered upon a new stage in its development".[152]

Thus a change in Soviet policy was envisaged. The friendship between India and the Soviet Union was further deepened. This was marked in the beginning of 1971.

References

1. J. David Singers, "International Influence: A Formal Model" in James Rosenau, ed., International Politics and Foreign Policy: A Reader in Research and Theory (New York: The Free Press, 1969) revd edn, p.383.
2. For details see, James N. Resenau, "Theorizing Across System; Linkage Politics Revisited", in Jonathan Wilkenfeld, ed., Conflict Behaviour and Linkage Politics (New York: David McKay, 1973), p.43.
3. Jawaharlal Lal Nehru, India's Foreign Policy: Selected Speeches, September 1946- April 1961 (Delhi: Government of India, 1961), p.22.
4. Louis J. Cantori and Steven L. Spiegel, The International Politics of Regions: A Comparative Approach (New Jersey: Englewood Cliffs, Prentice Hall, 1970), p.5.
5. Nehru's Speech in the Constituent Assembly of India on 8 March 1948, Constituent Assembly of India Debates (CAID), vol. III, no.2, 8 March 1948, p.1768, see also Nehru, India's Foreign Policy, n.3, p.35.
6. Bimal Prasad, " An overview", in Bimal Prasad ed., India's Foreign Policy: Studies in Continuity and Change (New Delhi: Vikas, 1979), p.483.
7. Nehru, n.3, p.39.
8. Nehru's Speech in the Constituent Assembly of India on 4 December 1947, CAID, Vol. II, pp.1262-3. See also ibid., p.28.
9. India, Lok Sabha Debates (LSD), Series 2, vol. XXIII, 1-12 December 1958, Col.3959.
10. Bimal Prasad, n.6, p.485.
11. Nehru's, Indian Foreign Policy, n.3, p.35.
12. Nehru's inaugural address to Asian Relations Conference on 23 March 1947, Asian Relations (ARS), (New Delhi, Asian Relations Organisation, 1948), pp.20-27.

13. Indira Gandhi's address to the World Peace Council, New Delhi, on 18 October 1970, in the Years of Endeavour: Selected Speeches of Indira Gandhi, August 1969-August 1972, (New Delhi: Government of India, 1975), p.699.
14. John Spanier, American Foreign Policy since World War – II (New York, 1973), edn. 6, p.27.
15. For details see Ibid., pp.45-69.
16. Russell H. Fifield, South East Asia in United States Policy (New York, 1963), p.74.
17. W.W. Rostow and others, An American Policy in Asia (New York, 1955), p.5.
18. Hans J. Morgenthau, American Foreign Policy: A Critical Examination (London, 1952), pp.125-201.
19. T.V. Kunhi Krishnan, The unfriendly Friends: India and America (New Delhi: Indian Book Company, 1974), p.133.
20. Adi H. Doctor, Essays on India's Foreign Policy (New Delhi: National 1977), p.67.
21. B.K. Shrivastava, "India and the United States" in Bimal Prasad, ed., International Studies, Vol. 17, no.3-4, July-December 1978, pp.759-60.
22. S.L. Poplai and Phillips Talbot, India and America: A Study of their Relations (New Delhi: Indian Council of World Affairs, 1958), p.121.
23. Dinesh Singh, "Indo-U.S. Relations, "The Institute for Defence Studies and Analyses Journal (New Delhi), Vol.6, July 1973, p.6.
24. SCOR (Security Council Official Records), yr. 17, mtg 1016, 22 June 1962, p.4.
25. Foreign Affairs Record, Vol. 8, no.6, June 1962, p.117.
26. India, House of the People, Parliamentary Debates, Part 2, Vol. 1, no. 12, 1 March 1954, col.971.
27. See Theodore C. Sorensen, Kennedy (New York, 1965), p.664. W.M. Dobell, "Ramifications of the China-Pakistan Border Treaty", Pacific Affairs (Vancouver, Canada), Vol. 37, Fall 1964, pp. 286-7. Chester Bowles, Promises to keep; My Years in Public Life 1941-1969 (New Delhi, 1972), p.472.
28. SCOR, yr. 18, Supplements 1963, Doc. S/5437, pp.5-6.
29. For details see B.N. Chakravarty, India speaks to America (Bombay, 1966), pp. 112, 114-17. John Kenneth Galbraith. Ambassador's Journal: A Personal Accounts of the Kennedy's

Years (London, 1969), p.286. SCOR. Yr. 16 mtg 988, p. 27. The Department of State Bulletin, vol. XLVI, 22 January 1962, p.149.

30. Sorensen, n.27, p.578.
31. Arthur M. Schlesinger Jr. A. Thousand Days: John F. Kennedy in the White House (Boston: Houghton Mifflin, 1965), p.528.
32. Adi H. Doctor, n.20, p.75.
33. Foreign Affairs Record (FAR), Vol. 7, no.9, September 1961, pp.259-60.
34. New York Times, 28 October 1961, see also K. Rangaswamy, " A letter from New Delhi: Why Menon irritates the West", The Hindu, 18 November 1961.
35. J. P. Jain, India and Disarmament: Nehru Era: An Analytical Study (New Delhi, 1974), Vol. 1, p.98.
36. *Ibid.*
37. GAOR, Session 16, 1 cttee, mtg 1178, 26 October 1961, p.79.
38. Dean Acheson, Present at the Creation: My Years in the State Department (New York: W.W. Norton, 1969), pp.334-36.
39. Harold W. Chase and Allen H. Lermen, ed., Kennedy and The Press (New York, 1965), p.496. See also Shivaji Ganguly, "U.S. Military Assistance to India 1962-63: A Study in Decision Making", India Quarterly (New Delhi), vol. XXVIII, July-September 1972, p.221.
40. Galbraith, n.29, p.504. See also Chester Bowles, n.27, pp.440-82.
41. Ganguly, n.39, pp.221-22.
42. T.N. Kaul, Reminiscences: Discreet and Indiscreet (New Delhi: Lancers Publication, 1982), p.280.
43. Benjamin I. Schwartz, "The New Turn in Sino-U.S. Relations: Background and Significance", Pacific Community, Vol. 3, no.1, October 1971, pp.19-31.
44. Chester Bowles, "America and Russia in India", Foreign Affairs (New York, N.Y.), vol.49, July 1971, p.638. "The United States Government however has never considered India to be of major political significance to the future of Asia".
45. Kaul, n.42, p.270.
46. Surjit Mansingh, India's Search For Power: Indira Gandhi's Foreign Policy 1966-1982 (New Delhi: Sage, 1984), p.75.
47. For details see Lloyd I Rudolf and Susanne Hoeber Rudolf, The Regional Imperative (New Delhi: Concept Publishing House,

1980), Introduction: "The Coordination of Complexity in South Asia", pp. 1-100.

48. Memorandum Department of States, 15 May 1965, quoted in Mansingh, n.46, p.78.
49. K. Subrahmanyam, Bangladesh and India's Security (Dehra Dun: Palit and Dutt, 1972), p.11.
50. Thom A Travis, "United States – India Relations: Obstacles and Opportunities", India Quarterly (New Delhi), Vol. XLII, no.4, October-December 1986, p.382.
51. Norman D. Palmer, "Ups and Downs in Indo-American Relations", Annals of the American Academy of Political and Social Science (Philadelphia), Vol. 294, July 1954, pp.119-20.
52. For details see Kaul, n.42, pp.273-4
53. Mansingh, n.46, p.77
54. Cable from Ambassador Bowles to Secretary of State Dean Rusk 31 March 1965, National Security Files, Lyndon B. Johnson (LBJ) Library, Austin, Texas, cited in Surjit Mansingh, "India and the United States: What Price Partnership"? Towson State Journal of International Affairs, Vol.13, no.2, Spring 1979.
55. Government of India, Ministry of Commerce Report 1980-81 (New Delhi, 1982), p. XVF.
56. See Mansingh, n.46, p.106.
57. Baldev Raj Nayar, "America and India: The Roots of Conflict" in K.P. Misra, ed., Foreign Policy of India (New Delhi: Vikas Publishing House, 1977), p.281.
58. Subimal Dutt, With Nehru in the Foreign Office (Calcutta: Minerva Associates, 1977), p.217. For the statement of Chester Bowles, see "Mr. Bowles' American Report", Eastern Economist (New Delhi), vol. 18, no.5, February 1953, p.197. India "needs help and deeply appreciates it, provided it comes without strings and from one equal partner to another partner".
59. Kaul, n.42, p.271.
60. Dean Rusk, Memorandum to the President, 28 March 1966, Briefing papers for the visit of India's Prime Minister, White House Files L.B.J. Library, quoted in Mansingh, n.46, p.79.
61. Indira Gandhi to Lyndon Johnson, 12 May 1967, White House Confidential Files, L.B.J. Library, quoted in Mansingh, Ibid., p.111.
62. Harold R.Issacs, " Neutralism in Perspective" in Selig S. Harrison, ed., India and the United States (New York: N.Y. Macmillan, 1961),

p.36, Henry Kissinger, White House Years, produced in India Today, Vol. IV, no.19, 1-15 October, p.1979, p.13, remarked that "By 1971 our relations with India had achieved a state of exasperatedly strained cordiality, like a couple that can neither separate nor get along".

63. Nehru, n.3, p.3.
64. Report on the Indian Constitutional Reforms (Calcutta, 1918), p.14.
65. K.P.S. Menon, Lenin Through Indian Eyes (Delhi, 1970), pp. 54-55. Since the revolution was " against imperialism it might somehow help the movement for Indian independence which, with Mahatma Gandhi's advent on the Indian scene was taking a new turn".
66. Jawaharlal Nehru, Soviet Russia: Some Random Sketches and Impressions (Bombay, 1929), p.4.
67. Report of the Forty Ninth Session of the Indian National Congress (Allhabad, n.d.), pp.9-12, quoted in M. Saleem Kidwai, Indo-Soviet Relations (New Delhi: Rima Publishing House, 1985), and p.21.
68. M.M. Rahman, The Politics of Non-alignment (New Delhi: Associated Publishing House, 1969), p.54.
69. See the statement of Jawaharlal Nehru in his Soviet Russia, n.66, p.91. "The Tsar has gone but the rivalry between England and Russia continues and we are now told that India is threatened by the Soviet Government".
70. Nehru, Soviet Russia, Ibid., p.34.
71. Quoted in K.P.S. Menon, Many Worlds: An Autobiography (Oxford: Oxford University Press, 1965), pp.229-30.
72. The Statesman (New Delhi), 16 April 1947. See also Hindustan Times, 14 April 1947.
73. Kessing's Contemporary Archives (London), 21-28 June 1947, p.8908.
74. Some autobiographical accounts would show lack of reciprocity to India's initiative for establishing friendship. See Vijayalakshmi Pandit, The Scope of Happiness: A Personal Memoir (New Delhi, 1979), pp.240-41, T.N. Kaul, Diplomacy in Peace and War (New Delhi: Vikas, 1979), pp.8-15.
75. Quoted in J.A. Naik, Soviet Policy towards India (New Delhi: Vikas, 1970), p.33.
76. Ibid., p.36.
77. Mahatma Gandhi was criticized as a 'bourgeoisie reactionary' who "aped the ascetics" to liberate India, helped the imperialists and

betrayed" the people. Quoted in K.S. Murthy, Indian Foreign Policy (New Delhi, 1964), p.103. Also see for Soviet Union's silence on Mahatma Gandhi's assassination, K.P.S. Menon, The Flying Troika (London: Oxford University Press, 1963), p.18. The Great Soviet Encyclopedia held Gandhism ' a reactionary political doctrine". Quoted in M.S. Rajan, India in World Affairs 1954-56 (Bombay: Asia, 1964), p.300. See also M. Saleem Kidwai, n.67, p.29. Nehru was held as a "lackey and running dog of British imperialism".

78. Quoted in A.Z. Rubinstein, The Foreign Policy of the Soviet Union (New Delhi, 1960), p.93. For details also see New Times no.22, 31 May 1950, p.30., no.32, 4 August 1948, pp.9-15., no.3, 12 January 1949, pp.8-12.
79. A. Appadorai and M.S. Rajan, India's Foreign Policy and Relations (New Delhi: South Asian Publishers, 1985), p.261.
80. New Times, no.6, 6 February 1949, p.17.
81. SCOR, yr. 2, mtg 217, no.102, p.2698.
82. New Times, no.40, 29 September 1948, p.30. See also K.M. Pannikar, In Two Chinas : Memoirs of a Diplomat (London George Allen and Unwin, 1951), pp.10-11. "It was clear that Russia had become uncertain of India's attitude and was generally suspicious of our approach to questions of vital interest".
83. See T.N. Kaul, Reminiscences, n.42, p.150.
84. Nehru, n.3, p.47. See also his statement in Parliament on 17 March 1950. India's policy of non-alignment "does not mean that in our economic life or in other spheres of life, we do not incline this way or that way". Nehru, Speeches, 1949-53(New Delhi, 1954), Vol. II, p.221.
85. Nehru Press Conferences (New Delhi, 1950), p.122.
86. S. Gopal, Jawaharlal Nehru: A Biography 1956-1964(New Delhi: Oxford University Press, 1979), vol. II, 1947-56, p.23. As pointed by Nehru, "India does not charge the Soviet Union with responsibility for communist activities in India, but we have little doubt that Russia has encouraged them and can certainly stop them if it so chooses".
87. See Kaul, n.42, p.152.
88. Tass (Moscow), 18 July 1950.
89. Kessing's Contemporary Archives, 15-22 July 1950, p.10847.
90. Vyshinsky, General Assembly Official Records (CAOR), session 7, 1 Cttee, mtg 623, p.751. See also New Times, no. 33, August

1953 supplement, p.15. Soviet Premier Malenkov stated in Supreme Soviet on August 1953: "In the efforts of peace loving countries directed towards ending the Korean war, India made a significant contribution".

91. New Times, Ibid., The slogan of the CPSU Central Committee on the occasion of 37 anniversary of the October Revolution wished " friendship and cooperation" between the two countries for "the protection of peace through out the world". Cited in Naik, n.75, p.79.
92. New Times, no.24, 1954 Supplement, p.4.
93. Hindustan Times, 20 April 1954.
94. Times of India, 26 November 1953.
95. Quoted in J. Vibhakar, A model Relationship (New Delhi, 1972), p.17.
96. K.P.S. Menon, Many Worlds: An autobiography (Oxford: Oxford University Press, 1965) pp.282-7. The Indian embassy was reported to have stated about the lavish reception and facilities provided by the Soviet Union.
97. Washington Post, 7 June 1955. See also The Statesman (Calcutta), 8 June 1955. " ...This was the most enthusiastic demonstration staged for any foreign visitor since World II, not excluding Mr. Chou-En-lai and other ideological allies of the country". See also M.S. Rajan, n.77, p.308. "He (Nehru) received a fantastically popular and affectionate reception".
98. For full Text see Foreign Policy of India: Texts of Documents 1947-59 (New Delhi: Government of India, 1959), edn. 2, pp.183-87.
99. Quoted in Saleem Kidwai, n.67, p.49.
100. Hindustan Times, 11 December 1955, Khrushchev declared at Srinagar on December 9 that Kashmir People have already decided to join the Indian Union. Also see Foreign Policy of India, n.98, pp.185-87. See also N.A. Bulganin and N.B. Khrushchev, Visit of Friendship to India, Burma and Afghanistan: Speeches and Official Documents. November-December 1955 (Moscow, 1956), p.112.
101. The Great Soviet Encyclopedia, 2nd edn. 10, p. 203. Quoted in Kidwai, n.67, p.55.
102. Ministry of Commerce and Industry, India's Trade Agreements with other Countries: As in Force on December 15, 1953(New Delhi, 1954), pp.146-56. See also FAR, Vol.1, no. 2 February 1955,

pp.32-37. An agreement was signed to install a steel plant at Bhillai. See also J. Vibhakar, n.95, p.17. The Statesman, 5 June 1955.

103. K.P.S. Menon, India and the Cold War (Bombay, 1966), p.48.
104. The Hindu, 1 November 1956. Nehru's address to Congress legislators and workers in Hyderabad. "I have come across no grosser case of naked aggression than what England and France are trying to do".
105. F A R, Vol. II, no.11, November 1956, pp.74-75.
106. GAOR, Emergency Session II, 4-10 November 1956, 569 mtg. p.44.
107. Ibid., 571 mtg. p.68. Menon said: "We cannot subscribe to the idea that any sovereign state can agree to elections under the UN Organisation".
108. Nehru, n.3, p.556. See also GAOR, mtg. 608, p.529.
109. For Indian delegate A. Lall's abstention from voting see GAOR, Emergency Session II, 614 mtg, 8 December 1961, p.1428-29.
110. See V.K. Krishna Menon's statement in UN General Assembly II Session, 6 December 1956. Produced in FAR, Vol. II, no.11, November 1956, p.205.
111. Lok Sabha Debates, Vol. IX, no.4, part II, 19 November 1956, col. 388. It was obvious that Nehru meant Kashmir. See Kidwai, n.67, p.78.
112. For details see Ibid.
113. See For the statement of Krushchev, The Hindu, 20 July 1958. "We consider it essential that the representative of India in the person of Nehru should take part in the Security Council meeting".
114. The Hindu, 6 September 1957.
115. K.P.S. Menon, n.77, p.208.
116. Keesing's Contemporary Archives 1961, p.1860. Quoted in A. Appadorai and M.S. Rajan, n.79, p.273.
117. See SCOR yr. 16, mtg. 988, 18 December 1961, pp.25-26.
118. Michael Brecher, India's Foreign Policy (New York, 1957), p.4.
119. F A R, Vol. IX, no.9, September 1963, p.3
120. S. Harrison, "Troubled India and Her Neighbours" in Foreign Affairs, Vol. 43, no.2, January 1965, p.325.
121. The Hindu, 10 September 1959. See also Pravada, 1 November 1959.
122. H. Getman, Communist Strategies in Asia: A Comparative Analysis of Government and Parties (New York, 1962), p.116.
123. Quoted in The Hindu, 12 September 1959.

124. R. Vaidyanath quoted in Saleem Kidwai, n.67, p.91. Also see for details Charles H. Heimsath and Surjit Mansingh, A Diplomatic History of Modern India (New Delhi: Allied Publisher, 1971), pp.441-2.
125. Pravada, 5 November 1962.
126. Nehru's statement in Rajya Sabha on 2 September 1963. Produced in FAR, Vol. IX, no.9, September 1963, pp.194-5.
127. Prime Minister on Chinese aggression, Ministry of External Affairs (New Delhi, 1962), p.87.
128. Mansingh, n.46, p.138.
129. Appadorai and Rajan, n.79, p.272.
130. See V.P. Dutt, India's Foreign Policy (New Delhi: Vani Educational Books, 1984), pp.104-5.
131. F A R, vol. XIV, no.7, July 1968, pp.160-63.
132. For Piloo Mody and M.R. Masani's comment see Hindustan Times, 12 and 23 July 1968. A.B. Vajpayee and Nath Pai's comment see also Hindustan Times, 14 and 16 July 1968.
133. Indira Gandhi, Replying to debate on Soviet arms supply to Pakistan on 22 July 1968 in Lok Sabha Debates, V ol. XVIII, 22 July 1968, col. 466.
134. Appadorai and Rajan, n.79, p.279.
135. Asian Recorder, Vol. XV, no.33, 13-19 August 1969, p.9076.
136. Free Press Journal (Bombay), 2 October 1970.
137. Hindustan Times, 31 October 1970.
138. F A R, Vol. XVI, no.11, November 1970, pp. 224-45.
139. For Swaran Singh's statement see India, Rajya Sabha Debates, Vol. LXXIII, no.9, 6 August 1970, cols. 128-33. For general debates, cols. 128-62.
140. Yearbook of International Trade Statistics 1965 (New York, 1967), p.361.
141. The Statesman's Yearbook 1968-69(New York, 1968), p.381.
142. B.R. Bhagat, "Indo-Soviet Trade: Promising prospectus Ahead", Commerce, April 11 1970.
143. Figures from Government of India, Economic Survey 1979-80, pp.131-38.
144. See V.P. Dutt, n.130, pp.112-3. See also K.Subrahmanyam, "Quarter Century of Indo-Soviet Friendship", National Herald, 20 April 1972.

145. V.P. Dutt, "Indo-Soviet Relations: Convergence of Interest", in V.D. Chopra, ed., Studies in Indo-Soviet Relations (New Delhi, 1986), p.52.
146. Henry Kissinger, The White House Years (Boston, Little, Brown, 1979), p.187.
147. Dinesh Singh in the Lok Sabha, 8 April 1969, produced in F A R, Vol. XV, no.4, April 1969. Quoted in Mansingh, n.46, p.141.
148. Swaran Singh in the Loksabha, 25 May 1972, quoted in R.K. Jain ed., Soviet-South Asian Relations 1947-78(New Jersey, 1979), Vol.1, p.386f.
149. Mansingh, n.46, pp.139-40.See also Robert C. Horn, "Indian Soviet Relations in 1969: A Watershed Year"? Orbis, Vol.19, no.4, Winter 1976.
150. See for details Kaul, n.42, pp.254-56.
151. Tass despatch, March 15 1971 in T.V. Kunhi Krishnan, Chavan and the Troubled Decade (New Delhi: Somaiya, 1971), pp.385-6.
152. E.N. Komaraov, Indo-Soviet Cooperation: Historical Background and Present day Developments (New Delhi: Allied, 1976), p.106.

3

American Pakistan Tilt: A Constraint on India's Power During Bangladesh War and Beyond

During the Bangladesh crisis it was plausible to argue that the Indian leaders were hopeful of a political settlement without war in the initial phase. Because the severity of military atrocities on the people of East Bengal and the fleeing of about 10 million refugees with all political, economic and social repercussion on India, would stir the moral conscience of the super powers, and Pakistan military ruler Yahya Khan would be forced to a settlement. But the Indian leadership was soon disillusioned as no response came from the world community. As Indira Gandhi stated in the Lok Sabha on 4 December 1971:

> We repeatedly drew the attention of the world to this annihilation of a whole people, to this menace to our security. Everywhere the people showed sympathy and understanding for the economic and other burdens and the danger to India. But Governments seemed morally and politically paralyzed. Belated efforts to persuade the Islambad regime to take some steps, which would lead to a lasting solution, fell on deaf ears.[1]

From the above analysis, it can be said that the failure of world community to understand the Indian line of approach to the crisis, was an important variable, which made war a near certainty and close other options to resolve the crisis. Thus, Indira Gandhi announced in the Lok Sabha on 24 May 1971: " If the world does not take heed, we shall be constrained to take all measures as may be necessary to ensure our own security and the preservation and development of the structure of our social economic life". [2]

During the Bangladesh crisis in 1971, the United States policy towards the Indian subcontinent was marking a turning point. Yahya Khan's contribution to Nixon' s new China policy was not confined to the arrangement of a secret trip of Henry Kissinger to China in the midst of the Bangladesh crisis. Since Nixon became President in 1969, Yahya Khan was closely associated with this policy. According to one authority, during his visit to Pakistan in 1969 Nixon had a long dialogue with Yahya Khan requesting the latter to let him know the Chinese reaction to his new China policy. As a result, Yahya Khan visited America in October, and China in November 1970 and discussed the problems of Sino-American relations with both Nixon and Chou-En-Lai.[3] In complementarities to the successful role of Yahya Khan, Nixon announced the lifting off the embargo on Pakistan of lethal and military weapons to Pakistan. Even during his earlier visit to Pakistan as Vice-President in December 1953, Nixon was reported to have inclined " to favour military aid to Pakistan as a counter force to the continued neutralism of Jawaharlal Nehru's India".[4]

It has been held by some that the favourable impression formed by Nixon of Pakistan during his visit as Vice-President, continued to influence the content of American policy towards this subcontinent even after his becoming President of America in 1969. As one authority remarks "Nixon's warmer attitude towards Pakistan as Vice-President had not completely cooled during the intervening years". [5] Nixon was reported to have complimented. Yahya Khan during the latter' s visit to Washington in October 1970: "Nobody has occupied the White House who is friendlier to Pakistan than me". [6] It has been argued that the United States' policy should not be explained in terms of Nixon's personal friendship with Yahya Khan.[7] But the impact of Nixon's "subjective feelings" on the policy formulation of the United States cannot be denied. [8] Nixon's pro-Pakistan attitude was nothing but a reward for Yahya Khan for his contribution towards Nixon's China visit.[9]

According to another journalist, " A pro-India posture would have abandoned any role in Pakistan damaging improved relations with China, and still leave uncle Sam second fiddle in India. A pro-Pakistani posture would have destroyed the remnants of our position in India, perhaps recapturing some role in Pakistan, but certainly would improve chances of Nixon's project to gain friendship in Peking". [10] Another version expresses also the similar undertone that establishment of a rapprochement with China would tilt the balance of power in favour of the United States and this as a major foreign policy objective would enhance his personal political fortune. [11] Thus, it can be said that Nixon's concern with China was the main force behind his pro-Pakistani foreign policy. As Nixon and Henry Kissinger "who so largely controlled US foreign relations were to be found in the Lincoln Sitting Room or the Executive Office Building, not reading the cables from Dacca or New Delhi but absorbed in the nuances of the latest Chinese note, planning their reply, contemplating the historic stroke ahead". [12]

Thus, it can be said that during the eruption of Bangladesh crisis the relations between the United States and Pakistan was cordial and close, while the relations with India were not cordial yet hostile. The United States policy was to reduce the tension between Pakistan and India, which would not escalate into a war and peaceful political accommodation within the framework of United Pakistan. A reference to the official statement in June 1971 by Joseph J. Sisco, the Assistant Secretary of the US Government for Near Eastern and South Asian Affairs, in this regard, would explain the basic objectives of the United States' policy, "The first is that we are fully supporting international efforts to provide humanitarian relief assistance to the people of East Pakistan who have been affected by the civil strife". He said similar assistance was also flowing to India for looking after the refugees and secondly, "because of the possibility that the situation in East Pakistan and eastern India could escalate dangerously, we have counselled restraint on both sides". Thirdly, we have made clear our belief that normalcy can be restored in East Pakistan only within the context of a peaceful political accommodation". [13] Like India, the United States also found in the political settlement between East and West Pakistan the key to the solution of the crisis. As Nixon himself has said: "We knew that political settlement between East and West Pakistan was the key to ending the crisis. Our relief programme was an effort to gain the time for a process to work". [14]

But both the United States and India differed about the nature and content of a political settlement.

After the eruption of the crisis, the United States neither divulged publicly the content of the political settlement it wanted nor condemned the military brutality of Yahya Khan. Whatever was conceived as solution to the crisis in terms of political settlement was confined to private diplomacy and secrecy. As Nixon has said: " The United States did not support or condone this military action".[15] This attitude of America was criticized by many scholars.[16] An excerpt from Nixon would reveal the real intention of the United States in not coming forward to a solution of the crisis: "Throughout the summer, we refrained from public declarations but continued to express our concerns privately to all parties. It would have served neither Indian nor Bengali interests for us to alienate ourselves from the Government of Pakistan, whose policy and action were at the heart of the problem".[17]

The United States feared that any public posture might offend Pakistan in view of latter' s importance as a factor in forging a cordial tie between the United States and China. As one US Journal editorially commented: "Washington refuses to do anything which might alienate Gen. Aga Mohammed Yahya Khan who was involved in the break-through in Sino-US relations".[18] It was the perception in the United States that a fresh war between India and Pakistan would vitiate the new international order going to be created by the rapprochement between China and America. Hence any public posture and pressure would antagonize Pakistan. Only through friendly persuasion a political accommodation could be brought about in Pakistan. This was exactly the statement of Christopher Van Holler, Deputy Assistant Secretary of State for Near Eastern and South Asian Affairs, in June 1971 that what was happening in East Bengal was the internal affair of Pakistan and the US government "through its quiet diplomacy" was trying to achieve political accommodation which would enable the return of refugees to their home.[19] Regarding this, Nixon similarly said:" We are not going to engage in public pressure on the Government of Pakistan. That would be totally counter-productive. These are matters we will discuss only in private channels".[20]

The United States overemphasized the humanitarian context to the neglect of a political settlement. In reaction to U Thant's appeal for economic assistance to the East Pakistan refugees, a spokesman of the Government of the United States said that this was the "approach, which we have encouraged and supported".[21] He shared the Secretary General's earnest hope that refugees in India would be " voluntarily repatriated at the earliest possible time", and further he stated: We stand ready to be of assistance in Pakistan, as India, in any international humanitarian relief effort".[22] It is not without a grain of truth that Pakistan which was totally opposed to the UN presence in the initial phase of the crisis, accepted fully the UN presence, because of the friendly persuasion and influence of the United States.[23]

In providing assistance to East Pakistan, the United States did not bring any distinction between the military atrocities on East Pakistan in March 1971 and the devastation caused to it by a cyclone in November 1970. Addressing the United Nations Economic and Social Council on 28 June 1971, George Bush, the United States representative stated: East Pakistan has been exposed to " immense tragedies, the great loss of life in the cyclone last November and the troubles of this spring which have uprooted millions of people and spread hunger and epidemic disease in large areas".[24] In a similar vein, in another address to the same Council on 7 July, he stated that the tragedies of Peru (devastated by earth quake) and Pakistan needed a streamlined international system" to cope with the emergencies of earth quake, flood pestilence and large scale personal dislocation".[25] It was also the strategy of the United States that restoration of economic 'life would facilitate the normalcy of political life. As Nixon observed: "The most constructive role we can play is to 'continue our economic assistance to West Pakistan and thereby to be able to influence the course of events in a way that will deal with the problem of hunger in East Pakistan, which would reduce the refugee flow into India and which will, we trust, in the future look toward a viable political settlement".[26]

But the Indian Government was apprehensive that such an aid to Pakistan would whet the military atrocities of the Pakistan military regime against the people of East Pakistan.[27]

Though the total aid given by the United States was more than that given by all other countries put together,[28] even Americans condemned the United States "over the failure, to give significant assistance to India in meeting even the growing financial burden of the relief of the millions of refugees from East Bengali which by December 1971 was costing India between two and three million dollars a day".[29] It was also considered by Indian leaders as being "woefully inadequate and addressed to the symptom rather than the cause of the trouble".[30]

India's major concern was in regard to a political settlement, which would enable the refugees to return home with safety and honour, than with the peripheral problems of refugee maintenance. As Indira Gandhi stated in the Lok Sabha on 24 May 1971:" ...the question of giving relief to these millions of people is only part of the problem. Relief cannot be perpetual, or permanent; and we do not wish it to be so. Conditions must be created to stop any further influx of refugees and to ensure their early return under credible guarantees for their future safety and well-being".[31]

As regards the concept of political settlement, United States and India differed from each other on means of achieving it but both agreed that a political solution of the crisis was essential. As Nixon wrote to Indira Gandhi on 28 May 1971: "We have been discussing with the Government of Pakistan the importance of achieving a peaceful political accommodation and of restoring conditions under which the refugee flow would stop and the refugees would be able to return to their homes".[32] Similarly in his letter to Yahya Khan on May 28 Nixon reiterated:" I feel sure you will agree with me that the first essential step is to bring an end to the civil strife and to restore peaceful conditions in East Pakistan, I believe, therefore, that it is absolutely vital for the maintenance of peace in the subcontinent to restore conditions in East Pakistan conducive to the return of refugees from Indian territory as quickly as possible".[33]

Despite such vouchsafing the divergence on methods to be used created a situation where as there was no meeting of minds, there could be no solution. This can be illustrated by the different approaches outlined. According to Nixon "It was obvious to us that a lasting political solution could be found only on the basis of some form of autonomy for East Pakistan".[34] Henry Kissinger's statement in a press conference in Washington on 7 December 1971 would explain the divergence of approach to the concept of political settlement of both countries. He said: "We attempted to promote a political settlement, and if I can sum up the difference that may have existed between us and the Government of India, it was this ... We all said that political autonomy for East Bengal was the inevitable outcome of political evolution and that we favoured it. The difference may have been that the Government of India wanted things so rapidly that it was no longer talking about political evolution, but about political collapse".[35]

From this analysis it can be said that while America favoured autonomy within Pakistan, India stood for complete independence of Bangladesh.

The Indian approach denoted a political settlement with the already elected members of Awami League led by Mujibur Rahman.[36] Swaran Singh was to state in the Lok Sabha on 28 June 1971 that, " the political solution is one which is acceptable to the elected representatives led by Sheikh Mujibur Rahman". The United States claimed to have prevailed upon Pakistan to take different conciliatory measures to restore normal life in East Pakistan.[37] But, it was doubtful whether the United States did anything to ask Pakistan to come to a settlement with the already elected members of Awami League, Yahya Khan's attempt to woo a section of the Awami League in close collaboration with the United States, would explain this point. The Financial Times of London reported that Begum Akhtar Suleman, daughter of the late H.S. Suhrawardy had a meeting with certain members of Awami League believing in Pakistan ideology in Dacca to form a new political platform to be led by Zahir-ud-Din, one close associate of late Suhrawardy.[38] Yahya Khan was understood to have offered a proposal for cooperation on the basis of the Awami League's six point demand except provincialization of foreign trade, to Zahir-ud-Din and Kamal Hussain, the constitutional adviser to Sheikh Mujibur Rahman.[39]

That all these were carried on with the collaboration of the United States, could be confirmed through Nixon's statement when he said that: " ... in August, we established contact with Bengali representatives in Calcutta. By early November President Yahya told us he was prepared to begin negotiation with any representative of this group not charged with high crimes in Pakistan or with Awami League leaders still in East Pakistan".[40] In a similar vein Henry Kissinger reiterated in a press conference on 7 December 1971 in

Washington that, the Indian Prime Minister during her visit had been told about our efforts to arrange negotiation between Yahya Khan and leaders of Awami League to be specifically nominated by Mujibur Rahman. In addition to this, on 19 November the ambassador of India was informed about the precise political autonomy for East Pakistan to be discussed with them. [41]

But Kenneth B. Keating, ambassador of the United States to India, challenged the veracity of these above statements. " Mr Keating said he was aware of our repeated statements that we had no formula for a solution, and our belief that the outcome of negotiations would probably be autonomy if not independence, but he regretted that he was not sanguine of any specific statement favouring autonomy". Further he said, " the only message he had on record of this conversation ... makes no reference to this critical fact". He continued that the "statement that Pakistan had authorized US" to contact Mujibur through his attorney seems an overstatement; since according to Islambad ... Yahya on 29 November told Ambassador Farland nothing more than that a Farland - Brohi meeting would be a good idea since Ambassador Farland would be able to obtain from Brohi at least his general impression as to the state of the trial and its conduct. Mr. Keating said he was unaware of any specific authorization from Yahya to contact Mujibur through Brohi ...In any case, as we are all only too unhappily aware, Yahya told Ambassador Farland on 2 December that Brohi allegedly was not interested in seeing him". [42]

From the above analysis it can be concluded firstly, that Yahya Khan was not genuinely interested in a political settlement with Mujibur Rahman, the leader of Awami League. His declaration of disqualification of members of the Awami League who had not participated in revolt or committed crimes and holding of by-election to those cases [43] and his final declaration of disqualification of 79 Awami League members of the National Assembly[44] and his getting fifty-five men elected uncontested[45] would explain this point. The reported statement of Yahya Khan to execute Mujibur Rahman[46] exposed the lack of initiative to reach a political settlement. Secondly, Keating's contestation of the above fact revealed that the United State's claim of exercising influence over Yahya Khan to reach a political settlement in terms of autonomy for East Pakistan was very doubtful.

The supply of economic and military aid by the United States to Pakistan during the crisis revealed the nonchalance of the former to exert any kind of pressure on the latter to come to a political settlement with the leaders of the Awami League. In the World Bank's Aid Pakistan Consortium meeting in Paris on 21 June 1971, Cargill (The head of the ten man team of World Bank officials which had been established in May 1971 to study economic prospects in both West and East Pakistan on behalf of the Bank) submitted his team's report recommending only humanitarian relief and held that "renewed international development assistance would serve little purpose". [47]

Most of the western countries accepted Cargill's recommendation by suspending economic aid to Pakistan. [48] The United States despite its allies' pressures, declined to suspend economic aid. Christopher Van Hollen stated in the Consortium meeting that the United States had decided to dissociate "itself with any decision to condition " its" economic assistance to Pakistan on political settlement". Further he remarked that the United States "did not plan to use aid as a lever to secure a political solution".[49]

It was held by the American press that the United States policy of refusal to use economic sanction against Pakistan and policy of counselling it for political accommodation seemed to be contradictory. [50] Also this policy of the United States was not liked by India, as it would not exercise any kind of pressure on Pakistan to come to a political settlement. The statement by Swaran Singh in Parliament on 25 June 1971 after his return from visits abroad, would explain the perception by India's decision makers that any kind of assistance to Pakistan would make the reaching of political settlement bleak: "I pointed out also that, in fact, any economic assistance, excepting that given on humanitarian considerations to the victims of oppression in Bangladesh under international surveillance, would have the effect of maintaining in power the military machine of the minority now engaged in oppressing the majority of the people of that country, and thus would constitute an unfortunate form of interference in their internal affairs". [51]

The United States' policy of supplying arms to Pakistan was the most preponderant variable affecting India's decision making. Indian leadership was convinced of the remote possibility of political settlement because of this policy of the United States. Certain newspapers in the United States reported evidence of use of US weapons by Pakistan against the East Bengalis.[52] Even this was admitted by David Abshire, Assistant Secretary of State for Congressional Relations in a letter dated 20 April to four senators, and reaffirmed that after the events of 25 March, supply of lethal items though ordered for delivery in October 1970, was suspended to Pakistan.[53] But in June reports appeared in the American news papers that two ships, Padma and Sunderbans, carrying American weapons had already left the United States for Pakistan.[54] What was most astonishing and disturbing was the fact that the news appeared at the time when Swaran Singh landed at Palam air port after his return from America, proving that when he was in that country attempting to solve the crisis, arms were being shipped to Pakistan.[55]

In addition to this fact, another report revealed that the sailing of another four or five ships of arms besides Kaptai to Pakistan was only for the shabbiest of political reasons".[56] Charles Bray, a Government spokesman of the United States stated on 23 June that the shipment of arms to Pakistan was prior to official prohibition.[57] Similarly Henry Kissinger stated in New Delhi on 6 July on his way to Islambad that the flow of arms to Pakistan was due to a "bureaucratic muddle".[58] On 7 July in Rawalpindi it was announced by Henry Kissinger that the United States would not interfere in the sailing of four or five shiploads of military hardware purchased by Pakistan from the United States under valid licenses.[59] In response to this report, the United-States officials expressed that the shipment of arms to Pakistan provided an opportunity to the United States to hold a 'private dialogue' with the Pakistan in order "to provide a political settlement to the East Pakistan crisis. The assurances given by the United States to India was that it was not supplying arms to Pakistan and whatever was in" pipeline was because of confusion in the administration. Washington Post in its July 5, 1971 issue stated, " Here we have a classic example of how the system really works; hidden from public scrutiny, administration officials have been supplying arms to Pakistan while plainly and persistently telling the public that such supplies were cut off".[61] This argument was not at all convincing and did not cut any ice with the India's decision makers. Henry Kissinger stated in his book, "Indian leaders evidently did not think it strange that a country which had distanced itself from most of our foreign policy objectives was asking us to break all ties with an ally over what was in international law a domestic conflict."[62] It appeared as if the Nixon administration was concerned more with its relationship with Pakistan as part of a global strategy rather than with the wishes and aspiration of the Bangladesh people. As Chester Bowles stated that the recent shipment of arms to Pakistan though stated to be "an unfortunate bureaucratic snafu which did not represent United States policy", in reality, " was official US policy and that the decision came directly from the White House", and Nixon's pro-Pakistan policy was responsible for this and it might be justified as "the price we paid to secure Pakistani cooperation in helping Mr. Kissinger set up the President's visit to China... Since there were other ways for Mr. Kissinger to get to Peking, this can only be described as one more devious and needless manoeuvre".[63]

This policy of the United States was resented in India and thus instead of easing the tension and paving the way for a political settlement, it could only lead to a continuation of the military atrocities of Pakistan's military regime which would be a menace to the peace and security of the whole Indian subcontinent. Swaran Singh stated this in the debate in Rajya Sabha on *23* June 1971.[64]

The explanation was always given by the United States that formal economic or military sanctions against Pakistan would undermine their efforts to persuade the latter to reach a political settlement. Senator Edward Kennedy asked with regard to the question of leverage through military aid: "where is that leverage? Where is the leverage to stop the use of US arms, which produce the refugees, and civilian victims that we then must support in India? Where is the leverage to halt the secret trial of Sheikh Mujibur whose only crime is that he won a fresh election? ... Why, if we have the leverage to influence the Government of Pakistan, must our great nation assist in this shabby and shameful enterprise?"[65]

Another factor, which impinged on the decision makers in India, was the failure of the United States to study the crisis as being one between the military regime of Pakistan and the people of East Pakistan. It tended to put it across as one between India and Pakistan. That is why; Nixon wrote to Indira Gandhi that Yahya Khan was ready to withdraw troops unilaterally in order to defuse the border situation.[66] Nixon was highly appreciative of Yahya

Khan's acceptance of stationing of UN observers in the border to facilitate repatriation of refugees. [67] The United States was resentful of India's refusal to withdraw forces from the border and rejection of stationing of UN observers and helping the Bangladesh liberation forces. It squarely put the blame on India for having failed Yahya Khan in reaching a political accommodation under US advice.[68] The suggestion of the United States to India to start negotiation with Yahya Khan was nothing but an attempt on the part of Nixon administration to sidetrack the main problem and equate India with Pakistan. [69] With reference to these above points Indira Gandhi stated in a press meet at National Press Club, Washington, 5 November 1971 : "Pakistan's pleas for observers from the United Nations, for bilateral talks with India, and for mutual withdrawal of troops seemed very plausible at first sight. But these are only methods to divert the attention of the world from the root of the problem to what are merely by-products. We cannot be sidetracked. We cannot have a dialogue with Pakistan on the future of East Bengal, because we have no right to speak for the people of East Bengal. Only Sheikh Mujib or the elected and accepted representations of East Bengal have that right". [70]

Even about political settlement and release of Mujlbur Rahman, the United States was not serious. After his talk with Indira Gandhi during latter's visit to the United States, Nixon was understood to have informed Congress that a time-bound programme for political settlement had been prepared and intimated to her. In an interview with NBC on 7 November when she was asked: "Did the United States suggest some plan of action which you felt you could not accept? " She replied: "No plan of action has been suggested to us".[71] But, Nixon claimed to have saved the life of Mujibur Rahman through his influences. [72] Bhutto contradicted this after he became President of Pakistan that "Mujib was to be executed by 16 December, but it was he (Bhutto) who saved his life. At a White House meeting to decide the course of action to be taken in the Security Council meeting on Indo-Pak war on 5 December, Kissinger said, as quoted by Jack Anderson: "We will go along in general terms with reference to political accommodation in East Pakistan, but we will certainly not imply or suggest any specifics such as the release of Mujib". [73]

Instead of hammering at the root causes of the crisis, the United States' intention was to exercise pressure on India to go back in its pledges to the Bangladesh liberation struggle. Indira Gandhi was reported to have been warned by Nixon that in case of an Indo-Pak war, America would intervene on behalf of Pakistan in compliance with a secret pact agreed between the United States and Pakistan. [74] Indira Gandhi later on, disclosed this in a speech in Delhi " that threats were being given to India and certain pacts with Pakistan were being mentioned". [75]

During Kissinger's visit to India, he was understood to have highlighted the possibility of China's intervention on behalf of Pakistan and reiterated America's neutrality. Kissinger made it clear to L. K. Jha, the ambassador of India to the United States. [76]

From the above analysis, it can be concluded that the United States approach to the solution of the crisis could make it apparent that peaceful political settlement with the already elected leaders of the Awami League was remote.

Though all countries Indira Gandhi visited, agreed with her about the need of a political settlement, the terms of settlement were certainly not to India's liking or perception of the situation. It was within a United Pakistan. [77] Their proposals for a dialogue with Yahya Khan and appointment of UN observers were rejected by her. [78] She pointed out that this would mean that the issue was being taken as one between India and Pakistan and as she pointed out, the UN observers would not solve the root cause of the crisis.[79] Despite Indira Gandhi's exposure of events in right perspective, Britain like United States also was inclined to study the crisis in terms of Indo-Pak conflict and equate India and Pakistan.[80] The British Foreign Secretary doubted the number of refugees cited by India who had entered into India.[81] She was reported to have been asked by Nixon to seal off the border for checking further influx of refugees, to stop all kinds of help to Mukti Bahini and entrust the return of refugees to UN, as a condition for starting negotiation between Yahya Khan and Mujibur Rahman.[82] Nixon's proposal for withdrawal of troops was also rejected by her as it would not solve the crisis and it would jeopardize security because of Pakistan's deployment of troops on the border.[83]

Indira Gandhi was asked by Nixon administration to exercise restraint and forestall armed intervention while steps were being taken to arrange negotiation between Yahya Khan and Mujibur Rahman. [84] It is not clear whether Indira Gandhi left Washington having refused to accept the American position. But it is certain that India was no longer willing to wait in the absence of definite settlement in Indian terms. As she remarked: "Everybody is busy telling us that we must show restraint. But where has the restraint taken us? With all our restraint, we are not getting any nearer to a solution ... People had asked me how long India can manage. Actually that date has long since been passed. I feel that I am sitting on the top of a volcano and I honestly do not know when it is going to erupt".[85]

The two countries differed with each other in regard to political settlement. The United States' concept was within United Pakistan.[86] India was accused of not being cooperative with the United States in itching some amount of autonomy for East Pakistan.[87] Her visit to the United States was a failure, according to News Week otherwise she would not have remarked: "Every nation has its own cross to bear".[88] The only thing she achieved was that she could highlight the justness of India's cause before the Nixon administration, which realized India's determination to solve the crisis at any cost.[89] The non-responsive attitude of countries Indira Gandhi visited to the solution of the crisis on Indian terms, can be marked from her speech at Columbia University on 6 November 1971: "We do not mind if there is no response. But we do think that the limit of our endurance has been reached when they think they can just put their troubles on us".[90]

Even if her visit could not yield any concrete result in terms of political settlement on India's terms short of war, she could not be blamed that she had not tried her efforts and options. If war broke out, it would be despite her best efforts.[91]

After her return from visiting these countries, it became clear to her that nobody was going to pull India out of fire; India was to solve the crisis alone. As she stated in Parliament after her return: " Having said this I must make it clear that we cannot depend on the international community, or even the countries which I visited, to solve our problems for us".[92]

Thus, it can be said that Indira Gandhi's visit to Washington was significant. On the eve of her visit, N.P. Firybin, the Deputy Foreign Minister of Soviet Union left India for Moscow with a joint statement under Art 9 of the Indo-Soviet treaty that both countries agreed that Pakistan was going to attack India. "This move had the appearance - intentional or not — of a diplomatic fait accompli that Washington had to accept, Mrs Gandhi had not come to ask for peace, but to tell the President of the United States what she had decided to do".[93] As a biographer remarked: "In contrast to the wild and non-controversial note she had struck on previous foreign visits, this time her tone was sharp and uncompromising. She spoke, not as a supplicant, but from a position of strength, which reflected both her increased self-assurance and her confidence in the political stability and military preparedness of her Government".[94]

India was left with no choice other than a military intervention to solve the crisis. Though Indira Gandhi could not succeed in overcoming the United States constraint, succeeded in exposing to the world community the circumstances under which India could be forced to choose the military solution of the crisis. For the impending war between India and Pakistan, it was not India rather the United States, China and Pakistan to be blamed. Indira Gandhi's historic letter to Nixon after the war would explain this.[95]

During this period the activities of Mukti Bahini in liberating areas of East Pakistan reached a crowning success. It succeeded in claiming the liberation of " Khulna in the South to Rangpur and Sylhet in north-Kalaroa in Khulna district, Chougacha in Jessore district, Amarkhana, Raiganj and Hatibanda and Barakhata in Rangpur district and Jakiganj and Al-gram in Sylhet district ... South of Faridpur was in the Mukti Bahini's hands long before November, while Madhopur in Mymensingh and Nawabganj, South of Dacca, were also ... brought completely under their control".[96] In addition to this the blowing up a train loaded with Pak troops at Karigram, and sinking of two ships the 'La siva' and ' Mini-labour', liberation of 512 miles territory of Kushtia district and shooting down a Pakistan helicopter in Kushtia district, testified the gathering momentum of the liberation war of Mukti Bahini.[97]

US Role in the United Nations

The attitude of super powers like the United States, the Soviet Union and China to the crisis has already been analyzed. In the light of their attitude the role these powers played in the United Nation can be analyzed.

On the outbreak of war on 3 December 1971 both India and Pakistan sent their complaints to the Secretary General. The Indian

Prime Minister wrote about the Indian towns being attacked by the Pakistan forces and refuted Pakistan allegations about the invasion of Pakistan by Indian armed forces. On the other hand, the Pakistan government informed the international organization about the aggression made by the Indian forces on its eastern and western front. While non-intervention from the United Nations was sought by the Indian Government, the Pakistan Government in pursuance of its long struck UN approach sought the intervention of the United Nation for the protection of its territorial integrity.[98] The Secretary General also informed the Security Council that the war in the subcontinent was "a threat to the maintenance of international peace and security".[99]

The United States also expressed its serious concern to call into session immediately the Security Council, even though it was aware of the ineffectiveness of the United Nations to bring an end to war, the Soviet Union's veto would help India liberate Bangladesh, At least the stance of the United States would be made known to the world.[100]

Thus, at the request of Argentina, Belgium, Burundi, Italy, Japan, Nicaragua, Somalia, UK and the United States, an emergency session of the Security Council was convened on 4 December, But controversy brewed over the issue of the letter addressed by Bangladesh representative Justice Abu Sayeed Choudhury to the Security Council for participation in the debates and supported by Jacob Malik representative of the Soviet Union. China's representative Huang Hua opposed the stand of the Soviet Union on the ground that it would constitute a gross interference in the internal affairs of Pakistan.[101] In view of this opposition by China along with the United States and other nations, the Soviet proposal was rejected by the President of the Security Council.[102] After this controversy both India and Pakistan accused each other of committing aggression against the other and put the blame on each other for the crisis.[103]

The United States ambassador George Bush submitted a resolution calling for an immediate ceasefire and withdrawal of forces to their own sides of the border. This proposal also asked the Secretary General to implement it and Pakistan and India to create condition for the return of refugees. Though the United States was stressing on a political settlement, it put forth that its proposal was essential for creating conditions for a political settlement.[104] The stand of the United States was in conformity with its known Pakistan tilt. The Soviet delegate called this proposal as " one sided" and "unacceptable ". He reiterated that the United States had not taken into account the root causes of the crisis in East Bengal and stressed upon the need of an immediate political settlement based on " will and the inalienable rights and lawful interests of its population". In Soviet Union's view political settlement would only create necessary conditions for cessation of hostilities in the subcontinent. [105] When the proposal of the United States was put to vote, eleven members including China and the United States countenanced this and Poland and the Soviet Union voted against it with Britain and France abstaining. Thus the Soviet veto killed the United States' proposal. The United States' attempt to overlook the main issue in India's perception and impede the work of liberation of Bangladesh by the United Nations could not be effected.

After vetoing the United States proposal, the Soviet Union submitted a resolution calling for "a political settlement in East Pakistan which would inevitably result in a cessation of hostilities" and calling upon Pakistan to cease all acts of violence in East Pakistan, which led to the deterioration of the situation".[106] On 5 December after the meeting was resumed two more resolutions one by China and another by eight non-permanent-members were put before the Security Council. The Chinese resolution called for ceasefire and withdrawal of forces and appealed to all states "to support the Pakistani people in their just struggle to resist Indian aggression".[107] The eight-member nation resolution was just the repetition of the United States resolution.[108] The Soviet resolution supported by Poland was opposed by China with 12 nations abstaining. The 8-member nation proposal received the same voting pattern as the United States proposal had, with a veto cast by the Soviet Union.[109] The Chinese resolution was withdrawn. On 6 December, a resolution for ceasefire was moved by Belgium, Italy, Japan, Nicaragua, Sierra Leone and Tunisia.[110] The delegate of the Soviet Union proposed two amendments to the draft, but it was not put to vote, as there was divergence of views among the three super powers. Soviet Union's amendment to give priority to political settlement in East Bengal was not countenanced by China and the United States. [111]

In view of the statement created by the Soviet Union veto and lack of unanimity among the members about the solution of the crisis in the Security Council, a six member resolution to transfer the matter to the General Assembly under 'Uniting for Peace Resolution' was moved and passed in the Security Council with France, Poland, the Soviet Union and the United Kingdom abstaining.[112] The Soviet Union was of the view that because of the recommendatory nature of the General Assembly, this proposal was only an extension of the attempt " to divert attention from the substance of the problem, from the main cause of the conflict, to muddy the waters, to confuse the United Nations, and to avoid the adoption of a solution to the problem".[113]

The General Assembly met on 7 December 1971 and a resolution cosponsored by 34 member states calling for an immediate ceasefire and withdrawal of forces and creation of conditions for return of refugees, was moved. During the debate Pakistan's delegate Agha Shahi castigated India as an aggressor and blamed it for exploiting the difference between two wings of Pakistan into a demand for liberation which was initially a demand for autonomy. China also supported Pakistan's stand and pleaded with members of the United Nation to put diatribe on India as an aggressor and condemn Soviet support to India. Samar Sen, India's representative pointed out that three things were to be taken into consideration: the genocide in Bangladesh, the peoples struggle against the tyranny and the existence of Bangladesh as an independent state. The proposal for withdrawal of forces, which should include the withdrawal of Pakistani forces from Bangladesh and cessation of hostilities and release of Mujibur Rahman.[114] The Soviet delegate stressed on the recognition of the will of the people of Bangladesh and cessation of bloodshed while not agreeing to a ceasefire between India and Pakistan.[115] The United State's delegate put the blame on India squarely for having complicated the crisis by denying the involvement of the United Nation in the crisis from the very beginning.[116] The general tenor of the debate was in favour of the territorial integrity of Pakistan, non-interference into its internal affairs, immediate ceasefire and withdrawal of troops.[117] When the resolution was put to vote, it was supported by 104 to 11 with 10 abstentions.[118]

After this resolution being passed by such a large majority, another draft resolution moved by the Soviet Union was not put to vote. Thus the resolution passed by the General Assembly was only recommendatory. The Secretary General forwarded the resolution to both India and Pakistan for acceptance. The Pakistan government on 9 December informed the Secretary General about its decision to accept the General Assembly resolution, which called " for an immediate ceasefire and withdrawal of troops".[119]

The reaction of the Indian Government was made known to the Secretary General on 12 December, which stated that the General Assembly resolution was unrealistic and inadequate as it had not given consideration to the creation of conditions for the return of refugees. Thus the calling for ceasefire and withdrawal of troops coupled with a hope that refugees would voluntarily return, seemed to be absurd, as the independence of Bangladesh as a separate state had become a reality. As the Indian note stated: "International law recognizes that where a mother state has lost irrevocably allegiance of such a large section of its people as represented by Bangladesh and cannot bring them under its sway, conditions for the separate existence of such a state comes into being".[120]

Being perturbed by the crushing of Pakistani forces by Indian armed forces and Mukti Bahini, the White House issued a statement on 12 December saying: "In view of India's defiance of world opinion expressed by such an overwhelming majority, the US is now returning the issue to the Security Council". It further stated: "with East Pakistan virtually occupied by Indian troops, a continuation of the war should take on an increasingly the character of armed attack on the very existence of a member state of the UN".[121]

The Security Council began its session on 12 December with a draft resolution from the United States' delegate Bush which noted Pakistan's acceptance of the ceasefire and India's rejection and called upon India to strictly adhere to the General Assembly resolution of 7 December.[122] The United States' delegate held India mainly responsible for the deterioration of the situation. It was India's involvement and non-cooperation with the United Nations, which further complicated the crisis. Even if Yahya Khan's military atrocities on East Pakistan on 25 March was a 'tragic mistake' that

" does not justify the actions of India to intervene militarily and place in jeopardy the territorial integrity and political independence of its neighbour, Pakistan".[123] Serious doubts were expressed about India's real intentions, after the virtual occupation of East Pakistan by Indian armed forces and Bangladesh Mukti Bahini. India was asked whether it had any intention to change the status quo in the western front by occupying the territory of West Pakistan. On December 12 and 13 December, India's External Affairs Minister Swaran Singh refuted the charges of the United States and disavowed the intention alleged to India of forcibly occupying the territories of Pakistan in the western front and change the boundary line.[124] Swaran Singh narrated in detail the genesis of the crisis, the problems created for India by Yahya Khan and the attitude of the United States, other super powers and the international community to sidetrack the root causes of the crisis and only study it in terms of an Indo-Pak conflict. On the issue of territorial designs he said: " We have no intention whatsoever of acquiring any part of West Pakistan or of Bangladesh by conquest or otherwise. Our recognition of the People's Republic of Bangladesh makes it quite clear that we have no territorial designs on Bangladesh". On the western front it was Pakistan, which attacked India first, and had been trying since 1947 to force the change of the boundary line into Indian territory, " We shall certainly use force to repel Pakistan's renewed aggression, whether it is in Kashmir or anywhere else in India".[125] About the draft he said: "The one sided approach in the statement of the representative of the United States to which I have referred is amply reflected in this draft. While preamble paragraph 6 pays lip service to the desirability of finding a political solution, there is nothing in the operative paragraphs to implement this pious wish. No resolution which does not recognize the existence and the rights and obligation of the people of Bangladesh in any ceasefire agreement can be effective or of any practical value".[126]

On 13 December meeting, the Soviet Union raised the issue of participation of Bangladesh's representative in the debate. The President of the Security Council rejected the appeal without a vote.[127] When the United States resolution was put to vote it received 11 votes in favour, Poland and the Soviet Union voted against and Britain and France abstained. Because of the veto of the Soviet Union, the draft resolution of the United States was killed.[128] After this on 13 December, a draft resolution by Italy and Japan was not taken up. On 14 December after mutual consultation among the members, the meeting was adjourned. On 15 December meeting Bhutto, Pakistan's representative accused the Council of legalizing India's aggression, subversion, and occupation of East Pakistan. "Dilatory tactics" and "filibustering" were attributed to the Security Council, while Pakistan was "dying". He tore up the draft resolution and walked out in deep anguish declaring that he would "not be a party to the ignominious surrender of part of" his country.[129] China also was vituperative and offensive in its tone against India and the Soviet Union. It said that at the behest of the Soviet Union, India vitiated peace in the subcontinent.[130]

Meanwhile on 16 December there was surrender of Pakistani forces and unilateral declaration of ceasefire by India and its acceptance by Pakistan on 17 December. On 16 December in the Security Council meeting a draft resolution was moved by the United States and Japan calling for "an immediate and durable ceasefire and cessation of all hostilities in all areas of conflict ... leading to prompt withdrawal of the armed forces from all the occupied territories". At the insistence of India a modification was brought about in the draft.[131] India accepted the resolution and promised to withdraw its troops as soon as possible.

India's unilateral ceasefire and Pakistan's acceptance of it took a dramatic turn. The Security Council on 21 December adopted a resolution cosponsored by six non-permanent members by 13 votes to none with Soviet Union and Poland abstaining which "took note of the unilateral declaration of ceasefire by India in the western sector and Pakistan's agreement thereto with effect from 17 December 1971" and called for "withdrawal of all armed forces to their respective territories".[132] India had nothing to lose by this resolution, as it had already declared as unilateral ceasefire. The issue of Bangladesh in the United Nations came to a close with Pakistan's acceptance of the ceasefire.

From the above analysis it can be concluded that the lines of battle were clearly demarcated while both the United States and China fought vigorously in the United Nations in favour of Pakistan the Soviet Union did so for India. Here though the United States wanted to avoid a war in the subcontinent by advising restraint by India and creating an impression that Pakistan was being wooed to democratic path and in the direction of a political settlement, decision makers in India did not allow themselves to be cajoled into such a grandeur delusion of assurance.

With the outbreak of war, the United States expressed its animosity against India in strong terms. As a spokesman of the United States' state department said: "We believe that since the beginning of the crisis, the Indian policy has, in a systematic way, led to the perpetuation of the crisis, a deepening of the crisis and that India should bear the major responsibility for the broader hostilities that have ensued". [133] The recognition of Bangladesh by the Indian Government was thought as a further deterioration in the situation by the United States policy makers.[134] As a first step, the Nixon administration suspended $ 87.6 million of aid to India that was in the pipeline.[135]

Further, a cancellation of arms and ammunition licenses worth about 2 million dollars was followed "by a decision to cancel about 11,500,000 dollars worth of licenses covering communications and electronic equipment and spare parts for transport aircraft. [136] But no such steps were taken against. Pakistan. The evenness of attitude shown to both India and Pakistan in the 1965 war was not adhered to by the United States in 1971 war. Rather the United States' supply of arms to Pakistan continued. [137] Signs of tilting towards Pakistan continued even after the outbreak of war. The Anderson Papers disclosing the minutes of Washington Special Action Group meeting held on 3, 4, 6 and 8 December 1971 as published by New York Times on 5 and 15 January 1972, would reveal Nixon's tilting towards Pakistan.[138] According to these reports Henry Kissinger was reported to have said: " I am getting hell every half hour from the President that we are not being tough enough on India. He has just called me again. He does not believe we are carrying out his wishes. He wants to tilt in favour of Pakistan".[139]

A passage containing the minutes of the same meeting on 8 December 1971 runs as follows: "Henry Kissinger said that we are not trying to be even-handed. There can be no doubt what the President wants. The President does not want to be even-handed. The President believes that India is the attacker. We are trying to get across the idea that India has jeopardized relation with the

United States".[140] An excerpt from the same papers underlines the fact: " We need to think about our treaty obligations. I remember a letter or memo interpreting our existing treaty with a special India tilt. When I visited Pakistan in January 1962 I was briefed on a secret document or oral understanding about contingencies arising in other than the SEATO context".[141]

While formal announcement of arms suspension to Pakistan was made, as the Anderson Papers disclosed, indirect supplies of arms to Pakistan continued through Jordan and Saudi Arabia. King Hussain of Jordan was allowed to supply P-104 fighter planes from his American supplies to Pakistan.[142] American arms in Vietnam were reported to have been diverted to Pakistan.[143] 75 US supplied military aircrafts were also despatched from Saudi Arabia to Pakistan. [144] Similar disclosures have been made by Anderson of the consideration of the requests by Jordan and Saudi Arabia for transfer of weapons to Pakistan by the Nixon administration from the WSAG meetings.[145]

The Seventh Fleet episode was another evidence of Nixon administration's tilt towards Pakistan and an attempt to balk the war for liberation of Bangladesh. As Nixon said: " If we had not taken a stand against the war, it would have been prolonged and the likelihood of an attack in the west greatly increased ... The complete disintegration by force of a member state was intolerable and could not be acquiesced in by the United Nations. The war had to be brought to a halt".[146] As has been shown earlier the attribution of a sinister design on Kashmir front to India was denied by Indira Gandhi. This is despite the fact that " not a shred of the alleged convincing evidence has ever been made public".[147]

Against this backdrop it can be thus said that the United States' role in the United Nation was tilted completely towards Pakistan, It has been seen already that China's support and sympathy to Pakistan was assured to Pakistan. Though the probability of China's military intervention on behalf of Pakistan was to a greater extent reduced by the Indo-Soviet treaty, it was still considered an important factor in the military strategy of India. After the war, China became more vituperative and scathing in its criticism against India and the Soviet Union. This time China took no time in announcing the attack of India on Pakistan, just half an hour after Pakistan attacked on Indian airfields.[148]

About India's recognition of Bangladesh on 6 December, Beijing Radio termed it as an act of expansionism on the part of India and compared it with Japan's puppet Government in Manchuria, which was recognized by German and Italy. [149] In its criticisms Russia was made the target and held as the main culprit behind India's war. [150] China was of the view that but for the help of the Soviet Union; Indira Gandhi would not have embarked on such a course of action. [151] In the United Nations the debates over the crisis were nothing but exchange of acrimonious words between China and the Soviet Union. Huang Hua said on 6 December "the Soviet social imperialists are carrying out aggression, subversion and expansion everywhere".[152] In reply Mallik of the Soviet Union retorted: "The Chinese representative, with his vicious pathological slander against the Soviet Union, is aspiring to the role of the imperialists' court jester".[153] The United Nation saw a close alliance between China and the United States over the issue of Bangladesh against India. Beijing's behaviour tended to show that they were inclined, "to attach equal importance to the development of their relation with the US and the role played by Pakistan in that development".[154]

The Soviet Union began to tilt more towards India after the outbreak of war. The official statement in Tass warned the United States and China not to interfere in the crisis and to "refrain from steps signifying in this or that way their involvement in the conflict and leading to a further aggravation of the situation in the Hindustan Peninsula". [155] Mutual consultations took place under Art IX of the Indo-Soviet Treaty, which was held between India's Foreign Secretary T.N. Kaul and Soviet ambassador Nikolai Pegov.[156] When Kosygin was in Oslo on 7 December he rejected all rumours about possibility of the Soviet Union's having opened the prospect of a Tashkent type approach to the Indo-Pak war. [157] The role of Soviet Union in the war in the Seventh Fleet episode, moving troops to the Sinkiang region to check China's intervention and above in the United Nation has already been analyzed. The exercise of three vetoes by the Soviet Union against all resolutions in the Security Council against India contributed a lot to India's strategy of liberating Bangladesh within the stipulated time period.

The Third World countries did not support India in the United Nations. Their own problem of minorities within their states precluded them from applying two standards - one for their own country and another for Pakistan. They were mostly guided by the urgency of containing the war. Though India has always supported the cause of African people, these countries did not support the liberation of Bangladesh as the "tribal structure of multi tribal states often with arbitrarily demarcated boundaries left behind by their erstwhile European masters have provided almost all the black African states with festering political secessionist problems within their own domains".[158] Another reason may be their abhorrence to any involvement in the super power conflict, which was inherent in the Bangladesh crisis.[159]

From the above analysis, it can be concluded that though the United Nations General Assembly put forward a resolution against India, the Security Council failed to pass one because of the Soviet Union's veto in support of India. Before the United Nations could intervene, the Indian policy makers brought the independence of Bangladesh successfully within the time frame.

Post Bangladesh Crisis

The rise of new power relations Sino-US-Pak axis with the Soviet Union at the back of India-increased the antagonisms between India and Pakistan. The Simla Agreement signed in 1972 did not heal the wounds suffered by Pakistan in the 1971 war. In an interview to a foreign magazine, Bhutto viewed the perspective of adjustment with India under the Simla Agreement, as "dim".[160] During the phase of implementation of the Simla Agreement, Bhutto's attitude seemed to have hardened by the United States' announcement of lifting of the arms embargo on Pakistan on 14 March 1973 and supplying it with 300 armoured personnel carriers, aircraft engines, military spare parts and parachutes. This move of the United States of America was very much resented by Foreign Minister Swaran Singh of India in the Rajya Sabha, that it would strengthen Pakistan's anti-India and militaristic policy.[161]

From the very day of signing the Simla Agreement onwards, though many other agreements were signed relating to trade, commerce and aviation between the two countries, the relation ship between them had not been cordial enough to avoid mutual conflict, suspicions and aggression for all times to come. It would be idle to say that Pakistan had forgotten its humiliation of 1965 and 1971. Kashmir was still a major cause for confrontation between them.[162] Pakistan only waited for time and opportunity to strengthen its bargaining position and get an edge over India by growing militarily with the help of external powers. This has always been the perception of India leaders that the external factor is the main stumbling bloc to durable peace between the two countries.[163]

In pursuit of its policy of gaining strength, Bhutto used India's Pokharan explosion as a card for getting the ban on United States arms supply lifted. President Ford announced this on a case-by-case basis on 24 February 1975. Bhutto said this move by the United States helped only remove an anomaly, which had deprived Pakistan of its right to purchase arms from its ally for self-defence. Further he stated, Pakistan lacks necessary resources or will to join an arms race with India.[64]

Pakistani Armed Forces Expanded with American Aid

On the other side Indira Gandhi, the Prime Minister of India, resented the American move, as it would "amount to reopening the old wounds." She further admonished that Pakistan's " new belligerence" coincided with this fresh flow of arms and the repercussion of this coincidence should not be overlooked.[165] The real expansion of Pakistan armed forces took place between January 1972 and December 1979 with a pledge given to armed personnel and officers of Pakistan that "we would under any circumstances, take revenge against India" for Pakistan's humiliation in 1971.[166] This was also revealed by General Zia-ul-Haq to an Indian Journalist; three reasons were advanced for Pakistan being anti-India and aggressive: (i) India dismembered Pakistan in 1971; (it] The Kashmir problem was still alive and (iii) India's attitude remained unfriendly as evidenced from India's hostility to Pakistan acquiring new weapons from abroad.[67]

Another opportunity was provided to Pakistan's General Zia to obtain more military aids from the United States, by Soviet Union's intervention in Afghanistan in 1979. Thus, a new geo-political scenario was created by the Soviet move on India's border. Despite Pakistan's burning of the American Embassy, United States President Carter offered a $500 million military aid to Pakistan; an offer spurned by Zia-ul-Haq as "pea-nuts'.

The main motive behind United States' policy of expanding Pakistan's Armed Forces with all modern sophisticated weapons was to cultivate Pakistan as a military ally in its pursuit of global strategy in South Asia, South West and West Asia. [168] Giving an interview to News Week, General Haq revealed that Pakistan would not hesitate to comply with the American request for military bases in Pakistan. [169]

The Reagan Administration has also upgraded the continued supply of military aids to Pakistan by formalizing an agreement in September 1981, on a United States $3.2 billion military and economic assistance programme over the next five years. This would give to Pakistan 155 mm guns. Cobra gunships, Tow anti tank missiles and upgrade the M48 tanks to A3 standards, artillery fire locating radars, electronic warfare equipment and so on. But the prize catch was the United States commitment to sell 40 F-16 planes "on a cash basis" of $ 1.1 billion, 7 of them before October 1982, that were not included in the assistance package. The NATO allies were requested by United States to supply Pakistan with a requisite number of planes by reducing their demands to the United States. [170]

The reasons adduced by Reagan Administration for supplying military aid to Pakistan were an expression of concern to withstand Soviet expansion. But the communiqué issued on the occasion of the arms aid programme from Islamabad did not make any reference to the Soviet threat. The State Department Spokesman, replying to newsmen, explained: "This administration believed that addressing those security concerns which motivated Pakistan's security programme, and establishing a relationship of confidence with it, offers the best opportunity in the long run for our overall security objectives in the region." The United States policy makers are well aware of the perception of Islamabad that the threat came chiefly from India. [171]

In the wake of the Afghanistan crisis during 1980s India was initially critical of Pakistan's position. But in the hope of reducing constraints on India's power because of the introduction of new weapon systems into Pakistan, India favoured a regional consensus to the crisis. To begin with, India's special emissary, Sardar Swaran Singh assured President Zia about the non-existence of India's threat along its border and encouraged him to divert its 17 divisions facing India to the Afghan border. [172] Talks with the Soviet Union and the Kamal Government in Afghanistan were pursued. As a result, the non-aligned Foreign Ministers Meet on Afghanistan in February 1981 found a merger of Indian and Pakistani views. There was good understanding of each other's problems. [173]

But this assuaging mood was interrupted because of President Reagan's presentation of the military package to Pakistan. This was an exact repetition of the events of 1953. Nehru and Mohammed Ali were on the verge of agreeing on several post-partition problems and on the appointment of a plebiscite administrator in Kashmir when reports of an American offer of 25 million dollars of military aid in October 1953 vitiated the whole environment in which the relationship between India and Pakistan was to grow. [174] Reagan was probably guided by the post-Second World War cold war moorings to isolate India in order to ultimately force it to identify with the West.

US Supports Pakistani line to Contain India's Nuclear Power

India's nuclear explosion in 1974 raised consternation in Islamabad. It was informed to Indira Gandhi on 6 June 1979 sounding concern over India acquiring nuclear weapons. [175] But it was not unknown to Indian leaders that it was Bhutto who had embarked upon a plan to detonate a nuclear bomb as early as 1972. [176] India's development it can be said was in response to this Pakistani move rather than vice versa. While the former United States President Carter ordered stoppage of aid to Pakistan in April 1979 following disclosures of its nuclear device, President Reagan got the Symington Amendment waived in 1981 for six years to provide military and economic aid to Islamabad without commit ting it to non-proliferation, [177] though there were reports of Pakistan having devised the nuclear bomb. [178] On the contrary severe legislative restrictions were put on supply of enriched Uranium to Tarapur despite Indira Gandhi's assurance that it would be, for peaceful purposes. During Indira Gandhi's visit in July 1982 an agreement was declared by Reagan to pass the buck of supplying Uranium from the United States to France without renewing the 1963 agreement. [179]

This had the effect of encouraging a pro-nuclear lobby in India to advocate the need and time for India to produce nuclear weapons. According to Leonard Spector, a leading American expert on nuclear proliferation, 'The next time India and Pakistan go to war, each side must presume that they have a bomb."[180]

Pakistan advocating a nuclear free zone in South Asia is believed to have aimed at containing India's nuclear power. The United States putting pressure on India to sign the Nuclear Non-Proliferation Treaty (NPT) has already the Pakistani approach. Pakistan whenever faced with United Stated Congressional pressure in regard to its clandestine nuclear programme, has urged on a regional approach to the issue with India, the United States is supporting the Pakistani line. [181] A nuclear weapons race thus started between India and Pakistan.

New Military Aid Package to Pakistan

The next aid package of $ 4.02 billion starting with 1988, without conditionalities to certify its non-nuclear weapons capability, can be seen in its security dimension to India in the context of United states and Soviet Union signing a Nuclear Disarmament Treaty at Geneva and Soviet withdrawal from Afghanistan. According to an Indian Air Commodore, by this, "The United States, incidentally has started shifting the emphasis for the rationale for aid to Pakistan beyond the Afghanistan crisis scenario, where Pakistan would continue to play a larger vital role including Its "security needs' along its eastern borders with India, as a "frontline state' falling within the area of jurisdiction of the United States Central Command established in 1983." [182]

This new aid package seemed to have included AEW/AWACS, more F-16 fighters, P-3 Orion long-range maritime patrol aircraft, armour and armoured fighting vehicles (AFWs). [183] During 1987 an additional aid of 2386 Tow-II Missiles for $ 78 million came from the United States. In addition to this, in early 1988 Pakistan was to obtain another 200-300 tanks of M 48-A 5 class from its existing stocks. [184] According to a report in Pakistan's daily Jang, the United States is to supply Pakistan 4 to 5 p 3c nuclear submarines each estimated to cost $ 3 million. This is reported to have been done in response to India's recent acquisition of a nuclear submarine from the Soviet Union.[185] This report however has been denied by India's Ambassador P.K. Kaul. India he said, had acquired this on the basis of lease for training purposes. With the completion of the lease, it would be returned. The notable difference is that it is without nuclear weapons.[186] This growing offensive capability of the Pakistani" military forces in close collaboration with the United States cannot simply ignored by India's policy makers.[187]

Another constraint on India's security is the permission by the Pakistan rulers to the United States for use of its airfields for the purpose of perceiving Soviet Union's threat to the Persian Gulf from Afghanistan. This could be well used by the United States AWACS, SR-71 and RC 135. If the United (States shares this intelligence gathering with Pakistan over India, a security threat is easily posed to India. There is little doubt that the United States is in a position to provide Pakistan intelligence about India based largely on satellites, high-level air reconnaissance (SR 71). What would be most disquieting to India if the United States decided to supply digital maps to be fed into the navigation computers of the F-16 for air strikes against Indian targets. The position would be more serious if Pakistan becomes a beneficiary of the LANTIRN system, which will bestow an all-weather low-level navigation capability. The submarine Harpoon could be a serious threat to the Indian naval forces even in the South Arabian Sea and the Indian Ocean, if target intelligence is supplied to Pakistan by the United States."[188]

Up to now the United States has remained the major supplier of military aids to Pakistan besides China, the Western Countries, Saudi Arabia and the Gulf countries. This had the effect of encouraging India to divert its resources towards defence. Thus, an arms race is encouraged between India and Pakistan. According to a report, Pakistan is spending 6.4 per cent of GNP for defence while India is spending 3.8 of its GNP.[189] Per capita expenditure towards defence in Pakistan is $ 23 and $ 9 in India. 33.6 per cent of the total budget is diverted towards defence in Pakistan, while in India it is 15.6 per cent.[190] Pakistan's expenditure on defence is nearly double that of India's.

As a result of this massive military build up, Pakistan attained a near equality with India in military balance during 1987-88. The following Table[191] would show, in spite of inequality in size and resources, Pakistan has been able to come up to India in defence.

Indo- Pak Military Balance (1987-88)

Army	*India*	*Ratio*	*Pakistan*
Total Manpower Active	1,000,000	2.4: 1.0	450,000
Inclusive reserves Division	I,30,000	1.3: 1.0	980,000
Armoured	2	1.1	2
Infantry / Mechanized	29	1.6: 1.0	18
Independent Brigades			
Armoured	7	1.4: 1.0	5
Infantry	12	1.5: 1.0	8
Artillery	10	1.25: 1.0	8
Armour Regiments	NIL	NIL	6
Equivalent total	42	1.5: 1.0	28
Maximum deployable Tanks	28	1.1: 1.0	25
Total (Excl. Reserve)	2,250	1.3: 1.0	1700
of which MBT	350(T-72)	I.0: 1.3	450 (M48-A5)

In the context of an agreement between the Reagan Administration and the Zia regime in 1981, Indira Gandhi told a public gathering in Patna that "war clouds\are gathering all over the world." Pakistan's acquisition of lethal weapons "beyond its legitimate defence requirements", was a grave threat to India's security.[192]

Because of this massive military aid, chiefly from the United states, Pakistan felt confident by about 1984 to launch an attack on Siachen and has kept up this attack at intervals which ultimately led to Brasstacks crisis in 1987.[193] Now both India and Pakistan have their guns pointed at each other on the Siachen Glacier, In spite of many round of talks at ministerial and diplomatic level no possibility of disengagement of forces on either side has yet been seen.

The geo-strategic objectives of Pakistan's military offensive at Siachen was to go beyond the NJ 9842 the 1972 demarcation line of control to the Indracol region wedged between its illegally occupied parts of Kashmir and the 4,500 km of territory ceded to China. It would enable Pakistan to dominate the Nubra Valley and routes going down to Leh thereby sharing a common border with

China. The attitude of the United States in this case has been pro-Pakistan. Its official maps and atlases showed the line of control extending from NJ 9842 to areas claimed by Pakistan in the Karakoram pass.[194] The Indian side, on the other hand, claimed the Siachen glacier as part of Indian territory.[95]

The acquisition of most modern, sophisticated and latest weapons by Pakistan from the United States and other countries enabled Pakistan to exercise Zarb-e-Momin in response to India's Brasstacks, which ended on 23 December 1989. Its Army General, Aslam Beg reported to have remarked: "The broad strategy that we are going to follow is that while defending all territories of Pakistan including Kashmir, the Pakistan Army plans to launch a sizeable offensive, thus carrying the war into enemy territory."[196] Thus, the noticeable shift from defensive to offensive in Pakistan's military strategy would mean a grave challenge to a non-nuclear India and a need for a drastic overhauling of its old military strategy to face a nuclear attack from Pakistan, even though India has to act against heavy financial constraints.[197]

It is the perception in Pakistan that its military capability in collaboration with the United States and other countries was in response to India's not vice-versa. Pakistani fears of security threats from the dominant India were found to be dominating the Pakistan policy makers.[198] This has been expressed by General Zia-in an interview:

India... is at the present moment in the process and has been for the last five years — of inducting sophisticated weapons through France . . . Britain . . . Soviet Union. Can India convince us today that these arms are not meant for war against Nepal, Bhutan, Bangladesh, Sri Lanka or Pakistan? Against whom are these arms going to be used?[199]

Can Indian policy makers underplay the security threats that heavily military built-up Pakistan would pose to India by effecting" a downright cut in its defence budget to alleviate the fears of a dominant, regional bully, or big brother India?[200] The Indian policy makers cannot be accused of having not attempted at removal of such fears. Pakistani rulers rejected Nehru's offer of a Non-Aggression Pact in 1949 and Indira Gandhi's offer of the same in 1980. Paradoxically in the event of India acquiring French Mirages and British Jaguars in response to Pakistan receiving F-16 planes,

M-18 tanks and Harpoon missiles from the United States, General Haq offered a No-War Pact which the Indian leadership found an absurdity in the environment of Pakistan going for unprecedented arms acquisition. The policy of Pakistan's dualism meant probably to halt India's military expansion was soon exposed when Haq ordered the border attack on India's Siachen Glacier.

References

1. Indira Gandhi, The Years of Endeavour: Selected Speeches of Indira Gandhi August 1969-August 1972(New Delhi: Government of India 1983), p.591.
2. Foreign Affairs Record, Vol. XVIII, no.5, May 1971, p.77.
3. G.W. Choudhury, "U.S. Policy towards the subcontinent" Pacific Community, Vol. 5, no. I, October 1973, p.107.
4. Ralph Toledano, Nixon (London: Sidwick and Jackson, 1957), p.164. Also see V.B. Kulkarni, 'Mr. Nixon's Indophobia', Indian Express, 12 January 1972.
5. William J. Barnds, India, Pakistan and the Great Powers (New York: Praeger, 1972), p.233.
6. G.W. Choudhury, n.3, p.100.
7. Usha Mahajani, "India, Bangladesh and U.S.A- Illusion and Reality", United Asia, Vol. 24, no.1, January-February 1972, p.19.
8. Francis G. Hutchins, " The Birth of Bangladesh", The Atlantic, vol.229, no.2, February 1972, p.24.
9. Homer A Jack, "US, India and Bangladesh", Motherland, 6 September 1971, quoted in S.R. Sharma, Bangladesh Crisis and Indian Foreign Policy (New Delhi: Young Asia, 1978), p. 218.
10. C.L. Schulzberger, "Why Nixon chose to be pro-Pakistan", The Hindu, 12 January 1972.
11. The Hindu, 9 January 1972 from Easwar Sagar in Washington, also see The Hindu, 17 July 1971 from G.K. Reddy.
12. Roger Morris, Uncertain Greatness: Henry Kissinger and America's Foreign Policy (London, 1977), p.215. Henry Kissinger, "White House Years", produced in India Today, Vol. IV, no.19, 1-15 October 1979,p.16. Opined that "we had, moreover, every incentive to maintain Pakistan's good will. It was our crucial link to Peking..."
13. Department of State Bulletin, Vol. LXIV, no.1661, 26 April 1971, p.554.

14. Richard Nixon, United States Foreign Policy for 1970s : The Emerging Structure of Peace, A Report to the Congress, February 1972 (United States Information Service, New Delhi, 1972), p.162.
15. Ibid., p.158.
16. See Norman D. Palmer, "The United States and the New Order in Asia", Current History, Vol. 63, no.375, November 1972, p.194.
17. Richard Nixon, n.14, p.161.
18. Christian Science Monitor, 31 July 1971.
19. Relief Problems in East Pakistan and India. Part I (US Government Printing Press, Washington, 1971), p.16.
20. Department of State Bulletin, Vol. LXV, no.1678, 23 August 1971, p.189.
21. Ibid., Vol. LXIV, no.1668, 14 June 1971, p.764.
22. Ibid., p.765.
23. Richard Nixon, n.14, p.162.
24. Department of State Bulletin, Vol. LXV, no.1674, 26 July 1971, p.100.
25. Ibid., Vol. LXV, no.1677, 2 August 1971, p.124.
26. Ibid., n.20.
27. Asian Recorder, Vol. XVII, no.25, 18-24 June 1971, p.10218.
28. The total contribution of the USA up to 24 February 1972 was $ 89,157,000, Bangladesh Documents, Vol. II, no.4, p.85. Also see Nixon's Press Conference on 4 August 1972, Department of State Bulletin, n.20.
29. Norman D. Palmer, "Indo-American Relation in the Seventies" United Asia, Vol. 24, no.1, January-February 1972, p.7.
30. William J. Barnds, n.25, p.247.
31. Foreign Affairs Record, n.2, p.77. See for Swaran Singh's statement in the Lok Sabha, India, Lok Sabha Debates, series-5, Vol. IV, no.26, 28 June 1971, p.230. Also Foreign Affairs Record, Vol. XVII, no.6, June 1971, p.98, "I never raised this question of aid. In fact whenever this was mentioned, I always took the precaution to point out that this to me is a peripheral matter and it touched only the symptom and did not go to the root of the problem, and unless the root of it is tackled by simply tackling the symptom or touching the periphery of the problem and not the basic problem, it was no use".
32. Richard Nixon, n.14, pp.160-1.
33. *Ibid.*, pp. 159-60.

34. *Ibid.*, p.162.
35. Verbatim report of Kissinger's press briefing on 7 December 1971, in Vinod Gupta, Anderson Papers: A Study of Nixon's Blackmail of India (Delhi: An ISSD Publication, 1972), Appendix I, pp.189-204.
36. FAR, Vol. XVII, no.6, June 1971, p.99.
37. Richard Nixon, n.14, p.162.
38. Financial Times, 8 June 1971.
39. The Hindu, 7 June 1971.
40. Richard Nixon, n.14, p.162.
41. Vinod Gupta, n.35, p.193.
42. New York Herald Tribune (Parish edition), 6 January 1972. Also see Vinod Gupta, n.35, pp.185-7.
43. The Dawn, 25 May 1971.
44. Ibid., 8 August 1971.
45. See Assam Tribune, 21 December 1971. This did not in any way mean that Yahya Khan was at all prepared to come to a political settlement with Mujibur's Party.
46. Indira Gandhi's Message to Heads of Government, 10 August 1971, FAR, vol. XVII, no.8, August 1971, p.156.
47. Robert Jackson, South Asian Crisis: India, Pakistan, Bangladesh (New Delhi: Vikas, 1978), and p.62. See also The Times, 12 July 1971. Times of India, 13 July and 17 July 1971.Bangladesh Documents (Government of India, New Delhi, 1971), Vol. I, pp.515-9.Pakistan Horizon, Vol. XXIV, no.3, pp.142-3.
48. New York Times, 29 June 1971. Sir Alec Doughlas Home said in House of Commons on 23 June: "that there can be no question of new British aid to Pakistan until we have firm evidence that real progress is made towards a political solution". Quoted in Bangladesh Documents, Ibid., p.509. Sweden, Holland and West Germany also announced their decision that further aid to Pakistan would remain suspended. Times of India, 9 July 1971.
49. Relief Problems in East Pakistan and India, n.41, p.24. See further Tad Szulc, "US says it will continue aid to Pakistan despite cut off urged by other Nations", cited in New York Times, 29 June 1971.
50. Flora Lewis, "The isolation of Forward Pakistan", Washington Post, 11 July 1971.
51. FAR, vol. XVII, no.6, June 1971, p.93.
52. "Pakistan's Made in USA Arms", New York Times, (Weekly Review), 18 April 1971.

53. Full Text of the letter in Relief problems in East Pakistan and India, part I (Washington: US Government Printing Press, 1971), Appendix IV, pp.81-82.
54. See Tad Szulc, "US military goods sent to Pakistan despite Ban", New York Times, 22 June 1971.
55. See Motherland, 9 December 1971, ed., 'A Dirty Word'.
56. "US Arms for Pakistan: A shameful Record", Washington Post, 5 July 1971.
57. Asian Recorder, vol. XXVII, no.30, 23-29 July 1971, p.10270.
58. Times of India, 8 July 1971, See also Times, 23 August 1971.
59. Hindustan Times, 8 July 1971.
60. Ibid.
61. Chester Bowles, "US Arms for Pakistan", Washington Post, 15 August 1971.
62. Swaran Singh stated in Lok Sabha on 28 June 1971: I think it is my duty to report to the House that I am completely dissatisfied with the explanations that have been given by the United States or by their Spokeman...."Quoted in FAR, n.51, p.102. See Henry Kissinger, The White House Years in India Today, Vol. IV, no.19, 1-15 October 1979, p.25.
63. See also for details Chester Bowles, "Five Major Blunders by US in Asia" United Asia, Vol. 24, no.1, January-February 1972, pp.36-47.
64. India, Rajya Sabha Debates, vol. LXXVI, no.24, 24 June 1971, col.3, for details see col. 2-50. See also FAR n.51, pp.97-102.
65. Bangladesh Documents, n.25, Vol. I, p.598.
66. Amrita Bazar Patrika, 2 December 1971.
67. Sucheta Ghosh, Role of India in the Emergence of Bangladesh (Calcutta: Minerva Associates, 1983), p.106.
68. Nixon, n.14, pp.162-3.
69. The Hindu, 29 June 1971.
70. Indira Gandhi, The Years of Endeavour: Selected Speeches of Indira Gandhi, August 1969-August 1972, n.1, p.551.
71. Quoted in Pran Chopra, India's Second Liberation (New Delhi: Vikas, 1973), p.86.
72. G.W. Choudhury, "US Policy towards the Subcontinents", n.3, p.97.
73. Quoted in Pran Chopra, n.71, p.87.
74. Indian Express, 21 December 1971.
75. S.R. Sharma, Bangladesh Crisis and Indian Foreign Policy (New Delhi: Young Asia, 1978), p.230. See Indira Gandhi, speech at

the University of Delhi, 10 December 1971 in The Years of Endeavour, n.70, p.606.

76. G.W. Choudhury, India, Pakistan, Bangladesh and Major Powers. (New York: The Free Press, 1975), p.94.
77. Statesman, 20 November 1971.
78. Hindustan Standard (Calcutta), 10 November 1971.
79. Indira Gandhi interview on B.B.C. by Mark Tully on 1 November 1971. The Years of Endeavour, op.cit, p.539.
80. Times of India, 6 November 1971. Indira Gandhi, India and Bangladesh: Selected Speeches and Statements: From March to December 1971(New Delhi: Government of India, 1972), p.55. At a Foreign Press Association luncheon she warned; "Nothing ... will work if people continue to equate India with Pakistan. We are tired of this equation, which the Western World is always making... We are not equal and we are not going to stand for this kind of treatment". Zareer Masani, Indira Gandhi: A Biography (New Delhi, 1975), pp.240-1.
81. Ibid.
82. Tribune (Chandigarh) 9 November 1971.
83. Hindustan Times, 26 November 1971 by Prithvis Chakrabarty.
84. US Foreign Policy for the 1970's: The Emerging Structure of Peace, A Report of President Richard Nixon to the Congress, 9 February 1972(Washington, 1972), pp.140-7, makes it quite explicit that Washington expected the $4.2 billion of aid given or loaned between 1965 and 1972 to weigh heavily on Mrs. Gandhi's action.
85. India Speaks (Government of India), 31 October 1971, p.49. Cited in Zareer Masani, n.80, p.240.
86. Times of India, 8 November 1971, Indira Gandhi, Press meet at National Press Club, Washington, 5 November 1971 in The years of Endeavour In.1 p.553. "... I would say that we have a similarity of approach with the United States, we could never an absolutely identical approach neither with the United States or, for that matter, with any other country".
87. See Christian Science Monitor, 6 November 1971: "There is nothing sacrosanct about the British settlement of India into two different powers. But Washington presently supports a continued partition and continued strong Pakistan...".
88. Hindustan Times, 8 November 1971, edit: Limited Gains.
89. Times of India, 9 November 1971.

90. The Years of Endeavour, n.1, p.568.
91. Indian Express, 10 November 1971 by T.V. Parasuram in Washington.
92. India, Lok Sabha Debates, vol. VIII, no. I, Session 3, 15 November 1971, p.244.
93. A Wayne Wilcox, Emergence of Bangladesh: Problems and Opportunities for a Redefined American Policy in South Asia (Washington, 1973), p.45.
94. Z. Masani, n.80, p.241. Commerce, vol. 123, 13 November 1971 in its editorial column commented that as a result of Indira Gandhi's visit "no one can complain now that he does not know what India wants to do in the present crisis".
95. FAR, vol. XVII, no.12, December 1971, pp.393-4.
96. D.R. Mankekar, "Pakistan Cut to Size" (New Delhi: Indian Book Company, 1972), p.42. Also see D.K. Palit, The Lightening Campaign (New Delhi: Thomson Press,1972), p.71.
97. D.R. Mankekar, Ibid., pp.42-43.
98. UN Documents S/10410/Addl. 1, Security Official Records, Supplement for October, November and December 1971 (United Nations, New York, 1972), pp.85-86.
99. Ibid., p.80. Full text of his report in pp. 80-85.
100. See Kissinger's statement in Washington Special Action Group meeting on 4 December 1971. Vinod Gupta, Anderson Papers: A Study of Nixon's Blackmail of India(New Delhi: An ISSD Publication, 1972), pp.53-54.
101. For text of his speech see UN Doc. S/PV 1606, Security Council Official Records, mtg 1606(New York, 4 December 1971), pp.22-23.
102. Ibid., pp.1-7. For the letter of Justice Choudhury see UN Doc. S/10415 Security Council Official Records.
103. For text of Pakistan delegate Aghashahi's statement, n.98, pp.89-90. See UN Doc. S/PV 1606, Security Council Official Records, pp.7-14, and for Indian delegate Samar Sen's statement, pp.14-18.
104. Ibid., pp.18-19. Full text of the statement is reprinted in the Department of State Bulletin, Vol. LXV, no.1697, 27 December 1971, pp.721-2.
105. UN Doc. S/PV 1606, Security Council Official Records, n.101, p.10.

106. UN Doc., S/10418, Security Council Official Records, p.91.
107. Ibid., p.92.
108. UN Doc. S/10423, Ibid., p.93.
109. See SCOR, S/PV 1607, 5 December 1971, p.126.
110. UN Doc., S/10425, n.106, p.94.
111. See SCOR, S/PV 1608, 6 December 1971.
112. The resolution was moved by Argentina, Burundi, Japan, Nicaragua, Sierra Leone and Somali.
113. UN Doc. S/PV 1608, Security Council Official Records, mtg 1608, December 1971, pp.5-6.
114. See GAOR, A/PV 2022/7, December 1971 and A/PV 2003/7, December 1971, pp.68-82.
115. Ibid., A/PV 2003, pp.176-90.
116. Ibid., A/PV 2002, 7 December 1971, pp.42-43.
117. See S.R. Sharma, Bangladesh Crisis and Indian Foreign Policy (New Delhi: Young Asia, 1978), p.191.
118. Resolution No. 2793(XXVI) of 7 December 1971. India, Bhutan and nine communist countries-Bulgaria, Byelorussian Soviet Socialist Republic, Cuba, Czechoslovakia, Hungary, Mongolia, Union, opposed the resolution. Four Communist Countries viz: Albania, China, Rumania and Yugoslavia supported the resolution. Afghanistan, Chile, Denmark, France, Malawi, Nepal, Oman, Senegal, Singapore and the United Kingdom abstained.
119. UN Doc. S/10440, Security Council Official Records, p.103. Also circulated in the General Assembly as A/8567.
120. UN Doc. S/10445, Security Council Official Records, p.106. Also circulated in the General Assembly as A/8550.
121. UN Monthly Chronicle, vol. IX, no.1, January 1972, p.27. See also SCOR Doc. S/10444, 12 December 1971.
122. UN Doc. S/10446, Security Council Official Records, p.106. Later on the resolution was revised and called upon both India and Pakistan for ceasefire and withdrawal of forces. For full text of the revised draft see UN Doc. S/10446/Rev.I, Ibid., p.107.
123. For full text of the speech see UN Doc. S/PV 1611, Security Council Official Records, mtg 1011 (New York, 12 December 1971), pp.2-4.
124. For the text of his speeches see UN Doc. S/PV 1611, Ibid., p.5-14, UN Doc. S/PV 1613, Security Council Official Records, mtg 1613, New York, 13 December 1971, pp.19-23. Also see

Reproduced in Bangladesh and Indo-Pak war: India speaks at the UN (New Delhi, 1972), pp.1-58. Also FAR, vol. XVII, no.12, December 1971, pp.325-48.

125. FAR, Ibid., p.347.
126. Ibid., pp.347-8.
127. UN Monthly Chronicle, Vol. IX, no. I, January 1972, p.32.
128. See SCOR, S/PV 1631, 13 December 1971. Mallik's speech, pp.36-41, 55-57 and 72-93.
129. SCOR Doc. S/PV 1614/Addl., 15 December 1971, pp.6-26. Also see The Times of India and Hindustan Times of 17 December 1971.
130. Peking Review, 24 December 1971, pp.11 and 16.
131. UN Doc. S/10459/Rev. I, Security Council Official Records, n.98, pp.1123. India objected to the draft on the ground that he was not "occupying" Bangladesh by force as implied in the proposed resolution.
132. See SCOR, S/PV 1621, 21 December 1971, SCOR, mtg 1621, New York, 21 December 1971, pp.8-10.
133. The Statesman, 6 December 1971.
134. Amrita Bazar Patrica, 7 December 1971.
135. Times of India, 7 December 1971.
136. Washington Post, 4 December 1971.
137. See Md. Ayoob and K. Subrahmanyam, The Liberation War (New Delhi: S. Chand &Co), p.227. "On 29 November 1971, after the United States announced a suspension of all arms supplies to Pakistan, a US Air Force C-141 Starlifter, was reported to have flown in urgent military supplies. This was taken up by the Indian Chief of Army Staff with the US Ambassador in India".
138. Vinod Gupta, n.35.
139. *Ibid.*, p.98.
140. *Ibid.*, p.151.
141. Quoted in Md. Ayoob, n.137, p.228.
142. Motherland, 18 December 1971.
143. Indian Express, 17 August 1971, Quoted report of the Laos Angels Times, "Correspondent William Coughlin", Senator Kennedy asked for investigation into its reports that the Nixon Administration has diverted arms being withdrawn from Vietnam to Pakistan. See also Amrita Bazar Patrika 19 August 1971, edit: Another Source.
144. Financial Times (London) 29 October 1971.

145. See Md. Ayoob, n.137, pp. 230-1. " Kissinger said that the President might want honour those requests. The matter had not been brought to presidential attention but it was quite obvious that President has not inclined to let the Paks be defeated. David Packard, Deputy Secretary Defence then said that they should look at what could be done. Sisco agreed but said it should be done very quickly".
146. Richard Nixon, United States Foreign Policy for 1970s: The Emerging Structure of Peace, A Report to the Congress, February 1972(United States information Service, New Delhi, 1972), p.166.
147. Norman D. Palmer, "The United States and The New Order in Asia", Current History, Vol.63, no.373, November 1972, pp.195-6.
148. See Statement, 4 December 1971, Also News Review on China (ISDA), December 1972.
149. Ibid.
150. See Guardian (London), 6 December 1971, Daily Telegraph (London), 7 December 1971.
151. See 'The Dream of Nehru's Great Empire will end in Smoke" in Peking Review, no.52, 24 December 1971, p.12. Also Tsung Wen," Indian Reactionaries will never realize their Expansionist Ambitions", Peking Review, no.52, 31 December 1971, pp.14-16.
152. For Chinese criticism see Hsinhua dated 13, 20 and 27 December 1971.
153. For Soviet criticism of China's role see Pravada, 22 December 1971. Also Izvestia, 23 December 1971.
154. Md. Ayoob, n.137, p.234.
155. Text in Bimal Prasad, ed., Indo-Soviet Relations 1947-1971: A Documentary Study (New Delhi, 1973), pp.427-9.
156. Hindustan Times, 5 December 1971.
157. Ibid., 8 December 1971.
158. S.R. Sharma, n.75, p.202.
159. See Motherland, 14 December 1971.
160. Washington Post, 15 November 1972.
161. Foreign Affairs Record, Vol. IX, no. 3, March 1973.
162. See for the raising of the Kashmir issue in the united Nations by Pakistan contrary to Simla Agreement and India's strong protestation, Times of India, 20 October 1988.
163. Indira Gandhi's interview to Surjit Mansingh in July 1981, quoted in Mansingh, n. 17, p. 235.

164. Asian Recorder (New Delhi) 9-15 April 1975, p. 12532.
165. Ibid, 21-27 May 1975, p. 12597.
166. Times of India (Bombay), quoted in Asian Recorder, Ibid.
167. Interview with Kuldip Nayar, Indian Express (New Delhi) 21 January1980.
168. See Indian Express, 8 March 1981, Statesman, 16 March 1981, Times of India, 23 March 1981 and Statesman, 22 April 1981.
169. Quoted in Indian Express, 9 June 1981. See also US News and World Report, 21 September 1981, pp. 45-46.
170. Times of India, 17 September 1981.
171. See J.N. Parima's Despatch from Washington in Times of India, 19 June 1981.
172. Swaran Singh's interview with Surjit Mansingh, March 1980 in Mansingh, n. 17, p. 237.
173. See Inder Jit, "Zia seeks Friendship But...", Times of India Sunday Review, 1 March 1981. Rajendra Sareen, "India's Pragmatism has Prevailed Over Principles", Sunday (Calcutta), 14 June 1981.
174. See Escott Reid, Envoy to Nehru (New Delhi: Oxford University Press, 1981) p. 118F. The Government of the United States, British and Canada were made aware of "the deplorable effect this would have no Indo-Pak relations."
175. National Herald (Lucknow) 8 June 1979.
176. See Bhutto, If I am Assassinated (New Delhi, 1979), p. 137.
177. Times of India, 13 September 1988.
178. News Week quoted in Times of India, 4 July 1988. See also Times of India, 17 November 1988. The United States was not unaware of the clandestine nuclear device of Pakistan at Kahuta with China's active support. See Nilofar Suhrawardy, "Sino-Pak Nuclear Link", Mainstream, Vol. XXVII, No. 21, 18 February 1989, p. 6. See also, Warren H. Donnelly, "Pakistan and Nuclear Weapons" Strategic Digest (New Delhi), 17(12), December 1987, pp. 2273-82.
179. See for details, Mansingh India's Search for Power: Indira Gandhi's Foreign Policy 1966-1982(New Delhi: Sage Publication, 1984), pp. 96-105.
180. Quoted in Times of India, 4 July 1988. Dhirendra Sharma of Jawaharlal Nehru University is quoted as saying that his assessment was that, "within two to three weeks we could assemble 20 to 40 nuclear Weapons and that India's aim is to have a ballistic, missile capacity by 1990." See for Pakistan producing nuclear bombs by

importing components of two nuclear centrifuges and extracting enough plutonium from its heavy water reactor at Kanupp, Sunil Sondhi "Indo-Pakistan Nuclear Equation", Mainstream, Vol. XXVI, no. 14, 16 January 1988, p. 32. See also K. Subrahmanyam, "Indo-Pak Nuclear Stand-off: A challenge and Opportunity," Times of India, 6 June 1988.

181. Times of India, 9 August 1988.
182. Jasjit Singh, "Pakistan Army: Growing Offensive Capability", Mainstream, Special Number, 26 January 1988, p. 26. See also Times of India, 1 July 1988 for Government of India's concern over the growing security links between Pakistan and the United States Cent-Cm-Forces.
183. R.K. Bhonsle, "AWACS-the Force Multiplies", USI Journal (New Delhi), 117 (490), October-December (New Delhi), 1987, pp. 377-85.
184. Jasjit Singh, n. 93, p. 29.
185. Quoted in Times of India, 1 July 1988. See also 9 September 1988.
186. Quoted in Times of India, 9 August 1988.
187. R.G. Sawhney, "Pakistan: Military Capability," Strategic Analysis, Vol. 8 no. 7, October 1984, pp. 607-33. Nikhil Chakravarty, PM Cannot Afford to Ignore US Arms Supply to Pakistan," Telegraph 26 October 1987, (Calcutta) and Aabha Dixit 'Study of US-Pak Strategic and Military Collaboration," Strategic Analysis, Vol. 11, no. 12, March 1988, pp. 1393-1413.
188. For details see Surya (New Delhi) Vol. 13, no. 11, August 1989, pp. 14-16.
189. World Bank, World Development Report 1988, World Bank Reports on India No. 7185 of April 19 1988. Pakistan No. 7118-Pakof21 March 1988: US Arms Control and Disarmament Agency, World Military Expenditure and Arms Transfers 1987.
190. Quoted in Times of India, 9 August 1988. For Pakistan's defence policy, see Hasan Askari Rizvi,. The Military and Politics in Pakistan 1947-86 (Lahore, 1987). Rodney W. Jones, 'The Military and Security in Pakistan," In Craig Baxter (Ed.) Zia's Pakistan (Boulder, 1985).
191. **Military Balance**: 1987-88 (IISS, London).
192. **Indira Gandhi**, Patna, 26, June 1981, Times of India, 27 June 1981.

193. Inder Malhotra, "Blood on Siachen Snows." *Times of India*, 8 October 1987. Jasjit Singh. "Siachen: the Himalayan Battlefield," Hindustan Times, 18 October 1987.
194. American Alpine Journal 1981, p. 298, Quoted in Surya Vol. 13, no. 11, August 1989, p. 13.
195. Jasjit Singh, "No Pak Claim to Siachen," *Times of India*, 19 May 1988.
196. Answering Brasstacks reports Babar Ayaz from Karachi, Frontline (Madras), Vol. 7, no. 2, 20 January - 2 February 1990, p. 30.
197. See K.S. Pendse, "Future Shock," Illustrated Weekly of India, 14 January 1990, pp. 30-33.
198. K. Sarwar Hasan, Pakistan and the United Nations (New York, 1960), pp. 49-50, stated that, "The foreign policy of Pakistan ... has been dominated by considerations of security and independence from its neighbour India."
199. Interview to Atul Dev, Gentleman, 31 August 1988, p. 76.
200. See Sa'adat Rizvi, "Call to Big Brother," Mainstream, Vol. XXVI, no.31, 14 May 1988, p. 7. 30.

4

Myths and Realities in Indo-U.S. Relations

Indo- U.S. relations have always traversed a path zigzag, surfeit with more downs and less ups ever since Nehru modelled a non-aligned foreign policy being impervious to super power alignment. Notwithstanding a commonality of their being vast democratic nations and natural affinity that many in both countries want their relations to grow into harmony and unanimity, their postures and postulates on international and bilateral issues have not infrequently been divergent, conflictual and incongruous rather than supportive of and countenancing each other's views and perceptions. They have distanced themselves from an idyllic closeness due to their conflicting interpretations of and strategic approaches to the cold war, economic dissimilarities, nuclear non-proliferation treaty, Kashmir imbroglio and more significantly United States massive economic and military build up of Pakistan as a global bulwark against Soviet communism showing short shrifts to India's security concerns and anxieties. Not that there was lack of any will and effort on both sides to put their relation on an even keel but what seemed to have queered their pitch was the ingrained proclivity in U.S. to study and approach events and issues in various part of the globe and more particularly the Indo-Pak conflicts not in their own merits but mechanically in terms of cold war logic and derivatives.

No sooner had the ink on the ornate lines declaring the burial of cold war, Soviet Union and Communism dried up than the entire world was exposed to a millennium of vast uncertainty and tremendous potential. The flames of new hopes and vision about a new world order based on more democratization and regional primacy to resolution of conflicts in the third world without the danger of being dialectically linked to super power global conflicts, seem to have flickered in view of the emergence of a unipolar world with U.S. pontificating its own version of world order and security with other super powers like Germany and Japan kowtowing the U.S. line however reluctantly as was evidenced from the manner with which U.S. peremptorily stage managed the entire U.N. during the Gulf War putting on a veneer of conducting a U.N. War against Iraq. The countries particularly in the third world are not comfortable with the role to be played by them in a world of uncertainty and fluidity during a time when the very relevance of non-alignment movement is at the nadir.

This does not mean that there are no moves and readiness to respond on the part of national actors to this changing world. Though there were some moves on both sides during the eighties to have a review of what had strained their relations, the eclipse of cold war and disintegration of Soviet Union undeniably urgented the replacement of old logic and imperatives.

Indo-US Relation During the Cold War

Aversion to super power alignment

In the cold war phase, given its size, population, geo-strategic location and greatness of its own culture and civilization Nehru wanted India to play a major and influential role, not a second fiddle to super powers in world politics especially in Asia arrogating to itself the monopolistic right of casting moral judgments on things and happenings in the world on its own idealistic and civilization denominations. As Nehru pointed out in one of his speeches : "For too long we of Asia have been petitioners in western court and chancelleries. That story must now belong to the past. We propose to stand on our own legs and cooperate with all others who are prepared to cooperate with us. We do not intend to be the play thing of others"[1]. Keeping this in view Nehru chiseled non-aligned foreign policy for India in terms of independence, autonomy and aversion to any superpower alignment. The Indian protestations articulated by Nehru and subsequently by his successors had always been against both the united States and Soviet Union for their expansionist and interfering tendencies in Asia and Africa. This was stated very candidly by Indira Gandhi in one of her speeches in 1970.[1]

India could not acquiesce in what the dominant view in the United States portrayed of Soviet Union as only one expansionist aggressive power intending to spread its tentacles of communism to all parts of the globe. Having experienced the historical trauma of colonial exploitation, India wanted to take up the cudgels for all national liberation movements in the third world. But the United States continued to misinterpret these nationalist movements as the manipulation of and susceptible to Soviet influence. Thus, a perceptual incongruity and strategic divergence occurred between India and the United States firstly, when the former cocked a snook at Washington's fear of Soviet communist expansionism and suggestion to India to play an American surrogate in its global strategy of containment of communism, secondly, when India was to disapprove of the United States' policy of containment of communism and opposition to the rise of nationalist movements in Asia and Africa. On the other hand, an identity of stand between the Soviet Union and India was perceived on the issues of nationalist liberation movements. In pursuance of its policy of containment of communism, when the United States searched for allies to its alliance system, a non-aligned ambitious India was found to be too big to conform to its strategic procrustean bed. Washington tended to see in British eyes two things in Pakistan to be taken advantage of. One is its geo-strategic location as the 'fulcrum of Asia' in the northern tier of subtropical states having all the appropriateness of being a western ally. Second is its fear of India's alleged expansionist ambition to redress the wrong done in the partition of the United India[3], which ultimately impelled Pakistan to be an accomplice in U.S. strategic syndrome. In practice while Pakistan occupied a prominent place in America's global confrontation and by eighties became the 'frontline' state[4] India was at a discount in U.S. strategic outlook. Improvement in Indo-Soviet relations, a convergence of interests between them can be justifiably said as the consequence of this U.S. placement of India in it strategic order. If one is to explain the U.S. lukewarm interest and reluctant responsiveness to woo India when Soviets were tarnishing Nehru as a "lackey and running dog of British imperialism"[5] and Gandhi "a bourgeoisie reactionary aping the ascetics to liberate India" [6], it would be only on the indices of the refusal of a non-aligned India to toe the American line. When Pakistan became a signatory to U.S. sponsored military pacts and received massive military and economic wherewithal from Washington, the attempts of Indian policy makers at insulating South Asia from superpower intrusion were reluctantly to prefer Soviet Union for its economic and military build up. In 1962 Chinese war the United States could have corrected the Indian Soviet leaning by favourably responding to India's request for military help. Rather Nehru's request for supply of modern supersonic jet fighter—available to Pakistan — were turned down. His subsequent requests for military assistance to the United States were tied with strings like dialogue with Pakistan on Kashmir, lowering its ceiling on rupee and foreign exchange for defence expenses, delaying its decision on purchase and manufacture of fighter air craft and acquiescing in the supervisory role of the United State personnel. The U.S. gave up the idea of a joint air defence pact, which could have achieved for it a major break through in relationship[7]. Behind Washington's reluctance to come to India's rescue was to allay Pakistan's anxiety and fear of India's growing military power with the American help. As and Indian diplomat perceived it:

> It was an opportunity America could have utilized to bring India closer to herself, but she missed it. The U.S. administration tried to tie down in a joint defence pact with Pakistan, which went directly against India's potential value and strategic importance. US experts treated us as if we were a client state and wanted us to make impossible concessions to Pakistan on Kashmir [8].

As a consequence of America nurturing up Pakistan militarily and economically to contain Soviet communism, India's dependence on Soviet Union increased. Since Pakistan stood prominent in the United States strategic scale it was logical on their part not to envisage any step, which would reduce India's dependence on Soviet Union antagonizing Pakistan. Resentful of American policy towards Pakistan, where India had been always vocally critical of the United States policy towards Vietnam, Middle East, Africa and Latin America, it had never condemned rather condoned Soviet policy towards, say, Czechoslovakia, Hungry, Yemen, Afghanistan.

Pakistan and Military aids Constraint

The Kashmir issue marked immediately the pro—Pakistan tilt in U.S. policy. Without looking to the merits of the crisis a linkage between U.S. global strategy and regional imperatives was established justifiably. U.S. stood solidly behind Pakistan on the question of plebiscite in Kashmir in all international forums to the chagrin of India. In 1965 Indo-Pak war though it was apparently neutral, its arms supply to Pakistan and treating equal both India — the victim and Pakistan — the aggressor by suspending arms aid to both lend credence to the view that it was a partisan neutral to the advantage of Pakistan. In 1971 Bangladesh war the Indo-US relation was at its lowest ebb when Nixon, the American President showed a complete Pakistan tilt in his foreign policy approach[9].

Whatever justifications Kissinger adduced for U.S. tilt as a counter to Soviet Union's highly inflammatory role[10] were not convincing to India as the arms flowing unabated to Pakistan were never to be used against Soviet Union. As it did wheedle out a promise from New Delhi in 1962 Chinese war that American weapons supplied to India would not be used against any adversary except China, it could not extract the same assurance from Pakistan that its weapons shall not be used against any adversary except Soviet Union. This ' double standard' approach in the U.S. redounds to the apprehension in New Delhi that it was a well-planned strategy of US to contain India's growing as a major regional power[11]. Where India perceived arms aid to Pakistan as a menace to India's security and enticement to arms race in the sub continent diverting sizable resources from developmental process, the U.S. has justified continuance of this as a mellowing force on Pakistan to conserve what the limited ability it had to restrain Pakistan[12].

Another pretext was provided to Pakistan's General Zia to obtain more military aids from the United States by Soviet intervention in Afghanistan in 1979. Despite Pakistan's burning of American embassy, States president Carter offered a $ 500 million military aid to Pakistan, an offer spurned by Zia-ul-Haq as- peanuts. Reagan administration also upgraded the continued supply of military aid to Pakistan in September 1981 on a United State $ 3.2 billion military and economic assistance encompassing 155 m guns. Cobra gunship, TOW anti tank missiles, upgradation of M 48 tanks to A3 standard with a prize catch containing US commitment to supply 40F-16 planes on a cash basis of $ 1.1. billion, 70 of them before October 1982. [13] The reasons adduced by Reagan administration for supplying military aid to Pakistan were part of his global strategy to withstand Soviet expansion. But the communiqué issued on the occasion of arms aid programme from Islamabad did not make any reference to Soviet threat. The United State policy makers were well aware of the perception in Islamabad that the threat came chiefly from India[14]. Afghanistan issue widened further the perceptual incongruity between India and U.S. [15]

Efforts to arrive at a regional consensus in the non-aligned foreign ministers meet on Afghanistan in Feb. 1981 were intercepted by Reagan's announcement of aid package to Pakistan[16]. It was the exact repetition of events of 1953 when Nehru and Mohammad Ali were on the verge of agreeing on several post-partition problems and appointment of a plebiscite administrator on Kashmir, reports of American aid policy has put on a veneer of containment of Soviet communism over its intent either explicitly or implicitly to undermine India's position and capability and to forestall it from growing into an influential regional power[17]. The next aid package of $ 4,02 billion starting with 1988 without conditionalities to certify its non-nuclear weapons capability comprising of AEW/AWACS, more F-16 air craft, P-3 Orion long range maritime patrol air craft. 200-300 tanks of M 498-AS class besides an additional aid of 23S6 Tow-II missiles during 1987 was of serious concern to Indian policy makers in an era when Soviet withdrawal from Afghanistan was almost ensured and a nuclear disarmament was signed at Geneva[18].

Nuclear Irritant

On the issue of nuclear device the United States was mainly guided by the logic and imperatives of keeping Pakistan in its global strategic orbit. Despite India's assurances given out since 1974 explosion for harnessing it for peaceful purposes Reagan did not feel any compunction to renege on US commitment on the supply of Uranium to India on the basis of 1963 agreement and to get the Symington amendment waived in 1981 for another six years to provide military and economic aid to Islamabad without committing it to non-proliferation, though there are reports of Pakistan having devised nuclear capability[19] and attempted at achieving this before India thought over it[20]. Pakistan whenever faced with United States congressional pressure regarding: its clandestine nuclear programme, had urged on a regional approach to the issue with a clear cut prompting and support from Washington. During the cold war phase when Zia and Reagan were sharing the same strategic bed, the usual argument emanated from the White House that aids to Pakistan were meant to act as a restraining force on it, which would prevent her from crossing the nuclear threshold. America had leverage with Pakistan because of the linkage between aid and Pakistan's nuclear restraint. The sole motif behind the whetting of Pakistan's hunger for being nuclear through military and economic aids was to strike a nuclear deal between India and Pakistan on a line suggested by Zia the support of US thereby bringing nuclear non-proliferation in the bakdoor[21].

Indo-US relation during the eighties — signs of improvement and de-ideolization

As the cold war ebbs out, the spectre of Soviet communism would no longer haunt the American strategists[22] thereby fostering a shift in the "Western image of the Soviet Union as the enemy, a perception that created formidable opposition and had what the current Soviet leadership sees as counter productive consequences for Soviet Power" [23]. Consequent upon this the imperative and compulsions of anti Soviet tinge in Indo-US relations declined to expose India to new possibilities and manoeuvrabilities. A shift in the perception of both US and India also marked to reassess Indo-US relations. According to an analyst "US policy makers concluded by 1934 that despite Indian willingness to condone Moscow's invasion of Afghanistan, the country remained a strategic barrier to Soviet expansion to the South", And also the strategy of maintaining a cordial relation with India emerging as a major naval power in the region, which would be conducive to US strategic interests in the Gulf and the Arabian sea, was highly appreciated by then[24]. The other consideration was the realization in US and its western partners of the potential of India as a growing power in South Asia in coming decades providing a prospective boom for their civilian and military hardware in Indian markets.

On the other hand in India's perception its relation with Soviet Union had already reached the apogee and India had become the center-stage of its strategic interests with Gorbachev's perestroika having made a bonfire of its ideological rhetoric and shift of emphasis towards geopolitically important third world states. In the words of Francis Fukuyama the Deputy Director for policy planning in the U.S. State Department: "The practical implications of the (New Gorbachev) policy are evident in a variety of regions around the world, no where more so than in India Gorbachev clearly views India as the center piece of his policy towards the developing world" [25]. The Soviet leaders seem to have projected Indo-Soviet relations as a model unto the third world countries not on already worn out pristine Marxian parlance rather than on geopolitical denominations. Instead of Indo-Soviet relations being viewed n the eyes of others as a smirch on India's non-alignment Gorbachev's new entente with U.S. on the rubbles of cold war and the prospect of a good relation with China would release the non—aligned India from its Soviet tilt to forge diversified relations with other superpowers[26]. India's non-alignment policy, which stands discredited and seems to have lost its favour, with the crumbling of its very historical foundations, and postulates that India's good relation with one superpower never precludes her forging the same with other superpowers.

From confrontation to cooperation: Economic and defence: Signs of shifts

Economic concerns, which tended towards reversal of stand in both U.S. and India, are also likely to lessen India's dependence on Soviet Union for economic and military build up. A coincidence of the need to reassess mutual perception of each other's strategy and policy occurred when Rajiv Gandhi coming to power in 1984 galvanized the process already set in the early eighties by a major liberalization of Indian economy at one swoop. The very logic and consequence of this policy was to depend on western market for its non-traditional manufactured products in order to stave off the further slide in its balance of payment situation. A memorandum of understanding (MOU) was signed in November 1984 leading to transfer of technology and easing of American restrictions on trade. The Indo-US relation marked an improvement when restrictions on the supply of duel use technology were lifted. To take a decision to grant India a license to buy of the line General Electric F 404 Jet engines for its light combat aircraft was significant in view of the earlier U.S. denial of the same to China. Another decision to sell India a Cray XMP-14 super computer though less powerful than the XMP-24 was significant in view of its sale to a country outside the western alliance. As confirmed by the then U.S. Defence Secretary Frank Carlucci in his visit to New Delhi in April 1988, Washington agreed to sell India a ring-laser Gyroscope for use for its newly designed light combat air craft (LCA). Indo-US defence cooperation encompasses the provision of United States radar components for Indian surface-to-surface missile tested in January 1988. As a quid pro quo American naval vessels have been allowed to visit Indian ports and United States defence officials have been permitted access to Indian defence facilities. [27] In the recent Gulf war, the permission to American airplanes for refueling on its airports by the Indian Government would not be surprising in the light of the above defence cooperation.

These transformations in US cold war attitude towards India surfaced during Reagan's administration and Rajiv's ascension to power after Indira Gandhi's assassination, were the result of an understanding of India by the US Administration to de- ideologize their relation with lowering same barriers in their mind. India began to be understood as a highly active regional power pursuing hegemonic policies and seeking the legitimacy and material cornucopia to pursue such policies. A perceptual transformation in understanding India appeared in US assisted by no doubt the gathering welter of evidences of decline of Soviet Union as a major threat to US interests [28].

Indo-us relation during the post cold War: Whether tilt towards an identity and convergence of interests positive ?

Delinkage Strategy

As analyzed above the strategic linkage between US and Pakistan has always been an overriding concern in Indo-US relations.

With the disappearance of the wall between East and West a reversal of stand in US over the issue affecting Indo-Pak relation can be noticed. Bush administration's pronouncements on terms approximating to India urging upon Pakistan to settle Kashmir issue on the basis of Shimla agreement and desist itself from morally and materially egging on secessionists in Punjab and Kashmir are candid enough to smack a change in the tone of Washington in contrast to the White House's earlier pro-Pakistan stand on Kashmir ensuring the dependability of Pakistan as an ally on it. But the Indian Policy makers must have the reason enough to expect a categorical statement from the White House that Kashmir is part of India and not a disputed territory. They cannot simply brush aside the concerns shown by the American Congress about human rights issues raised by international as well as Indian activist.

So far as the supply of military aids to Pakistan is concerned there has not been any noticeable shift in American strategy, which the Indian policy makers expressed their concern with. Pakistan has been emboldened by $ 1.5 billion in renewed aid provided since 1981 and by another $ 1.4 billion, which was scheduled for delivery by 1991 including 60 F-16 higher aircraft in addition to 40 already in Pakistan arsenal.

Even the Soviet withdrawal from Afghanistan had not reduced the flow, however reluctantly the Indian government swallowed it with a view to not straining its own technology flow from the United States[29] After the Soviet withdrawal the flow of aid to Pakistan would pose a security dilemma to India. As has been pointed out by an Indian Air Commodore, by this, "the United States, incidentally has started shifting the emphasis for the rationale for aid to Pakistan beyond the Afghanistan crisis scenario where Pakistan would continue to play a larger vital role including security needs along its eastern borders with India, as a 'frontline state' falling within the area of jurisdiction of the united States Central Command established in 1983". [30] With Soviet retreat the possibility of these sophisticated weapons being used in-Afghanistan appears to be remote whereas the prospect of their use against India in any future war like 1965 and 1971 war cannot be simply undermined. This would be the overriding concern of Indian policy makers while making a deal with US. With the possible losing *of* Afghanistan scenario, Reagan administration justified the flow in the name of restraining

Pakistan's growing nuclear power but it appeared to be misleading to India, as the White House's repeated certificate that Pakistan was not in possession of nuclear device, which was based on mere technicalities as Pakistan was clandestinely possessing nuclear devices without any public explosion.

But a change in Washington's use of aid as a leverage of influence and restraint of Pakistan was marked when congress pronounced to suspend an annual economic and military aid of $ 580 million dollar to Pakistan in view of President Bush's inability to certify as required under the Pressler amendment that Islamabad did not possess a nuclear device. [31] Reagan strategy of linkage between Pakistan Nuclear restraint and American aid disappeared in Bush administration. But the possibility that Pakistan may go nuclear independently of Washington's pressure cannot be simply ignored in India. In that case the United States would envisage the idea of a regional NPT between India and Pakistan in the Model of Argentina and Brazil with he superpowers guarantee encompassing Russia, China and U.S. So then in this context the Indian policy makers cannot but exercise nuclear option without pandering themselves to political gimmicks like disarmament and nuclear free zone. Exercise of pressures on India in the event of Pakistan going nuclear irrespective of whether Bush certifies or not, not to exercise this option with a promise of superpower guarantee against nuclear attack, would not only add to Pakistan's strategic superiority posing a danger to India's strategic environment, would be an outright sellout to U.S. old game of cajoling India into its NPT strategy. [32] On this vexed issue the tension between India and US persists. The Indian position on this is that it does not view regional solutions to nuclear non-proliferation a sensible way to approach the problem. It has to be looked at globally, and include a process of general nuclear disarmament. How far the policy makers in India would withstand the pressures exerted on them by US to sign the NPT can set the tone for Indo-US relation.

Another aspect of the delinking nuclear restraint from American aid seems in propinquity to Indian thinking. In all earlier wars with Pakistan though US denied having supplied military and economic aid to the former there were enough evidences of the latter's clandestine help. How far policy makers in India would succeed in compelling Washington to apply its delinkage strategy to Pakistan's stand on Kashmir and Punjab by cutting of aids to Pakistan, depends on the extent and degree to which Pakistan has plummeted down in the strategic calculation of US. It may be said that a noticeable point of departure from U.S. earlier stand to contain India's growing as an independent centre of power in South Asia was the recognition of India's skilful managerial role in Sri Lanka according to the Indo-Sri Lanka accord and its subsequent withdrawal on the request of Sri Lanka government and Maldives to suppress the attempted coup, and in Mauritius and Seychelles against externally organized coups not as aggressive, expansionist or ambitious. It was a major consideration in the United States to allow India more elbowroom for a managerial role in South Asia except Pakistan. A stress on the need for a reversal in the cold war portrayal of India even during Afghanistan crisis can be gleaned from the following extract:

> Above all, Washington needs an Indian polity that will facilitate New Delhi's difficult role of building a regional consensus on security issues in Asia - including a response to the Soviet presence in Afghanistan ... A U.S. policy recognizing India's position as the natural arbiter on political conflicts in the area can create more room for problem solving through negotiation, India's preferred style, and provides the best hope for stability in a potentially explosive environment. A new India policy comparable to the bold China opening of the 1970s would highlight common interests that are almost entirely obscured by the bi-lateral Pakistan-India US framework. At stake is America's interests in the emergence of a strong, stable, democratic and non-aligned India, an interest that America until now, was able to relegate to the distant long term. That long term is upon us [33].

Strategic low profile of Pakistan: A rebuttal

Of course in the context of changing international scenario there has been marked tendency in US to attribute a low profile to Pakistan in its strategic system. As Richard N. Haass, special assistant to US President and senior Director for Near East and south Asian affairs, had acknowledged that the US penchant to see South Asia in East-West terms and to apply extension of containment of communism to this region were no longer items in the United States strategic menu. It emphasizes a shift in US foreign policy from looking to issues between Indian and Pakistan in South Asia as derivative and mechanically connected and weaved into its global strategic fabric in a dialectal way to perceive issues and South Asia as a region as separate and distinct not as a subset of its global whole. To quote him, "It is important to note that we will do every thing possible to resist making our relation with India and Pakistan an either/or zero sum proposition ... In the modern age it is neither prudent nor possible to have a successful relationship with only one of these two states. We will require good relations with both or we will likely end up with good relations with neither" [34].

In the present uncertain and indistinct configuration of relations in world politics it would be too early a proposition to write off Pakistan either as preponderant factor in Indo-US relations or a reliable mentor of US strategic interest. One may not completely endorse what the Indian diplomat P.K. Kaul said in an assessment of Indian thinking: "Pakistan will always remain a problem"(In-Indo-US relation) "but instead of making it the key determinant one should make it one of the 50 items". [35]

If New Delhi cannot simply disown what Soviet Union has contributed during the last decades towards India's relative autonomy at a low cost and regional aspirations in response to Pakistan's, how one would expect that the US would simply ignore Pakistan which has allowed itself unhesitatingly to play a surrogate to US global strategy in blatant disregard of its sovereignty and independence? To quote Haass again :

"At the same time, the United States has a special relationship with Pakistan. Pakistan's valiant support for the Afghan resistance was and is much admired by Americans- That said ours is a relationship that predated the conflict in Afghanistan and one that survives its end" [36]

The Indian tilt: Pay offs and constraint

On Indian side there have been remarkable tilts towards the United States with P.V. Narsimha Rao becoming the Prime Minister, The end of both cold war and Soviet Union crumbled the very foundations on which non-alignment perched so far. India's security alliance with the Soviet Union got a jolt and became dysfunctional in view of the Russian federation, the successor or state of the erstwhile Soviet Union being reluctant and which was not in a position to play the dead cold war game. It may continue supplying the weapons to India on commercial basis without showing any commitment to defend India against external aggression. The dominant role that the US played in the Gulf crisis and its performance since in regard to the extradition of two Libyans suspected to have bombed a Pan Am aircraft in December 1988 are symptomatic of the invincible clout that US with other powers like Germany, China and France treading the US furrow beling all hopes of the third world and pronouncement of Bush about the democratization of UN and new world order. In such a changing international scene, there was no other rational option but forging security links with the US available to Rao's government, with NAM waning in its significance and relevance to take cudgels up on behalf of the third world against US was not a pragmatic choice for India, when many of the non-aligned countries are prepared to knuckle down to US pressure tactics. In pursuance of this choice India forged military and security links with US. Strategic and military co-operation are being wrought on the proposals of Lt. Gen. Claud Kicklcighter, formerly of the US Army Pacific, viz. visits by chiefs and staff, a joint army executive steering council, staff information exchange, exchange of Personnel, collective training information exchange, combined training activities or co-hosting of a Pacific armies Management seminar. To combat Pakistan's abetting and aiding terrorists in Punjab and Kashmir and to rebuff Pakistan's diplomatic offensive on the Kashmir issue, India's establishing military and security linkages with US and its allies seems to be the Hobson's choice for India. In the absence of planks of political understanding and congruity of interests and without being translated into their respective foreign policy objectives, such military cooperation may hamper India's security interests from a longer term prospective. The naval cooperation between them has its links with the US Pacific Command that covers the Indian Ocean littoral and the Asia Pacific Region. Having accomplished a triumphant hold in its Central Command Region in West Asia, the US aims at securing a similar hold over the Asia-Pacific Region. Whether India's allowing itself to be a partner in US strategy in this region to deter other hegemonic powers like Russia or Hanoi can be conducive to India's national interest.

The Congress Government under the steward of Narasimha Rao on entering office found the Indian economy in deep financial straits with foreign exchange reserves depleting, prices of essential commodities spiralling and balance of payment situation worsening. In order to salvage India from such a debt trap, the policy makers found that dependence on World Bank, IMF and other International financial institutions running under the tutelage and dictates of US is ineluctably necessitous. When the curtains whether of bamboo or iron were raised in the Soviet Union and other Eastern European communist states, the sordid economy afflicting millions of people shaped on Marxian parlance exposed the Indian policy makers to doubting the very rationale of conforming to the Nehruvian economy. Impelled by these forces Rao Government ushered in drastic economic reforms with liberalization and market economy orientation. US administration has expressed satisfaction over India's economic reforms which, according to them, seem to be on the track and enabled India to receive substantial amount of developmental loan from World Bank, IMF and ADB. Aid consortium seems to have favoured India a small-interest loan from IDA ad ADB.

In India's foreign policy pronouncements and formulations is found absence of its old cold war tradition of belching fires at rhetoric like anti colonialism or anti imperialism. India supported all resolutions in the Security Council, US mooted either against Iraq or Libya, and US move in the UN rescinding its 1975 resolution which had equated Zionism with racism.

The above analysis points to some of the quid pro quos and tilts on both sides, which are not without constraints and inherent limitations. During the cold war phase Indo-Pak relation was closely linked with US policy in South Asia. With the demise of cold war, it was prophesized in many circles that there would be a dramatic improvement in Indo-Pak relations bringing a quietus to the age long hostilities between them. US pro- India pronouncements and insistence on Shimla accord to solve the Kashmir tangle, its asking Pakistan to desist from aiding terrorism in Punjab and Kashmir and suspension of military aids to Pakistan under the prescriptions of Pressler amendment may have created this apocalyptic impression about an immediate improvement in Indo-Pak relations. But there has been yet no sign of any improvement. Behind all rhetorics, and cackles about having reached an agreement at prime ministerial or secretariat level to improve bilateral ties, only sabre rattling is being heard in both these countries. There has been yet no sign of the pro-India pronouncement being translated into foreign policy objectives of formulation of US. Irrespective of Pressler amendment being applied to Pakistan, can or will the United States adhere to a policy of suspending military and economic aids to Pakistan so far as and until the latter continues egging on terrorism in Punjab and Kashmir morally and materially? It would remain a formidable question to Indian policy makers to answer. It has been platitudinous to attribute a low profile to Pakistan in US strategic outlook. But whether US is prepared to ditch its old and reliable ally in order to court the new ally, which has not shown that lavish gratitude to US, remains intrigue. In spite of the Pressler amendment, commercial sale of spare parts of F-16s and other weapons to Pakistan continues. Once the arms embargo on Pakistan over the issue of its clandestine nuclear weapons programme lifted, Pakistan is likely to get from US six P-3c aircraft which carry "Harpoon" antiship missiles, "Side winder", air to air missiles and sophisticated sensors for antisubmarine war fare posing a security threat to Indian navy with their long range attack capability. The recent joint naval exercise between US and Pakistan assumes significance and raises concern in India. What is the guarantee that US will not resume supplying military and economic aids to Pakistan? The US recently by conceding the Saudi Proposal to gift over 300 main Battle Tanks and other unspecified weapons to Pakistan, would certainly create doubts in Indian mind about the real US intent and cause the euphoria in India over Indo-US military build up to die down.

Pakistan's utility as an ally to US is at a discount owing to end of cold war and Soviet withdrawal from Afghanistan. But the dethronement of Najibulla Government, formation of an interim Mujahidin Government in Kabul and terrible infighting among the various factions have provided new elbow rooms for Pakistan to impress upon the United States the need not to downgrade Pakistan's regained strategic importance in this region. The upsurge of an Islamic fundamentalism in Central Asia and Europe to the chagrin of US seems to have provided a sheet anchor to Indo-

US relation. Whether it would redound to American long term strategic interests to ditch Pakistan — a reliable and close ally of US located close to the strategic regions of Gulf, Central Asia and Commonwealth of sovereign states of erstwhile Soviet Union, remains to baffle the US policy makers. But there has been strong pro-Pakistan personalities in Congress, Pentagon and CIA and other decision making organs lobbying for restoring to Pakistan its prominence in the US strategic chess board. A strong pro-Pakistan lobby in American military establishment is of the view that Pakistan is the only country between Israel and Thailand that can serve as support for US forward policy shoring up American interests in the Gulf and Indian Ocean. They are prepared to pay high cost, political as well as financial to develop Pakistan as a reliable agent of US policy in this strategic region. The United States would prefer a strong Pakistan to countervail a strong "hegemonic" India and not countenance any policy, which is likely to disturb the local balance in South Asia.

The recent divulge of secret strategy paper circulated to the top brass of the Pentagon though disowned by the American administration enjoins upon the White House to put a premium on Pakistan's strategic importance and thwart the emergence of new rivals to American military supremacy in the post cold war era. Seven nations were identified as potential rivals not barring India thus contesting strongly the view that US has departed considerably from its earlier policy of containing India's growing as a strong dominant power in South Asia. However officially denied these Pentagon papers certainly carry the ingrained view of an influential section of American decision-making, which cannot be ignored by India. According to Michio Kaku, Professor of Nuclear Physics at the City University of New York-, it was deliberately released as a veiled warning to friends and foes alike that the US would not tolerate threats to its military supremacy. US putting Pressure on India to sign NPT, which India castigates as unequal and discriminatory is a revelation of US desire to nip in the bud rise of any other power centers challenging US unrivalled supremacy.

Pakistan Prime Minister Nawaz Shariff's proposal for a 5-nation meet on the de-nuclearization of the Indian subcontinent has its mouthpiece in the United States, which India has opposed from the very beginning on the ground that a regional NPT would not solve a problem which is global. India's posture boils down to what gives you the right to have nuclear weapons and tell us not to have any? The success in US in having persuaded India to agree to Pakistan's regional approach demonstrates US determination to contain a nuclear India. On the issue of clandestinely producing nuclear weapons Pakistan no doubt has irked US. India has also no less incurred the wrath of US by declining to sign NPT. Pakistan having its 5-nation meet theory on de-nuclearization propounded by US appears to be closer to US than India.

United States forbidding Pakistan from aiding terrorism in Punjab and Kashmir and admonishing it to solve Kashmir tangle on the basis of Shimla agreement, may have produced some diplomatic vantages to India. But United States expressing concern over violation of human rights in Punjab and Kashmir appears to be contradictory and heavily loaded against India as and when the latter's policy of fighting Pakistani sponsored terrorism in Punjab and Kashmir decimating the lives and property of men and women would be calumniated as violation of human rights, even though the US has asked Pakistan in public to desist from such activities.

On economic front India has been able to receive loans from World Bank IMF, ADB and IDA owing to having its economy reformed on the lines suggested by US. But these are not without strings and conditionalities. US wants India to develop economically and militarily but not too strong to challenge US. The reluctance of US to sell or transfer some of double use technologies urgently needed by India, will create not only road blocks to their bilateral ties but also doubts about genuineness of US intention to cement ties with India. All attempts at improving their relation will come a cropper as a result of US initiation of punitive action against India under special 301. There are significant discordant notes between them regarding the patent law and the intellectual property rights. When China has submitted to American will to avoid trade sanctions, the question is how long India will resist such mounting pressures to concede concessions to US?

Apart from these constraints, there is ideological dissimilarity between the two countries. Ideology seemed to have constituted the copingstone on which promotion of their national interest was based. During cold war India was averse to US sponsored alliance system to contain communism and launched a non-alignment movement with the third world countries as its members remonstrating super power intrusion into their autonomy, independence and sovereignty to the utmost disenchantment of US. India throughout went on crusades for the cause of third world development and independence on the rostrum of anti colonialism and imperialism.

It has always been vouchsafing for democratization of international institutions, which would form the pitch, and substance of a new international order causing irascibility in US. With the end of cold war and Soviet Union, the hopes and envision of third world countries about the inauguration of new a world order based on justice, equity and democratization, soon dissipated by Bush's preferring a unipolar world in opposition to the emergence of new centers of powers in various part of the globe. The involvement of US in Iraq during the Gulf war and after the war suggests how US is intent on resorting to force to prevent proliferation of nuclear, biological, chemical and missile weapons. The values of justice, equity, independence and democracy so dear to India inherited from its history and culture cannot be bargained away ostensibly to court the friendship of US.

Long accustomed to this habit of carving out a niche of status and dignity in its struggle against imperialism and colonialism as pertaining to a major power of considerable political and military clout in the international realm, India would not be expected to be an accomplice in what US would do jettisoning the proclaimed values which India has upheld even at the risk of bedeviling its relation with the United States. If the contours and contents of new world order will be according to the dictates and prescriptions of US, there is bound to be an ideological collision between India and US.

At the psychological level there will be an inherent conflict between a super power and a regional power. Though the United States was appreciative of the managerial role that India played in South Asia as a pre pre-eminent power, it would not do any thing that contributed to India's growing as a big power in South Asia. Given its size, population, geo strategic location, natural resource and level of industrial and technological development, India would not relish such a regional power status as would be dictated upon it by the United States. During the cold war India was ruefully critical of the regional balance between India and Pakistan being maintained by US by supplying Pakistan all economic and military wherewithal to match India. It would be irksome to India and strain the bilateral relation between India and US, if this Kissinger advocated local balance of power theory continues to apply to South Asia. To many in India there is a logical incongruity between what US preaches and what it practices. If international peace and security will be guaranteed by one super power dictating terms according to its own specifications, why peace and security will be vitiated in South Asia by India emerging a dominant power?

In addressing this question the much publicized and officially disowned Pentagon papers assumed significance. Irrespective of what the current events are, there will remain an inherent tension between the two at the psychological level. Each has its own magnified view of its place in the international world and high expectations from the world, which are most likely to come in conflict with each other. According to an analyst, "The United States, the globally dominant military power with its economy on the slide, sees long range threats developing to its supremacy and wants to scotch them in the egg. India with the bitter history of colonialism behind it, and before that the memory of foreign invaders succeeding by dint of superior military technology, is unwilling to let itself be scotched".[37]

Why various strands before weaved into a harmonious Indo-US bilateral tapestry, do face many disarrays and breaks? It is largely because of US negotiating from a position of strength. What India needs from America is more than that US needs from India. This built in inequality of support and needs from each other puts India always at a disadvantage. The United States, has always struck to a policy of "one step forward and two steps backward" by imposing conditionalities and strings on India and wresting concessions from it more than what India is in a position to concede without risking its pronounced objectives, and compromising its pride and honour as a dominant power. The strength of India's protestations against US and other powers in international forums like disarmament/non-proliferation and Uruguay round soon petered out as other developing countries one after another are submitting to American pie how long India's stand on trade related patent intellectual property rights would remain unshaken? With

France, China, Brazil and Argentina signing the NPT, India stands alone. Unless and until the United States appreciates and gives due credence to the historic role that India has been playing for international peace and security, and incorporates convincingly the values which India and other third world countries cherish into what is couched as New World Order, Indo-US relation cannot unfold into a relation of intimacy.

Any bilateral relations in order to take off depend to a large extent on mutual understanding, co-operation and give and take. In the absence of sense of equality and mutual respect the bilateral relation is likely to get a set back. Much depends on the stronger party to exonerate the weaker party of the fears and suspicions it has nurtured up about the real intents of the stronger state. This is more or less true of the United States. To impose or dictate terms to the weaker party at the cost of its honour and pride as a nation would be psychologically a hard pie to be swallowed. American exertion of pressure on Russia not to sell cryogenic Rocket technology, which it had once agreed to sell and its blatant refusal to sell wheat to India on the ground that it had sold rice to Cuba, were indicative of hegemonic tendencies in the stronger power to bound bilateral ties with umpteen strings. To hold the view that US is no longer averse to India's growing as a major dominant power both economically and militarily can be rebutted on this score. The agreement with Russia does not by any means constitute an infringement of the Missile Technology Control Regime (MTCR) which formidably flawed and discriminatory against the haves not countries. This would gravely impair India's legitimate economic and commercial aspirations in terms of education, communication, weather and space-achievement for civilian purposes can India be bound by an agreement, the effect of which is to deny access to all kinds of modern technologies for industrial and technological advancement to the developing countries? Any discriminatory step that aims at consigning the developing countries to constant poverty and subordinate status, relics of an imperialistic era, would certainly dampen the efforts to improve bilateral ties. This has helped rekindle fear and suspicion of Indians about the US. The scope and prospects for better Indo-US ties depends on how and to what extent US erases such fears and suspicions from the Indian mind.

In the absence of Soviet Union, communism and cold war India would find no more the occasion to use worn out rhetoric like colonialism or imperialism. It would take more time and wait for an opportune moment to devise new slogans and shibboleths, which would attribute a new role to India while finding new bases and justifications for a leadership in third world countries. This interregnum and wobbles in an Indian policy can be exploited by the United States in order to woo India into its ambit of confidence and friendship.

September 11 Terrorist Attack and Transformation in Indo-US Relation

American crusade against terrorism in the wake of Sept 11 terrorist attacks was immediately supported by India with a view to transforming the long 50 years of Indo-Pak conflict into part of the global war against terrorism. With the end of the cold war and crumbling of Soviet Union into independent sovereign states, the priority of Pakistan in the strategic agenda of US plummeted on expected lines. But it was not exactly a zero sum improvement in Indo-US relation. The US stumbled to toe the Indian lines on Kashmir issue being guided by the geopolitical situation of Pakistan, an old time cold war friend and a gateway to Afghanistan and central Asia where America recently discovered a repository of oil and natural gas.

Given all hopes and expectation revolving round the two largest democracies, for most of the last 50 years, the relation between the US and India has been far from friendly. The end of the cold war provided an impetus to improving their relation in defence and economic field, but there was no convergence of strategic interest between the two and specifically on Kashmir issue a perceptual incongruity marked their relations. In no uncertain terms it can be said that introduction of liberal market economy in India and India's "bound to be dependent on US" situation created by disintegration of Soviet Union brought the two nations closer than they were in the cold war. Ties between them slid down only recently when the US imposed sanctions on India after It conducted nuclear tests in may 1998 being caught in a nuclear sandwich between China and Pakistan. In the final years of Bill Clinton's presidency a marked rapprochement was found in their relations. The turning point was when Bill Clinton prevailed upon Pakistan's Prime Minister Nawaz Sarif, to withdraw its forces it had sent across the line of control in Kashmir near Kargil. Sidetracking the assumption in some Indian sections that US could come to Pakistan's rescue like the one it orchestrated in 1971 war, that the US could prevent Pakistan's Kargil conflagration from catapulted into a major, even a nuclear war between India and Pakistan, very much impressed India. Close on the heels of this came President Clinton's five-day visit to India in March 2000 with a perfunctory five-hour stopover in Pakistan, followed by Vajpayee's return visit to US in September 2000. What denied warmth to Indo-US relation is the reluctance of US to buy the Indian placement of facts and figures before the world community about Pakistan's sponsorship of terrorism in Kashmir across the border. Rather than understanding the Indian reality, the US has preferred to think in terms of what Pakistan called the crisis in Kashmir as an independence movement. In the last two decades Pakistan has fought proxy wars against India using Kashmir Islamic fundamentalists bent on independence from India. They are trained in terrorist incubators on the Pakistan side of the so called Line of Control that separates the two countries in the Jammu and Kashmir regions supplied with material and logistics by Pakistan's army and intelligence service, and funded by the multibillion dollar narcotics trade. This no cost war reflects Pakistan's hope of administering death to India by a thousand cuts. Since the Soviet withdrawal from Afghanistan, many of the victorious Mujahidden have joined with Kashmir freedom fighters in their armed struggle for independence. Three major rebel groups, the Hizbul-Mujahideen, Harkat-Ul-Mujahidden, and Lashkare –Taiba, have formed a loose coalition to coordinate and execute terrorist attacks including suicide bombings, in India from their sanctuary in Pakistan.[38] General Musharraf; Pakistan's current President gives this organisation free rein to operate within Pakistan's border, as did his predecessor, Nawaz Sharif. Not until September 11 terrorist attacks, the US did not consider the Pakistani sponsored terrorism in Kashmir a global terrorism and a threat to world community. What created a misgiving in India is that where as attacks on World Trade Center on Sept.11 could be termed as global terrorism by US, the Pakistan sponsored terrorism in India killing hundreds and thousands innocent civilians could not be termed so. Before the September 11 incident, this hesitancy on the part of US to take up the cudgels with the support of the nations against the Pakistan sponsored terrorism is what queered the pitch for any kind of peace process that American intended to foster between India and Pakistan.

Repetition of cold war leverage approach

The US ad-hoc, and lukewarm approach and failure to initiate stronger action to convince its former allies in Islamabad to forswear the cross- border terrorism before any dialogue is held between India and Pakistan was reflective of America's cold war parity approach looking at both the victim and perpetrator alike, an orchestration of what US did in1965 and 1971 wars. Taking the leaf from cold war strategic outlook of looking at South Asian politics from its own perspective, it continued to exercise restraints on India and testify its patience and forbearance with the damage and loss of human beings wreaked by Pakistan in Kashmir valley. For example, when America imposed sanctions on India for its nuclear tests, it did not take into consideration India's security concerns about nuclear threats from both China and Pakistan. What triggered India to acquire nuclear weapons was not unknown to US. US had strong evidences in its hands about Pakistan's clandestine productions of nuclear weapons in collaboration with China and North Korea. But it pretended to overlook the difference between cause and effect just in repetition of its cold war style in order not to jettison the influence it has had over Pakistan, which US believes would be the basis of its peace mediation in Kashmir imbroglio between India and Pakistan. This is exactly what US did in1971 Bangladesh crisis. Instead of accepting Indian line, US continued supplying military and material help to Pakistan military ruler to justify its " tilt towards Pakistan"[39] as a kind of influence on Pakistan to come to a political settlement. But American leverage in Pakistan did not work.

It is said a blunt refusal by Clinton to stop over Pakistan on his South Asia tour of March 2000 could have signaled the right message that US wants Pakistan stop sponsoring and aiding terrorism in Kashmir as a viable condition for dialogue with India. A pointed snub during the first presidential visit to that part of the world since President Carter's in 1978 might have sufficed to jolt Musharraf into starting a peace process by stopping terrorism [40]. The same conventional American " influence over Pakistan " syndrome which ran the only likely effect of a cold shoulder from Clinton would have been to drive the Pakistan's further away from American influence. It was preposterous to hold that with such a snubbing from America, Pakistan would have drawn itself into embrace of Islamic fundamentalism, and into another war with India. What is irony is that it was American influence over Pakistan that hurtled Pakistan into American strategy to fight American war against Soviet Communism in Afghanistan by organizing its jehadis, terrorists and radical Muslims ' Afghan Mujahidden and Talibans under the leadership of both ISI and CIA '. What has remained enigmatic between Indo-US relations is the very fact that the US has always utilized its influence over Pakistan to its interests contrary to Indian expectation that it would be used to the best interests of India, specifically on Kashmir issue.

Bush attempts at intensifying rapprochement: No zero sum approach

On assuming office in January 2001, George W. Bush revealed his intention to intensify the rapprochement that has already begun between India and US. While India's Foreign Minister Swaran Singh was holding talk with National Security Adviser Condoleezza Rice in April 2001, Bush's dropping by and holding a cordial 40-minute talk in the Oval office demonstrates America's alacrity to strengthen ties between them. In the same tone and vein, India was eager in response to the overtures of US to promote better relation between them, casting aside its cold war anti-US diatribes. Prime Minister Vajpayee's portrait of the two countries as natural allies may be overstated, but reflects the growing consensus in New Delhi that the end of cold war has made US, the arbiter and architect of the world order pontificating to the world in its own political and economic terms and improved ties with US will help enhance India's status in the power structure and itch a global role for India. The compulsions of globalisation and liberal market economy have made it imperative to depend on US. During cold war India carved out an international image and status for itself by expressing comments on international issues from a moral stand point, demonstrative of an ascetic India motivated by India's civilization and culture which were perceived by US as against itself. The major aim of US foreign policy was to frustrate all efforts of India to grow in power and status, as it would hurt its cold war ally Pakistan. In the present changed scenario a shift in India's foreign policy took place when India decided to cast its lot with US which will ensure India's ascension to great power status including a permanent membership in Security Council. India's relationship with US will bolster up its dealing with Pakistan. On the other hand, the American policy makers consider India as an emerging great power and hence a strategic partner for the US in Asia. A closer Indo-US relation would restraint China's growing dominance in Asia, which is not palatable to US interests. During cold war Washington's link with Pakistan was an obstacle to Indo-US relation. This zero sum or linkage approach at present stands discredited. It is said, Bush administration has now decided not to balance its relation with two rivals; instead it will allow relations to run on their separate tracks[41]. This is nowhere evidenced than in America expressing no concerns as it used to, over India's large-scale military purchases from Russia. What India considers lifted the principal barrier to improved Indo-US relation was the cut off of all military aids to Pakistan in 1991 for reasons ranging from latter's covert nuclear programme to its alleged soft corner for religious militants. The issue of nuclear non-proliferation, which has earlier infected relations between India and US, was rendered irrelevant with India's nuclear tests in 1998. Further, with the issue of stopping such nuclear tests becoming redundant, the Bush administration's lack of emphasis on such issues appears to have made Indo-US relation a smooth sailing. 1.7 million strong flourishing Indian – American community has become a force for better relation.

All said above does not mean that there was almost a convergence of interests between US and India; it was rather the commonality of desires on both parts to better their relation in the changed international situation. Till the September 11 incident, American statements on Kashmir issue have not been conducive to Indian interests, and seemed to have betrayed the impression that the Pakistan ghost is still stalking through the corridors of Pentagon.

War on Terrorism Put to Test Indo-US Relation

The American declared war on terrorism, in the words of Robert D. Blackwill, US ambassador to India transformed Indo-

US ties[42]. It has greatly strengthened political dialogue between the United States and India and enhanced cooperation on sensitive issues such as Afghanistan and Pakistan. An array of official visits at defence, foreign affairs, military and intelligence and political level between the two countries took place. This overenthusiastic cooperation and interaction between the two led former Secretary of States, Colin Powell to echo the Indian Prime Minister's description of our nations as ' natural allies" to American Senate on October 25, 2001.

Defence Cooperation

The immediate visible effect of war on terrorism was in security relations. In the wake of September 11, the US lifted nuclear sanctions. It eased export controls on so called dual –use technology to secure both civilian and military purposes against which the proponents of nuclear non proliferation fought strenuously but lost out to those in US administration who wanted a broader security relationship with India. Talks on arms sale from US to India for the first time including P-3 naval surveillance, aircraft, sophisticated counter battery radars, and General Electric engines for India's Light Combat Air Craft started. It also permitted Israel to include US technology in the radar system it proposes to install in Russian made planes to provide India with air surveillance and early warning capability. Programmes for joint exercises, improved technical coordination and expanded training of US and India armies, navies and air forces were undertaken. Cooperation between the two navies moved faster not surprisingly in view of their parallel interests in keeping Indian Ocean open for the flow of oil.

Muting mutual public reaction and avoidance of diplomatic pinpricking

Muting mutual public reaction and avoidance of diplomatic pinpricking not symptomatic of cold war period marked an improvement in their relations. When President Bush criticized Iran as part of the "axis of evil", India desisted form publicly reacting, despite Indo-Iranian ties, rather privately conveyed doubts about Bush's statement. On Bush's rejection of Kyoto protocol India emphasized on positive, though it endorses the protocol. Similarly in a subdued and careful tone America reacted when New Delhi tested its intermediate range ballistic missile, the Agni, in late January 2002.

Given the reality, the improved ties between the two countries would prove ephemeral, if US takes a stand on Kashmir unfriendly to India and supplies military equipment as F-16 fighter bombers to Islamabad. In the wake of Sept 11, US promised such military supply with a view to engaging Pakistan in US led global war against terrorism. A moderate, democratic and economic build up of Pakistan, India considers not a threat to Indian interests. The end of cold war has considerably waned the strategic significance of Pakistan to US. But the sudden re embrace of Pakistan as a partner after General Musharraf joined the war against terrorism created deep concerns in India. The US strategy to cultivate Pakistan in the war against the Taliban makes eminent tactical and strategic sense.

Pakistan: a subservient partner

Geographically adjacent to and having a long common border with Afghanistan, Pakistan is in a position to provide logistical, intelligence and other support to US and is the only logical choice for bases to mount operations in Afghanistan. Why did Pakistan agree to play this role? In a briefing to foreign ministers, retired Generals and heads of think tanks, Musharraf said on September 18 that the decision to extend unstinting support to the US had been taken under tremendous pressure. A refusal could have serious consequences including the possibility of the US, India and Israel jointly taking military action against Pakistan and Afghanistan. The threat of being branded as a terrorist state loomed large in Musharraf. The economic promises made by US to mitigate its economic crisis by lifting sanction and providing economic assistance lured Pakistan into US network against terrorism. As a token, US rescheduled over $ 550 million debts to Pakistan and announced an outright cash grant of $ 50 million, though seems not enough to counter balance the external debts of $36.5 billion, which Pakistan has and nearly a billion dollar worth of economic loss due to Afghan war[43]. Pakistan's post September 11 relationship with the US is subservient .It is obvious from the fact that its views on excluding the Northern alliance from the post Taliban set up, conducting a short war in Afghanistan and ceasing operations during Ramadan have all been rejected by the US. Pakistan might have taken note of some Americans being sympathetic about Pakistan and citing about Pakistan's loyalty as an ally. This gratitude of US, Musharraf thought would reap dividends while settling scores with India on Kashmir issue. Adding to these is the speech made by Musharraf in which he made it clear that he was yielding to the US demand to join the coalition only in the same spirit in which the holy Prophet made tactical compromises with his enemies to bide his time to vanquish them later. It is a tactic of running with the hare and hunting with the hound [44]. This can be basis to lend credence to the news that Bin Laden's Taliban and Al Qaeda have been hiding in Pakistan in connivance with Musharraf after being hounded out from Afghanistan.

These tactical compulsions of both US and Pakistan did not get unnoticed in India. But India could not relish US putting encomium on Pakistan for its strategic help to US despite its having been harbouring terrorism in Kashmir. What it sincerely wants US weave Pakistani sponsored terrorism into the nexus of global war against terrorism in Afghanistan and elsewhere. The flowing of assurances from Washington that India's terrorism problems would not be ignored and would be taken up after Afghanistan, could not be relied on convincingly when India's foreign minister Singh was in Washington, the terrorists attacked the Kashmir state Assembly, killing 38 people. With Pakistan playing such a key role in the war in Afghanistan, many Indians feared that the Americans would turn a blind eye to continuing ISI support for cross border terrorism in Indian held Kashmir. The failed attempt of terrorists allegedly belonging to groups linked to ISI to blow up India's political leadership by attacking the Indian Parliament on December 13, 2001 put the US to the test and India's patience with US petered out. This immediately spurted India into putting diplomatic pressure on Pakistan- interruption of rail and air links, the thinning of diplomatic staff, and the recall of India's high commissioner. Vajpayee and his key advisers decided that India's patience with Pakistan provocations has come to an end, and India has to fight Pakistan's terrorism alone. Accordingly, India ordered amassing forces along the entire border with Pakistan and strengthening existing troop concentrations along the Line of Control in Kashmir with preparedness to resort to retaliatory strikes against Jehadi training camps on the Pakistani side of the Line of Control. Pakistan's continuing terrorism provoked world leaders to condemn Pakistan asking it to desist from such activities. With such military stakes on the verge of nuclear brinkmanship having serious impact on the global war against Taliban and al Qaeda, and staring in the face, the US immediately sprang into action and put pressure on Pakistan to meet Indian demands. At the same time in line with its traditional policy it cautioned India against any precipitate military moves.

Differential Focus

There was differential focus-America's focus was on Afghanistan, where as India's was on Pakistan. To assuage India being hurt at the US and the world community failure to restrain Pakistan, the United States also took an action that it had previously scuttled: putting the Jaish-e-Mohammed and the Leshkar-i-Taiba, the two militant Pakistani Islamic groups that India blamed for much of the conflagration in Kashmir – on its list of foreign terrorists. In the wake of this, came Musharraf's major policy announcement on January 12,2002 which promised not to allow Pakistan a base for foreign terrorism, ISI for terrorist attacks on line of control and took swipes at domestic Islamic fundamentalists that have infested Pakistan in recent years. But India did not take these words seriously knowing very much that Pakistan has the track record of reneging on its own words. Despite lavish praises showered on Pakistan, US kept up the pressure on Musharraf and accepted India's insistence on having proof that ISI backed infiltration into Kashmir has stopped. It is said due to diplomatic engagement by Washington following the attack on Parliament, de-escalation of the crisis along the line of control has resulted in withdrawal of military forces along the line of control by both India and Pakistan. But frequent infiltration of militants from the side of Pakistan into Kashmir continues unabated killing innocent people to the chagrin of India. India sincerely wants that US direct its second frontline against terrorism to Pakistan. With the installation of a pro US government at Kabul, US hunt for Bin Laden has not come to an end. In spite of strong evidences of Taliban and al Qaeda having safe sanctuary in Pakistan, the US has not been able to take strong action against Pakistan, to the great dissatisfaction of India.

No zero sum relationship

During cold war the relationship between US, India, and Pakistan was zero sum. US-Pakistan relationship was against India. The September 11 incident has brought a considerable rapprochement between India and US. But it was not a zero sum relationship. To America, Indo-US relation can coexist with US-Pakistan relationship. A peaceful resolution of Kashmir imbroglio between India and Pakistan without US mediation is what America sincerely desires. India expects that US utilizing its leverage in Pakistan take stronger measures that would decimate all sanctuaries of terrorists harboured in Pakistan. On this point there has not been a convergence of interests between India and the United States. In the cold war the US leverage in Pakistan was redounded to America interests to the disadvantage of India. The Pakistani military debacle in 1971 and the independence of Bangladesh should have settled the entire conflict. Whether it was the unwillingness or inability of India to decimate the Pakistani military machine in the western sector during the 1971 war remains intrigue and enigmatic till today. Similarly in Shimla peace conference India could have forced Bhutto to accept unconditionally the LOC in Kashmir as the international boundary [45]. But it was a matter of fact that the United States got assurance from India though Soviet Union that the status quo in western front would in no case be altered by India.

Conclusion

As the September 11 situation shows, the US leverage in Pakistan acts to some extent in favour of India but not completely. India strongly opposes to America's double standard in combating the plague of terrorism. Nowhere such a contradictory stand is seen than in America which put lavish praises on Pakistan being a strategic partner with US in bringing an anti Taliban group to power to Afghanistan, while Pakistan itself remains actively sponsoring terrorism from its territory against India. If Pakistan is not put to task or Pakistan does not stop terrorism there will some difficulty in Indo-US relation. As India strongly demands, America rolling up its cold war leverage policy take strong action against Pakistan either, whether the US is going to dispense with that or take retaliatory measures against Pakistan like the one it is taking against Iraq, Libya or North Korea, is yet to be seen. America's stake in India so far as countering terrorism, managing nuclear proliferation and containing China are concerned. US strategic and political interests seem to be compatible with those of India[46]. As most Indian strategic analysts perceive, China as the principal security threat to India and many in Washington consider China as the principal strategic competitor to the US both in Asia and world wide, the convergence of both India and American interests takes place[47]. Thus the Unites States has a fundamental stake in the growing capability of India to provide a major counter weight to forces in Asia that are clearly antagonistic towards American interests. " Washington has yet to realize that India can play the role of a major friendly power only if it is able to secure-and preside over- a stable and legitimate order in South Asia"[48]. To the attainment of this objective what enjoins on the US is to neutralize Pakistan's capability to continue stoking the fire of terrorism in Kashmir. To what extent America succeeds in decimating Pakistani instigated terrorism has a telling effect on Indo-US relation.

References

1. Nehru's inaugural address to Asian Relations Conference on 23 March 1947, Asian Relations (New Delhi: Asian Relations Organisation, 1948), pp. 20-27.
2. Indira Gandhi's address to the World Peace Council, New Delhi 18 October 1970. The Years of Endeavour : Selected Speeches of Indira Gandhi, August 1969—August 1972 (New Delhi: Government of India, 1975), p. 699.
3. See Michael Brecher, Nehru: A Political Biography (London, 1959), pp. 377-8 which quoted Nehru: 'India cannot and will not remain divided. This is my conviction on matter how much I am criticized for having accepted the partition". See also Evening Star, 22 December 1962, which stated, "Mr. Nehru's aim is not a matter to be taken lightly. It confirms the suspicion that Vishal Bharat, comprising Afghanistan, Pakistan, Ceylon, Burma, Thailand, Indonesia and even beyond it is not mere a fantastic dream of

mediaevalist Hindus but is "a well planned national scheme which has the support of the highest in India."

4. Richard Nixon, 1989 : Victory without War produced in Gentleman 31 January, Vol. 9. No. 1, 1989 who said Pakistan today holds the front line against Soviet expansion into south Asia, see for details, Surjeet Mansingh, India's search for power : Indira Gandhi's Foreign Policy 1956-1982 (New Delhi: Sage, 1984) P. 75. Lloyd I. Rudolf and Susane Rudolf. The Regional Imperative (New Delhi: Concept Publishing House, 1980), pp. 1-100.
5. M. Saleem Kidwai, Indo-Soviet Relations (New Delhi: Rima Publishing House, 1985), p. 29.
6. Quoted in K.S. Murty, Indian Foreign Policy (N. Delhi, 1964) p. 103. K.P.S. Menon. The Flying Troika (London, 1963) p. 18. M.S. Rajan, India in World Affairs: 1954- 64 (Bombay, 1964) p. 300.
7. Chester Bowles, Promises to keep: My years in public life 1941-1969 (New Delhi, 1972) pp. 440-82, Shivaji Ganguli., U.S. military Assistance to India 1962-63 : A study in Decision Making," India Quarterly, Vol. XXVIII, July-September 1972. p.221. John. Kenneth Galbraith, Ambassadors Journal: A personal Account of the Kennedy years (London, 1965), p. 504.
8. T.N. Kaul, Reminiscences: Discreet and Indiscreet (New Delhi. Lancers Publishers, 1982), p. 280.
9. See for the reverse view Christopher Van Hollen "The Tilt Policy Revisited: Nixon Kissinger Geopolitics and South Asia," Asian Survey, Vol. 20, No. 4, April 1980, pp. 339.41.
10. Henry Kissinger, The White House Years (Boston, Little Brown 1979), p. 866.
11. Baldev Raj Nayyar, "American Policy towards India : The Larger Framework", Economic and Political Weekly (Bombay), Vol. 11, No. 12, 20 March 1976. See K. Subrahmanyam, "U.S. Policy towards India, China Report, Vol. III, Nos. 1 & 2, January-February, March, April 1972.
12. Department of State (DOS), Kissinger statement to the Washington Special Action Group dates 2 September 1971, Freedom of Information Document.
13. Times of India, 17 September 1981.
14. See J.N. Parima's despatch from Washington in *Times of India*, 19 June 1981.

15. See Walter K. Anderson, "Policy towards India and the Indian Ocean" in James C. Hsiung and Winberg Chai ed., Asia and U.S. Foreign Policy (Praeger, Praeger special studies, 1981), pp 194-96.
16. See Inder Jit, "Zia seeks friendship But Times of India, Sunday Review, 1 March 1981. Also Rajendra Sareen, "India's Pragmatism has prevailed over principles", Sunday (Calcutta), 14 June 1981.
17. See Baldev raj Nayar, "A World Role The Dialectics of Purpose and Power", in John Mellor ed., India: A Rising Middle Power (Boulder: Westview 1979)
18. See for details R.G. Sawhney, "Pakistan : Military Capability", Strategic Analysis, Vol. 8, No. 7, October 1984, pp 607-33.See also Abha Dixit, "Study of U.S. — Pak strategic and military collaboration", Strategic Analysis, 11(12). March 1988, pp 1393-1413.Nikhil Chakravarty, "P.M. cannot afford to ignore US arms supply to Pakistan", Telegraph, 26 October 1987.
19. Warren H. Donnelly, "Pakistan and Nuclear Weapons", Strategic Digest, 17(12), December 1987, pp 2273-82. See also Nilofar Suhrawardy, Sino-Pak Nuclear Link", Mainstream, Vol. XXVII, No. 21, 18 February 1989, p. 6. Sunil Sondhi, "Indo-Pakistan Nuclear Equation", Mainstream, Vol. XXVI, No. 14. 16 January 1988, p.32. K. Subrahmanyam, "Indo-Pak Nuclear Stand off" : A Challenge and Opportunity", Times of India, & June 1988. On the contrary A 1988 report sponsored by the Carnegie Endowment for International Peace concluded that while it is possible that neither country has so far made complete nuclear bombs, by 1991 Pakistan could have as many as 15 Hiroshima size bombs and India could have more than 100. Carnegie Task Force on Non-Proliferation and South Asian Security (Washington, DC: Carnegie Endowment for International Peace, 1988), p. 56..
20. See Z.A. Bhutto. If I am assassinated (New Delhi, 1979), p. 137.
21. Ashok Kapur, "India's Nuclear Agenda", Indian Express (Orissa edn.), 24 January 1991.
22. Charles W. Maynes, "America without the coldwar", Foreign policy, No. *78* Spring 1990, p.8.

23. Lawrence T- Caldwell, "Soviet American Relations. The Cold war ends" Current History, Vol. 89, No. 549, October. 1990, p. 306.
24. Nayan Chanda, "A New Indian Summer" Far Eastern Economic Review, 25 February 1988, p. 34. For an analysis of Indian naval expansion: See Ashley J. Tellis, "India's Naval Expansion: Reflections on History and Strategy". Comparative Strategy. Vol. 6, No. 2, 1987, pp. 185-219.
25. Francis Fukuyama, "Patterns of Soviet Third World Policy", Problems of Communism, Vol. 36, No. 5, September — October 1987, p. 7.
26. Zalmy Khalizad, "The United States in South Asia", Current History, Vol. 88, No. 542, December 1989, pp. 419-20.
27. See for details Nayan Chanda n. 24, p. 3. Khalizad, Ibid.
28. See Stephen Cohen, in Harold Gould and Sumit Ganguly ed., The Hope and Reality: US — India relations from Roosevelt to Reagan (Boulder, West View Press, 1992).
29. Selig S. Harrisan, "US must prevent war in sub- continent", Washington Post, reproduced in Mainstream, Vol. XXVIII, No. 29, 12 May 1990, pp. 7-8.
30. Jasjit Singh, "Pakistan Army: Growing Offensive Capability". Mainstream, special number, 26 January 1988, p. 26.
31. Times of India, 17 January 1991.
32. See Kapur, p-21.
33. Francine Frankel, "Ply the Indian Card", Foreign Policy, No. 62, Spring 1986, p. 66.
34. Richard N. Haass, "US and South Asia", Strategic Digest, Vol. XX,No. 4, April 1990, p. 2178.
35. Nayan Chanda, op. cit., p. 35.
36. Richard N. Haass, op.cit. p. 2182.
37. Bhaskar Menon, India, and US: looking for their souls". Times of India, 12 July 1992.
38. Pamila Constable, " Radical Cleric's Message Alarms U.S., Pakistan," Washington Post, 21 February 2000.
39. Henry Kissinger, White House years, Vol.I (Boston: Little, Brown and Company, 1979), pp.913-14 (a phrase used by him in a White House National Security Council Meeting on Dec 3 1971 later on leaked to Columnist Jack Anderson.
40. Joel E. Starr, "Can the U.S. and India Be Steadfast Friends?" Orbis, Vol.45, No. I, Winter 2001, p.119.

41. Dennis Kux, " India's fine Balance ." Foreign Affairs, Vol.81, No.3, May-June 2002.
42. *Times of India*, November 2, 2001
43. *Times of India*, November 4, 2001.
44. K. Subraymanyam," Allies for the moment: But US not Blind to Pakistan's Ploys", Times of India, October 9, 2001.
45. Mohammed Ayoob, " South Asia's Dangers and U.S., Foreign Policy ", ORBIS, Vol.45, No.1, No.1, Winter 2001,p.129.
46. Mohammed Ayoob, "India Matters", Washington Quarterly, Winter 2000, pp.27-39.
47. David Shanbaugh, " China's Military Views the World: Ambivalent Security," International Security, Winter 1999/2000, pp.52-79. And Brad Roberts, Robert A. Manning, and Ronald N. Montaperto, " China : The Forgotten Nuclear Power," Foreign Affairs, July/August 2000, pp.53-63.
48. Mohammed Ayoob, "South Asia's Dangers", op.cit, p.133-34.

5

Indo-US Relation From Containment to Engagement

One of the startling ironies in Indo-US relation is that democracy being the most universally agreed, widely vouchsafed for, and an ideal means of founding a political society and achieving humanistic ends- a commonality in their societies, could not bind them together as natural allies expected of them in their respective societies, rather enmesh them in a maze of divergent, often conflicting and incongruent strategic approaches, perception and global outlook of cold war, economic dissimilarities, nuclear non-proliferation, Kashmir imbroglio and more significantly US massive military and economic build up of Pakistan as a plea to provide bulwark against Soviet communism to the great discomfiture of India.

Not that there was dearth of any will and effort on both sides to put their relations on an even keel but what seemed to have balked at these was the entrenched proclivity in US to study events and issues in various part of the globe and more particularly the Indo- Pak conflict not objectively and in their own merits but mechanically in terms of cold war logic and derivatives and also India's saintly image befitting its legacy of history, great civilization, culture and vast democracy to play a moralizing role in world politics and no less significantly its jumping into the embrace of Soviet Union as its principal arm supplier and moral supporter in international realm, despite New Delhi's professed commitment to non- alignment.

Democracy instead of acting as a glue to bind their relations turned out to be a chink in the armour of India's foreign policy, as its geo- strategic and geo- political vastness and uniqueness always putting independence, freedom and unencumbered sovereignty as uncompromising values on a high premium, could prove to be too large to fit into the American global strategic procrustean bed.

A commonly held belief was that America could have corrected the Indian Soviet leaning by favourably responding to India's request for military help. But America knew very much that a country recently unfettered from the shackles of British colonialism, remaining dazzled in the euphoria of its greatness of its glorious civilization and uniqueness of its independence movement through an extraordinary way i.e. non violent means, and taking up the cudgels for other countries in Asia and Africa would not like to play second fiddle to America, which Pakistan was very much willing to play at any cost. It was not surprising Nehru's request for supply of modern supersonic jet fighter available to Pakistan was turned down. The very illusion of believing that America as a great power is a messiah and would act in transcendence of immediacy of its national interests and global strategy, and judge things in their rightness proved pernicious when India succumbed to Chinese attack. In zero sum American understanding of India and Pakistan, US did not like to take any step that would further India's interests and anger Pakistan, its close accomplice in containment of communism. Thus, to the great advantage and delight of Pakistan, American policy of containing India's potential into an independent power in relation to Pakistan and later on China after a thaw in their bilateral relation at the regional level was dovetailed into its grand strategy of containment of Soviet Union. This American policy was a blend of active involvement and wilful prevention. In Chinese war American rejection of India's request for military help prevented India from rising to power in South Asia. In 1965 Indo-Pak war America feigned being neutral but in reality its weapons to Pakistan supposed to be used against Soviet communism fought the battle against India and as a token of support to Pakistan America retaliated by suspending military and economic aids to India. In 1971 Bangladesh war US policy of active involvement was evident when its warship carrying nuclear weapons moved into Bay of

Bengal to prevent India from adventuring into Pakistan in the western front. It was American active intervention and threatening posture to stem the further truncation of Pakistan that balked India of the opportunity to bury ever the Kashmir imbroglio by pushing through the western frontier and unconditionally demanding from Bhutto to accept permanently LOC at Kashmir as international border. This would have certainly removed India's Pakistani obsession standing always in its way to look beyond South Asia. But America succeeded in clipping the wings of India by miring it further deep into the labyrinthine abyss of Kashmir issue. Not yet frozen in time these events remained eloquent in explaining India's inability to settle the issue permanently, and American insidious role as a great constraint on India's journey to a big power status in world politics as apocalyptically eked out by its illustrious civilization and derived moral posture. Thus, Indo –US relationship was contentious and sometimes more turbulent during cold war. They were at odds on many issues. At regional level their differences centered round Pakistan, India's principal adversary. India was acerbic to US military assistance to Pakistan and its ambivalent stance on Kashmir. India's preference for state controlled economy in the place of liberal market economy was not palatable to US. At the global level India could not acquiesce in the policy of containment of communism- a central element of American grand strategy. The differences in strategic outlook were evident in India's dependence on the Soviet Union as its principal arm supplier, despite New Delhi's professed commitment to non-alignment.

Both attempted cautious moves to improve relations even before the end of cold war. Reagan administration dangled before India the promise of expanded technological cooperation to wean India away from its military dependence on Soviet Union. Yet the palimpsest of the past weighed heavily on both sides. America was under the strong impression that India would not sever its military ties to Soviet Union and jettison its commitment to the creation of global regimes based on regulatory as opposed to market mechanisms.

End of the cold war and disintegration of Soviet Union led to gradual withering away of most of these irritants in Indo- US relations. After the disintegration of Soviet Union, India embraced

American liberal market economy and showed little intransigence on issues ranging from trade to global climate change. Differences on key issues continued to mar their relationship however. During Clinton administration, the two sides could not bury their hatchet as both sides remained at loggerheads over Kashmir and over India's pursuit of nuclear weapons and ballistic missiles.

A new warmth in Indo- US relationship emerged after the Kargil war towards the waning days of Clinton administration. Only when the military confrontation between India and Pakistan broke out in the disputed territory of Kashmir at Batalik, Dras, and Kargil, and America condemned Pakistan for having sent troops across the line of control and played a pivotal role in brokering a cease fire agreement, a warmth in their relations dawned.

Indian policy makers perceived a shift in American ingrained stance towards India in their unequivocal condemnation of Pakistan and key role-played to resolve the crisis. India's assessment of the shift was reinforced when Clinton in his visit to subcontinent in March 2000 spent the bulk of his time in India and upbraided Gen. Musharraf during his only one day visit to Pakistan for having engineered the October 1999 coup and Pakistan for its inexorable slipping towards becoming ungovernable. This was further evidenced when Indian Prime Minister Vajpayee visited the United States later that year in September and had cordial discussions of contentious issues such as Kashmir and nuclear proliferation, which were remarkably devoid of any acrimony. In spite of this US- Indian dealings remained stuck in the same nonproliferation straitjacket.

The belatedly panned out Clinton policy towards India continued by Bush. Even prior to assuming office, the key policy makers and advisers of Bush signalled that India would be accorded a higher priority in America's foreign policy calculus.[1] Most importantly, what incensed America was Pakistan's stubborn unwillingness to snap extensive ties with Taliban regime in Afghanistan and stop supporting unremittingly and abating militarily and morally Muslim insurgents who were terrorizing Indian controlled Kashmir. On the other hand, US administration downplayed the issue of nuclear proliferation much to the delight of both India and Pakistan. After coming to power president Bush lifted many of the proliferation related sanctions that had been placed on India after the Indian nuclear tests of May 1998 and soon after lifted the sanctions on Pakistan.

The tragic terrorist attack of September 11,2001 provided the occasion to America to reexamine its policies towards Pakistan. This worked like the 1979 Soviet invasion of Afghanistan and transformed the US- Pak relations. Pakistan is what can be called a geo- strategic rentier (Hussain Haqqani). Had it not been for 9/11, Pakistan would have remained in the backwaters in American policy. In Ganguly's opinion, Musharraf has been a parsimonious ally and not as staunch as the US would like him to be or as he portrays himself to be.[2] Its geographical proximity to Afghanistan means its cooperation would be quintessential for launching the military onslaught against both the Taliban regime and Osama bin Laden's al-Qaeda terrorist network. The much hyped and talked about decline of Pakistan in the American scale of priority just after the end of cold war plummeted to trickles just when Washington came to understand Pakistan's geo-strategic significance because of its extensive links with Taliban and geographical proximity to Afghanistan, in its global war against terrorism. To avoid a rupture in Indo-US relations, senior American officials sought to assure their Indian counterparts that a closer relationship with Pakistan would not come at India's expense.[3] However, a series of terrorist acts against Indian targets carried out by Pakistan sponsored insurgents ignited skirmishes of words between India and Pakistan. Very much an imminence of war between the two countries was in the offing.

Pakistan based Lashkar- Taiba extremist group's brazen attack on Indian Parliament on December 13,2001 having incontrovertible links with Pakistan intelligence services[4], which was ultimately foiled by India, spurred it to snap diplomatic ties with Pakistan and demanded that Pakistan hand over some 20 individuals wanted in India for acts of terror, and shut down road and air links between the two countries.[5] India also embarked on a massive military mobilization designed to pressure Pakistan to end its support for Kashmiri separatist organizations. Senior Indian officials put pressure on America to induce Musharraf government to concede to Indian demands.

The terrorists' attack on Indian Parliament and India's subsequent demands threw American foreign policy into a dilemma. It could not simply show short shrift to Pakistan's complicity in terrorist activities of Kashmir separatist groups in its much-proclaimed war against terrorism. Logic of the war against terrorism and logic of the terrorist attack in Kashmir demand that America wage a war against Pakistan much to the delight of India. But the immediacy of its global strategy in Afghanistan impelled America not to be benevolent enough to completely side with India rather to develop a two- pronged strategy: it counselled restraint on the part of India while placing Lashkar-I-taiba and Jaish-e – Mohammed, another Pakistani terrorist group on the department's list of terrorist organizations and freezing their assets in the United States.[6] It also urged Musharraf to renounce his government's avowed support to insurgents in Kashmir. In this strategy America while addressing India's concerns tried to protect its interests. Caving in to American sustained pressure Musharraf denounced the activities of a number of radical Muslim organizations operating from Pakistan's soil and arrested some of their leaders as made clear in a speech on January 12, 2002. But he refused to renounce his government's support for the Kashmir cause, insisting, "Kashmir runs in our blood". America perceived this as a substantial shift in Pakistan's policy but some among the Indian leadership referred to the speech as little more than a sop to the American Cerberus[7]. Indo- Pakistani tensions remained high as both sides bolstered their forces along the line of control to the great discomfiture of the policy makers in Washington.

An avalanche of visits from US including that of Secretary of State Colin Powell and Secretary of Defense Donald Rumsfeld to both Pakistan and India continued over these months to preserve good relations with both states amidst sporadic terrorist attacks on India. But Indo-Pakistan relations continued on their downward slide and reached its nadir when Pakistan sponsored terrorist attacked an Indian military base at Kaluchak in the state of Jammu and Kashmir on May 14. It appeared that war was imminent. Again America stepped in to stop the escalation.[8] But it was an open question whether it was American intervention, the lack of adequate Indian conventional military capabilities, or the fear of a nuclear holocaust that whisked away the two from the brink but war was averted.

In reality, right up to the end of the Clinton administration, US- Indian dealings remained simmering in the same non-proliferation fire that had made a toll of all efforts at bilateral rapprochement since the inception of Indian nuclear test in1974. All successive governments in Washington were under the crusted impression that India was an inextricable part of the problem of proliferation because its nuclear capability and the existence of that capability outside various global regimes stood in the way of U.S nonproliferation efforts internationally.[9] New Delhi's close alliance with Soviet Union, its opposition to virtually every U.S position at the United Nations, and its activities within the nonaligned movement during those years further portrayed India in American eyes as unfriendly to American interests. Consistent with this entrenched perception, beginning in the early1970s every US administration, including that of President Clinton sought to erect higher and more robust policy, legal, and international regime obstacles between India and various strategic commodities so long as New Delhi persisted with its nuclear programme.[10]Thomas Pickering, under secretary of state for political affairs in the Clinton administration while acknowledging this in the midst of warming Indo- US relation clearly said that the "new and qualitatively closer relationship with India... cannot realize its full potential without further progress on non- proliferation" with further reiteration that "we cannot and will not be able to concentrate on military issues until there is substantial progress on non- proliferation."[11]

A new strategic partnership

During cold war America was justifying its military build up of Pakistan on the pretext that it would provide Washington the leverage on Pakistan to settle amicably the Kashmir issue with India. By that America was preventing India from becoming tough against Pakistan. Thus, while whetting up Pakistan's desire to be equal with India in military terms, America was denying India the same military and economic wherewithal to become powerful and independent enough to challenge its close ally Pakistan on Kashmir issue. Marking a departure from its cold war strategy Bush administration decided to extend its leverage strategy to India and improve its ties with it. Accordingly, while America exerted pressure on Pakistan to curb its support for the insurgents in Kashmir, it decided to offer inducements to India. With this objective in mind it undertook to initiate military to military cooperation with India and renewed discussions with the Indian government on the transfer of dual-use technology, which culminated in a new technology – transfer regime in early 2003.[12]

Given the two sides' history of mutual acrimony, distrust, and petulance, the military to military cooperation was dramatic and a shift in American policy. The foundation of these cooperative endeavour was laid during Clinton's administration when Secretary of Defense William Perry signed the "Agreed Minute on Defense Relations" with his Indian counterpart, S.B. Chavan in January 1995.[13] However Clinton administration's preoccupation with nuclear nonproliferation hamstrung any significant expansion of military to military cooperation or dual use technology transfers. What made further such ties impossible and prompted America to impose economic and military sanctions on India was the Indian nuclear tests of May 1998.

Bush administration took a more pragmatic and measured view of India's nuclear and ballistic missiles programmes. India's restraint in the light of Bush administration's decision to abandon the anti- Ballistic Treaty came as a most welcome surprise in Washington.[14] This new willingness of both sides to pursue a non-ideological approach to bilateral relations opened the path to greater security cooperation. Bush administration's quest to develop better security ties emanates in part from concerns about China's future role in Asia and limiting its strategic influence with India's cooperation. What was ideologically obnoxious from Indian point of view to become an accomplice of America policy of containment of Soviet communism during cold war has become now strategically ethical to India to jump into the American bandwagon of containing China by forging a defense relationship with it. This is indubitably a grand departure from India's proclaimed Nehruvian non-aligned posture during cold war shrouded in the mystery of supposed independence from both super powers. America departed from its cold war policy of preventing India from growing into a power to a policy of cooperation with it, and extended its policy of leverage, which was confined, to Pakistan, to India. Apart from expanding the scope of military to military cooperation Bush administration signalled a willingness to sell India various forms of weapons technology, including previously embargoed air craft engines and artillery locating radars. On matters of common interest as terrorism, peacekeeping operations, the protection of sea-lanes and piracy both sides continued regular diplomatic consultations.[15]

This military to military cooperation with India was initiated by America with the sole objective of assuaging India that America's reliance on Pakistan in the war against terror will not be to India's detriment. But India's publicly and privately vented grouse about America's coddling of Pakistan in view of its persistent support to terrorists in Kashmir and its proliferation connection with North Korea continued.

A small segment of India's public remains suspicious of American moves, goals and objectives. They termed the recent warming trends in Indo- US relations as window dressing. In their assessment, despite the end of cold war, the United States mistakenly remains persistent in its view of Pakistan as India's equal, has failed to recognize India's economic and political resilience, and is deeply opposed to India's preferred vision of a multipolar world in which regional powers should have some room for manoeuvre.[16] In their view India should avoid falling into the orbit of American influence by establishing good relations with regional powers such as Iran, Russia, France and China. Constellations of middle- range powers could offer a credible alternative to American global dominance. This post-Nehruvian vision of the multi polar world in which a country has more freedom of manoeuvrability than in a unipolar world cannot be effective if that country has not the required military and economic capability. Accordingly, the ruling elites in BJP were not nearly as concerned about upholding multilateral norms where India's perceived vital interests are concerned.[17] Consequently, marking a departure from the premises of Nehruvian foreign policy, the Vajpayee government embarked on vigorously and quietly producing nuclear weapons and ballistic missiles and bolstering its conventional capabilities along with flinging its door open to economic reforms and acceptance of market oriented principles of economic growth. India also very tactfully avoided confrontation with America on Iraq crisis.

Next Steps in Strategic Partnership (NSSP)

From 2001 to 2003 the courtship between the US and India grew in ardour and expectations. After a series of breakthroughs in bilateral diplomatic collaborations, military to military relations, counter terrorism cooperation and public diplomacy the way was paved for one of the Bush administration's major first term diplomatic achievements, Next Steps in Strategic Partnership (NSSP), which was announced in January 2004. Despite differences between two countries on other issues such as trade, Iraq, and the United Nations, they agreed to work together in four difficult arenas- civilian nuclear energy, civilian space programs, high – technology trade and missile defense.

This revolutionary step in American foreign policy is a sign of turning Washington's long-standing approach to New Delhi on its head. Contrary to its earlier position, America showed the proclivity to portray India as a part of the solution to nuclear proliferation rather than a part of the problem. President Bush resorted to a course of action that would permit India more access to controlled technologies even though New Delhi persisted in its nuclear programme, declined to concede to the principal nuances earmarked by the Clinton administration, and subsisted in its position formally outside the global nonproliferation regime. If this was the quid in terms of change in American foreign policy, the pro demanded of India was that India institutionalize comprehensive export controls in conformity with the best international standards, and New Delhi not use the technologies made available to it under NSSP to advance its own strategic weapons programmes. This change in foreign policy is derived from three evolving perceptions within Bush administration[18]:

First, the administration had come to realize that India would not give up its nuclear weapons so long as various regional adversaries such as China and Pakistan continued to possess comparable capabilities. During cold war America was simply glossing over Pakistan's clandestine nuclear programme, and rebuffed India's allegations as baseless. With Pakistan going nuclear American policy makers became sympathetic to New Delhi's predicament.

Second, the administration was now of the understanding that India's weapons did not pose a threat to US security and the

United States' larger geo- political interests, and could in certain circumstances actually advance American strategic objectives in Asia and beyond. American antipathy to nuclear arms control agreements such as the Comprehensive Test Ban Treaty and the Fissile Cut-off Treaty coalesced with its expectations of an eventual renewal of great power competition impelled the realist and neo-conservative factions within Bush administration to take a more lenient view of India's emerging nuclear capabilities.

Third. New Delhi's ownership of the range of technological resources associated with weapons of mass destruction and their delivery system that are present in India would not be a threat to American safety rather their leaking deliberately or inadvertently to hostile or non- state actors will be a serious threat to America. No doubt it is a change in America's previous policy of prevention or abstention. It is rather an extension of leverage policy to India, which was earlier applicable to Pakistan only. The dominant perception in America is that from America security point of view by courting partnership with India it would be more able to tighten the Indian export control regime than putting pressure on India to roll back or cap its strategic programmes by remaining outside or following the policy of prevention.

NSSP though was revolutionary from the viewpoint of radically transforming U.S. – Indian relations but hesitant because of the constraints imposed by U.S. law and the United States existing commitments to various non-proliferation regimes[19]. So the dilution of American stringency in applicability of its commitment to nuclear nonproliferation that took place to accommodate India seems to be precarious and asymmetrical not well weaved into its global interests. Further, NSSP demonstrated a degree of strategic hesitancy even in the realm of policy shifts because of concerns about the disruptive consequences for U.S. global anti- proliferation activities arising from any effort to accommodate India. While carving out a new approach to New Delhi it failed to provide a definitive answer to the question at the heart of any further transformation in Indo-U.S. relations. The same cold war understanding and perception of India stepped in to question whether an increase in Indian power conducive or pernicious to America and its global interests. This uncertainty and doubt hovering on American baptism of India into its global strategic orbit is derived from the fear that India is still bashing in the hubris of Nehruvian nonalignment, and does not relish any strategy that will cap its ambition to become a great power matching its glorious history and civilization and enhanced military and economic status. It is not lost to America that India while seeking to improve relations with Washington is simultaneously trying to avoid being coddled in its embrace.

Not Zero Sum Relation but Moving Beyond NSSP

The United States decided to establish good relation with both India and Pakistan. Accordingly, it bestowed a major Non – NATO Ally status to Pakistan because it is an active collaborator in the U.S. led action in Afghanistan and Operation Enduring Freedom. It became a prominent beneficiary of U.S. economic assistance and the recipient of significant arms transfers from the United States. This renewed centrality of Pakistan in American policy with arms supply to Islambad and the threat of paralyzing India- Pakistan hyphenation in American bureaucratic habits created skepticism in India about U.S. intentions and behaviour both globally and in South Asia. To kick start the process of good relations between India and America agreed to in NSSP, Secretary of State Condoleezza Rice visited India on March 16,2005 in the context of a larger visit to South Asia and East Asia. While replying to an Indian interlocutor's question on the significance of making New Delhi her first stop, she said, "It really is emblematic of how far this relationship has come in the last several years. The President very much values the enhanced relationship between the United States and India, the fact that we are becoming in many ways important global partners as well as regional partners. And he wanted me very much to come here, and I am glad that I was able to come here first". Asserting that " we have tried very hard, as a matter of fact, to make the point that this is not a hyphenated relationship," Rice declared that U.S. ties with New Delhi ought to be viewed on their own terms: " This is a relationship with India. We also have very good relationship with Pakistan and we are concerned about the well-being of both."[20]

Resumption of the sale of F- 16 fighter aircraft to Pakistan was in continuation of its old strategy of military build up, and exercise of leverage on Pakistan. President Bush after months of secret deliberations finally telephoned Prime Minister Manmohan Singh, on March 25, 2005 to inform him personally that the United States would resume sale of F-16 fighter aircraft to Pakistan. Indian Prime minister Manmohan Singh expressed his "great disappointment at the decision, which could have negative consequences for India's security environment"[21]. US wanted to have good relations with both India and Pakistan simultaneously because of the conviction that both countries represent different kinds of strategic opportunities for the United States. As Rice put it, "India is looking to grow its influence into global influence and Pakistan is looking to a settled neighbourhood so that it can deal with extremism inside its own borders"[22]. Unfolding a potentially far more radical initiative with respect to India in a background briefing, the senior officials on the very day of Bush's announcement, the United States had in fact reached a decision "to help India become a major world power in the twenty- first century". By further asserting that " we understand fully the implications, including military implications, of that statement"[23], the administration effectively gave clarifications that it would take to its limits the strategy advocated in an influential RAND report prior to Bush's election in 2000, namely, that the United States ought to " systematically decouple India and Pakistan (in its strategic calculations): that is, U.S. relations with each state (should) be governed by an objective assessment of the intrinsic value of each country to U.S. interests rather than by fears about how U.S. relations with one would affect relations with the other."[24]

Thus, resumption of sale of long overdue F- 16s to Pakistan and proclaimed commitment to advance India as a global power represent remarkably a radical shift from a zero sum to differentiated relationship while dealing with both India and Pakistan. But continuance of the same cold war strategy is found when America decided to assist Pakistan to transform itself into a successful and moderate state by rewarding General Pervez Musharraf through military and economic assistance. In relation to India America also concluded that a strong and independent India represents a strategic asset even when it remains only a partner and not a formal ally. No intrinsic conflict of interests exists between India and United States.

US new strategy with respect to India and Pakistan on two distinct tracks

Where Islamabad is concerned, the administration is committed to providing $3 billion economic and military assistance package that will be disbursed from 2005 to 2009. As a mark of gratitude for Musharraf's efforts in the war of terror the administration will proceed with the sale of F-16 aircraft to Pakistan.

Where New Delhi is concerned, first it has decided overcoming the hesitation of the past to take a more liberal view in regard to supplying India with advanced defense equipment. Accordingly, it has permitted Lockheed Martin and Boeing to offer F-16s and F-18s respectively as candidates for the Indian Air Force's multi role fighter program, with the assurance that Washington would be favourably inclined to license even more sophisticated sensors and weapons than those made available to Pakistan and to consider co- production of these platforms in India. It has stated directly that it will support Indian requests for other transformative systems in areas such as command and control, early warning, and missile defense[25].

Second, More important to India the administration has expressed willingness to discuss a range of difficult and highly contentious issues through separate high level dialogues with New-Delhi on strategic, energy, and economic concerns.

The strategic dialogue relates to global security issues, including India's quest for permanent membership in Security Council, future defense cooperation, high-technology trade, and space-related collaboration, as well as regional issues pertaining to security in and around South Asia. The energy dialogue hinges on energy security matters including the proposed Indian- Iranian-Pakistan gas pipeline, cooperation on nuclear safety and most important of all, ways of integrating India into the global nuclear regime so as to address New Delhi's desire for renewed access to safeguarded nuclear fuel and advanced nuclear reactors. The economic dialogue focuses on greater Indo-U.S. economic interactions for a hike in India's economic growth.

"On balance, therefore, the Bush administration's decision to expand relations with both its South Asian partners, but in a differentiated way commensurate with each state's geostrategic attractiveness to the United States, implies that Washington has placed its biggest bet on New Delhi, expecting that transformed bilateral relations will facilitate the expansion of Indian power in a manner that ultimately will advance America's own global interests with respect to defeating terrorism, arresting further nuclear proliferation, promoting democracy worldwide, and preserving a stable balance of power in Asia over the long term"[26].

The importance of what Washington is offering India for its future strategic trajectory helps explain the Indian government's muted response to US decision to sell F-16s to Pakistan[27].

Risks and Challenges to the New Strategy

The first and greatest calculation is that Islamabad will use the security provided by enhanced U.S military assistance to pursue its own aggressive agenda vis-à-vis India. This could take the form of expanded state support for anti- Indian terrorist groups, increased obduracy in Indo- Pakistani negotiation over Kashmir or more provocative needling of India through low intensity conflict. The outcome of such events disrupting the current thaw in Indo- Pak relation would bedevil the relation between U.S. and India, thus sabotaging the larger goal of transforming Indo- U.S. relations. During cold war period, when Pakistan was its close ally, America did not attach any conditionality to its supply of arms and ammunitions to Pakistan, knowing very much that these weapons would be used against India, though supposedly meant against Soviet Union. On the contrary, any such supply to India was attached with many conditions, one of which was that India would not use them against Pakistan. But in a changed context and with differential strategic values of both India and Pakistan to America, to supply weapons to Pakistan without any conditionality runs the risks of arms race in South Asia, and questions the sensitivity of U.S. to Indian concerns. This would bolster up Pakistan to increase its terrorist activities with renewed vigour against India. The pretext that these military supplies and defense tie with Pakistan would act as leverage on the latter forcing it to soften its stand on Kashmir, has yet to reap dividends so long as Pakistan continues sponsoring terrorism against India. This has led some commentators in India to castigate this new approach as being little more than an effort to stoke Indian pride and obscure the "deeply unfriendly act"[28] of selling F-16s to Pakistan. The challenges staring the Bush administration to have successfully a transformed Indo- U.S. relations require that Bush administration rivet sufficient attention both to the kinds of weapons transformed to Pakistan in the future and to the progress made in satisfying New Delhi's quest for critical technologies. It is said that the transfers will take years to implement, and the need for annual Congressional approval is a tacit conditionality put on Pakistan to behave responsibly on matters of vital importance to American interests[29]. Since U.S. and India do not converge on Kashmir issue and combating terrorism, Pakistan's behaviour in Kashmir may not come within the benchmark of what constitutes responsible behaviour on the part of Pakistan, and will vitiate the vital interests of America.

The second danger is that Pakistan's military rulers might read the renewed US willingness to supply them with major combat systems as evidence that Washington cares little about democracy in Pakistan and would tolerate further retreats from restoring it. America has till today maintained silence about Musharraf's broken promise to restore democracy in Pakistan. Hence, this reticence on the part of U.S. could spur Pakistani ruler to treat American interest in democracy as a mere euphemism. Further, America has not yet termed Pakistan a rogue state despite its complicity in sponsoring terrorism in India. The combinations of 9/11 terrorist attacks on America and 13/12 attack on Indian Parliament would have spurred the United States to recognize, respect and integrate the Islamic Jehadi threats against India with the overall American operations against global terrorism. The incongruence between Indian perception of terrorism and that of America, and lack of will and efforts on the part of Washington to weave the Pakistani sponsored terrorism into the global operation, will be the greatest challenge to American policy makers. The success of envisaged transformation in Indo- U.S relation depends on the celerity with which America moves toward the Indian line.

Third danger is that when Pakistan's record on eschewing terrorism, curbing proliferation and moving toward democracy is not entirely impressive, recommending F-16 sales could enhance the prospect of failures in these issue areas. The issue of strategic arms transfer to Pakistan could throw the relationship off track. Low-level supply will not be a big problem. The issue here would be largely the political fall out of any large-scale arms transfer to Pakistan.

The fourth risk and challenge is the ongoing peace process between India and Pakistan and its impact on Indo- U.S. relation. What is most conducive to American interests is avoidance of any kind of violent conflict or war between the two countries, as current arms transfers to Pakistan are more likely to embolden it to intensify its hostile activities against India. By the exercise of the leverage it enjoys over Pakistan, America can make Pakistan set out in candid terms its political objectives in the ongoing peace process, which is nothing but a political accommodation with India over Kashmir. As a sine qua non of transforming Indo- U.S. relation, this political accommodation would mean to America not thinking in terms of Pakistan's old welter of verbiages but in terms of Pakistan resigning to the current political facts of life in the subcontinent, and accepting the fact that it will never be able to secure a change in the status quo in Kashmir by any means. " Consequently, Pakistan will have to make its peace with reality by redefining the meaning of victory in terms of some criterion other than territorial control or fundamental changes in the existing patterns of sovereignty"[30] Given the effervescence surrounding the rhetoric about the history of their mutual acrimony, festered distrust, and entrenched misperception on which largely depends the political fortunes of the bureaucratic- military establishment in Pakistan, the question crops up whether American influence in Pakistan through its massive military and economic help will play the magic wand on expected lines in binding the Pakistani military ruler to the pragmatic requirements of a truce with the current political reality. It is certainly not through an Afghanistan or Iraqi type unipolar approach but through a crass political process hinging on dialogue and fostering moderation and bringing all to the path of democracy, American heavy weight in terms of its enviable influence may act as a catalyst. On the Indian side America will have to push New Delhi to satisfactorily address the sources of burgeoning discontent in Kashmir. The success of America in heralding a political settlement between India and Pakistan will certainly propel Indo- U.S. relation to exultant new heights.

Finally, Bush administration's new security objective to advance the growth of India's power implies to accommodate India on the issues of nuclear, space, and high technology cooperation by negotiating with the stringency of the international nonproliferation regimes, which Washington has been trying during the past several decades for implementation. The benefits India seeks are bound to come in direct collision with many of the restrictions enshrined in these universal regimes. Concerned, as with the augmentation of India's power, America cannot abide by its commitment without an infringement of the obligations of these regimes. The central question haunting the American policy makers is whether its avowed commitment to the growth of Indian power is worth risking blatantly reneging on its unflinching adherence to the nuances of nonproliferation regimes. If promotion of American national interest is the guiding star of its foreign policy, then Washington will not mind risking a compromise of its holistic allegiance to the long hallowed principles of nonproliferation regimes. What looms large and cannot be perilously overlooked by the U.S. policy makers, is India's increasing geopolitical importance, the role it can play in counter proliferation activities in the Indian ocean, its potential utility as a bulwark against a rising China, and its importance for global energy stability and environmental protection. One pragmatic option as a solution to this dilemma is not in terms of total rejection of the nonproliferation regimes but in terms of their selective and preferential applicability. This means, what Richard Haass once put it a proliferation of proliferation policies, where different countries are treated differently on the basis of their friendship and value to U.S. Otherwise, keeping India's presence outside the global nonproliferation regime will be increasingly dangerous for U.S. interests, given India's vast and growing indigenous capabilities. Rather, through the strategy of cooperation and leverage with India America can be more successfully able to control the proliferation than the cold war strategy of preventing. All current regime members receive material incentives and have access to nuclear energy. If Pakistan and Israel receive their subsidies in different forms, namely through large aid programmes and privileged political relations with U.S., then keeping India out of the circle of inducements will prove to be pejorative of American interests.

Prescriptions for America

In order to carry through his new policy toward India President Bush needs changing policy seeking appropriate waivers from various legislative constraints in close collaboration with Congress. In case it is infeasible, the other option is to establish coordination with the international community to develop the appropriate carve outs for preferential treatment of New Delhi as a legitimate exception to the existing rules. American steps in furtherance of these options will certainly prove that not eloquent words but deeds are important at present to carry India into confidence, and mute those who tend to doubt America's sincerity and commitment to India's ascension to great power status. Another ingrained constraint in American foreign policy formulation that needs to be overcome is the complex, often festering inter-agency brawling among the policy makers within the U.S. government further, aggravated by the proclivity of bureaucracy to pursue its own interests irrespective of how these are congruent with political preferences.

The July 18 nuclear agreement between India and the United States and Indian Government's imprudent decision to support the European-US resolution against Iran at the IAEA mark a palpable change in India's stance and represent a dramatic reversal of Washington's earlier proliferation policies towards New Delhi. The formidable irony of India's capitulation to American wishes on Iran is that its display of political weakness comes at a time when America becomes aware of India's strategic weight and strength. With this agreement India shows its acceptance to cap its nuclear programme through agreements to stop further testing, limit the production of missile materials, and allow International Atomic Energy Agency inspections. With this agreement signed, India's decision to defend itself through minimal deterrence was permanently blocked[31]. The question is, will the American president be able to pull the law governing nuclear exports required to supply nuclear fuel as assured to India through Congress and persuade the Nuclear Suppliers Group to go along- before he leaves office in 2008?

July 18 Nuclear agreement and American double standard

Though India insists the identification and separation of military and civilian nuclear facilities is its decision alone, the U.S. is insisting on having a say, as Mr. Burns told the Congressional panel in September 2005. The irony here is that the U.S. produces its tritium at civilian facilities. For decades, the U.S. has been the only nuclear weapon state to effect a civil- military separation more or less successfully thanks to billion of dollars spent on it. But in 2003 formal separation in the U.S came to an end when the Tennessee Valley Authority's commercial Watts Bar Nuclear Plant started producing both tritium for nuclear weapons and electricity for civilians. The Department of Energy, which oversees the U.S. military nuclear programme, stopped making tritium in1988 when its reactors at Savannah River were shut down for safety reasons. Since the gas has a short life span, the U.S. administration authorized the use of civilian facilities as a cheaper option to the establishment of a DOE- run dedicated extraction facility.

In other words, even as it expects India to separate its civilian and military nuclear activities, the U.S. is turning its back on separation because of the costs involved. None of the nuclear powers has effected such a separation. French civilian power reactors like the Chinon, Bugey and St-Laurent series are believed to have produced as much as 2000 kg of military plutonium for France's nuclear weapon stockpile over the years. In China, the China National Nuclear corporation oversees military and civilian nuclear activities and tends to run them as an integrated whole. In view of this India submitting to American will has grave implications on India's security. In Russia, Oleg Bukharin in Science and Global Security 1994, says, "The military and civilian nuclear fuel cycles are highly integrated at the level of both uranium flows and individual facilities."[32] Averse to such a hard and unfair demand on India put by the American policy makers Selig S. Harrison, an U.S. expert suggested that Indian negotiators guard against hardliner American nationalists who are reluctant to accept India's nuclear status. The idea behind demanding for in-perpetuity safeguard on all civilian facilities is to establish the fact that America is entitled to exercise a dominant global position through its nuclear dominance. The hardliners in Bush administration have zeroed in on in- perpetulty safeguards because this is what most clearly defines for them the fact that the U.S. is a nuclear power and India is not. Then this demand for in-perpetuity safeguards on all civilian facilities is an attempt to Indian sovereignty. According to him, " the obvious compromise is that any imported nuclear fuel or reactors could be placed in safeguards in perpetuity as a pragmatic adjustment, necessitated by the importance of getting civilian nuclear cooperation."[33] Another influential U.S. nonproliferation think tank, members of Institute for Science and International Security (ISIS) has recently come up with its own plan for effecting nuclear and civilian separation in India. In their opinion all of India's nuclear facilities not directly associated with nuclear weapons production or deployment should be placed under international safeguards, which should apply in perpetuity. An expert A.N. Prasad, former director in Bhabha Atomic Research Centre in India while denouncing these proposals is of the view that the basic idea in all these unofficial and official U.S. approaches is that India cannot be treated as a nuclear weapon state. The proposal by America to place all power reactors, naval fuel cycle rare metals plant under safeguards is simply outlandish.[34] Indian government presented a plan to separate the country's civil and nuclear facilities in response to U.S. proposal saying fast breeder reactor programme is not included in civilian facilities. India has no objection if the U.S. side shared the separation plan with the U.S. Congress. During his visit to Washington, the Indian Foreign Secretary made it clear that India could not accept safeguards on the non- nuclear state model.Further, clarifying he said that " the objectives of the safeguards is not to address India's strategic programme; it is to give our partners the assurance they legitimately expect that, one, civil nuclear cooperation with India would not be diverted to assist India's strategic programme and two, it would not result in diversion to third countries"[35]. As said above, if separation of nuclear from civilian facilities has not taken place in other countries and the use of civilian facilities for nuclear weapons is in practice, then India's acquiescence in America's proposal will result in independence of decision making in strategic programmes. An understanding on the separation of New Delhi's civilian and nuclear facilities between the two countries was hammered out on 2 March 2006 on the occasion of President Bush's visit to India, which Washington will have to push through the U.S. Congress and the Nuclear Suppliers' Group (NSG). Full implementation of separation plan will take till 2014. About 65 per cent of India's nuclear power capacity would come under international safeguards. The fast breeder programme however would not be subject to safeguards. On safeguards in perpetuity, another knotty issue in the negotiations, India would have no problem if these were linked to permanent supplies of nuclear fuel. The Americans have conceded that India would have the right to take corrective measures if fuel supplies were suspended as had happened in the case of Tarapur. On the negotiation of safeguards with the IAEA, India would pitch for a middle path. It did not fall in the category of the five recognized nuclear weapons states, nor it would agree to a protocol as a non-nuclear weapon state[36].

Increasing Defense Cooperation

In the strategic dialogue between India and US, defense cooperation remains important. The defense relation between the two countries witnessed an explosive rise since the waiver of U.S. sanctions imposed after India's May 1998 nuclear tests. Bilateral exercises, personnel exchanges, high level and unit visits, military education and training, and officer and unit exchanges are some of the remarkable achievements to mark their military to military ties.

In contrast to these developments, there remained three areas, which remained uncultivated: sales of major combat systems, bilateral defense industrial collaboration, and combined military operations. America's preponderant concern for maintaining regional military balance with Pakistan coupled with India's traditional lack of trust in Washington's reliability as a supplier could be the reasons explaining America's reluctance to license high leverage military technologies to India, and expand defense trade as much as military to military cooperation has. The very decision of US to offer sophisticated aircraft such as the F-16 and the F-18, as well as other transformative capabilities such as command and control, early warning, and missile defense systems stems from American understanding of India as relevant to a larger canvas of US interests than South Asia. In an attempt to address India's concerns about US reliability, Washington has even expressed willingness to consider licensing co-production of some of these technologies in India. Some important items currently of great interest to India such as P-3 Orion anti submarine warfare aircraft, utility and attack helicopters, jet engines, minesweeping vessels, amphibious ships, and excess surface combatants remains in American cupboard yet to be opened for expeditious licensing for sales or co-production or hot transfers to India. America has not yet offered the Patriot PAC-3 missile as opposed to merely the Patriot PAC-2 for sale to India, which will enable India to acquire an American anti-tactical ballistic missile system. America still persists in its traditional reluctance to militarily strengthen India when the former disapproves the Israeli sale of Arrow anti-tactical ballistic missile. To defend a few critical conurbations against missile attacks, India will almost certainly require at least two-layered terminal defense architecture. Given the density and diversity of the missile threat, New Delhi has to counter, a single layered late terminal defense system,, even if configured around the advanced PAC-3, will simply be insufficient for high- confidence protection of the small target set of interests to India. Since the Arrow has been designed for high endoatmospheric defense- and could be integrated with the Patriot for low endoatmospheric protection- a two-layered architecture would provide the perfect technical combination for Indian defense planners. Apart from sales of these items, flow of more technical information unreservedly to India will be helpful to both in building a strengthened missile structure in India. According to Ashley J. Tellis

> So long as Washington abides by its new intentions to facilitate the growth of Indian power, and, accordingly, does not limit the sale of U.S. weaponry to India to comport with some illusory criterion of maintaining a military "balance" with Pakistan- an untenable proposition, given the disparity in national capabilities between the two sides, and a dangerous one as well, insofar as it disregards the Chinese security threat to India- there is every reason to expect the U.S.- Indian defense trade will grow in much the same way military to military cooperation has thus far.[37]

The Pentagon also approved the lease of two P-3C reconnaissance aircrafts for India and notified the US Congress of a $133 million military sale to provide logistical support for the deal that included training devices, test equipment and spare parts. Announcing the deal, the Pentagon's Defense Security Cooperation Agency (DSCA) said the proposed sale would help " improve the security of an important ally and strengthen the US- India strategic partnership." The P-3C aircrafts, built by Lockheed Martin would replace the Navy's Soviet IL-38 May aircrafts which are quickly reaching the end of their operational service life. This modernization would enhance the capabilities of the Navy, support its regional influence, and meet its legitimate needs of self defense, said the DSCA.[38] At the meeting of the Defense Policy Group (DPG) in Washington in September 2005, the two sides agreed to further strengthen bilateral defense cooperation and stressed on the importance of service- to –service ties. Under the Indo-US Defense framework agreement inked in June 2005, both countries agreed to further strengthen bilateral defense cooperation as an important facet of the India-US global partnership reflected in the India-US Joint Statement of July 18,2005. A 12 day joint exercise of Indo-US Navies called SALVEX began at Kochi on 13 September and concluded on 23 September 2005.[39]

In a step up of service- to- service engagement, India and the US conducted the biggest ever army level exercises near Ranikhet, in Uttaranchal in January as American officials indicated that Washington was working to open doors to high technology transfers. A company force of the US army also conducted joint exercises with a thrust towards anti- insurgency operations in the mountainous terrain near Choubhatia. US Pacific Command wants to expand its military level interaction with India over a broad front to enable the two armed forces to share experience in doctrines and higher formation- level exercises. Officials said that, though Indo-US defense trade stood at USD 287 million, they expected a big jump in arms sales through major deals with the Navy, the Special Forces and the Air Force.[40] The Indian efforts during the Straits of Malacca patrols in support of Operation Enduring Freedom and the closely coordinated activities in relief operations in the aftermath of the December 2004 Tsunami in Southern and Southeastern Asia provide examples of how both countries could cooperate in ad hoc coalitions of the willing outside any formal UN mandate. The Indian Navy's escort operations at Malacca in the aftermath of the 9/11 attacks were precedent setting in this regard. The question is whether India is ever willing to send its military division to fight an American battle. For example, was it acceptable to India in the case of American- Iraq war? When Vajpayee government was just toying with the idea of sending its troops to Iraqi stabilization operation, strong opposition in the domestic front nipped the proposal in the bud. Unless there is convergence of national interests of the countries, joint military operation or India joining American forces in its battle against a third country, is a remote possibility. "In many ways, much of the U.S- Indian defense cooperation thus far has been oriented to increasing mutual familiarity between the two armed forces in order to advance the goal of interoperability. But with furthering the growth of Indian power, now a conscious U.S. objective more heed should be paid to how New Delhi's military resources could be used collaboratively to advance the national interests of both countries."[41]

Strategic Relationship on Space

India's space programme, the crown jewel of its technological achievement began in 1962 with the specific objective of pursuing only scientific and developmental endeavours under the stewardship of Vikram Sarabhai, a committed pacifist in the Gandhian mold. From the very beginning, the Indian space programme, which was insulated from the nuclear programme taking leaf under Homi Bhabha sought and maintained strong links with the U.S. National Aeronautics and Space Administration. This close affinity helped the Indian Space Research Organization (ISRO) grow into a world-class venture characterized by a strong culture of professionalism, internal accountability, and high technical standards. Within three decades of India's unmitigated efforts, ISRO acquired an impressive end-to- end space capability that included production of a variety of launch vehicles and remote sensing, communication, and meteorological satellites; acquisition of systems engineering expertise; and maintenance of the organizational and technical infrastructure necessary to control space assets.

With American non-proliferation regime growing during 1970s and 1980s, Indo-US space cooperation got a set back. The program in regard to space launch vehicles (SLVs) came a cropper, as American successive governments continued to perceive this as more or less synonymous with ballistic missiles. In the face of US nonchalance, misperception, and non cooperation, India continued its indigenous efforts to develop its SLVs, and consequently rode on the crest of its crowning glory when it became capable of launching larger and larger payloads into space and in the process was transformed into a serious competitor in commercial launch services involving low earth orbits. While civilian activities related to communications, broadcasting, remote sensing, meteorology, distance education, telemedicine, natural resources management, space science, and satellite launch services constituted the main items in the programmatic agenda of ISRO, the organization was compelled by Indian policy makers during the 1980s to help the Defense Research and Development Organization (DRDO) develop the solid-fuel rockets needed by India's missile program. This connectivity, which materialized in the form of inter-organizational personnel exchanges, sharing of facilities, and ISRO production of the Daisy solid propellant motors for India's Agni series missiles, oppugned the organization's avowed pretensions of involvement solely in the peaceful uses of space, thereby providing afortiori pleas to America to constrain cooperation with ISRO even on what were admittedly nonmilitary and civilian.

NSSP (Next Steps in Strategic Partnership) resulted in US taking serious efforts to review these constraints on U.S.- Indian space cooperation. This became easier for Washington as the US legislative restraints and international regime commitments were comparatively less stringent and arduous than nuclear technology. NSSP made major policy decision to permit India to acquire a variety of dual-use technologies needed by its space program; to jointly develop, produce, operate, and market commercial satellites; and eventually to launch either foreign satellites containing U.S. components or U.S. satellites themselves upon successful conclusion of a space cooperation agreement. "This enhanced collaboration was premised on the belief that U.S.-Indian space partnership was possible in a wide range of areas, except for SLV technology and high- resolution remote sensing, so long as New Delhi met two conditions: agreeing to undertake a comprehensive upgrade of its export control system and promising not to use the artifacts acquired through NSSP liberalization to advance its own strategic weapon programs"[42].

The first condition appears sensible, as this is a precondition for enhanced U.S.-Indian space cooperation. The second condition proves hollow the Bush administration's promise to enhance the growth of Indian power. If America really intents to see India grow into a major player on the Asian stage to its strategic advantages, and its promise has any meaning, it should come forward to extend its ungrudging hands with respect to developing its national power comprehensively. But this is not so. Its help is only confined to supporting India with its conventional military capabilities, economic growth, and energy production but not beyond this. This American policy is continuation of its cold war stand that India should not be allowed to grow beyond the confines US wanted India to be fenced in, and not in a position to challenge Pakistan, its close ally. If it is the real intention of US to build up India as a counterweight to China, then what prevents it from lifting off the shutters? It is to be partly explained by the fact that America is yet to be cured of its inveterate paranoia of apprehension of India's undying predilections for independence in foreign policy, and avowed distaste for playing a second fiddle to any outside power. The other reason is that India ascending to great power status propped up with unbounded America help is unlikely to play the American card against China, as India has already demonstrated its strong penchant for forging a multi pronged relationship with all nations in general and more particularly with China. Awake to such American reasoning, the Indian policy makers will certainly try to warm up relationship but not too intensive and impulsive to fall into US embrace. As Ashley J.Tellis is eloquent on American inhibitions against witnessing India grow into a major power status:

> "...Existing U.S. policies threaten to crimp India's ability to develop certain strategic assets, an outcome that would at the end of the day undermine the larger American objective of advancing the growth of Indian power in Asia."[43]

Such a selective, sectoral, conservative and highly prejudiced approach by Washington to build up India will prove illusory and not grandly germane to American strategic interests in Asia. If the United States really aims at concretizing its geopolitical objectives in Asia, then it should not feel constrained or outrageous in any way to clear its mental deck of the ingrained prejudices, beliefs, and past apprehensions it casts about India, and come forward uninhibited to help India develop its strategic capabilities, weaponry system, and associated delivery systems, which would impregnate it with a built in confidence and prowess to deter against the growing and utterly more capable nuclear forces Beijing is likely to possess by 2025. If Washington does not follow such proactive policy, then it should refrain itself from proclaiming any statement or policy decision that are likely to hamstring India in its efforts to become a major power. That means to leave India and its international partners alone, and pursue a policy that will have the same effect as its active indulgence in strengthening Indian strategic capability would have. This would convey India hints about the larger canvas of American interests in Asia, a prospect which propelled former US ambassador to India Robert D. Blackwill to ask recently, " Why should the U.S. want to check India's missile capability in ways that could lead to China's permanent nuclear dominance over democratic India?"[44]

Apart from the current US prejudices against India's strategic weapon programs, the issue of internal versus external proliferation remains central to US policy toward India, and needs to be reinvented. Internal proliferation prohibits India from using American technology and resources to produce strategic weapons. External proliferation means an export control system that prevents all kinds of leakage, either deliberate or inadvertent to foreign entities. India has already proved its credentials as a responsible power pronouncing its commitment to and belief in the proliferation of weapons to other countries. According to Ashley, the conditions put on India pertaining to internal proliferation need to be extinguished for four reasons:

"First, the ban on using U.S.- origin technologies to advance Indian strategic program is in fact strategic, in that it is inconsistent with the objective of advancing the growth of Indian power in those critical technological arenas important to the preservation of geopolitical balance in Asia.

Second, it imposes unreasonable burdens on India, in that it requires New Delhi to sustain artificial firewalls within its national technological system with the enclave focused on strategic programs... Such firewalls even if they could be erected, would be difficult to sustain indefinitely and would become the object of constant circumvention even assuming the Indian government's best intentions.

Third, it creates gratuitous irritants in the bilateral relations with India: By preventing Indian national organizations that are formally assigned by their government to develop certain strategic capabilities from meeting those programmatic goals, the emphasis on preventing internal proliferation puts the United States and India at odds, with no discernible benefit to American interests.

Fourth, If Indian national interests demand the acquisition of certain strategic capabilities such as nuclear weapons and their associated delivery systems, and American national interests do not permit a complete technological quarantine of India, then the current U.S. obsession with preventing internal proliferation will only become increasingly unsustainable over time"[45].

Ebullient in the glow of Indo-U.S. friendship and American eloquent and assured promise of help to India for its untroubled ascension to great power status, the Indian policy makers should not put the epochal thaw in their relations above national interest, which is always defined in terms of independence of decision making, freedom of will and untrammelled sovereignty. Given the objectives of hardliners and neo-cons having enviable influence in Bush administration to convert world into a unipolar world where America would pontificate to all other power centers as a great master not as equal partners, New Delhi's caving in to American proposals will certainly mark a departure from its Nehruvian foundation of foreign policy, making a toll of its long term perspective of promoting India's long cherished lofty ideals and goals found enshrined in its history, culture and great civilization, buoyancy of economic and political development. Indian policy makers should not remain oblivious to the fact of whether American move is a renewed version of its cold war strategy of preventing India from rise to power and also to the fact of how clipping the wings of a bird will enable it to fly to great heights. The resolution of this American contradiction between words and deeds must remain central to a reliable foundation in Indo- U.S. relation. No where this contradiction is seen more glaringly than in American reticence on India's claim to permanent membership in Security Council. India strongly believes that its historical transition to democracy and its successful imbibing into the mainstream of society, exemplary cultural and linguistic diversity, its large population, growing economic prowess, nuclear power, distinguished record of participation in international institutions and commendable role in peace keeping operation justify global recognition through membership in Security Council. During Indian Foreign Minister's visit to Washington on April 14, 2005 when matter was pressed, Secretary Rice evasively responded:

> " The United States wants to be supportive of what we see as a positive trend in India's global role because India is a democracy and that matters to us in the global role that it is beginning to play. We are demonstrating that we support that aspiration by the breadth of the relationship that we have with India.... Now, in terms of the UN Security Council, the United States has said that we believe UN Security Council reform needs to take place in the context of broader UN reform, that it is important, of course, to reform the Secretariat, the institutions of the UN, the organizations of the UN, it needs management reform and, of course, we should also look at Security Council reform. I said when I was in India that international organizations in general will have to take into account India's growing role in the world in order to be updated and to be effective"[46].

This carefully deliberate reluctance on the part of U.S. is conditioned by two fundamental considerations: one is U.S. very much knows, India's ingrained predilection for an independent foreign policy often couched in moral verbiage and most times at odds with American preferences would not be conducive to American interests. Second, the very idea of an expanded Security Council, which comes in direct clash with its own notion of world order, is repugnant to American interests. If past records and recent examples in Afghanistan and Iraq are to be believed in, showing short shrifts to and gradually moving away from the UN system by U.S. has been an effective instrument for advancing its national interests. Membership in Security Council represents a symbol of power status in world politics. American startling silence in endorsing India's candidature makes its high sounding promise of bestowing on India a high power status hollow, and the hiatus between words and deeds will awaken the Indian policy makers very convincingly to what intent really remains significant in the minds of America. Doubts about the real intention of America will persist asking New Delhi to remain wary of whether it is the orchestration of Washington's same cold war strategy of prevention or abstention by which America stood in Indian's way. America remaining obscure about its preferences with respect to expansion of Security Council is quite reflective of its vision of unipolar world. But if U.S. settles for a strategy of neglecting the UN because that body is too unwieldy and unhelpful to American objectives, supporting permanent membership for India will entail no costs to U.S. If America fails to stem the tide of worldwide movement for reform of the UN system, and in the event of an expansion and reconfiguration of UN becoming a fait accompli, throwing its weight in support of Indian cause will be beneficial to American interests. In such a changing situation of democratization and multilateralization of the UN system, it will be pragmatic of America to endorse Indian cause as there will no longer be any inherent conflict of interests between the two on fundamental issues starting from democracy, human rights to trade, development and environment.

To unfold a new chapter in Indo-US relation both countries first need to estrange themselves from the moorings of the past. Given India's non-aligned stance despite the end of the historical factor originally responsible for its emergence, America should tolerably recognize New Delhi's preference for independence of will, freedom of action and sovereignty. To expect India's overt collaboration with American global design at the cost of these cherished values will be illusory. Within the explicit recognition of India's preferences America should come forward to forge its strategic partnership with India. In order not to make its words of promise for the growth of indian power escape into the repertoire of lofty rhetoric, America should create exceptional carve-outs for India. In case it fails to do so or considers these not worth the costs in relation to other objectives, the critics charge of containment of India by America holds good. In a similar vein, India also needs to fashion its supportive policies that would spur Washington's incentives to support India's preferences. In the absence of required transformation in their respective stance toward each other, the opportunity to forge a durable strategic partnership between them will soon slip away to prove the cynics right.

References

1. On this point see Condoleezza Rice, "Promoting the National Interest", Foreign Affairs, vol.79, January/ February 2002, pp.45-62
2. Sumit Ganguly, " The Start of a beautiful Friendship? The United States and India", World Policy Journal, Vol. xx, No.1, Spring 2003
3. Patrick E. Tyler and Celia W. Dugger, Powell's Message: America's Courting of Pakistan will not come at India's expense", New York Times, 18 October, 2001.
4. Celia W. Dugger, "Group in Pakistan is Blamed by India for Suicide Raid", New York Times, December 15, 2001.
5. Tara Shankar Sahay, "India Hands over List of 20 wanted terrorists to Pakistan", India Abroad, 11 January, 2002, p.1
6. David E. Sanger and Kurt Eichenwald, "Citing India Attack, US Aims at Assets of Groups in Pakistan", New York Times, 21 December 2001.
7. B. Raman, "Will He Walk the Talk?", Outlook, 14 January 2002, available at www.outlookindia.com
8. Farhan Bokhari and Edward Luce, "Bombers Kill 33 in Kashmir as US Envoy Visits India", Financial Times, 15 May 2002.
9. Ashley J Tellis, India as a New Global Power: An Action Agenda for the United States (Washington D.C.: Carnegie Endowment for International Peace, 2005), p. 6
10. *Ibid.*
11. Thomas R. Pickering, "US Policy in South Asia: The Road Ahead", address to the Foreign Policy Institute, South Asia Program, Paul H. Nitze School of Advanced International Studies, John Hopkins University, Washington, D.C., 27 April 2000, available at www. fas.org/ news/ Pakistan/ 2000/000427_ pickering_ sa.htm.
12. Chidananda Rajghatta, "US Opens High-Tech Tap to India", Times of India, 7 February 2003.
13. Sumit Ganguly, op.cit.
14. Dennis Kux, "A Remarkable Turnaround: U.S-India Relation", Foreign Service Journal, October 2002, pp. 18-23.
15. Celia W. Dugger, "Wider Military Ties with India offer U.S. Diplomatic Leverage", New York Times, 10 June, 2002.
16. See S.D Muni, "India and the Post- cold war: Opportunities and Challenges", Asian Survey, September 1991, pp. 862-74.

17. See Jaswant Singh, Defending India (London: Macmillan, 1999)
18. Ashley J. Tellis, n.9, pp.6-7
19. *Ibid.*
20. Secretary of State Condoleezza Rice, "interview with Shivraj Prasad of NDTV," New Delhi, India, March 16, 2005, available at www. State.gov/secretary/rm/2005/43511.htm.
21. Amit Baruah, "We are Disappointed: Manmohan", The Hindu, 26 March 2005.
22. Ashley J. Tellis, "South Asian Seesaw: A New U.S. Policy on the Subcontinent", Carnegie Endowment for International Peace, No.38, May 2005.
23. U.S. Department of State, "Background of briefing by Administrative Officials on US- South Asia Relations", March 25, 2005, available at www.state.gov/r/pa/prs/ps/2005/43853.htm.
24. Frank Carlucci, Robert Hunter, and Zalmay Khalidzad, eds., Taking Charge: A Bipartisan Report to the President Elect on Foreign Policy and National Security- papers (Santa Monica, California.: RAND, 2000), p.38.
25. U.S. Department of State, "Background Briefing", note. 23
26. Ashley J. Tellis, n.9, p.10
27. Ashley J. Tellis, n.22.
28. Siddharth Varadarajan, " F-16s for Pakistan will Fuel Arms Race", The Hindu, 27 March 2005.
29. Ashley J. Tellis, "South Asian Seesaw", *op.cit*.
30. *Ibid.*
31. Murali Manohar Joshi, "The U.S.- India agreement: Victory for Whom?" The Hindu, 22 October 2005.
32. Siddharth Varadarajan, "India- U.S. deal: negotiating the nuclear fine print", The Hindu, 21 October 2005.
33. Selig S. Harrison, quoted in Siddharth Varadarajan, "keep fast breeder reactor out of IAEA inspections: U.S. Experts", The Hindu, 17 December 2005.
34. Siddharth Varadarajan, "U.S. non-proliferation group ups the ante with draft separation plan", The Hindu, 21 December 2005.
35. The Hindu, 6 January 2006.
36. The Hindu, 3 March 2006
37. Ashley J. Tellis, op.cit., p.32
38. L. Venkateshwaran, Indo-US Relations: Recent Developments, IPCC Special Report 19, May 2006

39. Editorial, Daily Times, 13 September 2005
40. Editorial "India, US to conduct biggest ever military exercise", Deccan Herald. 10 December 2005
41. Ashley J. Tellis, op.cit., p.33
42. Ibid., p.35
43. Ibid.
44. Robert D. Blackwill, " A New Deal for New Delhi", The Wall Street Journal, March 21,2005,p. A16.
45. Ashley J. Tellis, Op.cit., p.37
46. Secretary of State Condoleezza Rice, Remarks with Indian Minister of External Affairs Natwar Singh Following Meeting, Department of State, Washington, D. C., 14 April, 2005, available at www. sstate. gov/ secretary/ rm/2005/44662.htm.

6

Indo-U.S. Strategic Engagement: Convergences and Divergences

The Indian policy makers tended to overrate India's weight in international relation as formidable disproportionate to its military and economic prowess, couched partly in civilizational power. Americans' understanding and definition of power is different from Indians in that they view it in material terms as one of greater military and economic capability in relation to others. In that sense, they always portrayed India as a feckless and minor global player. Civilizational value laden outbursts and preaching in international arena, non- aligned and independent foreign policy by Indian elites under Nehru, and Indira Gandhi's tilt towards Soviet Union in 1971 abandoning its much proclaimed neutrality, Pokharan nuclear test in 1974 and India's proven ability to pursue economic self sufficiency in its own strides, and taking up the cudgels on behalf of third world solidarity estranged the two "natural allies", and strengthened America's relation with Pakistan, the close adversary of India. The strategic significance of South Asia generally was not in the policy calculation of US except that Pakistan was to be cultivated as a frontline state against the Soviet communism and as a conduit to establishing relation with China. South Asia in general and India in particular earned a down gradation in the strategic menu of America. American military weapons supplied to Pakistan to fight Soviet communism in contingencies were actually used by Pakistan against India in 1965 and 1975 wars. Without addressing the concern and interests of India, America continued ignoring India to the greater advantage of Pakistan. Only when, there was a crisis in South Asia, America had risen to the occasion. For example, when the Soviets invaded Afghanistan in December of 1979, South Asia catapulted to American attention, but at that point US concern was focused primarily on Pakistan as a conduit for military aid to the Afghan Mujahidden. With Soviet withdrawal, South Asia again receded to the backburner but Indo-Pak conflict remained a peripheral concern to US to the point that it did not escalate to a situation inviting super powers into the imbroglio, which would likely marginalize US interests with active intrusion of Soviet Union and China in support of their allies. The nuclear tests by both countries in 1998 inviting American irked sanctions and later on, the Kargil war between the two in 1999 prompted again US into South Asia.

India's rise as an economic and strategic force since the mid1990s, epitomized by its crowning success of its information technology at the global level, and Indian immigrants contributing immensely to brain gain of America in all walks of life, suddenly occupied the centerpiece of American attention. Although India's going for the second nuclear test in 1998 provoked renewed American concern, it is unlikely that nuclear test alone could have led to same level of engagement. Because, as early as 1993 U.S. government's most important foreign policy priorities was geared to enhancing relationship with ten of the fastest growing markets in the world. India was among the top in this list, along with China. Rise of Asia as a new geopolitical theatre with American diplomatic and military engagements from the Middle East through Central Asia to the Pacific Rim for reasons ranging from the Iraqi and Afghanistan imbroglio to Iranian nuclear crisis to the emergence of vocal new regional institutions such as the Shanghai Cooperation Organization and East Asian Community prompted America to view India not through prism of cold war orthodoxy but beyond its South Asian confinement. India "can become a strong anchor in support of America's ambition to pursue a liberal order across Eurasia. Indeed, if the U.S. should welcome the emergence of any one Asian power, it should be India, which shares America's concern over the spread of Islamic fundamentalism, sub-state nuclear proliferation, and China's ambitions."[1] What the tests did unequivocally was to propel the two countries into vortex of engagement through dialogues for the first time providing sinews for jettisoning the biased past toward better understanding. As Talbott put it, for India, the nuclear tests were geared to "simultaneously stand up to the United States and sit down with the United States."[2] What again brought South Asia to lime light exacting American attention is the September 11 attacks. As a result, in the last two years of the Clinton administration, the Indian relationship enjoyed an unusual high- level focus, culminating in President Clinton's May 2000 visit to India, the first Presidential visit in 22 years. The subsequent meetings between his successor George Bush and Prime Minister Atal Bihari Vajpaee were crucial in charting out the future path, with Bush calling relations a strategic partnership and Vajpayee suggesting that India and the US were natural allies. Then followed George Bush 's visit to India and Indian new Prime Minister Manmohan Singh's visit to America in 2005 and 2006 culminating in historic July 2005 and March 2006 Nuclear agreement. Significant progress in foreign and defense establishment took place binding the two countries in a web of new obligations and engagements. All said does not mean that there has been complete convergence of interests of both countries. The following chapter depicts vividly about the nuclear deal and its problems and prospects. There are constraints and limits to their partnership. India's decision in July 2003 declining American request for sending its troops, as part of U.S. coalition in Iraq was not well received in America. Eight months later, even when there was a talk going on in New Delhi between the two countries, bestowing a Major Non-NATO Ally (MNNA) on Pakistan without any prior notice raised hackles in India. India's refusal was viewed by some American policy makers that India could not be counted upon. In the case of the MNNA, India's resentment had to do with both substance and style.

Different Security Perception

While a convergence of interests at the broadest level regarding potential threats in the global realm is marked in their relations, differences surface between them on how to deal with them. America's threat perception seems to rest on terrorism, weapons of mass destruction (WMD), and emergence of China with all cascading implications on the Asian balance of power. India's top security concerns find a rendezvous with those of America, but on terrorism and WMD, India differs from US. Many in policy making in India are opposed to being too closely identified with American version of war on terrorism on both ideological and substantial grounds. While extremist Islamic violence remains a great security threat to India, there is difficulty agreeing with American method of fighting it. This view has become stronger in the light of American experience in Iraq. This stance of India reflects its avowed disapproval of American scripted world order based on unchallenged preemptive exercise of military force.

With India pitch forked into a prominent place of American calculation, the policy makers in India expect that Indo-US relation be dehyphenated in relation to Pakistan. But this has not been so. India's views on terrorism or Pakistan involvement in terrorist attacks in various part of India, despite evidences in American cupboard, are not publicly acquiesced in by US. On the other hand, America goes public while putting pats on the back of Musharraf for his commendable participation in American war on terrorism. To say that India has already acquired the political leverage after forging the new partnership with US to cast a veto on U.S. policy toward Pakistan is highly erroneous. Even if it is said that the hyphenated relation is already thrown into the thrash can of history, it will be replaced in US policy toward India with caveats. It is too hard on the part of America to glutton the Indian version and perception of Pakistan. America still considers it important to persist in its cold war logic in relation to Pakistan. Any weakening of its position in Pakistan either through negligence or treading on an Indian path, would ultimately result in Pakistan being dragged into China's embrace, which America strongly disavows and tries to nullify by reinforcing its foothold in Pakistan, and cultivating India a great power as a foil to expansion of a non-democratic China. So on the issue of relevance of Pakistan to American strategy, and possible dehyphenation of its relation with India, both India and America stand apart.

Differences on Terrorism

A very view doing the round just after the September 11 that the two largest democracies would enliven themselves into a new bond on an issue of immediacy of security threats from Islamic extremists, was so prominent that the Taliban sponsored al Qaeda provided impetus for the spotlight on South Asia based violent extremism and terrorism, which India for its own interests and logic tried to highlight internationally. With Pakistan being baptized into American declared war on terrorism, India's expectations that Pakistan indulgence in terrorism in Kashmir got a set back. This might be one of the reasons compelling India not to devour American bait of fighting its war in Iraq. India's aversion to join American war in Iraq is symptomatic of the underlying differences over what they define terrorism and the effective means to combat it. No where this double standard is more candidly perceived than in America finding a difference between militants in Kashmir and extremists in the Middle East or Afghanistan to the alarming discomfiture of India. Contrary to Indian version, America strongly holds that India's position on terrorists in Iraq is misguided. Lack of convergence of approach to terrorism and more particularly in relation to Pakistan's involvement in terrorism in Kashmir, is likely to play a significant role in defining future Indo-US relation, and exacerbating existing Indo-Pak conflict. Given India's ever-burgeoning demand for energy, according to one former senior defense official, both India and US have a strategic interest in Middle East. As he averred, "Upon further examination, with regard to the Middle East, India should rethink its participation with regard to peace keeping in Iraq." This was not suggested " as a favour to the U.S., but because it is in India's interest for the pursuit of stability in the region."[3] A plethora of factors are alluded to Indian refusal to acquiesce in American proposal to send troops: lack of a United Nations mandate; domestic political opposition and finally, the need of troops in Kashmir. Elections being due in 2004, the Indian political parties did not like to risk their stakes in the Muslim votes if any Indian soldier died in Iraq. By stressing on the immediacy of troops in Kashmir, the Indian policy makers established a link between its ability to send troops to Iraq and American pro-Indian stance on Pakistan sponsored terrorism. "This was most likely an attempt by India to push the United States to step up pressure on Pakistan to stop cross border terrorism."[4] Rather the case for India's participation in American led forces in Iraq was espoused in other terms: "staking a claim in post- war Iraqi reconstruction; presenting

India as tough and trustworthy enough to go out on a limb for the isolated U.S.; not wanting to miss out an opportunity to play a role in the Persian Gulf/ Middle East and thus expand India's influence in a critical region; and gaining recognition as a major player at the global level".[5]

Another ground reality, which America should recognize, and actively support India in order to have an enduring strategic partnership with it, is India's specific geo-strategic context in relation to its role in Middle East. Like such other US allies as Turkey and Israel, India is located in a turbulent neighbouhood but has a robust military capable of affecting the outcomes of potential conflicts in South West and Central Asia. Also, the prolonged warfare in these regions has deleterious effects in India in terms of the damaging effects on environment and domestic political set up with a decisive Muslim vote bank being in a position to define stability in the country. According to one authority, " It has also a strong sense of national identity based on secular ideology, despite its tremendous ethnic and religious diversity. As a state with a large Muslim minority and heavy dependence on Middle Eastern oil, there are structural limits to India's cooperation with any aggressive American activity in the Gulf region. Like Turkey, it will not respond favourably to heavy handed American pressure."[6]

That Muslim is an important factor in India's foreign policy hardly needs any mention. Historically, India has always been sympathetic to the cause of Muslims in Middle East. This can be seen from the overwhelming support India has been lending to the cause of Palestinians. Its known sympathy for the Arabs and Iranians is well acclaimed in entire Muslim community, thus providing constantly an impetus to its domestic Muslim population to show allegiance and legitimacy to the governments' policy. In the secular fabric of Indian statehood, Muslim factor runs like a prominent thread, providing stability to the political system, and justifying India's claim for "unity in diversity". Apart from this domestic factor, India is economically 90 percent dependent on oil of Middle East for its industry and transport. It was only in 1992 India established relation with Israel, the archrival of Palestine but not at the cost of Muslims. India has been careful to couch its relation with Israel in terms of technical and narrow defense equipment cooperation, rather than as a broad strategic relationship that Israel wants to weave with India. India's interests in Middle East are tempered in part by the presence of nearly 3.5 million Indians working in the area who could become vulnerable to unpopular regional policies. On these counts it will not be startling to hold that Indian opposition to American military venture in Iraq started flowing from all walks of life in India. Shia, Sunni and even Hindu religious leaders congregated on one platform in New Delhi to condemn the US led coalition for "crimes against humanity"[7]. At the leadership and popular levels in India, Iraq tends to be viewed not as a Muslim issue, but rather as an example of America's aggressive unilateralism.[8]

Despite being the second largest Muslim populous state, India has never been a hub of al Qaeda recruitment or sanctuary of Muslim extremism to the high appreciation of the west. While allusions have been made to other countries like Hamburg, Madrid, Casablanca and Kuala Lumpur for al Qaeda cells in the report of the 9/11 commission, India remains unalloyed. In an expert's view, "It is a very privileged situation which India has." And he adds, " So when we want to cooperate with the United States, we have to do it in such a way that we preserve this."[9] Another growing concern centers on the view that American military venture in Iraq will not subside terrorism rather exacerbate it to the disadvantage of both US and India. India does not like to pay so heavy a price for American mistakes in Iraq.[10] Thus, to keep up the hallowed tradition of not hurting the Muslim interests in both domestic front and international front more particularly in Middle East by the way of any overt military support to any external power adventurism will set the extent and confines Indian government can come forward in extending support not at least in active military support but in playing a background role for political stability in the region like the one it plays in Iraq at present without any visible military support.

The United States and India converged on the issue of Iran's nuclear programme. It was highlighted then that both US and India differed widely about the dangers of WMD and terrorism from Teheran and it would be extremely difficult for India to support punitive action against Iran in the light of special Indo-Iranian ties in the nuclear and energy sector, India's traditional opposition to intrusions into a developing country's sovereignty, and differences with the US on how to approach nuclear proliferation, let alone fight it.[11] This was falsified when India voted at the International Atomic Energy Agency (IAEA) in favour of reporting Iran to Security Council, purportedly done at the behest of America. This pro-America stand of India showing obligatory returns to US for its nuclear deal at the expense of its long standing friendship with Iran came in for much broadside from all political parties at home. Though Indian government insisted that India voted in its own national interest, there appeared to be explicitly a close link between its decision and Indo-US nuclear deal. From the excerpts from "India, Iran, and the Congressional hearings on the Indo-US nuclear deal" it could be confirmed that America wanted seriously India vote against Iran as matter of reciprocity. America sternly warned India that India had to choose you are "either with we or against we". Representative Dana Rohrabacher said in the Congressional hearing: " The Indians need to know this is another time of choosing. In the past, they chose to be in a closer relationship with the Soviet Union during the cold war. And this is a time of realignment again, and a period of choosing for them. They can choose to be in a closer relationship with this outlaw mullah regime in Iran and radical Islam, or they can choose to be in closer ties with the people of the United States."[12] In the same vein, Representative Tom Lantos intoned: "I expect India to recognize that there is reciprocity involved in this new relationship, and without reciprocity, India will get very little help from the Congress. If we are turning ourselves into a pretzel to accommodate India, I want to be damn sure that India is mindful of US policies in critical areas such as U.S. policy towards Iran. India cannot pursue a policy vis-a vis Iran which takes no account of U.S. foreign policy objectives."[13] This was reiterated in a news-agency interview in January 2006, David Mulford pointed out that " If India were to vote against the referral, it would mean the end of the India- America nuclear deal. This was no more than a statement of fact. America's Congress would surely not agree to rewrite the non-proliferation regime for one exceptional country, were that country, India, to line up on the opposing side in the most important nuclear- proliferation argument of the moment". [14] This statement was considered a threat raising nationalist hackles in India. In its usual anti-American rhetoric the Left parties, a partner in United Progressive Alliance government in New Delhi castigated the Indian caving in to American pressure. Despite India's later on attempt to correct the American slant, the view stayed firmly in many circles that India did not hesitate to downgrade its relationship with Iran with a view to pandering to the wishes of America.

Limits to Cooperation on Terrorism

Even before 9/11 incident both countries tried to tackle the terrorism through joint action. For the purpose, in November 1999, the U.S. – India Counter –Terrorism Joint Working Group (JWG) was established and met several times, alternating between New Delhi and Washington. The 9/11 terrorist attack added urgency to the work of JWG. At the tactical level there was much left to be done as opposed to the strategic level. Major areas of cooperation include: strengthened intelligence sharing; upgraded and expanded anti-terrorism training programmes for Indian law enforcement officials; the launching of a Cyber security forum to focus on cyber-terrorism and information security; improving border monitoring, including equipment sales; enhancing measures against narcotics trafficking and implementation of the Treaty on Mutual Legal Assistance. Cooperation between the two countries seems to be constrained within these mechanisms as well. For example, the U.S. Federal Bureau of Investigation (FBI) has not even provided the transcripts of the interrogation of Afghan suspects in the December 2001 Indian Airlines IC-814 hijacking case to Indian authorities. "Ironically, one factor that seems to limit opportunities for a more strategic Indo-U.S. cooperation in this area is that India is a target for extremist violence and terrorism, rather than a base for terrorism against the U.S."[15] Cooperation then with India is less of a compulsion for the U.S. From the side of India, there are limits as well, particularly activities that might impinge on the Indian sovereignty and other long-standing sensible issues. US ambassador David Mulford's offer of FBI expertise made directly to the Assam state government to probe the serial bomb blasts in Assam and Nagaland spurred the opposition parties in India to lambaste US proposal as gross interference into India's sovereignty. Taking strong exception to this also one official of security establishment opined "If in the name of crackdown on the al Qaeda, the U.S. can do something in Pakistan, it should not think it can do the same in India."[16] Other Indian analysts viewed that this was an attempt by America to gain a foothold in India's sensitive Northeast region, abutting on Myanmar and China.

Expanding Cybersecurity cooperation between the two countries assumes strategic significance in the context of increasing menace from terrorism. The U.S. - Indian Cyberterrorism Initiative jointly announced by President Bush and the then Prime Minister Vajpayee in November 2001 represented an impressive beginning. "The enthusiasm for deeper engagement with India on cybersecurity matters was less than overwhelming on the U.S. side because of the perception that New Delhi's interests centered primarily on expanding its capacity for information warfare or interdiction of terrorism involving Pakistan. U.S fears about the first issue were exaggerated: Although India maintains an offensive information warfare capability, it is relatively small in programmatic terms and of uncertain quality, and has never been able to attract either the resources or the manpower that has flowed into the country's private sector dominated information technologies industry."[17] It seems, America has not been sensitive to India's interest in computer forensics, network surveillance, and the protection of supervisory control and data acquisition systems as means to defeat terrorism. This should be addressed by U.S. as a part of the U.S. global struggle against this menace.

Economic Relations

Given India's aspiration to ascend to the status of a developed country, the Indian policy makers decided unequivocally to improve its lopsided economic cooperation with America. In the same breath the America policy makers have begun to think seriously India in the same accent as China. In an allusion to both India and China, a report by the U.S. National Intelligence Council submitted to Congress in early 2005 states that:"The likely emergence of China and India as new major global powers- similar to the rise of Germany in the 19th century and United States in the 20th century- will transform the geo-political landscape, with impacts potentially as dramatic as those of the previous two centuries."[18] The prospects of India outpacing China in coming decades also riveted America toward India in economic front. In India, entrepreneurs in the private sector, not the government, are taking the lead in transforming Indian economy. It has succeeded in branding itself as the world's leading destination for business process outsourcing (BPO), and even high end operations such as GE medical labs and Hewlett -Packed research facilities are contributing to make India in technology innovation. India's biotech sector is set for even greater growth and has rapidly outpaced both China and South Korea in the filling of biotech patents. The potential in food processing and storage, telecommunications, financial services, and insurances is similarly vast. Micro credit enterprises have become stable in business propositions, even in the area of agriculture, enkindling hopes for a second, private-sector led Green revolution. These developments stand as a testimony to the vast potential to be harnessed for higher economic growth. No other developed country has such a post-industrial economic structure with 50 per cent of GDP derived from the services sector and manufacturing and agriculture comprising a quarter each. As a result of the outsourcing revolution, India has emerged as a major hub for international technology products and services, already accounting for 20 per cent of world software exports. India is also staking its economic future on the quantity and quality of its human resources. What oil is to Saudi Arabia, human talent is to India. Its mobile and ambitious youth will be the world's largest working age population segment by 2015 at which point it may even provide surplus labor to an aging China. India is aging gracefully while China is heading towards an unprecedented challenge of getting old before it gets rich.[19] India's growing prospects for higher economic growth in a liberal and free market society has been a preponderant factor working in the mind of America to enhance its economic relation with India.

It is pointed out that shortly after India's liberalization in 1991, there was a tremendous spurt in American interest in Indian economy. Comparisons to China in terms of actual investment still India is playing a second fiddle. But during these years India has made significant progress in improving its investment climate, and is rated among the top ten reformers of the world.[20] The Indian economy has become considerably more open, with the ratio of total trade to GDP reaching thirty percent in 2004 starting from 14 per cent in 1990, though falling behind China's at 50 per cent. There are some economists who believe that with wide and deeper reforms, India could easily attain an eight or nine per cent long term growth rate; if it is the latter, the country will be able to double its per capita income in just a decade.[21] Even those who are disenchanted with the current pace of reforms in India concede that " the buzz on India is fantastic."[22]

American businesses are not as excited by India as they are by China, for the obvious reasons that China's economy is two-and –half times bigger, is growing faster and is more integrated with the rest of the world. In each of the past four years, the annual increase in China's foreign trade has exceeded India's total merchandize trade. India's trade with America amounts to one tenth of latter's trade with China. Last year China received about ten times as much foreign direct investment as India did. In spite of India comparatively lagging behind China, it has become still the cynosure of American concern.[23] it is solely due to India's expertise in software development and other sorts of outsourced services. Nearly 400 of the Fortune 500 companies outsource some of their information- technology work to India.[24] The tremendous cost savings accruing to American businesses as a result of business process outsourcing to India almost certainly ensure the continued vitality of the U.S.- Indian information technologies market, a sector that today generates almost three per cent of India's GDP and which is expected to swell fivefold by 2008, becoming a US$57 billion a year export industry employing four million people and accounting for seven percent of GDP[25]. As former U.S. under secretary of commerce Kenneth I Juster told the India-U.S. Information Security Summit in 2004:

> " Information security- also known as cybersecurity- is one of the keys to unlocking the full potential of the trade and technology relationship between the United States and India. All levels of society today- from individuals, to companies, to governments- rely on information technology and information networks in their daily lives- to communicate, to manage activities, to transact business, and to provide essential services to the public. As commerce between the United States and India continues to expand, consumers and corporations will seek to ensure that their personal information and business propriety data are secure, and that information services are reliable and

> protected. Without an adequate level of security, we run the risk of backlash among consumers and loss of confidence among business people, which could severely limit progress in our trade and technology relationship."[26]

According to Promod Haque of Norwest Venture, a venture-capital firm, it is also suffering a "reverse brain-drain" as Indian and Chinese engineers go home. This, he argues, coalesced with the retirement of the baby-boomers, is creating a "shortage of intellectual capital" in America, which will eventually threaten its superpower status. Thus, America finds it pertinent to build a "strategic competitive advantage" through an alliance with an offshore base of intellectual capital as a solution to impending crisis. India is the obvious choice. Its pool of highly qualified graduates will be twice as large as China's by 2008, according to the McKinsey Global Institute.[27] The U.S. commitment to develop deep economic and commercial ties with India has never been stronger. U.S. exports to India are up by 50%, and India's exports to the U.S. are up by 15% for the first quarter of 2005. To boost trade and investment, the two countries are working cooperatively leaving behind many troublesome commercial disputes. The recent Open Skies Agreement with India is already increasing air traffic and creating new jobs, and India is finalizing a large order for Boeing aircraft. The revitalized Economic Dialogue focuses on trade, finance, commerce, energy and environment. A new business grouping called the CEO Forum has been constituted with 20 members, 10 prominent CEO members from each country to build business confidence and remove barriers to trade and investment and to propel growth, job creation, and delivery of social benefits to the people of both countries. As David Mulford opined, opening up sectors of the economy where private investment is now restricted, such as retailing, real estate, food processing, small – scale industry, and telecommunications will improve rural connectivity and help generate the growth and revenue streams necessary to provide positive returns to infrastructure investment. With proper roads, water delivery systems, and cold storage chains, the recently liberalized food processing industry, as well as other forms of agribusiness, could become important sources of consumer benefit and rural employment. This is one area America wishes to pursue under the newly inaugurated U.S. and Indian Agribusiness Initiative aimed at building partnerships among U.S. and Indian agricultural institutions.[28] American businesses have their own gripes about India. They would like to simplify its spaghetti-spill of bureaucracy, open up its markets faster and fix its rotten infrastructure.

In spite of all these developments ensuring prospects of India being in the center stage of American concern, the trade between United States and India has been very meager. But over the few years the trade between the two has increased. In 2004, US merchandise exports to and imports from India are estimated to have totaled US$6.1 billion and US$15.5 billion respectively, making India the twenty-fourth largest U.S export market and the eighteenth largest supplier of U.S. imports. In 2004, U.S. merchandise exports to India increased by 22.6 percent, over 2003, and imports by18.4 percent. Levels of U.S.-India, while relatively low, are blossoming; the total value of bilateral trade has doubled since 2001 and the two governments intend to see it doubled again by 2009. The U.S. exports to India in 2005 had a value of $8 billion up 30% over 2004 with business and telecommunications equipment, civilian aircraft, gemstones, fertilizer, and chemicals as leading categories. Imports from India in 2005 totalled $18.8 billion up 21% over 2004. Annual foreign direct investment to India from all countries rose from about $100 million in 1990 to an estimated $7.4 billion for 2005; about one-third of these investments was made by U.S. investors in late 2005 and 2006,the major U.S.- based companies Microsoft, Dell, Oracle, and IBM announced plans for multi billion dollar investment in India. Strong portfolio investment added another $10 billion in 2005. According to the 2006 report of the United States Trade Representative (USTR), India has moved to raise limits on foreign investment in several key sectors, however, despite significant tariff reductions and other measures taken by India to improve market access, and a number of foreign trade barriers remain, including high tariffs, especially in the agricultural sector. The USTR asserts that "substantial expansion of U.S.-India trade will depend on continued and significant additional Indian liberalization."[29] The United States also remains India's second largest source of FDI. U.S. cumulative FDI was US$4.1 billion in 2004, a 10.6 percent share of all such investment in India. Although these data are indicative of a dramatic gallop in U.S.- Indian economic ties, they nonetheless buttress only very modest degrees of interdependence. American trade turnover with India remains at less than one percent of the United States' global trade; India's percentage share of U.S. imports is less than one percent as well. U.S. government officials and business leaders have sniped at India's extensive trade and investment barriers, excessive regulatory and bureaucratic structures as being impediments to its own economic development, as well as to stronger U.S.-India ties.[30] For example, in 2004, the U.S Ambassador to India spoke to an Indian audience that " the U.S. is one of the world's most open economies and India is one of the most closed." Later that year, U.S. Under Secretary of State Larson opined that "trade and investment flows between the U.S. and India are far below where they should and can be,"adding that " the picture for U.S. investment is also lackluster."[31] Inadequate protection of intellectual property rights is a long-standing issue between the United States and India. The USTR places India on its special 301 Priority Watch List for "inadequate laws and ineffective enforcement" in this area. The International Intellectual Property Alliance, a coalition of U.S. copyright- based industries, estimated U.S. losses of $443 million due to trade piracy in India in 2005, three quarters of this in the categories of business and entertainment software. Estimated loss amounts for 2005 do not include motion picture piracy, which in 2004 was estimated to have cost some $80 million.[32] India's not yet becoming a fully free market society and its accent on socialistic policy in a coalition government surviving on the support of the Left parties has been a major U.S. concern.

A bilateral free trade agreement between the two countries would play a significant role in enhancing the growth of Indian power permanently. "The fear of being overwhelmed by high quality U.S. products- with all the associated consequences for domestic employment, resource allocation, and, ultimately, political survival- is why Indian leaders have shied away from comprehensive free-trade agreements involving the United States."[33] As Suman Bery, Director General of India's National Council of Applied Economic Research, has concluded, "If we are serious about liberalizing and becoming a global force to equal China, the idea of a comprehensive U.S.- India [free- trade agreement] has much to commend it."[34] According to Ashley J.Tellis, there are three reasons for which India should enact a free trade agreement with the United States;

"First, there is good economic analysis demonstrating that Indian gains deriving from preferential access to the United States, coupled with continuing domestic liberalization, are greater than those accruing from many alternative economic strategies, including current approaches, even when the disadvantages of trade diversion are taken into account. Second, because domestic reform is often difficult to implement in the face of objections by various rent-seeking constituencies- yet is vital to the continued growth of Indian power- a comprehensive free trade agreement that forced further reform by means of binding external commitments would be a useful means of pushing change in the face of popular resistance. Third, a comprehensive free-trade agreement with the United States would require India to implement many painful internal reforms as the price for constructing a more efficient and capable economy."[35] Due to sluggish economic growth in America burgeoning unemployment, the American policy makers will not be enthusiastic about allowing many benefits to India at the service sector. And in India the brunt of vitriolic opposition both from the people and Left parties to the internal restructuring of the Indian economy may not enthuse its leaders to go ahead with inking a comprehensive free trade agreement between the two countries.

India in a seesaw between socialistic undertone and liberal market economic thrust

The imperatives of liberal market economy replaced Nehruvian civilizational values as the edifying thrust of Indian foreign policy In 1990s. The impact of the footsteps of globalization is already resonated in all aspects of Indian society. Foreign direct investment (FDI) in India has gone up by stair-steps in the past two decades. The removal of many import restrictions has brought foreign goods within the reach of urban India. India is heading top news lines of The Economic Times under the rubric "the Global Indian Takeover": "For India, it is a harbinger of things to come- economic superstardom". India has emerged as the world leader in information technology and business outsourcing, with an average growth of about 6 percent a year. The highly touted information technology and business processing industries only employ about one third of one percent of India's work force, while optimists tout an Indian middle class of some 300 million people, and even greater number of Indians subsist on less than $1 per day. Growing foreign investment and easy credit have fuelled a consumer revolution in urban areas. Behind the proliferation of Starbucks-style coffee bars, increasing size of blackberry-wielding young professionals, spiraling shopping malls selling luxury brand names and large parts of Indian metropolis striving to resemble Manhattan is seen winking the stark realities of grinding poverty, swelling unemployment, spread of diseases like HIV/AIDS, diminution of forest cover, displacement of poor and tribal people, pollution of air and water resources and the problems of human security. The business-centric view of India spurred by the exuberant self confidence of a tiny Indian elites cornering a sizeable chunk of economic benefits, hides more facts than it reveals. The seamy side of Indian society is suppressed under the flaunted glamour of urban life. Recent accounts of the alleged meteoric rise of India suppress the fact that the country's $728 per capita gross domestic product is just slightly higher than that of sub-Saharan Africa and that, as the 2005 United nations Human Development Report puts it, even if it sustains its current high growth rates, India will not catch up with high-economic countries until 2106. India ranks 127 on the report's Human Development Index, just two rungs above Myanmar and more than 70 below Cuba and Mexico. Despite a slight plummeting in the incidence of poverty levels, nearly 380 million Indians subsist on less than a dollar a day. Half of all children in India are seriously afflicted by malnutrition. There is no shred of evidence to buttress the arguments of protagonists of globalization that they are being helped by the market forces, which have redounded to the aggrandizement of wealth in the few rich denying the poor access to health care and education[36]. Spawning of private medical colleges and engineering institutions has only helped the rich and not the poor and down trodden. Despite rise in economic growth 2.5 million children die annually in India, accounting for one out of every five child deaths worldwide. In the countryside where 70 percent of India's population inhabits, the government has reported that about 100.000 farmers committed suicide between 1993 and 2003[37].

Disenchanted with the urban and rich oriented economic growth under the aegis of liberal market economy, many insurgent outfits such as Naxalites, Maoists, People's War Group are growing in sophistication and lethality in Bihar, Andhra Pradesh, Orissa, West Bengal killing thousands and threatening India's democracy and way of life. The upsurge of similar movements such as Bodoland ,and ULFA movements in Assam and other insurgency in Nagaland, Manipur supported by outside countries has been a threat to the stability and security of India. In a country where there is yet to arise the labour intensive manufacturing boom, and imports reign supreme over exports, the spectre of growing unemployment is likely to haunt seriously the Indian government's alignment with the America scripted liberal market economy. This also means that as 70 million more people enter to bulge the work force in the next five years, most of them without the skills required for the new economy, unemployment and inequality could provoke even more social instability than they already have[38]. This shows that the potential for violent conflict looms large in India in terms of caste and class as the present economy has been successful in yawning the hiatus between the rich and poor. If all euphoria about the new economy are related to the employment of only 1.3 million out of a working population of 400 million in the information technology and business processing industries, then it is a heightened myth to find a panacea in liberal economy for all social ills in India. The involvement of bureaucratic-politico and industrialists nexus in corruption in India has further aggravated the situation. Berlin based Transparency International in 2005 placed India 88th out of 158 countries in its annual ranking of world corruption levels[39].

If Indian government fails to contain the surge of insurgency in parts of India, and its liberal market economy pervades the entire society without caring for the poor and the nature, then the threats to its stability and integrity loom large seriously over India's political scene. A country's ability to contain these fissiparous forces would be seriously doubted, and will be a matter of grave concern to America which is intent on building and presenting it as show model to other countries in Asia. Advocacy of western monitored liberal market economy in India has no doubt resulted in an upswing of unemployment, impoverishment and widening chasm between the poor and rich and upsurge of communist led insurgencies in various parts of the country. The question arises whether putting permanently socialistic path to backburner by policy makers in India is in the greater interests of its people. If India ever resorts to the socialistic path in response to the increasing social and humanistic imperatives of the majority people afflicted and infected seriously by the Indian jumping into western bandwagon to rectify its slant toward the western economy, this is bound to create a discordant note in their newly built strategic partnership. It is not nuclear weapons alone, but the sustained ability to provide human security to all the people in India as well, forms the crucible on which all justifications for India's claim to major power status with American help can be tested.

America Playing the Indian Card

The September 11 attacks on the United States brought South Asia into the limelight of American policy. From a long term perspective America considers it is in their best interest to give importance to India as it is a major Asian democratic power with the potential economic and military strength to counter the adverse effects of China's rise as a regional and world power. "It is indeed time to play the Indian card"[40]. China's neighbours- Japan, Korea, Taiwan, the Philippines, the countries of Southeast Asia, Australia, India are concerned about China's military build up, even if these countries shy away from explicitly bringing it to the public.[41] In addition to this, these countries consider China as an economic threat to their interest to the extent that China using its political leverage with the West, tries to corner a major chunk of allocation of foreign investment and get access to western markets and technology at the expense of other developing countries in Asia. Since many of these countries are democracies, America considers it important to support these countries against growing China.

America's trade policy solely chiselled to have a political leverage in China prodding it towards liberalization has proved to be ineffective. On the Chinese side, trade has ingrained the current political elite in authority, turning them into classic rent-seekers, increasing prices and creating substantial distortions in the domestic allocation of resources redounding to their own benefit[42]. Similarly, one prominent development economist in his analysis of China's current economic liberalization opined that it is neither liberal nor sustainable.[43] the influence of business tycoons and industrial caucus over the decision making in America is overwhelming. They are demanding that trade is not used as a political instrument. Caved into their pressure; the policy makers in America are no longer in a position to leverage its trade policy to promote Chinese liberalization. That does not mean that America would not use security policy to that end. One strategy, which America applies, is to exact a price for China's aggressive military and diplomatic behaviour by increasing its military expenditure to confront as many as external threats as possible. This was exactly the strategy, President Reagan so successfully used in case of former Soviet Union. According to Richardson, "The best security for the United States will come from surrounding China with successful, economically sound democracies. These nations will have the resources to sustain military spending and economies strong enough to retain political independence. They will also challenge China ideologically- reminding China every day of what it has been unable to accomplish politically."[44] As a part of its strategy, it has no problem to anchor its efforts to the south of China, because of its good relation with Australia and New Zealand. In the Northeast Asia the democratic tradition is very strong. To the west and north of China, Russia will play a significant role. Russia's Shanghai connectivity may embarrass America, but can be nullified as Russia's dependence on west is becoming stronger day by day. That is the reason America does not like to shed its leverage in Pakistan, which at best can play the cold war role to the disadvantage of Russia, and which does not fall into China's embrace. So far as India is concerned, it was the most overlooked of America's potential allies in a strategy containing China in this broader sense. During cold war, the strategic importance of India in continental Asia was obscured. With the end of cold war, and proliferation of missile technology, the threat to India has increased exponentially. In a new strategic environment, India, the most populous democracy confronts China, the world's most populous autocratic state. In other words, India finds itself vis-à-vis China in the same posture China was with respect to Russia thirty years ago during the cold war period.

During the cold war, due to strategic negligence of India, Indo-US relation was one of estrangement, indifference and short of friendship, though not exactly one of hostility or enmity. Nehru's monolithic ideology in favour of socialism, non-alignment, Indira Gandhi's Soviet tilt and taking up the cudgels for the third world and its anti west and anti- imperialistic pronouncements in international forums, and above all Pakistan factor played significantly in embittering Indo-U.S. bilateral relations. India's unwillingness to play American surrogate against Soviet communism and American difficulty adjusting a big democratic country having penchant for independence, and sovereignty into its strategic orbit, and failure to wean away India from Soviet Union even at the earliest opportunity when Nehru and Gandhi were maligned as imperialistic dogs by Soviet Union. Only when Rajib Gandhi came to power and India adopted American scripted liberal market economy, a change in the international scenario with the eclipse of cold war took place-forcing India out of U.S strategic fringe to which it was thrown by America during the last fifty years. America came to realize that in the changed environment to permanently relegate a large democracy and growing militarily and economically strong India to strategic fringe will be a strategic blunder and politically suicidal for America as it needs a strong bulwark against an undemocratic militancy of China.

So far as China factor is concerned, both America and India share the same strategic bed. India feels increasingly encircled by Chinese naval activity in the Bay of Bengal, both through its client Burma and through its massive investment in deepening the Gwadar port in Pakistan's Sindh province. Despite its current limited resources, India has been determined to engage in quiet competition with China in Southeast Asia even as the region is closely drawn into Beijing. Though China has already established its clout in Singapore, Vietnam, Indonesia and Japan or deeper involvement in Burma, India is not going to accord primacy to China[45]. Chinese efforts to keep India out of the core group directing the creation of an East Asian Community, and to lessen India's primacy in South Asia will remain preponderantly a factor to acquiesce in American strategy to build up India against China. Further, given India being hemmed in militarily by combinations of the Himalayan Mountains and undemocratic states from Pakistan and Nepal to Bangladesh and Burma, it is in the area of naval modernization where the U.S. strategy can best address India's geopolitical needs. "As China pursues a 'string of pearls' strategy to develop deep- water ports and stronger diplomatic and military relations with Pakistan, Burma, Indonesia", American strategy should be more focused on increasing the " the capacity of the Indian navy (through the project Seabird) to police and even deny access to the Indian ocean sea lanes" than the Indian army being strengthened.[46] Since both India and the United States face the danger of naval threats from terrorist groups like al Qaeda spanning the entire sea lanes from the Arabian sea to the Straits of Malacca, India being central to America's new strategic agenda, can very rightly take on to itself the onus of patrolling the entire sea lane[47].

For the reasons both from Indian and American perspective, the China paradigm not only marks the convergence of strategic interests of both countries but also provides the impetus to sustain long- term U.S. engagement with India. As Richardson states: " A strong India raises the price of China's military buildup and expansionist policies in Asia. A strong India would also send the message that democracy in a developing country is not incompatible with rapid growth and wealth. This is a message worth sending not just to China and other authoritarian states, but also to all the states of Asia troubled by Islamic fundamentalism. India has the unenviable distinction of lying at the heart of the Islamic world, spanning the globe as Islam does from North Africa through the Middle East to Southeast Asia and the Philippines. Not only can India deliver a positive economic message, but its success as a state composed of varying ethnic and religious groups is an important example for others."[48] Different from American cold war strategy of containment of Soviet communism, the current U.S. policy pertains to wearing out China through an erection of democratic states abutting China with strengthened military and economic buildup as a barricade against the expansion of an aggressive and undemocratic China. President Bush's pledges to facilitate Indian ascension to major power status through the strategic partnership with recent nuclear deal are consonant with America's policy of playing the Indian card. India is the ideal model to be imitated by all in Asia. As Katrin Bennhold observes: "India has been a beacon of democracy and stability in a region where both are the exception."[49] In a similar vein, Prime Minister Manmohan Singh in a meeting opines jettisoning India's traditional anti-imperialistic rhetoric: " If there is an idea of India that the world should remember us by and regard us for, it is the idea of an inclusive and open society, a multi-cultural, multi-ethnic, multi-lingual society... Liberal democracy is the natural order of social and political organization in to day's world. All alternate systems of authoritarian and majoritarian rule in varying degrees are an aberration. Democratic methods yield the most enduring solutions to even most intractable problems."[50] President Bush and Prime Minister Manmohan Singh's joint statement on July 18, 2005 on global democracy initiative and joint support for the United Nations Democracy Fund in September 2005 articulates their convergence of interests in showing adherence to universal democratization as a policy.

Pursuant to the declared objective of America to help India climb up to a major power status, the July 18 nuclear agreement is hailed as milestone in their strategic relations. But the Congressional draft bills with extraneous conditionalities not found in the original agreement run counter to American objectives. To close the options of India by these American bills to conduct nuclear tests in future in case Pakistan and China conduct nuclear tests is nothing but reinforcement of America's cold war strategy of containing India. If America remains true to its stated objective of creating a democratic barricade around China with a militarily and economically strengthened India as its steward, then it is the moral onus with the American President to see that the Congress pass the draft bills as exactly as enshrined in the July 18 agreement. Any attempt by America to sneak India into the NPT noose through the back door by curtailing its nuclear option would not likely to end the ingrained suspicion in New Delhi that America is not ready to see India rise in power potential, rather would fail as India being a what Stephen Krasner calls a "modified structuralist" state, continues believing in its long espoused non-aligned culture as relevant as its logical pronouncement to pursue a policy of multidirectional or multi alignment with all major powers to seek maximum interests.

If an enduring U.S. interest is at stake in India, and the stake is a successful democracy in Asia, building it with strength to offset

China's rising power In Asia, then one option was for U.S. to induct India into the NPT orthodoxy by making it as a member of their ranks, entitled to receive all privileges and responsibilities as five nuclear powers enjoy. This was very bleak to expect that China would cast an affirmative vote. Another option was the United States would withdraw from NPT on the ground that it was a failure as nuclear proliferation continued despite stringent rules. This would enable America to help India in its nuclear programme. The third option suggested America to pursue a policy of calculated ambiguity as it was used to China and France's nuclear programmes. At the very least, India to pay a price for American policy must not to engage in proliferation of its own, nor to develop missiles capable of targeting the United States.[51] But contrary to all these options, U.S. went for a deal with India inked on July 18, 2005 bestowing India a second class nuclear status with many restrictions and conditionalities as evidenced from the Congressional bills.

Divergences in Strategic Partnership

These restrictions have already created hiccups in Indian politics culminating in an upsurge of protestations against the deal. From Indian perspective, there is no gainsaying the fact that America has shown its commitment to promotion of civilian nuclear energy and space technology in India. The reality is that it depends on American will to provide or withhold supply to India according to its own interests. If American technology and equipment sales to China and handling of A.Q. Khan affair in Pakistan are any indication, then American steps give an inkling of the certitude with which it moves toward a fundamentally different relationship. The modifications to U.S. export licensing policies are castigated by many as cosmetics, pointing out they are to be reciprocal for India's "implementation of measures to address proliferation concerns and to ensure compliance with U.S. export controls."[52] On the issue of technology denial, the critics believe that "technology denial can work up to a point in the new knowledge economy, hence innovative sanctions against intangibles are likely to be developed, adding yet another layer of distrust between India and U.S." Further, they are of the view that, " the fundamental American goal of ensuring asymmetry in technology, including full spectrum dominance, will continue to dictate U.S. policies. This goal will lead the U.S. to try and put a ceiling on scientific development elsewhere. The defense technologists and scientists at least believe that as in the earlier period, the U.S. will only be able to slow down India, but not stop it in new arenas."[53]

While shaping the "new strategy for South Asia", the Bush administration responded positively to Indian requests for information on the possible purchase of F-16 or F/A- 18 multi-role fighters, and indicated that Washington is ready to discuss the sale of transformative systems in areas such as command, and control, early warning, and missile defense. "The top Indian officials express concern that the United States is a fickle partner that may not be always be relied upon to provide the reciprocity, sensitivity, and high technology transfers sought by New Delhi"[54].

From an American point of view, the NSSP "truly revolutionary", and suggests that what is really important is "a change in the U.S. strategic orientation towards India that in time will be more consequential than any of the minutiae encoded in the current agreement."[55] The pentagon supporters see bilateral agreements such as the General Security of Military Information Agreement and the Master Information exchange Agreement with India as the foundation for defense cooperation. But the defense transfer relationship is still described as embryonic. All major defense technology transfer deals continue to be stymied by existing restrictions that affect this area as well: the dual use technology controls in the Department of Commerce and the Department of State's licensing of Munitions List items directed at defense commodity trade.[56] Even defense officials favourably inclined to increasing high tech defense trade with India concede that " High tech defense trade with countries that do not have an established track record with the U.S. of protecting technology is extremely difficult and often a lengthy process. India is such a country."[57] High technology trade especially dual use technology transactions though very small in proportion to overall trade is considered very vital to India's national development. The issue of dual use technology trade has occupied such an elevated importance in the national debate over the extent of relations between the two countries that success or failure in this field defines the extent of their relations. The U.S. Commerce Department officials have sought to dispel the "trade-deterring myths" about limits on dual use trade by noting that only about 1% of the total U.S. trade value with India is subject to licensing requirements. It has as much to do with misperceptions as export controls or government restrictions. "The irony is that while the U.S. actually has more restrictive trade regulations vis-à-vis China, the U.S. has a more robust high technology trade and investment relationship with China than with India."[58] Further, the Commerce Department clarified that the great majority of dual – use licensing applications are approved more than 90% in 2005 financial year. The U.S.- India High Technology Cooperation Group (HTCG) in its inaugural session in July 2003 discussed a wide range of issues relevant to creating conditions for more robust bilateral high technology commerce. Since 1998, a number of Indian entities have been subjected to case by case licensing requirements and appear on the U.S. export control "Entity List" of foreign end users involved in weapons proliferation activities. In September 2004, as part of NSSP implementation, the United States modified some export licensing policies and removed the Indian Space Research Organization(ISRO) headquarters from the Entity List. Further adjustments came in August 2005 when six more subordinate entities were removed.[59]

Strategic Autonomy

The different stand on the role of export controls remains the main impediment in their commitment to the strategic partnership. American analysts are always inclined to view export controls as the foundation for technology transfers, and necessary for safeguarding national security. On the contrary, the Indian tend to view that export controls acceptable to America would infringe India's sovereignty if adopted. As an analyst opines, " Protecting India's perceived strategic autonomy has been a central driving motivation of Indian foreign policy, and high technology achievements are still seen as a critical tool in this regard."[60] The American invitation to join its unveiled the Proliferation Security Initiative (PSI) as a core member, which aims at interdicting WMD material including searches of suspected air, sea, and land cargoes, has received a lukewarm response from India. India's reluctance is based on the ground that there is no guarantee that the members of the core group shall not be targets of PSI. The members are to leave themselves open to spot checks of their own ships and aircraft. There is also the question of being consistent with the imperatives of international law. "Hypothetically speaking, if India were to try to interdict Chinese ships or aircraft heading for Pakistan, the risk of conflict with China would be high, without a clear idea of what the U.S. would be to avert or settle any such crisis."[61]

As analyzed above, there has not been yet a complete convergence of national interests of both countries though both countries have taken steps to break away from their past moorings and to move ahead by forming a strategic and defense partnership. On some critical areas of their foreign policy concerns, a discordant note is heard about their not getting a smooth sailing. The incompatibility between India's non-aligned political culture defined in Nehruvian idioms and America's penchant for a world order based on its own pontification demands of it a new vision and orientation to work out toward the resolution of this inherent antithesis. The foundational differences in their foreign policy is not going to be so easily obviated until and unless America shows the necessary stewardship in redefining its national interests not purely in its selfish and domestic imperatives at the expense of the interests of the poor, but in terms of planetary interests. As Indian Prime Minister stated in his speech at the University of Cambridge on October 11, 2006 on the occasion of his being awarded the honorary degree of Doctor of Law: "My appeal is that developed countries should not allow short term national interests to prevail at the cost of promoting freer trade and combating poverty. The prosperity of so many cannot be sacrificed for protecting the interests of so few. The price of myopia is heavy on the exchequers of the developed world. The issue also has profound moral dimensions". [62] India's stress on democracy, establishment of a new international order based on justice and equity, multilateralism and democratization of international institutions as opposed to American preachy unilateralism, would be the benchmark template on which New Delhi wants to chisel partnership with Washington. Prime Minister further stated in his speech: " As democracies we must also stand together in making governance across the world more democratic. As democracy we aspire to a world in which global institutions are more democratic and more representative of all the peoples of the world.... A more inclusive global process that carries the population of the world with it calls for a reform of these institutions, in which the developing world will have a greater voice."[63] This shows, while forging partnership with U.S. or establishing multidirectional relations with other powers, India will remain bound by its long and permanent commitment to promotion of democracy, democratic values, and taking up the cudgels for the developing world. To the extent America demonstrates the necessary political wisdom to mark a paradigm shift in its foreign policy away from its sole reliance on the narrow, consumerist and all acquisitive political culture, the newly carved out partnership will be enduring.

References

1. Parag Khanna and C. Raja Mohan, "Getting India Right", Policy Review, No.135, February- March, 2006, visited website, http://www.policy review.org/135/default.htm.
2. Strobe Talbott, "The Changing Nature of U.S.- India relations: The Clinton, Bush Eras and Beyond", remarks presented at " U.S.- India Bilateral Cooperation: Taking Stock and Moving forward" conference hosted by The Sigur Center for Asian Studies of the The Elliot School of International Affairs at The George Washington University, Washington, D.C. April 1-2, 2004.
3. Franklin Kramer, "Toward a Mature Defense Relationship: Limits, Possibilities and Lessons", remarks presented at ibid.
4. Deepa Ollapally, "U.S.- India Relations: Ties That Bind?", The Sigur Center Asia Papers19, The George Washington University, The Elliot School of International Affairs, Washington D.C.
5. *Ibid*.
6. Parag Khanna and C. Raja Mohan, *op.cit.*
7. The Asian Age, June 21, 2004.
8. The Hindu, July 8, 2004.
9. B. Raman, "Managing the War on Terrorism In South Asia", remarks presented at "U.S.- India Bilateral Cooperation: Taking stock and Moving Forward" a conference hosted by the Sigur Center for Asian Studies of The Elliot School of International Affairs at The George Washington University, Washington, D.C. April 1-2, 2004.

10. Swaminathan S. Anklesaria Aiyar, " Kush vs Berry", Times of India, October 10, 2004.
11. Deepa Ollapally, op.cit.
12. The Hindu, October1, 2005.
13. *Ibid.*
14. The Economist, 23 February 2006, " The great Indian hope trick" visited at website, http:// www.economist.com/ world/ displaystory.cfm? story_id=5545462
15. Deepa Ollapally, op.cit.
16. Quoted in The Hindu, October 7,2004.
17. Ashley J.Tellis, India As A New Global Power, Carnegie Endowment for International Peace, Washington, D.C., 2005,p.38.
18. Mapping the Global Future: Report of the National Intelligence Council's 2020 Project. National Intelligence Council. December 2004. http://www.cia.gov/nic/NIC_2020_project.html.
19. Parag Khanna and C.Raja Mohan, op.cit.
20. The report is entitled "Doing Business in 2005: Removing Obstacles to Growth", The Times of India, September 9,2004.
21. Arvind Panagariya, " Emerging India: A Threat or Opportunity?" paper presented at " U.S.- India Bilateral Cooperation: Taking Stock and Moving Forward", a conference hosted by the Sigur Center for Asian Studies of the Elliot School Of International Affairs at the George Washington University, Washington, D.C. April 1-2, 2004.
22. Adil Zainulbhai, Director, McKinsey and Company, " Taking Stock of U.S.- India Economic Cooperation", remarks presented at ibid.
23. The Economist, op.cit.
24. Parag Khanna and C. Raja Mohan, op.cit.
25. Ashley J.Tellis, op.cit. p.40.
26. Kenneth I.Juster, "Cybersecurity: A Key to U.S.- India Trade", a keynote address to the India-U.S. Information Security Summit 2004, New Delhi, India October 12,2004, available at http:/ www.state.gov/p/sa/rls/rm/37039.htm.
27. The Economist, Ibid.
28. David C. Mulford, U.S. Ambassador to India, Advancing U.S.- India Economic Relations, speech to the Indian Chamber of Commerce/ Indo- American Chamber of Commerce, Luncheon, Calcutta, 18 August, 2005, available at http:/ www.state.gov/p/sca/ rls/rm/2005/51317.htm.

29. K.Alan Kronstadt, India -U.S. Relation, CRS Report for Congress, updated July 31,2006,RL33529, Congressional Research Service, The Library of Congress, p.16
30. *Ibid.*
31. *Ibid*, p.17
32. CRS Report RS21502, India- U.S. Economic Relation.
33. Ashley J. Tellis, op.cit, p.48.
34. Suman Bery, " Needed: A U.S- India FTA", Rediff.com Business, November 9, 2004, available at http:/us.rediff.com/money/2004/nov/09guest1.htm.
35. Ashley J.Tellis, op.cit, p.48.
36. Pankaj Mishra, "The Myth of the New India", The New York Times, July 6,2006,p.3.
37. *Ibid.*
38. *Ibid.*
39. K. Alan Kronstadt, Indo-U.S. Relations, CRS Report for Congress, RL 33529, Updated July 31, 2006, p. 17
40. Lloyd Richardson, "Now, Play the Indian Card", Policy Review, no.115, October, 2002, http:/ www.policy review.org/Octo2/Richardson_print.html.,p.2
41. See, for example, A.D. McLennan, "Balance, Not Containment: A Geopolitical Take from Canberra", National Interest, fall 1997; and Gerald Segal, " "Asianism and Asian Security", National Interest, winter, 1995-96.
42. David Zweig, "Undemocratic Capitalism", National Interest, Summer, 1999.
43. Deepak Lal, Unfinished Business: India in the World Economy (New Delhi: Oxford University Press, 2000).
44. Lloyd Richardson, op.cit., p.4
45. Parag Khanna and C Raja Mohan, op. cit.
46. *Ibid.*
47. *Ibid.*
48. Lloyd Richardson, op.cit., p.13.
49. International Herald Tribune, December 7, 2004.
50. Prime Minister Manmohan Singh's India Today Conclave speech in New Delhi, India Today, February 25, 2004.
51. Richardson, op.cit., pp.14-15.
52. R. Ramchandran, "India, U.S. and trade in Technology", The Hindu, September 27, 2004.

53. Deepa Ollapally, op.cit., p.9.
54. K. Alan Kronstadt,op.cit., p.14.
55. Ashley Tellis, "Lost Tango in Washington", The Indian Express, November 15,2004.
56. Ashley Tellis, " Seeking the Breakthrough", Force, October 2004.
57. Peter Dougherty, "High Technology, Dual Use Technology and Critical Economic Issues", roundtable at "U.S.- India Bilateral cooperation: Taking Stock and Moving Forward", a conference hosted by The Sigur Center for Asian Studies of The Elliot School of International Affairs at The George Washington University, Washington, D.C., April 1-2, 2004.
58. Deepa Ollapally, op.cit., p.10.
59. K. Alan Kronstadt, op.cit., p.10.
60. Deepa Ollapally, op.cit., p.11.
61. Reshmi Kazi, "Proliferation Security Initiative and India", Peace and Conflict, Vol.7.no.7.October 2004.
62. Excerpted from the Prime Minister Manmohan Singh's speech at the University of Cambridge on 11 October 2006, The Hindu, October 13, 2006.
63. *Ibid.*

7

India and the United States Spinning the Nuclear Deal

One prominent reason why the nuclear factor has been an irritant in Indo-US relation stems from American disavowal of Indian great ambition to assume a great power status and pursue an independent foreign policy. Given the Indian non-aligned and independent stance in world politics and its reluctance to cling to American cold war logic, it is not surprising to expect that American would balk at any attempts by India to grow in military and economic strength to the discomfiture of Pakistan, a close cold war ally of America. A great India is certainly not to the liking of America, as this would hurt Pakistan and ultimately America's global strategy. Another reason American did not simply relish the emergence of another independent power centre, which would likely affect its strategic interests and challenge its supremacy in international realm. Pursuant to its cold war logic and strategy it tried to retain maximum control over nuclear materials and technology to promote peace and to maintain dominance and suppress the independence of countries like India. Given India's strong fulminations against systemic discrlmination of nuclear technology, long history of Indo-Pak conflict over Kashmir and finally, the bogey of big brother India ingrained in the Indian neighbors, the question is pertinent whether America doubted India's integrity and willingness to accept international safeguards on all its nuclear facilities as a matter of principle. When containment of Soviet communism was the sole objective of US foreign policy to see another nuclear India always inclined to focus on autonomy and independence, in Asia to the consternation of both Pakistan and China, the two allies of America was certainly not to the liking of Washington. Though neither side posed a direct threat to the other or denied compatibility of interests in the long run in view of their being largest democracies in the world their respective stances on nuclear issues raised doubts about their intent. Such doubts on both sides persisted and hindered the attempts and ability of both sides to maintain unbroken ties of cooperation on nuclear issues, which they had commenced in the 1950s. The legal instrument for the most tangible demonstration of Indo- US nuclear cooperation was the Agreement on the Tarapur Atomic Power Station (TAPS) signed on 8 August 1963. Disagreement over the interpretation of some of its provisions followed the controversy about the precedence of international agreements over domestic law after 1978. The enactment of the Nuclear Non Proliferation Act (NNPA) by the US Congress in the same year made it extremely difficult to honour its contractual obligations to India under the 1963 agreement. Though the Reagan administration decided to designate France as the supplier of fuel for TAPS in 1982, the controversy on the subject persisted.

The main objectives of India's nuclear policy were to reinforce its foreign policy of non- alignment and enhance its scientific and technological self-reliance. Always putting primacy on democratization of international system, India challenged the political and technological hierarchy of the international system, which was dominated by nuclear-weapons states. Always believing in peace and peaceful settlement of disputes, India was averse to production and deployment of nuclear weapons. Even it did not subscribe to the theory of international security through mutual assured destruction also known as nuclear deterrence. But that does not mean that India closed its options. While pursuing slowly and systematically the expansion of programme of nuclear research and the application of nuclear energy for peaceful purposes, India chose to exercise its sovereignty principle to keep the options open for the future direction of its nuclear and space programme in view of China assuming the status of a nuclear power in 1960s and Pakistan's prodding its way towards that with former's clandestine help in 1980s. Preoccupied with problems of military security and internal economic and political crises during the 1960s India depended overwhelmingly on US and Soviet Union. India was the first signatory to the Partial Test Ban Treaty of1963 after its sponsors, the US, the USSR, and Britain. India was also an active participant in UN sponsored negotiations to limit the proliferation of nuclear weapons and to ban chemical and bacteriologic warfare. The US contributed tangibly to India's nuclear programme and in 1963 loaned $80 million for the setting up of India's first atomic power station at Tarapur, north of Bombay. The Nuclear non Proliferation Treaty (NPT) discriminated against non nuclear weapons states and provided no sanctions against vertical proliferation of nuclear weapons by existing producers. V.C Trivedy, India's representative to the Eighteen Nation Disarmament Committee, once famously taunted the nuclear weapon states while stating the position of India: there was, in our legend, a king who drank to excess but forbade his subjects by edict from imbibing alcohol. Indeed the report of the Department of Atomic Energy for 1958-59 said: India is conscious not only of her own rights but of the rights of several other countries which, till recently, were subjected by colonial powers. The essence of non-alignment was independence of decision-making. On the nuclear issue India chose its own path. India always claimed to be an independent centre of power in a multipolar world. Nuclear capability was one of several criteria of power.

Nuclear test at Pokharan on May 18, 1974 by India expressed its challenge to an institutionalized hierarchy of privileged nuclear weapon states and the other unprivileged non- nuclear states. India first demonstrated its ability to conduct controlled nuclear explosions and asserted its right to have nuclear capability at par with that of the nuclear elite states. Different from the common notion India termed it a peaceful nuclear explosion (PNE). The excited euphoria of the common man in India as reported by Lewis Simons from New Delhi for the Washington Post ran as follows: We have the atomic bomb. Now we are the same as America, Russia and China. India goes nuclear at last.[1] Outside India; people also reacted at the same level. Among the developing countries India's prestige boosted. In 1973 George Quester discussed the technological and conceptual overlap between peaceful and military nuclear explosion and postulated a peaceful nuclear explosion in India because of the overlap. A PNE, he wrote, would allow India to join the nuclear powers club behind a euphemism avoiding too brazen an affront to the international community and behind a civilian economic rationale that may suffice to push the project through domestically.[2] America castigated India for having crossed the threshold. Many believed that India's action would propel other countries to follow the suit. In 1975, US Arms

Control and Disarmament Director Fred C. Ikle observed: " The right way to look at this next step in proliferation, the Indian explosion, is not that India is number six in a so called nuclear club, but in a way it is number one among a great many countries to come."[3] The public reaction was not to catapult India to pre Pokharan power position but to stem further slide in indefinite diffusion of that hierarchy. Symptomatic of its reaction to Pokharan test, America interrupted its fuel supplies to Tarapur Atomic Power Station. T. N. Kaul, India's Ambassador in his letter of 6 July 1974 to Secretary of State Henry Kissinger made it clear that the peaceful nuclear explosion had used only Indian materials, personnel and technology and did not violate any bilateral or international agreements to which India was signatory.[4] India's assurances that no materials from Tarapur had been or would be used for explosives were well received in America. Both countries tried to improve their bilateral relations downplaying the Pokharan explosion. India did not extend any pretensions to the distinction of being called a nuclear weapon state. India also desisted itself from conducting any follow up tests after Pokharan. It remained doubtful whether India remaining hostage to international pressure and constraints did not envisage any further nuclear explosion or its too much dependence on western countries for nuclear materials hindered its ambition. This shows, India under the leadership of Indira Gandhi failed yet to torn asunder the shackles of Nehruvian evangelistic idealism in order to understand that it is through realistic assumption of power through nuclear weapons that a country can think of ascending to a great power status. For this reason the hiatus in India between dream and action to realize it, in Henry Kissinger's grand design of Euro- centered ideas of a great power condominium in the world, China could find a place not India. The seemingly outward thaw in Indo- US relation was very much evanescent with a vocal group in America taking swipes at India's power of the nuclear industry at home and nuclear proliferation abroad. The Nixon- Ford administration was heavily criticized for not having pursued vigorously the cause of nuclear non-proliferation. The US nuclear industry wanted to dominate the world market in nuclear exports and protect its lion's share from any kind of inroads into its domain by western Europeans. So they were less concerned with enforcing stricture safeguards on the reactors and processes they sold. On the other hand, public interest groups took strong exceptions to the environmental and health hazards caused by nuclear plants and to the danger of terrorists capturing nuclear weapons, which were in abundant supply and inadequately protected. Vitriolic attacks on Nixon's 1974 promise of providing advanced nuclear technology to both Israel and Egypt, which would possibly cause a threat to world peace, were made. They stood solidly opposed to further shipments of enriched uranium fuel to Tarapur. A shipment of fuel to Tarapur was made in 1976 over the objections of some members of the Nuclear Regulatory Commission. Acting on behalf of several environmental groups, which demanded stricter regulation of US nuclear exports and firmer controls on nuclear plants within the US, the Centre for Law and Social Policy spearheaded the anti- Tarapur lobby. Similar groups also took hold of liberals in the Congress such as Senators Charles Percy of Illinois and Abraham Ribicoff of Connecticut, and representatives of Clement Zablocki of Wisconsin and Morris Udall of Arizona who were earlier friendly to India. These men wanted to transfer consideration of nuclear questions from the Nuclear Regulatory Commission to a subcommittee of the International Regulatory Commission chaired by their fellow reformist, Jonathan Bingham.[5] Further, they demanded that Congress have a share in deciding which nuclear exports were inimical to US security, and whether the assurances given by foreign purchases on physical safety and peaceful uses were adequate. After three years of bargaining, Congress passed the Nuclear Non Proliferation Act (NNPA) in September 1977, which became ultimately law after President Carter affixed his signature on 10th May 1978.

Tarapur plant came under the NNPA. On 20 April 1978 the Nuclear Regulatory Commission declined to recommend the license issued by the State Department for the export of fuel to Tarapur. American president Carter overruled this decision on 27 April. On 1 May a joint Senate house resolution was introduced in Congress to veto the President's decision. Public hearings were held with Prime Minister Morarji Desai addressing very frankly and candidly. Both the Senate and House foreign relations committee rejected the veto resolution with a directive to US executive and the Indian government- unless full scope safeguards were accepted by India within eighteen months as required under the NNPA continued exports would not be acceptable to Congress. A similar message was also transmitted to Euratom, which imported 50 per cent of its nuclear requirements from the US. It consequently decided to re-negotiate the terms of its agreement.

Morarji Desai well known for his articulated and principled stance against all nuclear tests accommodated the new demands of the US as far as it was possible for the Prime Minister of a sovereign country. He might have renounced the India's nuclear option had the super powers agreed in return to accept legal constraints on their own vertical proliferation of nuclear weapons. But Desai was unable to winnow from the US either a commitment to his idea of comprehensive test ban treaty or a guarantee of adherence to the 1963 TAPS agreement in regard to supplies of fuel. The deadline imposed by the NNPA was crossed with India continuing to resist full-scope safeguards, and the US continuing to obstruct fuel exports to Tarapur. Carter administration and Indira Gandhi's government decided to reopen negotiations in1980. The Indian Atomic Commission and the Ministry of External Affairs maintained a low-key approach to US. To meet the situation in case US reneged on its commitment to supply fuel to Tarapur plant, a substitute fuel (MOX) was prepared at Hyderabad. It was vauntingly said that India had full control and self-sufficient technology in every phase of the nuclear fuel cycle. India's capabilities in space technology, and its potential for manufacturing missiles, were demonstrated by the launching of the third Indian satellite in July 1980. The Prime Minister underscored India's right to keep its options open to conduct all kinds of nuclear explosions in the light of changing circumstances in the light of changing circumstances and the national interest. She also buttressed India's peaceful intentions in developing nuclear technology, and refused to panic in the face of reports about Pakistan's clandestine nuclear weapons activity.[6] Satisfied with India's assurances President Carter cleared the export of the two pending shipments of fuel for Tarapur, despite the objections of the Nuclear Regulatory Commission. America was convincingly of the view and guided by the strategic consideration that if US fails to maintain fuel supplies it would provide India the legal right and the political impetus to reprocess the unused spent fuel rods into plutonium which can serve both as a source for fuel and for weapons. By closing the dialogue with India US would deny itself the leverage it had over India to prevent the latter from pursuing the nuclear weapons option. From an economic point of view US did not have the monopoly in plutonium processing or fast breeder technology favoured by India and other countries. Withdrawing from the treaty obligations Senator Daniel Moynihan argued in favour of supplying fuel to India, as NPT was discriminatory and the latter being a non nuclear weapon state. Finally, the Senate clinched the issue and approved the President's decision to export the already licensed fuel by only two votes. India's representative to the IAEA warned that unless the misgivings of consumer nations were assuaged so as to give them confidence that supplies would continue to honour commitments, they would be forced to reconsider their own obligations and previous commitments. The controversy over the right to make decisions on nuclear policy remained stuck in the problems of fuel supplies and safeguards on reprocessing facilities, as these were not solved in1980. Surjit Mansingh's contention was that " India became the focus of the anti-proliferation drive within the US more because it openly challenged US prescriptions for world order than because it acquired a nuclear capability".[7] By outwardly subscribing to American prescriptions India could have produced nuclear weapons clandestinely as Israel and South Africa were alleged to have done. Being signatory to NPT if nuclear states could produce nuclear weapons without realizing their hypocrisy, what prevented India from doing so? Though it had the much-flaunted capability it failed to translate into reality. Ingrained clinging to words of promise or idealism permanently and hermitically sealed off from the prevailing international situation has been an obsession with India's foreign policy since Nehru founded it after independence. It was rather the lack of unity between realism and idealism and the spawning hiatus between the two that prevented India from pursuing its policy most boldly and explicitly, which was ultimately bridged in 1998 when Vajpayee, Indian Prime Minister decided to produce nuclear weapons. That India had long committed to peaceful use of nuclear energy remained not as a milestone rather a millstone in India's foreign policy. This obsession with words failed India in its rise to great power status. In contrast, US and other nations did not go by Indian words. They continued to persist in the impression that India had the nuclear weapons. As the US Senate Foreign Relations Committee noted, "India stands alone as the only nation which has overtly used unsafeguarded facilities to produce and test a nuclear device and which... refuses to rule out future tests."[8] To profess non-proliferation is as ludicrous as asking a bird of prey to kill by shedding its talons. Similar was the dilemma in India which was asked to profess non-proliferation as a crusade of its foreign policy without having the nuclear weapons in a changing security environment where its neighbours China was already a nuclear power and Pakistan was clandestinely producing nuclear weapons in complicity with the former. Though India did not overtly declare to be a nuclear power, it resisted full scope safeguards and declined to accept unilateral US or IAEA impositions of restraint on its choices. From 1975 onwards, New Delhi was subject to delay, restrictions and denial of consignments of fuels for Tarapur and even postponement of joint determination on how the spent fuel should be disposed as specified in the 1963 agreement. Consequent upon these delays by America and exacting high economic costs from India, Tarapur ran below the capacity and the Power Reactor Fuel Reprocessing Plant at Tarapur was forced to lie idle. The plant had been indigenously designed and constructed with the knowledge and approval of the US as part of India's early strategy to supplement scarce uranium by separating plutonium from the spent fuel of heavy water reactors and using fast-breeder reactors to produce new fuel. But US was sternly repugnant to any developing country acquiring the technology and facilities for the separation of plutonium and construction of fast breeder reactors. But India did not change its stand on the Tarapur Agreement. After 1980, it adduced strongly to establish its legal claims on the US. New Delhi firmly linked India's acceptance of IAEA safeguards on the facilities at Tarapur with US supplies of fuel for the efficient and continuous operation of Tarapur plant. The position of Reagan administration on nuclear exports and non-proliferation differed from that of Carter administration. The Republican Party platform in the 1980 presidential election denounced Carter's delivery to India of nuclear material, which feared might be directed to the manufacture of nuclear weapons.[9] On the other hand, President Reagan wanted to remove Congressional restraints on nuclear exports, allow US nuclear industry to recapture the markets it had lost to West European competitors, and re-establish the nation's reputation of being a "predictable and reliable partner for peaceful nuclear cooperation under adequate safeguards."[10] Further, it asserted its commitment to a defence strategy of multiplying the over-kill nuclear weapons capacity in the US, and waived restrictive legislation aimed at a potential nuclear weapons Pakistan. Countries not part of US security system but in possession of their own nuclear energy programmes were discriminated against with many denials and restrictions imposed on them. In other words, the immediate security and foreign policy concerns reigned supreme over the long avowed principles of means America was to lose in a highly competitive nuclear business. A prolonged debate went on in American Senate on President Carter's decision with thousands of pages from Nuclear Regulatory Commission being tabled before the committees in the House, countenancing India's stand and concerns, nuclear exports and non-proliferation. Nuclear programme was rightly a move toward greater power status and self-reliance but US tried to contain and discourage India by imposing many restrictions whereas it was lenient towards Pakistan. The controversy over supply of fuels to Tarapur came to an end by an agreement Reagan signed with Indira Gandhi on her state visit to US in July 1982. The buck of re-supplying fuels to Tarapur passed on to France and the 1963 agreement was not abrogated. India acquiesced in the transfer to another external supplier but declined to consider any additional safeguards of pursuit and perpetuity on its nuclear facilities. The issue of fuel supply remained like an albatross around the neck of Indo- US relation.

In 1998, when there was change of guard in New Delhi with Vajpayee becoming the Prime Minister, India exploded the second nuclear test at Pokharan for weaponisation as a sign of its declared ascension to nuclear power status and protection against nuclear weapon states- Pakistan and China. This invited strong reactions from US, which did not hesitate to impose immediately military, economic and technological sanctions against India. This was exactly a repetition of American cold war behaviour towards India glossing over the very fact that Pakistan had already nuclear weapons with connivance of both China and U.S. To say that U.S. was ignorant of Pakistan having nuclear weapons is a misrepresentation of fact. Moret revealed this. According to him, "while the George Bush administration was hyping the War on Terror, Defense Information Agency (DIA) officials believed that nuclear technology had been transferred to Pakistan and began investigating. Similarities between Pakistani and US weapons designs were of particular concern. A regular exchange of information was discovered between China and the Army Computer Lab at the Aberdeen Proving Ground in Maryland that took place during the 1980s and early 1990s. A .Q Khan was running the black market for distributing nuclear materials to countries as their key man. Countries that detained Khan were ordered to "look but do not touch" by the US, and he was released. Pakistani Nazir Ahmed Vaid was arrested in

Houston in 1984 attempting to smuggle out 50 krytrons, electronic switches for nuclear weapons. He received a very special deal and was let off on probation and deported. He continued to enter the country illegally and conduct business until 2004 when his son was warned by a Customs' Agent that there was a detention order on his father". In the 1980s, Congressman Charlie Wilson working with the CIA, told Pakistan's president Zia ul – Haq:

"Mr. President, as far as I am concerned you can make all bombs you want". [11]

Further as he stated, " It is hard to believe that the US intelligence community was ignorant of a massive secret atom bomb project funded by the Kingdom of Saudi Arabia through the failed BCCI bank. According to a Senate report George H.W. Bush's favourite bank was also used to covertly fund the anti- Soviet Afghanistan resistance, and the CIA has been aware since the 1970s of Pakistan's nuclear programme when Bush was Director. Among George W. Bush's "Axis of Evil" supposed enemies, many of his father's friend enemies are listed."[12] Since Pakistan was the belle of American strategic ball during cold war, it remained persistent in containing India not to disturb its strategic balance in South Asia to the discomfiture of Pakistan.

India's step was in response to changed regional security environment built around India. Pakistan had already had nuclear weapons with the active connivance of nuclear China and US. With two nuclear states adjacent to Indian territory having historical animosity against India, New Delhi perceived production of nuclear weapons was inevitably quintessential for its strategic national security. The onward march from idealism of Nehru to realism, which was half way during Indira Gandhi's regime reached the goal post during Vajpayee's time.

As said above, end of cold war and demise of Soviet Union ushered in a new era in international relation and a transformation in Indo- US relation providing opportunities to both powers to have a second look at what embittered their bilateral relation. In spite of having imposed sanctions against India for its second Pokharan test in1998, US tried to ease its relation with India. With Bush coming to power for the second time a new strategic partnership was established between the two.

US Undertaking

Noting the centrality of civilian nuclear energy to the twin challenges of energy security and safeguarding the environment, the two governments agreed on 18 July 2005 to undertake reciprocal commitments and responsibilities that would create a framework for the resumption of full cooperation in the nuclear field. As a part of this agreement, the United States undertook to seek agreement from the Congress to adjust US laws and policies to achieve full civil nuclear energy cooperation. It would work with friends and allies to adjust international regimes to enable full civil nuclear energy cooperation and trade with India, including but not limited to expeditious consideration of fuel supplies for safeguarded nuclear reactors at Tarapur. It would encourage its partners to consider fuel supply to Tarapur expeditiously. It also undertook to consult with its partners to consider India's participation in ITER and to consult with other participants in the Generation-IV International Forum with a view towards India's inclusion.

India's Undertaking

India conveyed its readiness to assume the same responsibilities and practices and acquire the same benefits and advantages as other leading countries with advanced nuclear technology, such as the United States. Accordingly, India for its part undertook the following commitments as stated by Prime Minister Manmohan Singh in the Parliament on 7 March 2006. [13]

- Identifying and separating civilian and military nuclear facilities and programmes in a phased manner
- Filling a declaration regarding its civilian facilities with the IAEA
- Taking a decision to place voluntarily its civilian nuclear facilities under IAEA safeguards, and
- Signing and adhering to an Additional Protocol with respect to civilian nuclear facilities

Other commitments undertaken by India have already been fulfilled in the last year. Among them are:

- India's responsible non-proliferation record, recognized by the US, continues and is reflected in its policies and actions.
- The harmonization of India's exports controls with NSG (Nuclear Suppliers' Group) and MTCR (Missile Technology Control Regime) Guidelines even though India is not member of either group. These guidelines and control lists have been notified and are being implemented.
- A significant upgrading of India's non-proliferation regulations and export controls has taken place as a result of the Weapons

of Mass Destruction Act of May 2005. Inter-Ministerial consultations are ongoing to examine and amend other relevant acts as well framing appropriate rules and regulations.

- Refrain from transfer of enrichment and reprocessing technologies to states that do not have them and supporting international efforts to limit their spread. This has guided India's policy on non-proliferation.
- Continued unilateral moratorium on nuclear testing, and
- Willingness to work with the United States for the conclusion of a multilateral Fissile Material Cut-off Treaty.

The joint statement acknowledges that India's nuclear programme has both a military and a civilian component. Both sides had agreed that the purpose was not to constrain India's strategic programme but to enable resumption of full civil nuclear energy cooperation in order to enhance global energy and environmental security. Such cooperation was predicated on the assumption that any international civil nuclear energy cooperation (including by the US) offered to India in the civilian sector should, firstly, not to be diverted away from civilian purposes, and secondly, should not be transferred from India to third countries without safeguards. These concepts will be reflected in the Safeguards Agreement to be negotiated by India with IAEA.

The Prime Minister further stated that India's nuclear programme is unique as it is the only state with nuclear weapons not to have begun with a dedicated military programme. It must be appreciated the strategic programme is an offshoot of research on nuclear power programme and consequently, it is embedded in a larger undifferentiated programme. Identification of purely civilian facilities and programmers that have no strategic implications poses a particular challenge. Therefore, facilities identified as civilian in the Separation Plan will be offered for safeguards in phases to be decided by India. The nature of the facility concerned, the activities undertaken in it, the national security significance of materials and location of the facilities are factors taken into account in undertaking the separation process. This is solely an Indian determination.

It was the considered opinion of New Delhi that under safeguards India will gain as the percentage of its thermal power reactor installed capacity under safeguards would rise significantly with addition of fresh capacity through such cooperation. Therefore, in assessing the extent of safeguards coverage, it would be important to look at both the number of reactors and the percentage of installed capacity covered. An average Indian reactor is of 220 MW and its output is significantly smaller than the standard reactor in a p-5 economy. So the small capacity of the reactors produced indigenously is to be taken into consideration.

To allay fear in many circles that separation plan and agreement to bring nuclear facilities under safeguards is likely to affect India's security, Prime Minister stated that a facility will be excluded from the civilian list if it is located in a larger hub of strategic significance, notwithstanding the fact that it may not be normally engaged in activities of strategic significance. Moreover, as India expands international cooperation, the percentage of its thermal power reactor installed capacity under safeguards would rise significantly as fresh capacity is added through such cooperation. India's approach to the separation of its civilian nuclear facilities is guided by the overarching judgment whether subjecting a facility would impact adversely on India's national security. A civilian facility would, therefore, be one that India has determined not to be relevant to its strategic programme.

India's acceptance of the safeguards is conditional and based on reciprocal actions by the US:

Thermal Power Reactors: India will identify and offer for safeguards 14 thermal power reactors between 2006 and 2014. This will include the 4 presently safeguarded reactors (TAPS1&2, RAPS1&2) and in addition KK 1&2 that are under construction. 8 other PHWRs, each of a capacity of 220 MW, will be offered. Phasing of specific thermal power reactors being offered for safeguards would be indicated separately by India. Such an offer would, in effect cover 14 out of the 22 thermal power reactors in operation or currently under constructions to be placed under safeguards, and would raise the total installed Thermal power capacity by MWs under safeguards from the present 19% to 65% by 2014.

Fast Breeder Reactors: India is not in a position to accept safeguards on the Prototype Fast Breeder Test Reactor (FBTR), both located at Kalpakam. The Fast Breeder Programme is at the R&D stage and its technology will take time to mature and reach an advanced stage of development.

Future Reactors: India has decided to place under safeguards all future civilian thermal power reactors and civilian breeder reactors, and the Government of India retains the sole right to determine such reactors as civilian.

Research Reactors: India will permanently shut down the CIRUS reactor in 2010. It will also be prepared to shift the fuel core of the APSARA reactor that was purchased from France outside BARC (Bhabha Atomic Research Centre) and make the fuel core available to be placed under safeguards in 2010.

Upstream facilities: List of those specific facilities in the Nuclear Fuel Complex, which will be offered for safeguards by 2008, will be indicated separately.

The Heavy water production plants at Thal. Tuticorin and Hazira are proposed to be designated for civilian use between 2006-2009.

Downstream facilities: India is willing to identify the following downstream facilities and separate as civilian:

India is willing to accept safeguards in the campaign mode after 2010 in respect of the Tarapur Power Reactor Fuel Reprocessing Plant

The Tarapur and Rajasthan Away From Reactors spent fuel storage pools would be made available for safeguards with appropriate phasing between 2006-2009.

American Safeguards

Consistent with the July 18, 2005 Joint Statement, the United States has also reaffirmed its assurance to create the necessary conditions for India to have assured and full access to fuel for its reactors. As part of its implementation of the July18, 2005 Joint statement the United States is committed to seeking agreement from the US Congress to amend its domestic laws and to work with friends and allies to adjust the practices of the Nuclear Suppliers Group to create the necessary conditions for India to obtain full access to the international fuel market, including reliable, uninterrupted and continual access to fuel supplies from firms in several nations.

To guard against any disruption or uncertainty of fuel supply:

- The United States is willing to incorporate assurances regarding fuel supply in the bilateral US- India agreement on peaceful uses of nuclear energy under section 123 of the US Atomic Energy Act, which would be submitted to the US Congress.
- The United States will join India in seeking to negotiate with the IAEA an Indian specific fuel supply agreement.

- The United States will support an Indian effort to develop a strategic reserve of nuclear fuel to guard against any disruption of supply over the lifetime of India's reactors.
- If despite these arrangements, a disruption of fuel supplies to India occurs, the United States and India would jointly convene a group of friendly supplier countries to include countries such as Russia, France and the United Kingdom to pursue such measures as would restore fuel supply to India.
- In the light of the above understandings with the United States, an India –specific safeguards agreements will be negotiated between India and the IAEA providing for safeguards to guard against withdrawal of safeguarded nuclear material from civilian use at any time as well as providing for corrective measures that India may take to ensure uninterrupted operation of its civilian nuclear reactors in the event of disruption of foreign fuel supplies. Taking this into account, India will place its civilian nuclear facilities under India-specific safeguards in perpetuity and negotiate an appropriate safeguards agreement to this end with the IAEA.

Indian Reaction to American Draft Bills in Congress

This epochal thaw and nuclear deal between India and US spurred a surge of debates in India from all walks of life centering on three things. "The first related to technology. Would the deal hamper India's indigenous three stage plans in the civil nuclear field by increasing India's import dependence and subjecting its reactors and research facilities to intrusive international inspections? The second set of concerns was linked to national security. To the extent to which nuclear weapons- rightly or wrongly- have come to occupy a central position in the country's security calculus, would the deal weaken or cap the Indian nuclear weapons capability? Finally, there were political and strategic concerns. What hidden costs did the US offer of nuclear cooperation bring with it? Was India running the risk of getting drawn into a web of alliances the US is building in Asia, thereby compromising its own strategic autonomy?"[14]

Coming to the implementation aspects of the nuclear deal when American President Bush introduced draft bills in Congress as a part of the agreement, the real intent of Washington came to the fore. A shift in goalposts was marked as far as India's obligations under the

July 2005 agreement are concerned. As found from the draft resolution submitted in the Senate, the changes made to the original agreement are problematic on four accounts: Whereas the first draft spoke of India filing a declaration with the IAEA regarding its civil nuclear facilities, the Senate Bill says the declaration must be 'complete' and include nuclear materials as well. The insistence on 'complete' is enigmatic since the word has been used internationally only in respect of the IAEA declarations filed by Iraq and Iran- countries accused of having a clandestine nuclear programme. Since the basis of the India-US agreement is the de facto acceptance of India's military nuclear programme, it is preposterous to speak of a complete declaration. This exposes American hidden intent to bring nuclear materials produced in the past by facilities going on the civilian list under the purview of safeguards.

Secondly, on safeguards, the original draft alludes to India accepting IAEA practices. The Senate amended this to add acceptance by India of IAEA standards and principles as well. As per the agreement, the assumption was that the country would sign an India specific safeguards agreement on the very acknowledgement of the fact that India is not a non- nuclear weapons state (NNWS) under the NPT. Thus, not all nuclear facilities would be safeguarded and those that were offered would be on the basis of IAEA practices whose precise contours would be the subject of negotiation with the agency. The new insistence on adherence to IAEA 'standards and principles' clearly speaks of American intention to bind India tightly into the stringent inspection regime presumably in line with the intensity meant for NNWS.

Thirdly, the original draft mentions of India making satisfactory progress towards implementing an Additional Protocol that would apply to India's civil nuclear programme. But the Senate deleted the reference to India's civil nuclear programme and replaced the reference to 'satisfactory progress with' substantial progresses. In the Senate Bill, the term 'Additional Protocol' has been defined as a " protocol... based on a Model Additional Protocol as set forth in IAEA Information Circular (INFCIRC) 540." But the Manmohan Singh Government has been giving the impression till now that it would sign only an additional protocol rather than the additional protocol. In a curious move the Senate by removing the reference to India's civil nuclear programme, has raised a question mark over Washington's willingness to allow India to invoke – as the US itself has done- national security exclusions to override the intrusiveness of INFCIRC540.

Fourthly, the July 2005 agreement insisted on India's support to international efforts to limit the spread of enrichment technology. The Senate has changed this to "supporting United States and international efforts". According to an analyst, " one of the efforts the US is considering to limit the spread of enrichment technology, for example, is to sanction or bomb Iran. Another is the Global Nuclear Energy Partnership (GNEP), in which President Bush told the Asia Society in February that India would be treated not as a fuel cycle state but as a recipient."[15] The question is whether India is going to be an accomplice in Washington's global strategy.

The July 2005 agreement clearly insists that US adjust its laws to enable full civil nuclear energy cooperation and trade with India. But what the Senate proposes is short of that full. It explicitly rules out the sale of enrichment related technologies to India. But the U.S. House of Representatives Bill 5682 passed in July says the U.S. President should seek to prevent the transfer to India of nuclear equipment, materials, or technology from other participating Governments in the Nuclear Suppliers Group or any other source. The draft Senate Bill 3709 also decrees that it shall be US policy to work with members of NSG individually and collectively to further restrict the transfers of such equipment and technologies, including to India. It also explicitly prohibits the sale to India of any equipment, materials or technology related to the enrichment of uranium, the reprocessing of spent fuel, or the production of heavy water. The Indian Prime Minister has assured in the Rajya Sabha on August 17, 2006 that any dilution to the July 18 agreement for full civil nuclear cooperation shall not be acceptable to India. In an interview to T.S. Subramaniam, Anil Kakodkar, Chairman, Atomic energy Commission says, India has always "been adopting the principle or philosophy of closed nuclear fuel cycle, which means that the spent fuel, after its use in the reactor, must be reprocessed, and uranium and plutonium recycled. This way, India has always had not only an environmentally benign radioactive waste management arrangement but also considerably enlarged energy that can be extracted from the given quantity of uranium. In the absence of closed nuclear fuel cycle, one ends up having to deal with the spent fuel as waste, which is not an acceptable solution even from a long-term credible waste management point of view. The spent fuel, if deposited in repositories for long term disposal, would over a period of time become a virtual plutonium mine once most of the radioactive components decay out. This can thus become a serious security issue over a long term. So India considers reprocessing is an extremely important part of full civil nuclear cooperation."[16]

In addition to these safeguards, the Senate Bill has incorporated another layer of supervision under the rubric of end- use monitoring. Any nuclear material, equipment and technology exported to India by the US would be subject to not just IAEA safeguards but an end use monitoring programme to be run by the US. The Senate is also insisting that this end use monitoring should involve US inspectors acquiring the same degree of access as IAEA inspectors in the event the IAEA inspectors fail to implement safeguards. Also by insisting that the President prepare an annual report on third country nuclear exports to India, which does not meet the standards applied to US exports, the attempt will be to force other suppliers and perhaps NSG as a whole to insist on similar conditions just in case India decides not to purchase equipment from American traders.

In an effort to circumscribe the nuclear strategic concerns of India, the US House of Representatives Bill of June 26, 20006 is that the President would have to submit periodic reports to the Congress beginning January 2007 and thereafter every year. The reports would have to describe in considerable details, India's nuclear related activities in the previous year and the extent to which progress in achieving US foreign policy objectives had been made. These objectives include achieving a moratorium on production of fissile material for nuclear explosive purposes by Pakistan, India and China; adherence to the FMCT to which both India and the US will be signatories; India's full participation in Proliferation Security Initiative and its interdiction principles; India's conforming to the Wassennaar Arrangements (conventional and dual use weapons) and the Australia Group Policies (chemical and biological weapons); and India's full compliance in the US policy on Iran's nuclear programme. Mandatory punitive action clause is also found in case India goes for the test. In the July agreement, India undertook to join in good faith the negotiations on a fissile material cut off treaty to be universal in nature. India supports now, as in the past, all measures towards universal nuclear disarmament, including an FMCT, but is opposed to a regional and segmented approach. India will accept only a multilaterally negotiated non-discriminatory and universally verifiable treaty negotiated at the Conference on Disarmament. American intention is unambiguously clear and designed to not only control India's nuclear capabilities, but also to ensure that Indian foreign policy is being outsourced to US and New Delhi's policy makers are answerable to the US Congress through the US president.[17] The whole efforts seem to aim at disciplining India so that it can never repeat a 1974 or 1998 or emerge as a full-fledged nuclear weapons state. Dangling before India the falsely contrived elation of being a great power with American help, Washington has been able to bring the NPT obligations in the backdoor, which India till date rejected as discriminatory. This led a nuclear scientist Homi Sethna to say that it would be better for India to renounce its nuclear weapons by signing the NPT than to subject itself to the deal's humiliating conditions.[18]

In the Senate resolution, there is a provision that any waiver on nuclear transfers to India shall cease to be effective if the President determines that India has detonated a nuclear explosive device after the date of the enactment of this Act. India has voluntarily agreed to a moratorium on tests in1998 and this position has been reiterated in the July agreement. It shows that India does not wish to embark on a future test unless the circumstances are compelling. However a totally new situation would arise if the US itself or China or Pakistan or some other country conducts a nuclear test. The disruption that would follow if the supply of nuclear fuel imported from the US or an NSG party were to be suspended for reactors that India may have imported would indeed be serious. The linkage of supplies to non-conduct of a test is understandable in the case of non-nuclear weapon states. If India as a de facto nuclear weapon state carries out a test under compulsions of ensuring its supreme national interest, there must be an opportunity or provision in the treaty of reviewing the situation between US and India prior to any suspension of supplies. In such a situation of India going for the test, the House resolution further stated that the president should seek to prevent the transfer to India of nuclear equipment, materials or technology from other governments in the NSG or from any other source. "This provision targets India unfairly even under unusual or exceptional circumstances when India is compelled to carry out a nuclear test, in response to actions of the US or some other nuclear weapon states carrying out a nuclear test."[19]

When India expands its civilian nuclear programme manifold, it expects to take advantage of global advances to gain the best economics and operating reliability. But what limits Indian options is the very fact that whatever input India may receive will be under IAEA safeguards. Hence the exclusion of these technologies not foreseen in the July 2005 and March 2006 agreements violates the spirit of these agreements and hamstrings India's options.

Another objection is regarding sequence of actions under the July 2005 agreement. India cannot agree to IAEA safeguards entering into force on the civilian segment of the Indian nuclear programme prior to the US lifting its restrictions and the NSG deciding on an exemption for India. All these three actions must take place simultaneously. It would be adverse to Indian interests if it accepts any US suggestion to de-link the three mutually interlocking actions.

In response to the moves in American Congress shifting goal posts in draft bills on nuclear issue, a group of Indian nuclear scientists headed by H.N Sethna put before the nation and government their views for serious consideration. In their considered views "India should continue to be able to hold on to her nuclear option as a strategic requirement in the real world that we live in, and in the ever changing complexity of the international political system. This means that we cannot accede to any restraint in perpetuity on our freedom of action. We have not done this for the last forty years after the Non-Proliferation Treaty came into being." In the face of stiff opposition from major powers after 1974 what India has been able to achieve building up capability in many sensitive technological areas, need not and should not be subject to external control. Safeguards should be strictly restricted to those facilities and materials imported from outside sources. Further, they are of the opinion that the Indo-US deal in the form approved by the US House of Representatives clearly infringes on India's independence for carrying out indigenous research and development in nuclear science and technology. Research and technology developments are the sovereign rights of any nation more particularly when these concern strategic national security and energy sufficiency. To satisfy an external power should not be at the cost of India's sovereign right and national interest.[20] What is deciphered from the Congressional discussion on President Bush's draft proposal is that India can secure both fuels and reactors only on condition that it roll back its nuclear weapon program and adopt full scope safeguards, which would mean making all current and future nuclear facilities subject to International Atomic Energy Agency (IAEA) inspection. It is like hoodwinking India into signing the NPT. India is unlikely to accept such a stance, which it has been resisting for many decades. In the context of the new partnership and American promise to India of its ascension to great power status, the challenge before the US will be to craft a solution that allows India access to peaceful nuclear technology even while it retains its nuclear weapon option as and when it feels necessary to go for explosion in a changed circumstance. Since history stands as a testimony to India always keeping its words unless forced to renege, India's unilateral moratorium on further nuclear testing should be construed as satisfying the NPT obligations.

Problems with US Strategy

The coping stone of a strategic partnership was not supposedly built on an emotional bond born of the euphoria over the fact that these two countries are the two largest and great democracies, but a sheer strategic dexterity employed by the advocates of the new US policy to build up India as a bulwark against the growing militancy of China. India is too vital, vast and independent mindset country for the United States to regard India as an accomplice against another country. To belief that India will play the role of an American surrogate is to put aside the past record of India's penchant for an independent foreign policy in the international realm, and will certainly come to a naught as and when it is asked to do so. If this were the strategic calculation of Washington to flesh out India militarily as counter to China, problems will arise when India inevitably chooses not to accede to a particular US preference. Indian outright rejection of American request to send Its troops to Iraq is not unknown. Recently, Manmohan Singh government's voting against its long time friend Iran on nuclear issue at the behest of America drew countrywide diatribes and later on he was forced to soften his stand. India also expressed its strong opposition to addition of a clause in the draft proposal in American Congress asking it to support American interest in Iran on nuclear issue. For example, in a contingency of war with China over Taiwan, it is natural on the part of America to seek Indian military help. It is very unlikely that Indian Parliament and people will support Indian direct military involvement in a US- Taiwan war against China. India's preference for multilateralism in place of Washington's unipolarism has enabled it to establish close relationship with Russia, China and other countries. India wants to be closer to America but not at the cost of China, Russia and other countries. The recent attempt to form a triad among India, China, and Russia as a counter to American hegemony is not to be sidelined. India prefers to reap the dividends of good relation with both America and China as a manifestation of its cold war period non- aligned posture. India's strategic interests consist more in forging close relation with China than kowtowing American line to the discomfiture of the former. These interests are more likely to be satisfied if India is close to America but not to jump into its embrace. But the American strategists are so much preoccupied with the "contain China strategy" that they have preferred to overlook India's long cherished non-aligned and autonomous political culture. "New Delhi is moving steadily to improve ties with Beijing along with Washington. India has not emerged from the shackles of colonial rule or the shadows of the cold war to do Washington's bidding against China. If this is Bush administration's game, it has misestimated its new strategic partner and chosen the wrong centerpiece for the partnership"[21].

Both India and America's strategic interests find a convergence in nuclear issue. While putting a premium on weapon sales, co-production, and military to military cooperation, there is little that would significantly increase India's economic prospects.[22] It is observed by many that economic competition, rather than military, is the most pressing political- economic challenge China poses to the United States, India and other developing countries. Economic build up of India in terms of energy generation, distribution and efficiency could have been the main focus in American strategy. Much more attention and assistance should be channeled to quicker and more efficient means to meet India's energy needs. But ironically, the United States is throwing spanners into a highly cost-effective way to get natural gas to India, via an overland pipeline from Iran through Pakistan. It is a fact that 60 per cent of Indians depend on agriculture for their livelihood. The most pragmatic course open to America is to strengthen India's development and therefore its long-term power. America could have devised trade rules and assistance programme to foster rural development and creation of social infrastructure to protect poor people, as they move off the land into urban economies that currently lack jobs, housing, and other resources to sustain them. Electricity grids do not reach many rural Indians and the best way to provide electricity to them will be through off-grid, distributed technologies. "But rural Indian interests lack the well paid and powerful lobbyists that defense contractors and nuclear industrial interests have mobilized in Washington and New Delhi to put military sales and nuclear cooperation at the top of the U.S.-India agenda."[23] But American stance in WTO, agricultural subsidy, pricing and trade regulation suggests that it is not willing to make developing countries self-sufficient in agriculture and food products as this will lessen their greater dependency on food aid and grain staples from the US and other western countries. Agricultural deficit and impoverishment in developing countries will redound to greater American economy, as these countries are dependent for food import on western countries and America.

All these years India stood firm on nuclear issue and strongly resisted all pressures put on it by America to sign the NPT. Deification of India's stand reached its apogee when it conducted nuclear weapons test in 1998 irking America and other European countries. Subsequently, India has deftly improved its relation not only with The United States, but also with China and Europe. Criticizing American double standard and policy of discrimination, India put forth its case more strongly for removal of all nuclear fuel and technology restrictions and full recognition as a nuclear weapon state. But they have been able to fulfill many of their interests by standing firm all these years. What led to such a reversal of stand in both US and India on nuclear issue? India's reversed preoccupation with winning nuclear energy cooperation resembles the earlier US obsession on non-proliferation. It seems as if America came forward to accommodate Indian interests by subordinating U.S non-proliferation interests. But the subsequent steps and the draft bills presented in the American Congress as discussed above, prove otherwise. The Bush administration has not made a strong case that U.S. interests would suffer significantly if Washington did not accommodate all of India's nuclear demands and end all non-proliferation restrictions on nuclear commerce with India. " It is strange and unexplained why an administration known for being exceptionally unaccommodating to most countries in most international discussions- climate change, Iraq, International Criminal Court, nuclear test ban and others- finds it wise to completely accommodate India in this case."[24] If end to restrictions on nuclear cooperation, and ascension to nuclear power status is the only motive spurring India to act in concert with US and establish friendship with it, then the foundation of such friendship is not well grounded as is American Congress digressing away from the mainstream of July 18 agreement signed between President Bush and Indian Prime minister Manmohan Singh. Strong opposition in India to such move by American Congress has led Singh to declare that in case America reneges on the terms of the July agreement, India is free to decide its course to be charted, on and draw its own conclusion. As per the agreement, after the nuclear cooperation deal with the U.S is signed, it will ensure complete and irreversible lifting of restrictions imposed on India during the past three decades. It will also take care of all aspects of nuclear cooperation in the field of energy, nuclear fuel, reactors, and reprocessing of spent fuel. While replying to a debate in Indian Rajya Sabha, Prime Minister Manmohan Singh stated candidly " autonomy of research and development activity, fast breeder reactors and thorium will remain unaffected. India will be free to build its own strategic nuclear fuel reserves as well." He also made it clear to Washington that " India would oppose any move to impose annual certification by the US President for implementation of the deal. If the U.S. legislation or the Nuclear Suppliers Group impose extraneous conditions, the government will draw the necessary conclusion consistent with my commitments to the Parliament and the people."[25]

A view doing the round giving a strong broadside to Indo-US nuclear deal is that American long adduced assessment that nuclear proliferation is the gravest threat to U.S. and international security, is falsified. If nuclear states fail in their commitment to enforce rules preventing such proliferation, the threat will grow. It has never been acknowledged in US that China poses a grave threat to the United States. If policies to contain China by bolstering India's nuclear power results in emasculation of non-proliferation regime, US security, on balance, will be in jeopardy. " A nuclear deal with India that sets precedents for China to seek similar rule changes or exemptions in the future could undermine U.S. efforts to contain Chinese power."[26] To help a party initially grow into unenviable military prowess even to the point of being challenged, and then try to contain it has been a recurrent phenomenon in American foreign policy. After Kissinger breaking the ice with China, America subsequently tried to strengthen China through establishing economic, trade and military relation with it. During cold war it was a strategic necessity for America to see China growing into a militarily mighty power as a bulwark against former Soviet Union. With the eclipse of communism and disintegration of Soviet Union, China once darling to America became its bete noire and competitor. Caving in to industrialists' pressure at home front, as documents show, American Presidents seemed to have given primacy to trade and economic interests over national security; otherwise they would not have feigned ignorance over China's clandestine role in proliferating nuclear power to countries like Pakistan. Adding to its intriguing role, President Clinton helped China grow into a mighty nuclear genie. Newly declassified 'Chinagate' documents reveal that in1996 under pressure from Hughes Aerospace CEO C. Michael Armstrong, US President Bill Clinton gave a waiver and personally approved the export to China of radiation- hardened specialized chip sets for a Chinese meteorological satellite. The special chips are necessary for advanced space technology and are critical for nuclear warfare in advanced nuclear warheads. "In all likelihood we will be glowing in the dark before we discover the true extent of Clinton decade of betrayal, stated Rick Fisher, Asian Security Fellow at the Center for Security Policy... If it was indeed intended for a new PRC weather satellite, then it is possible that it was used for their new polar orbit weather satellites. This is significant because the Chinese themselves acknowledge that their polar orbit weather satellites directly contribute to their long-range missile targeting capability. This becomes even more important for their new smaller but more accurate warheads, used on their new DF-31, DF-31A, DF5 Mod2 and JL-2 missiles. If they encounter significant weather, warhead accuracy degrades, reducing their utility", stated Fisher."[27]

This shows the extent to which the Clinton White House placed trade, specifically with China, above national security. Even more telling, the transfer took place during an investigation of Chinese espionage into missing US radiation-hardened satellite chips. Because of the greed of Hughes/Armstrong, the Commerce Department allowed the Chinese army to obtain a vast array of advanced missile, satellite and space technology. Several years ago, while the US space shuttle was grounded, the US space technology illegally sold to the Chinese army was used on China's first manned spacecraft.[28]

Further, as stated by Armstrong as Chair of the President's Export Council in1997, the US nuclear industry had to sell 100 nuclear reactors to China or the US nuclear industry and US Navy's nuclear programme would be threatened. From the 1970s through the Clinton era, China apparently got the entire classified portfolio on design and manufacturing of all US major nukes. Secretary of Defense William Cohen, commented on the transfer of nuclear weapons technology from Lawrence Livermore national laboratory to China: " They were not exactly spying in my view. We gave it to them."[29] According to Moret, the 'Nuclear Potlatch' legacy that President Clinton left for the twenty-first century is a modern Chinese army equipped for global nuclear war."[30] Further, Pakistan would not have acquired nuclear weapons without significant assistance from China, including provision of a tested nuclear-weapons design, which A.Q Khan then redistributed to Libya and other countries. Similarities between Pakistani and US weapons show that there was a nexus between CIA, US policy makers and China. A.Q Khan was used as a cover and acting as their front man secretly running a black market network for distributing nuclear materials to countries like Iran, North Korea, Libya, and Malaysia.[31] It was the considered view of the American policy makers that despite an international non-proliferation regime, China passed on nuclear technology to Pakistan clandestinely from America through A.Q. Khan. Rules and norms of NPT have not become effective to prevent nuclear technology from being transferred to a non-nuclear state. It is not the rules and norms that matter. Nuclear weapons per se are not a problem. The question is who possesses and uses them. If these nuclear weapons or nuclear capability fall in the hands of rogue states or terrorists, the norms and rules of NPT remain hapless and ineffective. Being signatory to NPT, both US and China did not show any qualms for their complicity in Pakistan becoming a nuclear power. By violating the rules and norms of NPT regime China instead of being chided in the international community, remained at the core of American economic and trade policy and received as mentioned above, nukes and chips for missiles. Where as India being a nuclear power and not recognized under the NPT was cast into a netherworld where it is denied the right to engage in the open technical and commercial collaboration on the peaceful uses of nuclear energy available to all other legitimate nuclear power states. That's why India was always critical of this 'double standard mode' and lack of morality and equity in foreign policy behaviour of nuclear power states. India, a strong opponent of NPT has behaved responsibly and put unilateral moratorium on its nuclear testing having the track record of its avowed adherence to peaceful use of nuclear energy and not having secretly passed on this nuclear know how to any other country. If Pakistan having all the required qualifications to be called a rogue state because of its complicity in terrorism, was entitled to be a nuclear power insidiously with the active connivance of China in contravention of the rules of NPT regime, why India being a responsible and democratic power cannot be entitled to have all restrictions on the supply of nuclear materials and technology lifted through friendship? A powerful India can stand in good stead to America in the latter's policy of containing China in its strive and competition for geopolitical supremacy with United States. Americans felt nuclear non- proliferation through a policy of restrictions, prevention and denial exacts a price that outweighs the benefits one would reap through a policy of negation of these restrictions and courting partnership. An India remaining outside of the orbit of NPT regime and always taking umbrage at what being meted out to it unjustly by the US, could prove during these years more robust, independent and yet responsible than it would be once it is brought under the strategic noose of America through charting a nuclear deal. India in US led orbit can be more malleably subject to the gravitational pull of American power than it is forced out. This might be one of the reasons spurring President Bush and his advisors to prefer a contravention and modification of the stringency of existing NPT regime while carving out a new path of partnership with India.

India has been among the chief targets of a worldwide technological denial regime designed to prevent states from acquiring various capabilities relating to the production of both nuclear power and nuclear weaponry. Not flummoxed by these constraints India has been able to prove its mettle by developing indigenous capability on both counts over these years. But these are insufficient to meet the national needs. In 1954, India's Atomic energy Commission declared that nuclear plants would provide 8,000 megawatts of electricity by 1980-81. Yet by 1970, only 420 megawatts of electricity were coming from nuclear plants, and that from the two US supplied reactors at Tarapur. In1971, Vikram Sarabhai, the Chairman of the Atomic Energy Commission sought to bring Indian nuclear planning down to earth and scaled back projections saying that by 1980-81, India would be producing 2700 megawatts of electricity from nuclear plants. Thirty-five years later Indian nuclear plants are producing roughly 2,700 megawatts of electricity. The only way to build and operate new plants would be rely to on imported fuel that existing nonproliferation rules prevent from being exported to India. Where nuclear power is concerned, questions about the safety of indigenous reactors continue to perplex the Indian Department of Atomic Energy. To meet the country's vast future electricity demands India will need many new, reliable, large reactors that will meet the safety standards taken for granted in developed states. Another relevant fact worth mentioning is that India though a vast country has been poorly endowed with natural uranium. As estimated, its modest reserve of about 70,000 metric tons can produce no more than approximately 420 gigwatt-years of electric power, if used in the pressurized heavy water reactors (PHWRs) currently operating or under construction. India's natural uranium deficiency has resulted in a commitment to an ambitious, technically challenging three stage programme designed to exploit the country's thorium reserve, which is estimated at 290,000 metric tons, the second largest in the world.

In stage 1 of this programme, a series of indigenously constructed PHWRs fuelled by scarce natural uranium have been used since the late 1960s to generate electricity and produce plutonium as a by-product. The stage 2 is concerned with constructing fast neutron reactors that will burn the plutonium produced in the stage 1 PHWRs in order to breed a uranium isotope, U-233 from the thorium blanket surrounding the plutonium in the fuel pellet. A major step toward stage 2 capability was taken when the 13- megawatt (electric) fast breeder test reactor (FBTR) at Kalpakkam, which uses uranium-plutonium carbide fuel, attained criticality in 1985. Another milestone was attained in 1997, when electricity from the Kalpakkam FBTR flowed into the Southern Indian power grid. This achievement, notwithstanding, India still does not have any fast breeder reactors operating on a commercial scale. This implies that India is still dearth of the requisite of quantities of U-233 required for achieving energy independence in the manner envisaged in the three-stage plan. Consequently, the 54,000 gigawatt (electric)- years of power potential believed to exist in stage 2 of the programme remains more or less notional today. Stage 3, which is many decades away from today will involve construction of advanced heavy water reactors (AHWRs) that will use the U-233 produced in stage 2, encased in a thorium blanket, to generate about two-thirds of these reactors' output from the thorium casing itself. Since fast neutron reactors are designed to produce more plutonium than they consume, and since India has enormous reserves of thorium, the stage 3 facilities currently being planned could in principle produce 358,000 gigawatt (electric)- years of electricity in total, sufficient to meet the country's energy requirements during this century and beyond.

Embedded in this grandiose scheme are technical and economic problems. Vast infrastructure needed to enable New Delhi to produce electricity in this fashion involves enormous monetary wherewithal, and it is yet to be clear whether India has mastered the techniques to separate U-233 on a commercial scale or handle the waste management issues associated with this process to an extent sufficient to guarantee the success of the three stage master plan. The scheme is further plagued by the high cost and technical complications of fuel fabrications due partly to the high radioactivity of U-233, which is invariably prone to contamination with traces of U-232. It is also beset by the difficulties of recycling thorium due to the presence of highly radioactiveTh-228 and the various technical risks associated with reprocessing in thorium- based fuel cycles, which have not yet been satisfactorily resolved. The World Nuclear Association dedicated to the promotion of nuclear energy is of the view that " much development work is still required before the thorium fuel cycle can be commercialized, and the effort required seems unlikely while (or where) abundant uranium is available."[32] These problems plaguing this grandiose scheme are likely to preoccupy India for many years to come. The critical shortage of natural uranium hamstringing India's efforts in this direction, which if remains unresolved could bring the operation of many stage 1 PHWRs to a gradual halt. This would seriously affect India's electricity production with all deleterious effects on Indian economy. Coming close on the heels of natural uranium scarcity what affects India worst is its long cherished aspiration for secured energy independence in the coming decades through this three-stage process. This might be the sole consideration behind Indian policy makers jumping immediately into the American nuclear bandwagon. According to Ashley J Tellis

> "Therefore, if India can be assured stable supplies of natural uranium over the long term, it is possible that national decision makers will not feel compelled to invest in the more risky stage 2 component of its nuclear energy

programme on any but an experimental scale. Alternatively, if India is provided unconstrained access to various types of advanced reactors together with their appropriate fuels, it is likely that new Delhi will postpone implementation of the three stage cycle, a program that would, incidentally, leave the country awash with more plutonium than it could ever use either for energy production or nuclear weaponry."[33]

Of course, India like all other states has the sovereign right to pursue their goal as independently as they can into the long distant future. In the absence of influx of supplies of uranium if India follows the above risky and dubious path, its large-scale separation of plutonium from spent fuel poses proliferation risks. The promise of steady supply of natural uranium and low enriched uranium fuel as outlined in 18 July agreements could serve this purpose.

Flaws with the Nuclear Deal

To cease production of highly enriched uranium and plutonium for weapon purposes has been the most important practice of five acknowledged nuclear weapons states from a nonproliferation point of view. Except China, all other nuclear states have a de facto moratorium on such production. It is said, India and the united States contravenes the basic principle and promise of their own agreement by failing to exact an Indian commitment to join the moratorium. As a responsible nuclear power, India has already declared unilateral moratorium on weapon production, keeping the option open into the future if and when the situation changes or other neighboring nuclear states produce weapons to its greater security threats. The difference between unilateral and common moratorium lies in the fact that into India's calculation has entered an element of context and strategic interest with reference to unarticulated and nebulous nuclear policy of both China and Pakistan. India is opposed to converting it into a bilateral legality.

Another criticism is that in the joint statement between President Bush and Prime Minister Singh, India states its readiness to assume the same responsibilities and practices and acquire the same benefits and advantages as other leading countries with advanced nuclear technology, such as the United States. The five recognized nuclear weapons states have all unilaterally ceased producing fissile materials for weapons purposes. This virtually propels them towards the goal of nuclear disarmament. Progress towards this goal is politically important to maintaining the global nonproliferation regime. " The U.S, - India joint statement hides India's divergence from the responsibilities and practices it has committed to uphold. Instead of ceasing production of bomb materials, the statement pledges India's cooperation in working with the United States for the conclusion of a multilateral Fissile material Cut Off Treaty. It is no secret that the Bush administration has an approach to such a treaty that eschews verification measures, which others do not accept. Offering the false promise of a treaty, as opposed to a moratorium, is so cynical that even administration officials laugh at it privately."[34] Hurling allegations like this at India for being insulated from nonproliferation obligations in the treaty is to fly in the face of the revelation of documents showing US- China complicity in nuclear and fissile material deal during Clinton Presidency. Further, asking India to sign the Comprehensive Test Ban Treaty as a part of fulfillment of the joint statement that India will assume the same responsibilities and practices as the established nuclear-weapon states should mean, which both US and China have disdained it, is like asking a cat to shed its claws whereas, the tigers and lions prefer to have theirs intact.

International politics has been a witness to the yawning chasm between what is agreed to and pronounced in treaties, and the practices that follow them. While strict adherence to NPT is demanded from both the five nuclear powers as well as the non nuclear powers, it is the five nuclear powers, which are first to violate the rules. It is US, which helped some non- nuclear powers like Iran, Pakistan, North Korea, Libya and Malaysia to acquire nuclear capability in glare infringement of NPT norms. " By illegally providing nuclear components arranged by the White House and Pentagon through middleman Asher Karni, the Bush administration and pro-Israeli neocons hoped to accelerate Iran's nuclear programme by ten years."[35] The Korea Times reported that the US military has 2.7 million depleted uranium bombs in South Korea, It is understandable why North Korea wants nuclear weapons.[36] After impregnating them with nuclear weapons, the US pontificating both Iran and North Korea in his unipolar stentorian command to stop producing nuclear weapons and open their facilities for international inspection seems to be riding on the crest of hypocrisy. From a nonproliferation critique point of view, the five acknowledged nuclear powers, non nuclear powers and developing countries have changed the rules of NPT regime. Thus, invoking "the sanctity of NPT related rules to deny nuclear technology and materials to a developing country - India - while doing little to defend the sanctity of disarmament commitments by the most powerful states, seems the height of hypocrisy".[37] It is said a nuclear deal with India could set precedents for China to seek similar exemptions or changes supporting its client states. It can use its positions in the UN Security Council and the Nuclear Suppliers Group to block Washington's attempt to change the rules only as the United States prefers and instead to open ways for China to sell nuclear favours to its friends. This argument seems preposterous, as China's complicity in making Pakistan and other states nuclear in contravention of NPT regime is well known. So it lacks the moral strength to contest American pro-India stand. In view of India's justifiable pretensions to have NPT regime modified enabling it to receive nuclear technology and uranium from US and other NSGs, the American Congress should try to adhere to the terms of July 18 agreement without putting in extraneous conditions.

To much of the world, especially non-nuclear weapon states and developing countries, the five acknowledged nuclear- weapon states have changed the rules of nonproliferation regime according to their convenience, and have not demonstrated any alacrity for elimination of nuclear weapons or disarmament as they promised in 2000. The Bush administration's disavowal of the Thirteen Steps that were negotiated by NPT parties in 2000 as benchmarks of the nuclear weapon states' fulfillment of their Article VI obligations comes as a testament to nuclear disarmament process receiving short shrift from them. The question is if the nuclear weapons states are not going to comply with their Article VI obligations, then why should non-nuclear states be subject to technology denial rules? Much of the world perceives this NPT regime as a form of 'nuclear apartheid', the term Indian leaders used in 1967. This is the reason, why much of the world is silent about the nuclear deal between India and America. They have seen this as an issue between rich and poor, technological haves and haves not. But what hurts India is that the rules applicable to nuclear weapons states are made inapplicable to it.

This is no where seen so prominently than in the central plank-that India would "assume the same responsibilities and practices and acquire the same benefits and advantages as other leading countries with advanced nuclear technology, such as the United States". It now insists that India cannot be allowed to pursue the same "practices" or enjoy the same "benefits" as the other nuclear powers do. As nuclear powers do, India will choose which of its nuclear facilities to designate as civilian and therefore to move under international safeguards and monitoring. The distinction between civilian and military facilities follows the practice of the US and other nuclear weapons states. It is understood that India will designate some facilities as military and that these will remain free of international safeguards or monitoring. It will have the same option that the recognized nuclear weapons states do of removing facilities from international safeguards if it wishes to, or of withdrawing nuclear material, such as plutonium, from safeguards if national security reasons are invoked. But the flaw lies in the stipulations that America is trying to incorporate in the deal divagating from the standards and practices of nuclear-weapons states. On the issue of breeder programme, when India negotiates facility-specific safeguards agreements and an Additional Protocol with the IAEA, the U.S. will insist on legally binding obligations for New Delhi that the other nuclear weapons states have not accepted. India will not be permitted to make the sweeping national security exemptions and exclusions that the other nuclear powers have built into their Additional Protocol with the IAEA. Further more, what curtails India's independence is the role of IAEA inspectors in India, which will neither limited nor token in nature. Rather, they will have the same lack of restrictions that they enjoy in non-nuclear states. U.S. Undersecretary of State Robert G. Joseph has testified that a "voluntary offer" safeguards agreement of the kind the U.S. has with the International Atomic Energy Agency (IAEA) will not be acceptable from India. The five acknowledged nuclear powers, under voluntary accords, offer nuclear materials and facilities for IAEA inspections in name only. The IAEA, in return, carries out token inspections or, often no inspections "to conserve resources." Out of 915 nuclear facilities the IAEA inspects world wide only 11 are in these nuclear weapons states. Not applicable to such nuclear weapon states, the US officials lay down another stipulation: IAEA inspections on Indian facilities "must be applied in perpetuity".[38]

Is it in the best interests of India to condescend to this stipulation? On July 29, the Indian Prime Minister assured Parliament that " predicated on our obtaining the same benefits and advantages as other nuclear powers is the understanding that we shall undertake the same responsibilities and obligations as such countries including the United States. Concomitantly, we expect the same rights and benefits". But Washington disowned this view saying India will not get equal rights and benefits.

What is military and civilian is to be decided by India as per the principles and standard practices of nuclear weapons states. While the deal merely states that India will begin "identifying and separating civilian and military nuclear facilities and programmes in a phased manner", Washington has attached specific conditionality- that such a separation plan be "credible", "transparent" and "defensible". This implies America is the sole judge to decide whether India acts in conformity with these stipulations.

In contravention of the rules and norms of the nuclear weapons states relating to separation of civilian and military, US insists that India make a watertight separation plan which it can monitor everlastingly. But it flies in the face of the fact that the other nuclear powers have not done the same, because in a majority of cases there is not even a semblance of civil-military segregation. In fact, as stated in preceding chapter, America produces tritium for its nuclear weapons in the civilian reactors of the Tennessee Valley Authority and conducts commercially marketable research in its weapon laboratory, a right it denies to India. When Indian Prime Minister stated in the Parliament that "it will be an autonomous Indian decision as to what is 'civilian' and what is 'military', Nobody outside will tell us what is civilian and what is military." US Ambassador, David Mulford insists that India open the great majority of its facilities to IAEA inspections.[39]

American real intention will be clearer after the bills came out of American Congress. To what extent the two Houses of American Congress have addressed New Delhi's concerns and glued to President Bush's promises made in July 18 agreement, can be a measure of whether Washington is at all serious to cement its strategic partnership with New Delhi on a permanent edifice. However, American unwillingness to baptize India into the rank and file of the five established nuclear weapons states with all concomitant benefits and privileges, and consequent upon this, the question of whether India will be ever willing to accept this much decried demotion lying low, will remain a stumbling block in the building up of this newly conceived strategic partnership between the two countries. Ashley J. Tellis outlined five illustrative options for Washington's consideration as a step to put Indo- US relation on an even keel on the vital issue of nuclear energy[40]

1. inviting India to participate in international research and development efforts pertaining to peaceful uses of nuclear energy.
2. offering India access to nuclear safety technologies for its reactors.
3. supplying India with various items for use within the steam cycle in safeguarded reactors
4. permitting India to purchase safeguarded nuclear fuel from the international market
5. permitting India to purchase nuclear technology including nuclear reactors from Nuclear Suppliers Group members or directly from U.S. suppliers.

So far as the first proposal relating to international research and development efforts is concerned, the three most important initiatives are Generation IV, ITER, and the Radkowsky Thorium Fuel (RTF) programme. Ten countries working together under the auspices of the U.S. Department of Energy's Office of Nuclear Energy, Science, and Technology to examine concepts that could lead to future reactor designs that are economical, safe, proliferation resistant and minimally waste producing, constitute the Generation IV. The ITER is comprised of six countries experimenting under the aegis of the IAEA with a hydrogen plasma torus, the goal being to design and build the nuclear fusion power plants needed to meet tomorrow's energy requirements. Several Russian research institutes, the Massachusetts Institute of Technology, and Ben Gurion University in Israel are working together under the direction of Brookhaven national Laboratory to develop proliferation resistant nuclear fuel cycles using thorium, which is plenty in India. Though India expresses its willingness to participate, America is avoiding on the ground that any access to civilian nuclear technology either tangible or intangible by a non-nuclear weapon state requires acquiescing in full scope safeguards under the NSG. New Delhi's integration into civilian nuclear energy research and development programmes depends on "a strong presidential commitment to making important policy changes that move the United States away from its currently rigid prohibitions against intangible transfers, as well as a willingness to pursue the relevant consultations within the NSG to minimize erosion of the international nonproliferation regime."[4]

The second option offering access to reactor safety technology relates to granting more intimate access to the technology used in nuclear reactors. These are presently on offer for India's safeguarded plants but are for the most part trivial and well within New Delhi's capacity to produce or procure indigenously. A nuclear reactor is a complex system of systems in which every component makes some contribution to safe operation. By this yardstick, meaningful safety cooperation would require that India get access to the entire range of reactor components. Adherence to this approach means abrogation of both the domestic law and international obligations of the United States. As the Carnegie Endowment recommended, " the Nuclear Suppliers Group should remove restrictions on transferring equipment that these states [meaning India, Pakistan, and Israel] need in order to bring safeguarded nuclear plants up to the highest safety standards. This should include trigger list technology if necessary."[42] Transfer of such safety related dual use technologies regulated by the Department of Commerce under NP1 and NP2 requires under NSG guidelines, full scope safeguards, which India will hardly comply with. America can transfer these to safeguarded reactors on the condition that these remain under IAEA safeguards, cannot be used for nuclear weapon programmes, and transferred to any country without the prior consent of the United States. Since India is unwilling to put all its reactors under safeguards for merely securing safety technologies, the formidable challenge waiting in the face of America is how to evolve a strategy that integrates New Delhi into its designed world nuclear order without compromising India's position.

The third option aimed at reinforcing Indo-U.S. Cooperation in the realm of civilian nuclear energy entitles India to receive various items restricted to the steam cycle in the present and future safeguarded Indian reactors. But Washington rejected this option because of strong objections from State Department's Non-Proliferation Bureau, which adopted a very conservative assessment of the presumed impact on US nonproliferation policy globally.

The fourth and fifth options face stiff opposition, because current U.S. law and international regime obligations permit such transactions only with legitimate nuclear weapons states those who have detonated nuclear device prior to 1967, or with non nuclear weapon states that will accept full scope safeguards. Since India is averse to accepting full scope safeguards what so ever, America finds it Herculean to entitle India to receive all supplies of nuclear fuel and imported nuclear reactors without devising ways to formally integrate India into the existing nonproliferation order.

On the negative side, nuclear deal with India will to a greater degree ensure dilution of India's non-aligned policy and its military and strategic independence will be lost to America by its constant interference. India's alignment with U.S. even if nominal, could provide the other countries scope to denigrate India as a U.S. lackey. This new found role under U.S aegis will delimit India's ability to intervene as an international player, especially in areas of non-proliferation. "Not only will it be seen as a U.S. ally, India will also serve as a shining example of to what some countries would aspire, establishing a nuclear weapons program outside of the NPT and later receiving acceptance and rewards. India may also wind up fulfilling the dire predictions of Indian analysts that see the United States attempting to dominate the Indian ocean."[43] Further, if the nuclear cooperation between the two assumes an unmistakable sign of a strategic unity, any evidence of U.S. sprucing up India as a counter weight to balance China or Pakistan could endanger India's own security through a regional arms race.

Hailed in America as historic and the Liberation Act 2006 for India, finally the Henry J. Hyde, United States- India Peaceful Atomic Energy Cooperation Act of 2006 was passed and sealed by the American President Bush. Many in India feel that there is little to reason to cheer[44]. India is caught in a totally indefensible position if its hands were tied under the Indo-U. S. deal, which would be the case if India had installed imported reactors using imported nuclear fuel. Were India to conduct a nuclear test in future in case other neighbouring countries pursue nuclear tests, the suspension of all cooperation will take place. It is not lost to India that the United States itself is indulged on the design of a "Reliable Replacement Weapon" (RRW) to modernize its nuclear arsenal and may indeed carry out a test in future, if it considers it necessary. China then may test its own improved design. Pakistan. too may carry out a test for its own reasons. This assumes important as the Senate in the past had already rejected the Comprehensive Test Ban Treaty. What is unacceptable to India is the very fact that

India is denied the option to test its design for all time to come, even when circumstances beyond its control require it to do so.

The uncertainty in fuel supply still remains to embarrass Indians. So far it was assured to India by America that it could maintain adequate stockpiles of nuclear fuel to tide over any possible disruptions in supply. America also agreed to work with other nuclear suppliers to enable India to secure nuclear fuel so that its nuclear power stations could continue to operate. To the great discomfiture of New Delhi, the Hyde Act has removed this protection calling upon the U.S. administration to work with the Nuclear Suppliers Group to ensure that India cannot get supplies of nuclear fuel if, for reasons contained in the Act, the U.S. is required to suspend supplies to India.

Full civilian nuclear energy cooperation namely enrichment of uranium and reprocessing of spent fuel was agreed to in July 2005. During the adoption of the Hyde Bill, U.S. legislators have argued that the U.S. Atomic Energy Act of 1954 specifically forbids exports of these technologies, as also heavy water production technology to other countries. Reprocessing of spent fuel to separate plutonium is extremely important in the Indian context. The Indian nuclear fuel cycle is crucially dependent on the use of Fast Breeder Reactors in the second stage and of thorium based systems in the third stage. Separation of plutonium is essential for the eventual use of thorium as a nuclear fuel. For this, the processing design remains crucially an India activity. But the denial of access to certain equipment or materials required by India, even when these activities are under IAEA safeguards, would be highly unreasonable. Though some exceptions are provided in the Hyde Act to the embargo on enrichment and reprocessing technologies. They are in respect of a multinational facility approved by the IAEA or bilateral or multinational programme to develop a proliferation-resistant fuel cycle. But this is uncertain and inconclusive on the "International Fuel Cycle Evaluation" scheme constituted in 1980s at the insistence of U.S. as there was no convergence among the countries on their nuclear policies.

India has always given primacy to universal nuclear disarmament. But the Hyde Act calls for achieving a moratorium on the production of fissile material for explosive purposes by India, China, and Pakistan. The Act outlines that the U.S. shall seek to halt the increase of nuclear weapon arsenals in South Asia and to promote their reductiou and eventual elimination. Opposed always to proposals for regional nuclear disarmamettt, India will lose all leverage to pursue the goal of universal nuclear disarmament and will be tied to elimination of nuclear weapons in South Asia

It was agreed that the approval of U.S. Congress and removal of restrictions on nuclear trade with India would take place simultaneously with NSG clearance to make exemptions in favour of India and with India placing facilities designated as civilian by India under IAEA safeguards. The present Act requires India to have concluded "all legal steps prior signature by the parties of an agreement requiring the application of IAEA safeguards in perpetuity..."; and also that" India and IAEA are making substantial progress toward concluding an Additional Protocol" among other conditions.

It is further clearly stated that the " Additional Protocol" is to be based on the Model Additional protocol of the IAEA applicable to non- nuclear weapon states, which is highly intrusive. The President of America is to satisfy himself that India is working actively on an early conclusion of the FMCT; that India is supporting the U.S. in preventing the spread of enrichment and reprocessing technologies; and that India adheres to the MTCR and NSG guidelines without actually being invited to be a member of these bodies. These actions India is obliged to take are not consistent with what a strategic partner should be taking[45].

In an effort to allay the Indian concerns about the several aspects of the nuclear Act[46], President Bush declared that he would not be bound by some of the law's provisions. About the directions to limit the amount of nuclear fuel India could store, and to seek to prevent the transfer to India of nuclear material by other countries in the event the U.S. cuts off supplies, the President clarified that given the constitution's commitment to the presidency of the authority to conduct the foreign affairs, the executive branch shall construe such policy statements as advisory.

Regarding the issue of denial of enrichment and reprocessing related equipment to India, built into Section 1 04 (d) (2) of the Act, President clarified that this restriction could give rise to a potential conflict between U.S. domestic law and nuclear Suppliers' Group guidelines, and raise a constitutional question.

Thus, in order to avoid such an eventuality, "the executive branch shall construe Section 104(d)(2) as advisory.

Finally, Bush said, he would "construe provisions of the Act that mandate, regulate, or prohibit submission of information to the Congress, an international organization, or the public" in a manner that would be consistent with his " constitutional authority to protect and control information that could impair foreign relations."

In response to the provisions of the Act that have not addressed all Indian concerns, the External Affairs Minister, Pranab Mukheljee stated in the Rajya Sabha that India would stick to its declared voluntary moratorium, and keep its option open on conducting nuclear tests if the national interest and priority so required.

References

1. Washington Post, 20 May 1974.
2. George Quester, The Politics of Nuclear Proliferation (Baltimore: Johns Hopkins, 1973), p.72.
3. In an interview with the Washington Post, 12 March 1975. Quoted by Charles Heimsath, "The American Quandary over Nuclear Proliferation in the Indian Subcontinent", USA Today, Washington D.C., January 1980.
4. A.G. Noorani, "Indo- US Nuclear Relations", Asian Survey, Vol.21, No.4, April 1981,p.404.
5. Thomas M. Franck and Edward Weisband, Foreign Policy by Congress (New York: Oxford University Press, 1979), p.111f
6. Indian Express, 24 September 1980.
7. Surjit Mansingh, India's Search for Power: Indira Gandhi's Foreign Policy 1966-1982 (New Delhi: Sage, 1984), p.103.
8. US Senate, Committee on Foreign Relations, Staff Report on Tarapur Nuclear Fuel Exports, 15 September 1980, p.35.
9. Republican Platform, Dedroit, 1980, reported in Newsweek, 21 July 1980.
10. Presidential Statement on US Non-Proliferation and Peaceful Nuclear Cooperation Policy, Washington D.C., 16 July 1981.
11. Joseph J. Trento, Prelude to Terror: The Rogue CIA and the legacy of America's Private Intelligence network, quoted in

Leuren Moret, "Planet Earth as Weapon and Target", World Affairs, Vol.9, no.4, Winter 2005,pp.78-79

12. Lauren Moret, op.cit., p.79
13. The Hindu, 8 March, 2006,p.13
14. Siddharth Varadarajan, "Assessing the nuclear balance sheet", The Hindu, July 7, 2006, p.11
15. *Ibid.*
16. Anil Kakodkar's interview to T.S. Subramaniam, The Hindu, September 8, 2006, p.11
17. Vikram Sood, "The Grand Illusion", Hindustan Times (New Delhi), July19, 2006, p.10
18. Brahma Chellaney, "Trick and trick", Hindustan Times, July 18, 2006, p.10
19. Excerpts from an interview with M. R. Srinivasan by Siddharth Varadarajan, The Hindu, July 27, 2006,p.11
20. Deccan Chronicle, 15 August, 2006,p.8
21. Michael Krepon, " The US-India Nuclear Deal: Another Wrong Turn in the War on Terror', The Henryl Stimson Center, Washington D.C., 2005. Visited website http:// www.stimson.org/pub.cfm?ID=283&print+yes, 9/19/2006, p.2.
22. George Perkovich, Faulty Promises: The U.S.- India Nuclear Deal, Carneige Endowment for International Peace, Carneige Nonproliferation/ South Asia, September 2005,p.6
23. Ibid.
24. Ibid.p.8
25. The Hindu, August 18, 2006
26. George Perkovich, op.cit., p.4
27. Charles R. Smith, "Clinton Gave China Chips for Nuclear War", Newsmax.com October1, 2003
28. Lauren Moret, " Planet Earth As Weapon and Target", World Affairs, vol.9, no.4. Winter 2005, pp.76-77.
29. Ibld, p.77-78
30. Ibid., p.78
31. Ibid., p.79
32. World Nuclear Association, "Thorium," Information and Issue Briefs, November 2004, available at www.world-nuclear . org/info/inf62.htm
33. Ashley J. Tellis, India As A New Global Power, (Washington: Carnegie Endowment for International Peace, 2005), p.18

34. George Perkorich, op.cit., p.8
35. Leuren Moret, op.cit, p.80
36. The Korea Times, 23 December 2005
37. George Pervorich, op.cit., p.11
38. Brahma Chellaney," Washington's ever-shifting goalpost", The Hindu, February 15, 2006 p.12
39. Ibid.
40. Ashley J.Tellis, op.cit., p.19
41. Ibid ., p.20
42. George Perkovich, Jessica T. Mathews, Joseph Cirincione, Rose Gottemoeller, and John B. Wolfsthal, Universal Compliance: A Strategy for Nuclear Security (Washington, D.C.: Carnegie Endowment for International Peace, 2005), p.48.
43. Lora Saalman, " The Implications of the U.S.-India Strategic Partnership", Power and Interest News Report (PINR), 5 August, 2005; visited website http://www.pinr.com/report.php?ac=view_report&report_id=341 on 10/19/2006
44. See Siddharth Varadarajan, "Indian has little reason to cheer", The Hindu, December 9,2006.
45. M.R Srinivasan, "India may lose control of its nuclear future", The Hindu, December 14, 2006.
46. The Hindu, December 20, 2006.
47. *Ibid.*

8

Globalization, America Crowning the Unipolar world: Challenges to Sovereignty and Independence of India

Globalization is mere a euphemism for engulfing the entire globe into the octopus grip of American designed and controlled economy. It is widely stated that the end of cold war, disintegration of Soviet Union and disappearance of communism erased the bulwark against the spread of capitalism, and made the latter a victor globally. But from a historical perspective, this is neither the first victory of capitalism nor the first era of globalization. Everyone now recognizes that the first period of globalization confirmed the economics of Adam Smith: the economy left alone, will produce the greatest wealth of nations and in the long run the state will wither or be pushed away, as though by an invisible hand. It also confirmed Karl Marx in a most particular way: every system of power tends to develop its own ideology and ideology guides and rationalizes the government policies that impose and sustain the system of power. Contrary to Smith and Marx way of thinking, it is not very hard to understand what happened in pre1914 globalization that seems to echo very much the present. The operative word then was imperialism that led to exploitation through colonization. At present it is exploitation through neo- imperialism or through global capitalism so in a way global capitalism has effectively taken the place of colonization to continue to exploit the developing countries for the benefit of the few developed ones. "As a result, it is within the realm of logical conclusion to observe that the ongoing ideology of globalization perceived from any angle is nothing but another name for colonial domination which still opposes as in the past, the redistribution of wealth and status to place all people and nations on an equal footing."[1] Thus, globalization does mean reorganizing or reordering of international relations, strategies and values with the same colonial logic and reasoning spelt out in the verbiage of democracy, liberalization and human rights and pushing all states more tightly into the American designed, dominated economic straight jacket, its net work of institutions- MNCs and TNCs. What started from the middle of the fourteenth century through the first half of twentieth century to extend the European power's political and economic influence throughout the world through the use of force typical of imperialism reached its crescendo with America scripting globalization. The imperial powers destroyed sovereignty, independence and freedom of will of all the colonies for the control of their resources. But as a result of post Second World War process of decolonization, many countries from Asia, Africa, the Pacific and Latin America have joined the community of nations by becoming independent.

> "Thus, having lost control over greater parts of the world resources, the rulers of the colonial past, in the name of globalization seem to have been successful in replacing all the nation states with what is called multinational corporations to continue to exploit as before from raw materials for exports and a source of cheap labour to readily available markets for their manufactured goods"[2].

In other words, globalization is the other name of replacing the colonial masters with the so-called multinational corporations. Looked at from any angle, globalization represents the same old order with new means of control, new means of exploitation, new means of oppression and new means of marginalization. Thus, the new corporate colonialism created is " likely to be more cynical and more ruthless than anything we have seen so far. It is likely to dispossess, impoverish and marginalize more people, destroy more cultures and cause more environmental devastation than either the colonization of the old or development of the last fifty years."[3] Today globalization means reinforcement of a new American empire engulfing the entire world.

> "This new empire with its command centre in the United States is the first truly global empire in the history of the world. Its subtlety has put the Roman centurions, Spanish conquistadors, and all the other imperialistic armies to shame. Unlike the empires that pervaded it, this contemporary version has managed to convince rather than force the conquered to accept every major aspect of its culture...the language of the empire is the global language of commerce, and diplomacy while its art, literature, movies, music, medicine, science, and communication network reach out to the remotest corners of the planet"[4].

Globalization: Projection of the Domestic Imperatives

The language and idioms the United States used to spell out its own script of world political and economic order seem to be largely ingrained in its own domestic capitalist, political and economic structure. The liberal market based polity and economy founded on Hobbes and Locke's possessive individualism aims at ensuring abundant economic growth, wealth production and luxurious, materialistic and commodious living. To this end science provided the ontological foundation. Newtonian image of particles in motion becomes the guiding metaphor in the emerging mechanistic worldview and liberal conception of possessive and atomistic individualism. Sharing the same ontological foundation with science, the political and economic thinking of the US as well as that of the West as a whole constitutes the ideological copingstone on which people legitimize the state authority as a guarantor of individual property rights, wealth production, market relations and inordinate life style. Acting in response to these domestic imperatives and compulsions means arming the state with the capability- the build up of masculine power in terms of conquest of nature and pursuit of pleasures in a competitive world.

Following the world war- II, the United States embarked upon a massive military build up which could enable it to have unimpeded access to resources in any part of the globe at a price it likes, and to countervail the forces opposing American world order. Former Soviet Union posed a challenge to the US world order by its own version of communism- the exact antithesis to capitalist liberal market economy. Soviet Union pronounced socialism; state controlled economy, and equal distribution of wealth and the principle "from each according to one's ability, to each according to one's needs" came in direct collision with the political and economic order as propounded by the United States. Both the super powers, thus engaged themselves in an ideological battle each trying to impose on the world its own version of world order as being universal one. Hence the military build up and arms race both conventional and nuclear resulted in a cold war between the two. Where as the domestic imperatives of wealth production and luxurious life style constitute the bedrock of America's foreign policy behaviour and engagement in various parts of the globe, the copingstone of Soviet Union's foreign policy was internationalization of communism.

The United States' political and military intervention in support of or opposition to the regimes in various parts of the globe during the cold war or post cold war period can be explained only in the backdrop of its domestic concerns. On the contrary, concerns for indigence of the working class in transcendence of any territorial and geographical confines could swing Soviet Union into intervention. In other words, the domestic concerns for affluence of its people are the idioms with which the United States defines its world order not only during the cold war, but also during post cold war. That means, squeezing the entire globe into its cocoon of concern for affluence and wealth production is what the US christens it as globalization. Thus, domesticisation of the universe is the other name for US world order. 'The domesticisation of universe' policy of US means compelling the South countries to dedicate themselves to the affluence, production of wealth and extravagant life style of US people.

To achieve this objective the United States constituted various institutions and structural arrangements for the exploitation of South. The Western frontier model of economics, trading system and the concomitant institutional and structural arrangements shaped at BrettonWoods on the indices of neo classical and liberal market economy are designed to legitimize and protect the monopoly of the US and its Western allies to expropriate the resources of the South. One of its major aspects is to permanently condemn the South to the periphery status in the world economic growth system and make them dependent on economic aid, assistance or loan from the rich industrialized North tied with many conditionalities or strings. The principal agency acting on behalf of credit institutions in the West is the IMF, which certifies debtor countries' continued credit worthiness. To qualify for loans, countries would have to carry out structural adjustments geared to the requirements of Western economic system. IMF's insistence of deregulation, privatization of government owned enterprises, elimination of tariff barriers to oversea imports, measures to boost export production, cut in deficit budgeting, devaluation of national currencies, removal of subsidies, and getting markets to work properly for efficient long run growth, has well been acquiesced in by the South countries in their bid to earn more foreign exchange, by exploiting their environment and adopting economic policies with only short term gains in mind. Similarly, the World Bank (WB) continues its traditional lending policies to the South for large capital-intensive projects without considering their impact on the local and regional environment. IMF and WB mostly financed and controlled by US are to a greater extent determining the economic policies of the South and developing countries. They are like states of US within the states of the South countries, which are already in debt traps. The total debt service and payment by the South has been so staggering that what led Willy Brandt to opine that resources flows from North to South has been reversed which can be likened to "blood transfusion from sick to the healthy".

The US and its allies are pressing hard in the GATT forums, WTO at Seattle or Doha or Hong Kong and other forums for greater protection and enforceability of corporate and private intellectual property rights including patents over genetic materials, and declining to make commitments to developing countries on access to biotechnology and other associated technologies on the plea that there is no way that they can interfere with private sector interests. For the reasons of US dictating and determining the world economic order, taking cue from Soviet Union nuanced socialism, public ownership and distribution of wealth, and equality, the NAM and South countries vouchsafed for a New International Economic

Order (NIEO) on the foundation of democratization of world trading and economic system, equality of sovereign states, transparency and disappearance of US protectionism during the cold war period. But to no avail, US continued enveloping all the South countries under its panoply of world order. The US view of world order comes a full circle with the occupation of the space left by the former Soviet Union. Information technology, Internet or PC may have brought about' death of distance' or 'end of geography' but it enables US to clamp over the entire globe with greater celerity and success to initiate the nations into its political and economic thinking. The global capitalist approach set by US comes closet to positing a globalization process in which the capitalist system as reconceptualised by Karl Marx is moving by its own internal logic and compulsions, to extend its institutions, processes and values as far a field as possible. In the name of globalization and New World Order, the US has through TNCs and MNCs succeeded in carrying out the economic practices and political values distinctive of US capitalist system to the reach of every nook and cranny of the universe.

Does this portray the glimpses of a New World Order? Is it different from US view of world order coming as it does since the post second world period? In the backdrop of the above analysis indubitably it can be said that the New World Order dreamt of after the end of cold war, is nothing but an extension, continuance and perpetuation of US version of world order shaped on its domestic imperatives. Globalization, a camouflage for American world order has not yet facilitated democratization of world economic and trading system equity in participation and access to resources, equality of sovereign states, collectivity security, decision making on the consensus of all members, objectivity and discarding of any moorings, dismantling of center-periphery status, sweeping away of barriers and protectionism attitude. All pomp, fanfare associated with the end of the cold war about the apocalypse of New World Order fade away into a religious acquiescence in things as they are, or still worse, into a slavish adulation of the US versed world order. With the exit of Soviet Union from the scene a unilinear occupation of space and time becomes complete by the US. The entire globe gets crammed into US version of world order without any challenge and an externalization of its scripted world order takes place as universal, dedication and total surrender to which is considered as the only standard of being called civilized. Hunchigton's clash of civilization is another expedient metaphor for earlier imperialistic notion of white man's burden to develop the South in the way the US defines as development. To propound on the one hand that the cold war competition between the United States and the Soviet Union defined the American foreign policy, often dictating choices at home as well abroad, and on the other, that there has been a change in America foreign policy beliefs and behaviour after the end of the cold war, is highly erroneous and seems to have undermined the substructural role of its domestic imperatives in the making of American foreign policy. Any asking on America to compromise its political and economic thinking is perceived as a threat and is very likely to create a popular upsurge, the backlash of which has a great bearing on its legitimacy to rule. American intervention be it in Vietnam, Nicaragua, Bosnia, Haiti or at present in Afghanistan, Iraq or in WTO or climate negotiation, can be explained only in this background of domestic imperatives. For instance, the United States reneged on its commitment agreed to at Kyoto to reduce emission of carbon dioxide to the atmosphere by 5 percent on the pretext that it would deleteriously affect its economy and the luxurious life style of its people-the promotion of which is the foundation of American foreign policy. These American interventions military or non-military as a world police are not that of a messiah but of a very hard possessive individualistic state concerned with its own domestic imperatives. The eclipse of cold war may have onset changes in the situation and context, but the pith and substance of American foreign policy remains unchanged and marks a constancy so far as the foundation of its foreign policy is strongly embedded to its domestic urges and imperatives of wealth production, inordinate life style and capitalist liberal political and economic order. The world order old or new is an American script; the drama to be played out is purely an American direction, keeping to itself the right to choose the actors, dialogue and even the tuning of the play.

The foundation of all encompassing globalization of American empire harks back to the 1840s when the Doctrine of Manifest Destiny (DMD) was invoked to justify the conquest of North America[5]. That means it is not man but God who had ordered the destruction of Indians, forests and buffaloes, the draining of swamps and the channeling of rivers and the development of an economy that depends on the continuing of exploitation of labor and natural resources. The context of Manifest Doctrine was also in vogue in the late 1800s and early 1900s to justify the US invasion of countries in Central and South America that declined to kowtow to American policies. Even the First World War, Second World War and the great depression compelled America to determinedly defend itself and spread its sphere of influence. The post second world war American onslaught on communism, military intervention in Vietnam, Iran, Indonesia, Guatemala or Nicaragua and the present military intervention in Afghanistan and Iraq after September 11 terrorist attack are some few examples to buttress the working of the Doctrine of Manifest Destiny in American Foreign policy to reinforce its empire. US President George Bush claimed that he was on a mission from God when he launched the invasions of Afghanistan and Iraq, according to a senior Palestinian politician in an interview to the BBC.[6]

What is gleaned from the above is that for the promotion of American and West's economic interests, globalization is the logical conclusion of the legitimacy that American state derives from its citizens on the ground that its policies redound to the inordinate consumption, profligate life style and production of wealth at the expense of both nature and rest of the world. So the ongoing ideology of globalization is nothing but another subterfuge for the continuing domination of the underdeveloped by the wealthiest America and Western countries and the funneling of resources and wealth from the less to the richest. The process of economic globalization espoused by the Bretton Woods institutions promoted the interests of the super rich so successfully that it also bound them to show short shrifts to the concern and obligations required of them to the less fortunate inhabitants in the developing world. Under the guise of globalization what is being practiced can be rightfully said as neo- mercantilism reinforcing the basic tenets of the mercantilism that the national economic welfare maximize the global economy when a state delivers greater economic wealth relative to other states. The doctrine of mercantilism is fundamentally in antithesis to the basic tenets of economic liberalism, which assumes that the interests of people, firms and states are fundamentally complimentary, where as mercantilism assumes that the interests of nation states are basically in conflict and competition. This is exactly the reiteration of what globalization aims at, heavily tilted in favour of American and western interests at the cost of rest of the world. Under the guise of globalization, what is being practiced can be rightfully characterized as neo mercantilism. Instead of nation states competing with one another to dominate world trade, under globalization the organized free traders of America and Europe are effective in advancing the economic dominance over the developing world.

> "The goal of neo- mercantilism can be defined as trade policy whereby a state seeks to maintain a balance of trade surplus and to promote domestic production and promoting exports. Under the managed trade of the western practice of globalization, the position of the state has shifted from direct control over the economy and trade to supporting the economic activities of multinational corporations with tariffs and trade regulations by staffing and managing military alliances and international organizations". [7]

The American empire is ruled not by a king, or emperor, not by a single person or a family. It is instead ruled by a group of men who control international corporations and banks, and through them the governments of the US and many other nations. "They are members of a corpotocracy. Beneath them, a pyramid of subordinates with a vast population numbering in the billion of workers who toil to channel most of the world's resources into the coffers of the corporations, people whom future history will classify as slaves."[8] The people at the helm of multi national corporations are called Economic Hit Men (EHM) whose job is to encourage world leaders to become part a vast network that promotes US commercial interests. In his recent book John Perkins points out:

> "Economic Hit Men (EHM) are highly paid professionals who literally cheat countries around the globe out of trillion of dollars. They funnel money from the World Bank, USA and other foreign aid organizations into coffers of large corporations and the pockets of a few wealthy families who control the planet's natural resources. Their tools include

> fraudulent financial reports, rigged elections, pay offs, extortions, sex and murder. They play a game as old as empire but one that has taken on new and terrifying dimensions in this time of globalizations". [9]

The current ingrained view doing round the globe is that the nation state which was intrinsically linked with capitalism for the last 200 years is in the decline with its place being usurped by the corpotocracy, a part of and parcel of globalization. It is said to be rendering the nation state obsolete, politics irrelevant and national sovereignty an empty shell.[10] It is further argued that the emergence of electronic and market globalization has receded the past into oblivion and suggests a future in which a part of the world will be wired, and dominant and the unwired rest left behind, with national governments made irrelevant. Kimon Valaskakis of the University of Montreal argues that the international system is escaping the control of national governments, and that the Westphalian system of absolute state sovereignty, which has ordered international relations since the thirty years war, now is falling without a replacement in sight.[11]

This alleged withering away of state and national sovereignty is considered due to the ubiquitous spread of capitalism to the remotest parts of the world and its universal acceptance as a global system. This view is particularly relevant in case of developing countries divested of national sovereignty by the all-penetrating globalization. But in relation to the people within the state, the state power has been redeployed in accordance with the logic of globalization to achieve economic growth at the cost of social hardship. Though in many parts of the world the state has shown the signs of its demise the fact remains that the supremacy of American state has not eclipsed in the new free market utopia. On the contrary, US hegemony and sovereignty have been reinforced spectacularly. The role of state has been redefined in the context of globalization. The stability and predictability of state guaranteed by a system of monetary regulation during the post second world war period and the role of state as a guarantor of social cohesion, coordinated economic, industrial and labour policy at national level has been torn apart by globalization.

Not an Apocalypse of Divine Will

Globalization is neither an apocalypse of divine will nor the result of automatic working out of invisible forces of market economy but is the outcome of American deliberate policy choice made to promote its own economy at the cost of the other. The creation of a worldwide free market is very much embedded in a series of important decisions taken by the US over the last 30 years, which included first, dismantling of post war international monetary system, second, liberalization of world markets and third, granting of autonomy and power to the financial sector unparalleled since the golden age of British imperialism.[12] Thus, financial sector diversified from its economic foundation now sets the pace, generates systemic constraints and imposes normative behaviour. With a strong and insidious economic motive the US authorities took decisions unilaterally in 1973, which included abandoning the system of fixed exchange rates established by the Bretton Woods Agreements in 1944, and introducing a system of generalized floating exchange rate. They sought to compensate for declining competitiveness and a growing national debt by exporting country's macro economic imbalances. The floating exchange rate system provided a flexible and efficient monetary tool that enabled them to avoid the adjustments that would otherwise have been required by American's new situation as a debtor. "In a system of fixed exchange rates and gold convertibility, the US would have been obliged like every third world country to pay for its indebtedness with a relative loss of sovereignty and highly unpopular domestic austerity measures."[13]

As said above, the new system was a US designed contrivance to remain persistent in a policy that would provide a very inordinate and luxurious standard of living at home from which it derives its legitimacy and rightness of authority by dipping deep into the planet's savings. Owing to its uncontested military supremacy and dollar power, the world's only reserve currency, the US has been able to keep its monetary sovereignty intact.

During the 1980s a decisive step was taken to deregularize the US finance industry paving the way for its globalization via the Wall Street banks, brokers, hedge funds and pension funds that dominate the world's financial flows. Worldwide liberalization in the 1980s and 1990s allowed the US finance industry access to the savings of the newly industrialized and emerging countries, where rates of return were very high. In short, the establishment of a global free capital market was essential for the economic and financial well being of the world's leading debtor US whose deficit now stands at $1.5 trillion i.e. 20% of GDP.

In continuation of US policy on financial liberalization based on consensus in1985, Ronald Reagan took decisions knocking down barriers to trade, foreign investment and free movement of capital between industrialized countries, especially in Japan. Then, his successor launched Enterprise for the American Initiative which was designed to support free markets and free movement of capital in the Western hemisphere. But under President Clinton it became a worldwide effort "directed in particular at the new area of wealth accumulation in East Asia, seen as a potential goldmine for American banks and brokerages."[14]

The liberalization of the Japanese financial system and the revaluation of the Yen under the 1985 Plaza Accords was accomplished through a mixture of coercion and cooperation typical of hegemonic power. When it came to organizing the forced march towards liberalization of the newly industrialized countries, the government set itself on a war footing. The overall plan, coordinated by the US Department of Commerce, identified 10 rising economic powers from the Pacific to the Atlantic whose economies were to be opened up, and it called upon all government departments from the CIA to US ambassadors abroad.[15] As Robert Keohane and Helen Milner have pointed out: "During the 1980s intense political pressure was exerted by advanced industrialized countries on developing countries to open their economies... the national economic regulations of developing countries were called into question."[16]

Three objectives set by America as a part of its hegemony and accomplished during the 1990s, were: to maintain the global balance resulting from the end of cold war, to ensure its technological lead and military supremacy, and to create an economic environment favourable to its own interests. No country or groups of countries appears able to constitute a political counterweight to US in the foreseeable future, let alone call into question its primacy in the hierarchy of nations. As Thomas Friedman puts it: " In the globalization system, the United States is now the sole and dominant super power and all other nations are subordinate to it one degree or another."[17]

The American scripted model is now unfolding throughout the world superimposing its will upon the rest of the world in the post industrial sectors of financial and cultural services, communications, leading-edge technologies and scientific-technological production. A normative world culture as built in by America is emerging in the realms of economic activity, social practice and private international law. It is the US, which is laying down the new ground rules i.e. the dominant economic norms (profitability, shareholder value) the regulatory criteria (ratings of companies and states) and the legal rules (international commercial arbitration). For instance, the behaviour of the markets is shaped by the ratings awarded by two major US private rating agencies, Moody's and Standard and Poor. Acting both as judge and party, they are imposing US normative criteria on the rest of the world.[18]

American capital plays a major and crucial role in redefining the universe of rules within which it operates, and also determines the constraints of international system without subjecting US to those constraints. The US has thorough control over the markets, no sign of its losing control. The Federal Reserve's decisive action following the stock market crash in 1987 and the US Treasury's intervention in 1994-1995 after the collapse of Mexican Peso are the cases in point to mark American supremacy over the markets of the world. Within this overall primacy of US hegemony, the other western powers participate to varying degrees in a broader pattern of western hegemony vis- a- vis the Third World. "Globalization is institutionalizing a new balance of power between states that hardens sovereignty of some while reducing the autonomy of others. The world wide free market accentuates the disparity between the centers of capital and the peripheries. The players with knowledge and power lay down the rules; the others fall into line."[19] The most vulnerable Third World countries trapped in the international division of labour are losing the last remnants of their sovereignty, while the new industrialized countries have become even more dependent over the last few years as recent experience in East Asia proves.

The West helps rich individuals and companies spirit away vast sums from the developing world. Raymond Baker, a committed capitalist in his new book, Capitalism's Achilles Heel, describes capitalism as "the greatest economic arrangement ever devised but he believes western governments and banks are failing catastrophically in their duty to police the system. Falsified pricing, haven and secrecy structures and illicit movement of trillions of dollars out of developing and transitional economies break the social contract... that Adam Smith incorporated into the core of the free- market system."[20]

Globalization: A Synonym to Unilateralism in American Foreign Policy

A bogey of militant communism and the assumptions of dangers emanating from it to American interests around which American Foreign policy was shaped and rationalized for the last four decades, dissipated with the eclipse of the cold war and disintegration of Soviet Union. The interlude between the end of the cold war and the nebulous script of new world order of the senior Bush witnessed an inter face between liberals like Clinton and Gore's penchant for global interdependence, economic liberalization, human security, transnational security challenges, citizen diplomacy and civil society and neo conservative's preferred pronunciation of national interest and national security in terms of power and military intervention.

The liberal market economy freed from its competition with communism geared its march towards globalisation Neo Conservatives forming the foundation of Ronald Reagan's foreign policy featuring star wars, roll back and strikes against the evil empire demurred that the US was squandering the moment- the unipolar moment.[21] What America needed was a neo-Reaganite foreign policy that would end US complacency and proudly proclaim US exceptionalism.[22] Recovered from the anti-communism tirade because of the end of the cold war during mid 1990s, these neo conservatives harped on a new aggressive foreign policy agenda. The outcome was the reborn of conservative internationalism adducing the extension of the unipolar moment throughout the next century- the "new American century". That means, the end of the cold war amplified the opportunity to globalize its domestic imperatives. The denouement of unipolarisim was enacted when America exercised pre-emptive strike against Afghanistan and Iraq flouting defiantly the United Nations and protestations of world public opinion and other powers. The September 11 terrorists attack on Wall street trade market made unipolarisim a mere fait accompli symptomatic of American foreign policy accent on prerogatives of its military supremacy heralding a fundamental shift in international affairs after Bush came to the helm of affairs in January 2001. On 9/11, the day that 3000 people died tragically in the United States at the hands of terrorists, 24000 died in the Third world from lack of nutrition as they do, on average everyday of the year.[23] But the former could be immediately catapulted into the security design of America as a global threat where as the latter remains sidelined not able to edge its way into its security design. Even the relentless killings of civilians in Kashmir by terrorists sponsored by Pakistan could not be a global security threat. This human dimension of security needs dismantling of American empire for securing people in the Third world from the scourge of poverty, malnourishment and environmental degradation. "They have an egotistic, autistic and solipsistic view of the world. They believe that whatever is good for America is good for the world."[24] What America considers a threat to its interests is espoused by it as a global security threat As Tom Barry points out "the Bush foreign policy is a melding of backlash politics and visionary grand strategy. The backlash is directed against all forms of feckless liberalism so detested by the neo- conservatives, and the vision embraces the opportunities and potential of US power"[25]. Backlash and vision dovetailed into conservative internationalist grand design of strengthening American nation state as the fulcrum of international affairs with utter disdain for the framework of multilateralism, liberalism and progressive liberalism as championed by liberal internationalists.

American Portrayal of International society as Hobbessian

The central assumption of Kenneth Waltz's Theory of International Politics is typically Hobbesian. He wrote: "The state among states, it is often said, conducts its affairs in the brooding shadow of violence. Because some states may at time use forces, all states must be prepared to do so- or live at the mercy of their militarily more vigorous neighbours. Among states, the state of nature is a state of war."[26] The conservative internationalists agreeing with this Hobbesian assumption hold that as an all powerful sovereign authority Leviathan is necessary to control its own population in the anarchic state of nature similarly an all powerful Leviathan is required in the anarchic international field to maintain the world order. Furthering their contention they argue that the liberal framework of multilateralism distorts the natural world order and stark reality of power relations. Listening to other states without effective power will diminish American role as a gendarme of world order. All said does not mean that America is dismissive of and averse to the framework of multilateralism as an instrument of foreign policy, rather subscribes to it very prudently and as a matter of political expediency when it feels doing so would unfold a world order enacted on the exact lines of its own political and economic script, and redounds to American interests. When liberal multilateralism in the form of rise of NGOs, greater participation of civil society, citizen diplomacy and multi dimensional forms of conflict prevention and resolution comes in to disavow American supremacy, the conservative internationalists insist that America sweep all these under carpet, as it did withdraw from Kyoto Protocol being signed by it and advocate alternatives to it by forging a partnership of expediency with six Asia Pacific countries- Australia, South Korea, China , Japan, India, and Brazil on clean development and climate. With this characteristic dis- ingenuity America has been able to duck global pressures to accede to Kyoto obligations. The most important reason for America not implementing Kyoto obligations is that it is not willing to bring compromises on Americans way of living – the building block of American legitimacy. The same can be cited of American military adventures into Iraq on the alleged and premeditated pretext of the latter's possession of weapons of mass destruction in the face of stiff opposition from all circles including its own people.

Globalization is Unipolarism

To America globalization is not a process of willingly self-withdrawal from the forcibly occupied spaces of the globe but an expedient and tactical usurpation of these spaces – political, social, economic, cultural at the global levels by any means even by resorting to force. In an essay written in 2000 for the Project for the New American Century (PNAC) Paul Wolfowitz, the then Deputy Secretary of Defense and a leading administrative hawk contended that unipolarism and globalization are really the same phenomenon. If there is a new global interconnectedness, it "occurs within the context of American global dominance."[27] So liberal and progressive notions of engagement, and webs of interdependence as instruments of peace and conflict prevention come in direct clash with US worldview. Dethronement of Saddam Hussein stands as a testament to neo conservatives' preference for regime change by military means- directly by US or through surrogate freedom fighters and utter rejection of liberal and progressive forms of conflict prevention. Where military adventurism is not an immediate and viable option as in China, Cuba or Iran, neo conservatives urge obstructing such rogues and peer competitors from addressing their internal contradictions and conflict, thereby hastening their demise.[28] Thus, American foreign policy approach marks a great departure from the liberal philosophies of Locke and Kant based on progressive assumptions of reason and social consensus, which once formed the keystone of American constitution. Antithetical to senior Bush's opaque outlines of New World Order and Clinton's vision of an interdependent world, the architects of current Bush's foreign policy envisions a Hobbesian world infested with constant conflict and war in which a Leviathan state is both necessary and good.[29] The proponents of American foreign policy describe America's grand global vision in terms of empire, benevolent global hegemony, Pax Americana or simply the American century. While putting emphasis on US cultural and political primacy, military domination and moral preeminence, the grand strategists of America reserves a major role for the nation state and national sovereignty in their total rejection of the framework of multilateralism, deepening global governance and emergence of civil society.

Conditional and Absolute Sovereignty

While ascribing a major role to nation state, the policy makers reserve absolute sovereignty for America and conditional sovereignty to other nations. As one PNAC scholar observed: "The conservative internationalist views the role of the nation –at least this nation – as being at the core of international relations today more than ever before."[30] International power relations are dismissive of John Austin's theory of sovereignty- "not in a habit of obedience to a like superior"- which implies equality of sovereign states. But in practice, in international realm, each country's degree and extent of sovereignty depends on the reach of its global power. For the most powerful nation state, sovereignty is complete and unchallenged. International law, treaties, conventions and humanitarian principles put constraints on the exercise of sovereignty. But in its grand strategy America rejects the idea of accepting these constraints on its absolute sovereignty, because US power and other associated global responsibilities exceed those of other nations. US supreme military power and global responsibilities entitle it to enjoy special privileges and prerogatives with respect to its global exercise of power even at the cost of other sovereign powers. Bush's foreign policy approach providing justification to its exceptionalism proclaims that America not only stands above all these constraints but also is the final arbiter of good and evil. In the wake of September 11 attacks, President Bush and his coterie articulated the doctrine of conditional sovereignty that " respect for the sovereignty of a nation state could be suspended if that state was deemed to be either sponsoring terrorism or developing weapons of mass destruction that might challenge US supremacy." [31] Under the doctrine of conditional sovereignty the US has arrogated to itself the right not only to judge whether nations are violating their responsibilities as sovereign authorities either by sponsoring non-state terrorists or by engaging in state terrorism but also to foster a regime change by exercise of its military power. Then, all means of international cooperation, multilateralism and engagement and respect for international law and norms and leaving space to civil society appear as anathema to American unilateralism in its foreign policy. John Quincy Adams, the sixth US President once admonished to the hawks: America ought not to go abroad in search of monsters to destroy.[32] But the present president Bush's grand design is to foster an imperial world order with America as a Leviathan nation ever in search of monsters to slay. The US is gearing towards a totalitarian design, which is the greatest possible threat to a decent existence of people around the globe in the decades ahead.

Globalization as unfolded, witnessed the enactment of an American script for crowning an imperial world order, pontificating its dictates to all the nations of the world. This constitutes the background against which the efforts of both India and America to build a new partnership are on. India's long hallowed non-aligned political culture of independence, autonomy and freedom of choice during cold war saw paling into insignificance with the end of cold war and disintegration of Soviet Union. India has no other choice but to leapfrog onto the American bandwagon. India's ascetic pronouncements and moral rhetoric largely outsourced from its hoary history and civilization on world issues involving both the super powers with a strength of argument derived from its durable democracy, its management of ethnic and religious diversity, its history of non-aggression, its contribution to international peace keeping, and its responsible stewardship of nuclear technology, material, and know-how for greater power and recognition in international realm, seem no longer virtues meriting consideration, and need to be replaced with emphasis on stark reality of power. This is the reason, India went for second test for ascension to great power status, and America extended its warm hand for a strategic partnership more particularly after the end of cold war and September 11 episode, to counter terrorism and contain China. Whenever America finds any nation grows in power enough to disturb its power structure, it tries to circumscribe it by a policy of cooperation and friendship. This exactly happened to India. Thus, Washington and New Delhi are caught in dialectic of power. But this is not without any price, the price being sacrifice of its long cherished non-aligned culture of independence, autonomy and sovereignty. With the collapse of Soviet Union and communism in 1991, the constitutional mandated socialism began to crumble in India giving way to American scripted globalization, and its liberal market economy. India opened all its doors with great hilarity to multinational and transnational corporations to occupy every nook and cranny of India for investment and establishment of industries destroying environment and displacing the poor from their land. In the process of globalization, which are mere an extension of American political economy, these MNCs and TNCs become states within Indian state. The World Bank and IMF which are the sole financier for development and other works laid down so many conditionalities that India is bound to adhere to, compromising its economic and political sovereignty. These TNCs, IMF and World Bank became the viceroy of America and other western countries in India and other poor and developing countries as found in halcyon days of imperialism, controlling the latter at former's behest.

Adapting to the new challenges of globalization became the new edifice of Indian foreign policy away from its constitutional dictum to usher in a socialistic and welfare state.

References

1. Ismail Shariff, "Growing Discontent with Globalization", World Affairs, Vol.7, no. 3, July- September 2003, p. 22
2. Ibid. P.23
3. Edward Goldsmith,"Development as Colonization", World Affairs, vol. 6, no.2, April- June 2002, p.36
4. John Perkins, "American Empire: Slaver or Saviour?", World Affairs, Vol.9, no.1,Spring 2005, p.14
5. Ibid. pp. 19-20
6. The Hindu, October 8, 2005
7. Ibid, p.46
8. John Perkins, op.cit.,p.15
9. Ibid, p.16
10. William Pfaff, "Despite Global Changes, National Sovereignty Remains King", International Herald Tribune, 30 March,2000
11. Noell Burgi and Philip S. Golub. April 2000, "Has Globalization Really made nations Redundant?", Le Monde Diplomatique, April 2000, p.1
12. Ibid. p.2
13. Ibid
14. Nicholas D. Kristof and David Sanger, "How US wooed Asia to let the Cash in", New York Times, 16 February 1999 . See also "Les – Unis et la mondialisation financiere", Nord- Sud Export, no.375, 30 April 1999
15. Ibid
16. Robert O Keohane and Helen V. Milner eds. "Internationalization and Domestic Politics" (Cambridge: Cambridge University Press,1996), p. 24
17. Thomas Friedman., The Lexus and the Olive Tree (New York: Farrar, Strauss and Giroux, 1997)
18. Saskia Assen Losing Control? : Sovereignty in an age of Globalization, (New York: Columbia University Press, 1996), pp. 14-18
19. Noelle Burgi and Golub, op.cit.

20. Duncan Campbell, "Where the rich hide their cash" , The Hindu, December 6, 2005
21. Charles Krauthammer "The Unipolar Moment", Foreign Affairs, Winter, 1990-91
22. William Kristol and Robert Kagan,"Toward a Neo- Reaganite Foreign Policy", Foreign Affairs, July- August ,1996 .
23. John Perkins, op.cit., p.15
24. Armand Clesse," America's Classical Security Dilemma: Search for a New World Order", World Affairs, vol.8, no.2, April- June 2004, p.173
25. Tom Barry, "Return of the Nation State- and the Leviathan", Interhemispheric Resource Center, November 2002, p.2
26. Kenneth W Waltz, Theory of International Politics (Reading, Massachusetts: Addision – Wesley, 1979), p.102
27. Paul Wolfowitz, "Statesmanship in the New Century" in Robert Kagan and William Kristol, eds., Present Dangers: Crisis and Opportunity in American Foreign and Defense Policy, (San Francisco: Encounter books,2000)
28. Summarized in William Kristol and Robert Kagan, "National Interest and Global Responsibility" in Present Dangers, ibid.
29. Tom Barry, Op.cit
30. James W. Cesar "The Great Divide: American Interventionism and its Opponents "in Present Dangers, ibid.
31. Tom Barry, op. cit.
32. Ibid.
33. George Manbiot, "IMF is still the rich world's viceroy", The Guardian Newspapers, quoted in The Hindu, September 6, 2006, p.13

9

Conclusion

No sooner had the Second World War ended than the United States, the major and dominant player started dictating to the world its own version of what world political and economic order would usher in. The language and idioms, the United States used to spell out its own script of world political and economic order seem to be largely ingrained in its own domestic democratic capitalist political and economic structure which was built by the consent of the people for a liberal market oriented polity and economy. This liberal market based polity and economy founded on Hobbes and Locke's possessive individualism aims at ensuring abundant economic growth, wealth production and luxurious, materialistic and commodious living. To this end of exorbitant wealth production and inordinate life style science provided the ontological foundation. Newtonian image of particles in motion becomes the guiding metaphor in the emerging mechanistic worldview and liberal conception of possessive and atomistic individualism. Sharing the same foundation with science, the political and economic thinking of US including the West constitutes the ideological foundation on which the people legitimizes the state authority to be a guarantor of individual property rights, wealth production, market relations and inordinate life style. Acting in response to these domestic imperatives and compulsions means arming the state with the capability-the masculine build up of power in terms of conquest of nature and pursuit of pleasures in a competitive world.

During the cold war both Indian and American foreign policy were divergent and incongruent with each other. Whereas America was solely guided by the domestic imperatives of liberal political economy, and providing a luxurious and inordinate life style to its people at the expense of both nature and other people, India was wedded to the path of socialism in order to improve the lot of the majority poor who were promised the basic human needs during independence. In contrast to Hobbes and Lockes' possessive individualism founding American foreign policy, India's enriched culture, glorious civilization and hoary past, and its unmitigated belief in humanity, democratization of international order, equality of sovereign nations, distributive justice and multilateralism became its guiding metaphor. It was then not unknown to America that a great country steeped in Buddha and Gandhi's philosophy and saintly values, and elated always in its history and culture driven role of moralizing the world, and believing unswervingly in independence and freedom of action could not prefer to play the role of a client state subservient to American interest. India was too large to fit into United States' straightjacket. It was not some eternal, universal, and moral principles but Hobbesian dictum that what is conducive to one's interest is morality, became the sine qua non of American foreign policy. Whereas military and economic supremacy America considered important means to frame its scripted world order, India believed in idealism and Gandhi's non violence and truth as the sole means to achieve greatness. An underdeveloped, poor, nascent democratic and independent country was highly ambitious to play a role as large as the greatness of its civilization even equal with American supremacy. But this was not in commensurate with its military and economic strength. A great mismatch between ambition and the wherewithal to translate this ambition was the weakness of India's foreign policy during the Nehru's era. A large, independent, non-aligned, socialist and ambitious country having universal designs antithetical to American national interest could not become a client state of U. S. This was the reason, which prompted Washington to prefer Pakistan, India's adversary into its global strategic network. Even the harsh criticism of Indian leaders by the Soviet leaders could not prevent it from jumping into Pakistan bandwagon. During the cold war, American foreign policy behaviour toward India was dictated by purely its global strategy of containment of communism not by any objectivity or realistic understanding of the situation.

Pakistan's strategic importance to the attainment of American goal outweighed any other consideration whether it is justice, objectivity or moral principles in Washington's dealings with New Delhi. India took up the cudgels for the south countries for democratization of the international institutions, ushering in of New International Economic Order, disarmament and establishment of a world free of exploitation, injustice and division on the basis of race or colour. India was conscious not only of its rights but of the rights of several countries in the South. On these issues both India and America differed and trod on different paths. In all Indo- Pak conflicts and wars during seventies and eighties, America sided with Pakistan already bolstered by the flow of weapons from its global strategic point of view. Nehru's internationalist face got a set back when America and its western friends played to Pakistan's gallery and trimmed the role of UN to the confines of their global strategy of containing communism. Pakistan, a frontline state to act as bulwark against expansion of communism received all modern and sophisticated weapons, which were ultimately used against India. Not to let Pakistan down at any cost in its war against India was the main plank of Washington's foreign policy during cold war.

It was felt, with the end of cold war; there would be a change of guard and the role of Pakistan as a playboy in the cold war would be soon discounted. Nothing of the short happened immediately after the end of the cold war because Pakistan was still considered a strategic conduit for establishing American foothold in Central Asia for energy, natural gas and oil along with the imperatives to stall rise of Talibans in Afghanistan and counter Russia emerging powerful from the embers of cold war. Gradually a change of perception and understanding of India thawed in America. Without discounting the value of Pakistan as an old guy, which has always stood it in good stead and in future will continue doing so, America decided to court friendship with India already shorn of socialistic rhetoric being a largest democracy, vast and most populous country next to China, and a huge market for investment and American goods. To respond to American overture positively was the Hobson's choice for India as it has already globalized its society and economy and legitimized American domestic imperatives as its imperatives of foreign policy. America felt, to look beyond the maze of Indo-Pak conflict syndrome and zero sum relation would be in its best interests. Hopes were raised about the prospects of a new friendship between the two largest democracies. India's second nuclear test in 1998 brought a set back to these hopes as America imposed economic, military, science and technology sanctions against India. Again Washington exhibited its cold war double standard strategy. Pakistan, which had already nuclear weapons clandestinely before India, went for it with the help of both China and America escaped with impunity. Only when Pakistan exploded in response to India, America imposed similar sanctions as used against India. Reciprocal visits of both the then Indian Prime Minister Vajpayee and American President Clinton to their respective countries prepared the ground for forging this new friendship. Clinton's role in resolving the Kargil war between India and Pakistan further strengthened the friendship and military to military and defense, science and technological cooperation harbingered a new chapter in their relationship. American military intervention in Afghanistan against Osma bin Laden directed Taliban again brought Pakistan into close proximity of US as the former provided the latter military base and intelligence and logistical facilities. In return, Pakistan received military and economic aids from US. This enabled Gen. Musharraf, the military head of Pakistan to continue in power. The 9/11 terrorist attacks on world trade center fostered a change in American approach. Death of 30,000 people in that attack made President Bush declare a global war against terrorism which India supported US as this would help it fight terrorism against Pakistan sponsored terrorism in Kashmir. During his two terms carried it further promising India a major world power status and seriously wanted India jump into its embrace under New Steps in Strategic Partnership (NSSP). As said in the preceding chapters, 18 July Agreement between Bush and Manmohan Singh is a land mark step as it promised India a major world power under the aegis of US. To make an assessment of the agreement it is necessary to understand the compulsions on both sides to reach the agreement. First, US feels the need to remold the political structure of Asia. India is an important 'swing state' in the sense that a strengthened Indo-US relationship would be a major gain for the US; conversely, an indifferent relationship would be a major loss. Second, US has reasons for having India work on multilateral security initiatives in Asia. The geo-strategic location of India astride major sea lanes and the utility of India as counter to China with which it can compete for power and influence in Asia. Third, the US could benefit greatly from gaining preferential access to the markets of the emerging third largest economy in the world, as is being widely speculated. Fourth, India is the most populous credible democracy in the world, and democracy is being advanced and exported as an essential national value by the Bush administration. For these reasons, Secretary of State, Condoleezza Rice, promised that the United States is intent on making India a major world power during her visit to India in March, 2005.The Indian compulsions were: first, it accepts that the United States occupies the apex of world power in its several dimensions-political, military, economic, technological and even popular culture. Second, it hopes to gain access to high technology, particularly defense technology, but also to nuclear technology, materials and equipment for its atomic energy program. Third, its desperate need for supplies of enriched and natural uranium needs greater appreciation and help. Fourth, India intends to enter into a closer relationship with US to deal effectively with the basket cases of Sri Lanka, Bangladesh, Myanmar and Nepal in its backyard. India needs the United States to face any eventualities that might arise from the tensions among its neighbours. The contours of the Indo-US nuclear deal might be seen in this perspective. A terminological inexactitude remains to question the efficacy of the deal. It recognizes India to be a responsible state with advanced nuclear technology, which is a euphemism for nuclear weapon states. This could apply to Israel and the members of Nuclear Suppliers Group with advanced nuclear technology, but hopefully not Pakistan. Rhetorically, it is being asked what about Pakistan, North Korea and Iran. How can the US be strict with these nuclear non-conformists but condone India for its nuclear tests. Pakistan's ambassador to Washington, Jahangir Karamat, has already lodged a demarche claiming that Pakistan is also eligible for receiving nuclear technology since it has cooperated with the US in its war against terror in Afghanistan. How will the United States reject Pakistan's claims? Russia and China may put similar concessions to their clients. They would feel free to cooperate with Pakistan, but also Iran, which is anathema to the United States. France and India are not very far from reaching a broad agreement on civilian nuclear cooperation as envisaged in their February declaration "on development of nuclear energy for peaceful purposes". But this is subject to condition that Nuclear Suppliers Group relaxes restrictions on New Delhi. The limitations and problems of the agreement have been very profusely dealt with in preceding chapters. From the draft bills in Senate and House of Representatives is gleaned that US is passing through rough weather as America has been shifting the goalposts constantly to the discomfiture of India. Unless India is fully assured supply of natural uranium in perpetuity without closing its freedom to detonate nuclear weapons in a changed circumstance not envisaged in the July 18 agreement, and privileges and rights of a nuclear power at present confined to five nuclear powers, the new partnership is likely to come a cropper.

Faces of Internationalism: Americans' Foreign Policy Beliefs

The Japanese attack on Pearl Harbour and the war that followed it were a turning point in American foreign policy. Prior to the war, being seemingly protected by the vast oceans that separated the United States from Europe and Asia, the nation designed an isolationist foreign policy strategy, one framed to protect its security and values by withdrawing from world affairs. After the war, isolation was jettisoned in favour of a globalist foreign policy posture sustained by domestic support for what Richard Gardner has called liberal internationalism, which he described as "the intellectual and political tradition that believes in the necessity of leadership by liberal democracies in the construction of a peaceful world order through multilateral cooperation and effective international organizations."[1]

By the end of the 1950s a consensus developed in American foreign policy among elite circles both in public and politics, which implied elements of both cooperation and coercion. The US hinted at a solution of both global and national problems through cooperation with other nations, and if need be it would not mind intervening in the affairs of others, using force if necessary to protect its self defined national interests. The Vietnam War after Pearl Harbour and World War II reoriented American foreign policy. Concern for cooperation and coercion, which founded the consensus among the people in respect of American foreign policy, now, divided them. The question was only hovering round whether America should be involved in the world, but now also of how it should be involved. In the wake of Vietnam crisis, internationalism came to wear two faces-a cooperative one and a militant one. [2]

During the cold war, "attitude towards communism, the use of American troops abroad, and relations with the Soviet Union, particularly the wisdom of détente, were critical in distinguishing proponents and opponents of the competing faces of internationalism – each of which became laced with partisan and ideological coloration" [3]. It was expected that the end of cold war would usher in a new world order then pledged by George Bush Sr., and bring changes in American foreign policy behaviour, as the logic of fear of communism, fear of the Soviet Union and a determination to contain both that gave structure and purpose to Post World War II American foreign policy, disappeared. The developments in the international system and American involvement in Bosnia, Haiti, Afghanistan and Iraq suggest that the core elements underlying the two faces of internationalism remain today as they were two decades ago.

As studied by Wittkopf, the intersection of the two faces of internationalism reveals four clusters of individuals with distinctive foreign policy beliefs in America, which can be described with the labels: internationalists, accommodationists, hard-liners, and isolationists.[4] Internationalists are willing to cooperate with other nations to solve global and national problems but they are also willing to intervene in the affairs of others to promote and protect American national interests. On the other hand, isolationists reject most if not all forms of global involvement. While internationalists embrace cooperative and militant internationalism, isolationists reject both. Accommodationists and hard-liners are internationalist but selective. They differ about how the US should be involved in world affairs not whether it should be involved. Accommodationists prefer multilateralism to unilateralism as a means of conflict management and resolution. Hard-liners, on the other hand keep faith in the utility of coercive diplomacy and prompting the US to the forefront of the global agenda. Making US the sole superpower is a label to be embraced, not to be sidelined. [5]

Rejection of multilateralism in favour of unilateralism in international relation by America would remain a formidable challenge before India, as the latter always stands opposed to US stand on international issues. The unilateralists in Bush administration "claim that because of the dire threats posed by terrorism and weapons of mass destruction, the United States must escape the constraints of multilateralism and abandon the structures of international cooperation it helped to build after World War II."[6]

Uncertain and indifferent public opinion behind foreign policy

The ease with which Presidents Eisenhower, Kennedy, and Johnson enjoyed consensus behind shaping of American foreign policy, could not be available to Nixon, Ford, Carter, Reagan, Clinton, and Bush to build coalitions of support for their foreign policy initiatives because of partisan and ideological division. The American people are divided about the nation's appropriate world role, but the term isolationism does not capture their mood. "Analysis who assume that America has a discernible national interest whose defense should determine its relations with other nations are unable to explain the persistent failure to achieve domestic consensus on international objectives."[7] This was no less evident in the 1990s when after the collapse of the Soviet Union; the American ascension to nonpareil global military, economic and cultural power was almost complete. The American easy victory in two Gulf wars against Iraq, and another one in Afghanistan, bombardment of Serbia without suffering a single causality and ever growing economy and booming stock market stood a testimony to show that "the United States resembled Britain in its mid-Victorian glory, but with even greater global reach".[8] Countering Soviet Union provided the North Star to guide American foreign policy during the cold war. In the post cold war period, the public in America is indifferent and quite uncertain about how to shape its foreign policy to guide this power. Polls showed the America public focused on domestic affairs and paying little attention to the rest of the world. In 1992 Presidential election domestic affairs dominated the election campaign. Clinton's victory depended on the irrelevance of foreign policy. It is striking to note, for example, that among the eight percent of voters who said foreign policy determined their vote choice, George Bush outpolled Bill Clinton by a whopping 11 to 1 ratio.[9] Similarly in the 2000 Presidential election foreign affairs played little role. Between 1989 and 2000, the television networks closed foreign bureaus and cut their foreign news content by two thirds. With the majority of American people being indifferent and uncertain about international affairs, the making of foreign policy has been left to those few who take keen interest in foreign affairs. In a recent poll in September 2006 in America before election to Congress over 70 per cent of the people polled are discontented with the state of economy. According to polls, Americans are far more concerned about the stagnant and the quagmire in Iraq than they are about terrorist attacks.[10] the result is a very narrow definition of national interest. Though a majority Americans were in favour of United Nations, America refused to pay its UN dues. It was the intensity of preferences of minority that Congress heard in shaping American interest[11]. American unrivalled rise to supremacy is not in response to what its majority of people want America to play in world politics. As Henry Kissinger pointed out," What is presented by foreign critics as America's quest for domination is very frequently a response to domestic pressure groups". The cumulative effects "drive American foreign policy towards unilateral and bullying conduct". [12] As the German commentator Joseph Joffe warns, " To the extent that the United States turns unilateralism into a habit or cuts its contribution to the production of public goods others will feel the sting of American power more strongly. And the incentive to discipline Mr. Big will grow."[13]

Attitudes towards globalization of American people is often more fragile than it appears. A wide range of public opinion surveys report that a plurality or majority opposes policies aimed at further liberalization of trade, immigration and foreign direct investment. These attitudes reflect not simply ignorance of the benefits but a feeling that costs of economic insecurity may be more important.[14] It is on terrorism Bush cashes to launch his unilateralism, and scores over Democrats at home front. But in India public opinion plays a major role in shaping foreign policy. Recent vitriolic public reactions from all walks of life and inside Parliament against nuclear draft bills in American Congress which purported to have incorporated many extraneous conditions not envisaged in July 18 Agreement forced Indian Prime Minister Manmohan Singh to candidly state that India will not accept any thing beyond the July 18 agreement at the cost of India's independence, sovereignty and freedom of detonating nuclear weapons in a changed circumstances.

America towards unipolarism

Defining national interest after the end of cold war became anomalous, problematic and uncertain. But in the wake of 11 September 2001,countering terrorism injected a new energy and focus to American foreign policy. Some critics see the successful campaign of America in Afghanistan as evidence that unilateralism works, and warn against entangling coalitions.[15] Many observers at home and abroad believe that the United States still purses a narrow and arrogant conception of its national interest. Some in the current foreign policy debates look at the US preponderance in power and see a modern empire. Self-styled 'neo Reaganites'advocate a foreign policy of benign American hegemony. Since American values are good and we have the military power, we should not feel restrained by others. In their eyes," Americans should understand that their support of American pre-eminence is as much a boost for international justice as any people are capable of giving. It is also a boon for American interests and for what might be called the American spirit". [16]

But according to many conservative realists and liberals, America by arrogating to itself such a pre eminence of power alienates others and goes against what the Declaration of Independence expresses in terms of "a decent respect for the opinion of mankind". According a substantial voice to others could mean we are acting truly not only in the interests of others but also in our interests. By doing so, we end up embracing some form of multilateralism.[17]

Americans are divided over how to be involved with the rest of the world. The current debate is taking place not only between isolationists and internationalists, but also between unilateralist and internationalists or what Wittkopt describes as between accommodationists and hard-liners. Isolationists, who advocate Monroe doctrine to buttress their point that America can avoid vulnerability to terrorism, fail to grasp the global realities and import of a global information age resulting in what telecommunication specialists call the death of distance. On the other hand, "the new unilateralists who urge us unashamedly to use American dominance of the information economy on behalf of self defined global ends are offering a recipe for undermining America's soft power- the power of attraction that is associated with ideals, cultures, and policies-and encouraging others to create the coalitions that will eventually limit our hard power".[8]

Lawrence F. Kaplan and William Kristol in their book, "The war over Iraq" argues that, in fact this invasion is just the beginning of a new era in American foreign policy. They are predictably critical of Clintonian liberalism but also deride Reagan and Bush Sr. for being narrow realists. Instead, they extol activist idealism – America sallying forth to make the world safer for democracy, actively following a policy of preemption against those who oppose its most cherished values. Instead of persisting with its historical isolationism, it must adopt a distinctly American internationalism.[19] As enunciated in America's national security strategy, this distinctive internationalism aims at creating a balance of power that favours human freedom and makes the globalized world a safer and better place. Richard L. Kugler of National Defense University has pointed out that while most countries address mainly own regions, the US strategy covers virtually the entire world.

Problems with a Non-aligned India

India's approach to various international issues, fighting terrorism, spread of diseases or poverty and removing structural inequality and increasing chasm between the rich and poor hinges on a multilateral approach, consensus of nations, an effective and decisive UN and other international regimes. While forging ties with US, New Delhi has not foreclosed its other options to establish relations with other powers. The famous Nehruvian dictum that India does not like to commit the folly of keeping all the eggs in one basket, still holds good for India. On his way to Brasilia to attend the IBSA (India, Brazil, South Africa) summit and Non-aligned summit, Indian Prime Minister Manmohan Singh, when asked how he proposed to play with so many pieces on the foreign policy board, he noted, " As have-nots of the world, we have to toss all the balls". [20] This visit will act as showpiece of an independent foreign policy to rebuff those critics who denounce New Delhi's strategic partnership with Washington as satrapising India's independence and sovereignty. While engaging with the

United States, India has lost no opportunity to establish ties with European Union, Russia, the ASEAN and China. The IBSA summit in Brasilia and Non- Aligned summit in Havana represents a different kind of engagement signalizing India's penchant for South-South cooperation as a necessary instrument to deal with North in international forums on issues of trade, globalization, environment and intellectual property rights. Thus, it is hard to believe that India will be always with America on all these issues affecting the south countries. The severest challenge before Indian foreign policy lies in how dexterously to move so that its multilateral ties with other nations and taking up the cudgels for the South on international issues does not come in the way of its warming up with US. Resuscitation of NAM to pursue the shared interests of its member states in a transformed world, not countenancing as emboldened in Malaysia NAM summit, United States' unilateral proclivities, claimed right to humanitarian intervention, export democracy, and characterizing some nations as belonging to an 'axis of evil' is emblematic of India's preference for multilateralism, and democratization of world order antagonistic to American pontificated world order, which certainly stands incongruent with American interest. More than that an ardent reassertion of South – South cooperation in trade, economic development, choosing an alternative path of development, exchange in science and technology and sharing of knowledge born out of their long individual experiences, and putting a common stand on international issues under the decisive leadership of India and other countries could reinforce India's independence and sovereignty in a better way than it thinks to do so in a blind alliance with US. The relevance of Non-Alignment Movement (NAM) is questioned today on the ground that the very historical context of cold war giving birth to it, has disappeared. Away from this narrow historical context and incidental confinement, if it means charting an alternative path of development by the South distinguished from the unquestioning adherence to the two paths – liberal market economy, and communism— irrespective of the merit of each block as propounded by US and Soviet Union respectively, then the relevance of NAM appears more justifiable than ever before in a changed world plagued by environmental crisis, disastrous climate change, terrorism, growing disparity and chasm between rich and poor, yawning trade imbalance, grinding poverty and gnawing injustice and inequity of resource distribution, increasing dominance of the west in decision making, nuclearization of security and rise of unipolarism. A new world order based on justice and equity can be created if South can work together as a bloc in the vital areas such as trade, finance, investment, energy, technology, and designing of development strategy, as the South has recently emerged as an important player on the world economic stage in terms of GDP, saving, investment, exports, imports, foreign exchange reserves, financial assets at home and abroad, quality and size of its corporate world, IT sector and capability in manufacturing. The revival of the old idea of a South Bank, a financial institution by the South for the South can play a crucial role in financing infrastructure investment, balance of payment support, and intellectual cooperation among the developing countries. There is an urgent need for enhancing South- South cooperation in the energy sector as it is the major producer and likely to be a major consumer of energy. This can overcome the resistance of the Northern multinational enterprises and provide a level playing field to the newly emerging companies of the South by providing them market oriented opportunities in obtaining prospecting development, transportation and marketing rights, thus, ensuring energy security. Increasing bargaining powers of the South in multilateral trade negotiations can be possible if they club together. The process of decision-making in the multilateral trade negotiations has been highly asymmetrical. Although the decision making should be by consensus, conventionally and by virtue of their indomitable power, the leading trade nations such as US and European Union exercise a disproportionate weight in agenda setting and decision making process. To level the playing field in the negotiations, coalitions of developing countries should begin to set agenda of the trade talks by bringing issues of their concern on the negotiating table and contribute to evolving a system that is more responsive to the development needs. Revival of NAM on these above principles provides India the opportunity to set an agenda for the new world order in sharp contrast to the dominant American version of it, and to clearly suggest Washington that its new partnership with it is not at cost of its long cherished non-aligned culture. This will also increase the bargaining power of

India while striking a civil nuclear deal with America. Any hard line stand in American Congress hamstringing India's ascension to nuclear power status agreed to in July 18 agreement, and freedom of the decision to produce nuclear weapons, is likely to reinforce Indian efforts to resuscitate NAM with new verve and vim.

Democratic within and Imperial Abroad: Incongruence with India

America's behaviour follows the classical pattern of imperialistic powers as history stands a witness to this. The Greeks were developing and practicing democracy even as they sustained slavery as indeed happened in the US too. The Romans who laid the foundation of rule of law practiced slavery and created a vast empire, the loot from which enriched Rome. The Americans became the first democracy with a written constitution emphasizing human rights but extended their territory to the pacific coast through the genocide of Native Americans. The British were evolving into a democracy as their empire expanded to cover the whole globe. So did the French. What America preaches in the country in terms of rule of law, equity and rights as eternal universal values denies them in the international system. This disconnect or dichotomy between the two is partly explained by the fact that international system lacks rule of law and is anarchic. In reality, there is no disconnect. The foundation of both internal and external policy rests on the need for promotion of exorbitant life style, wealth production and commodious living. On the application of this internal imperatives in relation to the external world, America is hell bent on having unimpeded access to resources with military forces at its behest to bully those recalcitrant or rouge or evil nations into accepting American terms, and imperatives of domestic policy remains the sheet anchor of its foreign policy. While substructural content of both domestic and external policy of the United States remains the same, in the application of its foreign policy to the external world, the United States marks an aberration from its domestic field. While consensus, tolerance, respect for others' rights and, freedom are found in the domestic field, in the external field it instead believes in the application of force as the only way in having access to resources found anywhere in the world. This dichotomous and paradoxical stand of US in the application of its policy in domestic and external realm, has been the cynosure of criticism and protestations from all the over the world. America's invasion of Iraq bypassing Security Council and in the face of stiff opposition from France, Germany and Russia is a classic example of Americans' belief in the use of pre-emptive strike as the only resort to protect its values and interests abroad. On what a Machiavellian double standard logic American foreign policy is founded to stonewall the widely held view that democracy can be implemented by democratic means only and by nothing else. This new conservative school puts a premium on an unrivalled military power and prowess of US to remove the antidemocratic and authoritarian regimes from power, and advocates active involvement in others' affairs to protect American interests and values. In other words, the Monroe doctrine has been expanded to make the entire world part of the American hemisphere. This is in consonant with the Machiavellian exhortation to the Prince to use force or war as the only medicine to a state of affairs where matter is diseased. The real poser boy of the neo-conservatives is military historian, classic scholar, author and columnist Victor Davis Hanson. At the centre of the Hansonian thesis is a belief that deterrence, backed by a credible show of strength is the only way to ensure lasting peace. In his words, "those who are the most educated, the most removed from the often humiliating rat race of daily life and the most inexperienced with thugs and bullies, are the likeliest to advocate utopian solution and to ridicule those who would remind them of the tragic nature of mankind and the timeless nature of war".[21]The British, a democracy at home, justified their colonialism as a civilizing mission, a white man's burden, or what Lodquard says a double mandate-civilizing the uncivilized and promoting the economic interests of the mentors. In a similar vein, Washington is talking of democratizing West Asian regimes. Such a thesis was acceptable to the British People then, as it would satisfy their economic interests, profligate life style and wealth production on the basis of which they have given legitimacy to the state. Similarly US assertion of its right to export democracy to West Asia and other continents by use of military power is symptomatic of the decadence and emasculated role of UN and other multilateral regimes. India disavowed American military adventure in Iraq from the very beginning. Unlike the cold war move, it failed to garner the South countries under the NAM to stand behind UN and the world public opinion against American and its allies move in Iraq. Further, possibly similar military intervention by US in Iran and North Korea because of their intransigence on nuclear issues could be a crucible to test India's balanced move between new partnership with US and its fraternity with NAM at a time when its relevance is seriously held as effete. Being held in Cuba, an inveterate anti-US campaigner, the 118 nations Non-aligned Movement in its conference on 17th September 2006 condemned unilateralism and attempts to exercise hegemonic domination in international relations, a favourite phraseology of Cuba for decades to attack Washington. It resolved to oppose and condemn the categorization of countries as good or evil based on unilateral and unjustified criteria and the adoption of a doctrine of pre-emptive attack including by nuclear weapons. In a veiled attack on the U.S, the summit opposed unilateralism in international relations as well as unilaterally imposed measures by certain states and the use of force and pressure to achieve their national policy objectives. But a startling exclusion in Indian Prime Minister Manmohan Singh's address to NAM was any reference to US unilateralism. This shows, New Delhi's long adduced adherence to independent foreign policy, advocacy of multilateralism, democratization, and non interference into sovereignty of another nation and peaceful resolution of conflicts is not going to be staunchest as it is already bound with US over a civil nuclear deal. The attempts to revive NAM with new élan with an objective to combat global crises are likely to collide with American global strategy, which inclines toward unilateralism. Being a founding member of NAM, India faces the challenge of how to dovetailing its pro-US posture with NAM's distaste for and vituperative attack on US unilateralism.

Unilateralism in Practice

Today US foreign policy stands exposed in all its Neanderthal crudity. In the existing political climate, it is impossible to talk about global rights to common property resources, or equity or social justice. The genuine claims of developing countries-addressing urgent problems like poverty, or the creation and sustenance of global democratic institutions – are simply not on the global agenda.

The United States rejected the Kyoto protocol in early 2002, a few months after Bush became President. This move could benefit US industry in the short term but at great cost to poor countries. With the biggest emitter of green house gases ducking out, the chances of dealing effectively with climate change are reduced considerably. The vulnerable least developed countries in Asia and Africa are sure to pay a heftier bill for unmitigated climate change exacerbating their scourge of poverty.

The grandeur irony is that the countries such as China, India, and Brazil whose exclusion from the Kyoto obligations is one of the reasons for which America withdrew from the Kyoto, have joined US in forging a six nation Asia Pacific Partnership in October, 2005 along with other three Japan, South Korea and Australia on clean development and climate. China and India are the two of the world's most populous nations requiring abundant quantities of energy to fuel their development. The group is led by the US, itself a huge energy guzzler and the world's biggest polluter, accounting for 36.1 per cent of global greenhouse gas (GHG) emissions. The US had elected not to join the Kyoto Protocol, citing non-inclusion of three large developing countries- China, India, and Brazil- in the first commitment round of 2008-12. Australia, which emits 2.1 per cent of global GHG, is a signatory to Kyoto but has not ratified the Protocol and as such is not subject to commitments. Of the other four Kyoto signatories in the Partnership, only Japan, with 8.5 per cent of global GHG emissions, is subject to emission reduction targets during the first commitment period. The signing of such a Partnership is curious and has great impact on the future of the Kyoto when European Union and other members were hoping to persuade the US to chip in. After all, without the US, the Kyoto Protocol is not really effective. Roping in the US might have meant imposing commitments on China and India as well. But the Partnership seems to have put paid to any hopes of getting the US into Kyoto. A perusal of the mission statement makes it clear that "the Partnership will collaborate to promote and create an enabling environment for the development, diffusion, deployment and transfer of existing and emerging cost-effective, cleaner technologies and practices through concrete and substantial co-operation so as to achieve practical results."[22] Firstly, Unlike Kyoto, the Partnership is envisaged as a loose non-binding coalition without any firm commitment or targets. Kyoto, on the other hand, has put in place a very complex mechanism to prescribe, measure, and enforce binding targets. Secondly, unlike Kyoto, the Partnership is forward looking- that is, only future green house gas emissions come under its purview, as it were Kyoto requires its rich members to bring down their GHG emissions by 5.2 per cent below 1990 levels because it is premised on the belief that global warming cannot be arrested without past damage alongside containment of future emissions. By one stroke India along with members of the Partnership has been able to absolve completely America of its past historic emissions and undoes what all nations participating in the Kyoto Protocol have achieved in terms of putting the onus on US and fixing a target. This proves to be costly in terms of the brunt of climate change and global warming due to uncontrolled emission of GHG by the US and other rich industrialized countries that will fall on developing countries. Further, this will likely to be a chink in India's widely held stand on environment and climate change. But very unwittingly, India along with China made themselves amenable to American calculated expediency of binding them to future emissions, which they were absolved of by the Kyoto on the ground that this would hamper their development and the very ubiquitous recognition that there is a difference between luxury emission and survival emissions. Finally, Partnership initiative makes a radical departure from Kyoto inasmuch as it includes nuclear power within the scope of the initiative. Despite its zero- emission, nuclear power has never been viewed as a clean source of energy because of the huge problems associated with waste disposal, decommissioning, and safety aspects. Kyoto's decision to keep nuclear power out of the list of clean energy source was an acknowledgement of these factors, and an adherence to the views held by scientists and environmentalists. While stress is put on finding out alternative resources, which are environmentally benign, the Partnership not only emphasizes the role of nuclear power in a future energy paradigm, but also took out the wind from the sail of India and other countries' move to put a strong front before the US and other industrialized nations on environment and climate change. Coming on the close heels of Indo-US nuclear deal, this move of India seems to be deliberate marking a shift from its South stranglehold on environment, climate change and other related issues like trade, intellectual property rights coming under WTO.

While US vouchsafes for a complete surrender to market liberalization at every global forum, yet continues to erect barriers that make it impossible for developing countries to compete in sectors such as agriculture and textiles. The United Nations Development Programme estimates that US farm subsidies alone cost countries about U $ 50 billion in a year in lost agricultural exports.[23] To earn more foreign exchange, the poorest countries rely mostly on the export of primary commodities, which are naturally resource based. High import duties on processed goods in industrialized countries keep developing countries out of the more lucrative market for processed goods. However, because global trade policies do not factor in social and environmental costs, the poor and their environment in developing countries end up bearing the ecological cost of consumption in rich countries.

The poor communities in developing countries are also bereft of the opportunity to benefit from biotic wealth. A crude estimate of the global annual market for products derived from genetic resources lies between US $ 500 and US $ 800 billion. The Convention on Biological Diversity (CBD) recognizes the rights of local communities to their biological diversity. It impinges on biotech, pharmaceutical and agricultural companies to compensate communities through benefit sharing agreements for use of this biodiversity, as well as the knowledge of its use. But this does not happen, primarily because the US-home to a majority of corporations, using genetic resources from the poor countries—has not ratified the convention. In a renegade's fashion, the US upholds the WTO's Agreement on Trade-related Intellectual Property Rights (TRIPS), which only recognizes the rights of corporations, and not developing poor communities. Any attempts at addressing the anomaly between the CBD and TRIPS have come a cropper due to its allies and US.

Global war on terrorism: American double standard

No sooner the Al Qaeda terrorists on 11 September in 2005 attacked the Wall trade centre in New York than America lost no time in giving a clarion call for global war on terrorism. Similar attacks by Pakistan sponsored terrorists on the people of Kashmir and other parts of India most particularly on Indian Parliament and series of blasts in Bombay did not receive any categorical response from America excepting some high sounding words exhorting India to restraint and start negotiating with Pakistan for an early and amicable settlement of Kashmir imbroglio. Even these Pakistan sponsored terrorist attacks were not considered as important as to assume the character of global terrorism. But after September 11, things changed and India joined America in its global war on terrorism with the hope that US will fight Pakistan terrorists on behalf of India. Nothing sort of this happened. American sword was pointed toward Taliban and Al Qaeda having stronghold in Afghanistan. President Musharraf of Pakistan has no option but to join America avoiding the danger of being US target because of his dubious stand on terrorism. Since Pakistan provided US the logistical and military facilities in its territory it highly requires for combating the Taliban forces in Afghanistan, it was naive to assume that America will attack Pakistan for Indian cause. Musharraf's words of assurances to cooperate America to fight Taliban, catch hold of its leader Osma bin Laden hiding in ravine mountainous ridges and hand over him to America were accepted by Washington as nothing but facts. Abundant military and economic help came flowing in to Pakistan to bolster the latter against the onslaught from Taliban terrorists. That Pakistan has banned terrorist organization in its territory and stopped helping them morally and materially has been highly appreciated by America. Except some stern admonition to Musharraf to exercise control over terrorist organizations in Pakistan's territory, American has done nothing-concrete favoring India in its fight against Pakistan terrorism. This American double standard approach to terrorism has been always to the chagrin of India. Since Pakistan is American prime military base, Washington is averse to taking any pro Indian step that will put Pakistan in trouble. Pakistan very dexterously has been using the Bin laden card to keep America close into its strategy of getting a free rider over India. The US believes that Osma bin Laden is hiding somewhere in Waziristan in the Federally Administered Tribal Areas (FATA), the frontline region in the US led war against terror and it is here that it wants Pakistan to do more meaning hunt him out by breaking the Taliban and foreign militant networks in the area. In simple terms, President Bush needs Pakistan for his war on terror. Pakistan, which received more than $ 3 billion from 2001 to 2005 from the US, needs the cash and international standing. The proposed sale of 36 F-16 aircraft to Pakistan as a part of an unprecedented security plan agreed with Pakistan has extracted muted response from India because of the reasons that these supplies are tied with many conditionalities. These military and economic packages are meant to establish an indomitable influence in Pakistan, which America considers important to its war on Taliban. John Hillen, Assistant Secretary, Bureau of Political-Military Affairs in the State Department, during a hearing of the US House International Relations Committee made no secret of this when he stated that the US believes in manipulating Pakistan in a direction that Washington believes is desirable and would result in an overall increase of American comfort levels in country, which has been proud of its sovereignty and independence. While the US only wants Pakistan to meet its present military objective, Pakistan the lesser partner, has always built into the relationship through what the former Foreign Secretary Tanvir Ahmed Khan, describes as auto-hypnosis expectations that were never agreed upon.[24] When these expectations have remained unfulfilled, frustrations mounts both in establishment and public and Musharraf has demonstrated signs of defiance towards America with double strategy in his mind- one is to reinforce legitimacy to his regime from the public and the second is to winnow further concessions from America. For instance,, in April 2006, when the US put the Jamaat –ud-dawa- it is linked to the banned Lashkar-e-Taiba- on its Specially Designated Global Terrorist list, the Pakistan foreign office said it was not obliged to follow suit. Other militant and extreme religious outfits banned by the Musharraf government have made a come back, especially after 2005 earthquake. The Herald Tribunal, a monthly reported recently that the Sipah-e-Sahaba Pakistan which was banned in 2002 and now goes by the name Millat-e- Islamia Pakistan, was allowed to organize a large public gathering in Islambad on April 2006. Now it has become clear that both Pakistan and America are playing hide and seek game in order to deceive India. When Pakistan received plaudits from America for its commendable role in war against terror, India did not take any more time to understand American lip service to combating terrorism against India from Pakistan side. To the allegations of Pakistani hand in the recent Mumbai serial bombings by India, United States assistant Secretary of State Richard Boucher demanded that New Delhi find evidence to support its claims, and asserted that no country has done more than Pakistan in the ongoing fight against terrorism. But what is matter of great concern to India is the feigned posture of ignorance maintained by America. Its Country Reports states that the Lashkar is based in Muridke near Lahore and Muzaffarabad. Further, it states that almost all Lashkar members are Pakistanis from madrasses across Pakistan or Afghan veterans of Afghan wars. On the Jaish – e-Mohammad, Country Reports is even more alarming. The Jaish continues to operate openly in parts of Pakistan despite President Musharraf's 2002 ban on its activities. The group is well funded, and is said to have tens of thousands of followers who support attacks against India. Put simply, Country Report renders Boucher's claims that Pakistan has acted against terror groups such as Lashkar and Jaish, absurd, proscription and after all means nothing when all these organizations have been operating in full public view. In March, the Federal Bureau of Investigation showed a court satellite images of a terrorist training camp near Balakot in Pakistan's North West Frontier Province which were taken by spy satellites in 2001 and 2004.[25] There is nothing startling in Boucher's statement bestowing accolades on Musharraf. This is in continuation of American pattern. What runs counter to American interest has all the qualifications to be christened as threat to American interest, and hence to be globalized. But the continuing decimations of hundreds and thousands Indian people by Pakistani terrorists since the creation of Pakistan much more than killed in American Wall Trade Centre, though threat to India are not threats to US and hence lack the raison detre to be called global threats. The US will never act against Pakistan for any thing it does to India. To make Pakistan absolved of all Indian allegations, the US destroyed forensic evidence related to the 1993 Mumbai bombings. Mired in the labyrinthine maze of an intractable war in Iraq and its energies spent in Afghanistan, at least a part of the United States' policy establishment seems to believe ignoring continued terrorism against India as height of its hypocrisy, is an acceptable price for whatever can be extracted from Pakistan. "On 9/11, the day that 3,000 people died tragically in the United States at the hands of terrorists, 24,000 died in the Third World from lack of nutrition. It is estimated that 30.000 children die every day from curable diseases simply because the current system is unwilling to provide the medicines they require."[26] Very sordidly, this pathetic death of children has never been defined as security threat to all nations of the world. The alacrity and celerity with which the terrorist attack on America was globalised as threat to the entire humanity, exposes the United States' dominant view securitizing the whole world under its canons, sidelining all other nations' security concern. It will be acme of India's delusion to believe that US will do India's work on Pakistani terror.

Nuclear deal a clipping of Indian's wings?

The legislative process in American Congress to translate the July 2005 and March 2006 agreements between President Bush and Prime Minister Manmohan Singh into a binding legality, should have received enthusiastic plaudits, instead received opprobrium and brickbats from all walks of life in India. During much of July and August 2006, politicians, Members of Parliament, media, public opinion, and the scientific community have been greatly agitated over the attempts of the U.S. Congress to incorporate extraneous conditionalities into what India perceived as a settled agreement.

As stated in the preceding chapter, the House of Representative Bill No.H.R.5682 urges upon America to achieve a moratorium on the production of fissile material for nuclear explosion purposes by India, Pakistan, and China at the earliest possible date. The Senate Bill talks of cessation of production only by India and Pakistan. These propositions are clearly unacceptable to India. India is willing to join only a non-discriminatory, multilaterally negotiated, and internationally verifiable Fissile Material Cut- off Treaty.

The very provision in the draft Senate Bill S.3709 that any waiver on nuclear transfers to India "shall cease to be effective if the President determines that India has detonated a nuclear explosive device after the date of the enactment of this Act", though consistent with the U.S. Atomic Energy Act 1954, clearly enjoins upon America to prevent non-nuclear weapon states receiving cooperation from the U.S. acquiring nuclear weapons. France's explosion of a series of nuclear tests some years ago did not balk at the existing cooperation between U.S. and France. It is not unknown to world that India has declared unilateral and voluntary moratorium on nuclear tests after the Pokharan II test in 1998. In a changing situation, for example if America, China, Pakistan and other countries conduct nuclear tests, it will be illogical and inconceivable to cling the wings of Indian option to detonate tests. India may also be required to carry out a test for technological reasons including ensuring safety of its arsenals. The long gap of 24 years between the two tests demonstrates India's sense of responsibility and restraint.

The provision in H.R. 5682 that the President " should seek to prevent the transfer to India of nuclear equipment, materials or technology from other participating governments in the NSG or from any other source" further worsens the dislocation to the Indian economy that will happen to nuclear reactors. These provisions are both unfair and unacceptable to India as it is a de facto nuclear weapon power.

The Senate Bill which excludes "export or re-export to India of any equipment, materials or technology related to the enrichment of uranium, the reprocessing of spent nuclear fuel or the production of heavy water" runs counter to the provision of civilian nuclear cooperation promised in July 2005 agreement. When civilian nuclear power heads towards a large scale expansion, India would like to benefit from global advances in nuclear fuel cycle technology. Denying this multilateral facility or a multilateral programme to develop a proliferation resistant fuel cycle will certainly clipped Indian wings to further expand indigenously.

As to an "Additional Protocol", the Senate Bill had stated that "Additional protocol means a protocol additional to a safeguard agreement with the IAEA, as negotiated between a country and the IAEA based on a Model Additional Protocol as set forth in IAEA information circular (INF-CIRC) 540". Applied to non nuclear weapon states, it is highly intrusive and requires extensive reporting practices. India sincerely desires that these specific safeguards be on the lines of IAEA INFCIRC-66, and some where between those applicable to weapon states and non-weapon states.

The provision in the Senate Bill requiring the President to make an annual report to Congress that India is in full compliance of its non-proliferation and other commitments, is likely to diminish a permanent waiver into an annual one and introduce uncertainty.

India is opposed to the provision for implementation of safeguards on the civilian facilities prior to lifting of restrictions on the nuclear commerce by US and other NSG. It wants simultaneity in implementing the provisions in the agreement. What is more intriguing is the very fact the Senate Bill while putting an overwhelming emphasis on nuclear non-proliferation, has completely ignored the impact of agreement on energy security and problems of mitigating greenhouse gases. The American intent is very clear to fence India with so many denial regimes that with its warped wings it could not move farther in nuclear weaponisation than where it is.

A wrong deal with wrong energy source

In support of nuclear deal with America it is claimed that civilian nuclear energy will make India less reliant on unstable sources of oil and gas. One obvious consequences of reduction of India's dependency on imported fossil fuels would be the stabilization of international oil prices at lower levels. These tall claims do not stand up to scrutiny. In 2005, only about 1 per cent of India's installed electrical capacity of 120 gigawatts electric (Gwe) was fuelled by oil, according to figures available at Indian President A.P. J. Abdul Kalam's website. Nuclear energy accounts for only about 2.7 per cent of India's capacity. Most of India's energy comes from coal (55 per cent) and hydroelectric power (26.4 per cent): some comes from natural gas (10.3 per cent). Wind, solar, and other renewable energy sources (5.2 per cent) produce more centrally generated electricity than both oil and nuclear combined. India prefers not to use its oil for centrally generated electricity, but rather reserves it for other uses such as transportation. So India's use of nuclear energy will do little to release more oil into the international market. And while nuclear energy could supplant coal energy, doing so would be far more expensive than raising the level of energy efficiency, not to mention the huge additional costs of storing radioactive spent fuel and disposing of nuclear waste. India's Bureau of Energy Efficiency reports that, in the industrial sector alone, more efficient use of energy could conserve 15Gwe of electricity a year. Further improvements in end- use efficiency of household appliances could save another 3-5 Gwe. That means an aggressive programme of improved energy efficiency could substitute for all the future power output from nuclear reactors currently being planned in India between now and 2020. One argument made in favour of building nuclear reactors is that nuclear energy reduces greenhouse gases. But if India were to go the route of increasing energy efficiency over more nuclear plants, the reduction of greenhouse gases would be greater, since such improvements can be made in a much shorter time. India needs additional energy to meet its economy and growing population. According to India's own picture, if it were to achieve energy independence by 2030, most of such production would not come from nuclear power. Under this scenario, the projected level of electric power production would be 456 GWe and would still be fuelled mainly by coal (43.8 per cent), followed by hydro (22 per cent), renewables (27.6 per cent), and finally, nuclear (6.6 per cent). It is clear that India does not find nuclear power as the solution to its energy problems for the next 25 years.

One approach to this problem is decentralized, distributed energy generation, in which small to medium sized facilities are located near sites of power demand, in contrast to relying on large central power plants. Because the electricity produced by distributed generation flows shorter distances to consumers, it is cheaper than relying on a vast transmission and distribution network, which has high capital, operations and maintenance costs, as well as significant energy losses. Distributed generation encompasses a number of options: wind power, biomass and waste driven fuel cells, micro- turbines, and solar photovoltaic. It includes the use of natural gas- fuelled turbines for combined heat and power installations for large facilities.

One of the most ignored or misrepresented issues in the current debate over the nuclear deal is the huge potential of India's alternative sources of electricity. According to a study by the international management-consulting firm Frost and Sullivan, India's untapped electrical generating capacity is 150 Gwe from hydro (the equivalent of 150 large nuclear plants), 85 Gwe from biomass, and 45 Gwe from wind power. India is already the world's fourth largest producer of wind power, which currently produces 50 per cent more electrical power than India's nuclear reactors. According to Leonard Weiss, "all of these facts lead to the conclusion the nuclear deal with India is the wrong deal with the wrong energy source at the wrong time."[27]

As stated above, nuclear scientists have not been able so far to meet the energy requirements of the people from nuclear reactors as promised by them. Exploration of alternative sources of energy from renewable sources or by clean coal technologies and coal gasification would certainly lessen India's overwhelming dependence on America for natural uranium for its reactors. This would free India ever from being bullied into many restrictions or conditionalities as recently put into Congressional draft bills reneging on what promised in July 2005 and March 2006 agreements. This would have reinforced India's non-aligned political culture vis-a-vis America.

Supremacy of US over multilateralism

In the absence of any Security Council resolution the US launched its invasion on Iraq. Not only that the World Summit on Sustainable Development (WSSD) in September 2002 and at the climate changes conference that followed in New Delhi in October the same year, the US was blatant in its effort to draw out countries from the UN process and to form "coalitions of the willing" instead. At the WSSD, Paula Dobriansky, head of the US delegation, accused governments of focusing too much on text. These words cannot save the earth, She said in a press conference. Instead, She called on governments to focus on voluntary partnerships between governments, regional groups, local authorities, non-governmental actors, international institutions or private sector actors. In the climate negotiations, the US chief negotiators disparaged the Kyoto Protocol as just a piece of paper while calling on countries to go with US, and sign bilateral deals instead.

As stated by Stephen Brooks and William Wolhlforth, American supremacy today is unparalleled in history. The US spends as much on military research and development as the next six powers combined. The US economy is twice as large as its closest rival Japan. California's economy alone is the fifth largest in the world, ahead of France and just behind the UK. It is also the world's leading technological power. US expenditures on R & D in the 1990s equaled those of the next 7 richest countries combined." The US has no rival in any critical dimension of power", as, stated by them. "The recent tendency to equate unipolarity with the ability to achieve desired outcomes single-handedly on all issues only reinforces this point; in no previous international system would it have occurred to anyone to apply such a yardstick."[28]

Preaching Democracy and Human Rights: Chimerical

The sincerity and genuineness of Americans truly taking up the cudgels for human rights, democracy and building a new safe world order, began to be doubted as the casus belli or raison detre for military intervention in Iraq with reports showing how CIA intelligence reports were deliberately distorted, monitored, sexed up and exaggerated to prove Iraq's possession of weapons of mass destruction (WMDs) and its links with Al Qaeda.[29] In a recent international relation committee report presented in Senate revealed that there is no connection between Saddam Hussein and Al Qaeda. This has embarrassed even, the Defence Intelligence Agency, the CIA and MI-6 Richard Butler, an unabashed war supporter, and former UN weapons Inspector says: " Clearly a decision had been taken to pump up the case against Iraq". [30] Sunday Herald reports that the Blair government ran a dirty tricks operation designed specially to produce misleading intelligence to give Britain an "excuse to wage war", [31] Operation Rockingham was set up to cherry pick and doctor intelligence. After the American successful war in Iraq, not even coming across a slightest evidence of the presence of WMS in Iraq exposes the invidious design of the US to carve out a world according to its own script with the ability to use force any where in the world, say after Iraq, it is the turn of Syria, Korea, Iran where Americans feel its self defined national interests are likely to be threatened or already threatened. US emphasis on human rights and democracy provided it new euphemism for intervening with its military might and genie to absolve the world of the powers that it considers as evil and not willing to conform to its strategic procrustean bed.

The post war world might see the US doing a lot more reinforcing its preeminent position and its interests by forming "coalitions of the willing to get what it wants and counter the moves targeted against it. The unwillingness of France, Germany, Russia and China to toe the American furrow in Iraq war and the tumult of world public opinion deter US from hurtling into any kind of harsh decisions it considers rightful in its view to reinforce its interests. The US will therefore be forced to seek out particular countries as allies and reward them with its protection. Recently signed two agreements with Singapore and Chile by US could be dangled as models of reward for countries that surrender themselves to American dictates. Nothing could be more worse for developing countries - for their problems, concern and demands for equity, justice and democratization of institutions will be consigned to the backburner – than the fact that they will continue to foot the bill for what the US is doing to the climate, and to implement the domestic imperatives of wealth production, inordinate consumption and profligate life style.

Need to redefine national interest in new planetary terms possible?

During the 2000 election campaign when, Condoleezza Rice, now the Secretary of State wrote that we should "proceed from the firm ground of the national interest and not from the interest of an illusory international community". What disrupts its European allies was "the assumption that a conflict between the pursuit of national interest and commitment to the interests of a far from illusory international community necessarily exists". [32] It is in American interest to preserve its preeminent position. But global commons such as terrorism which is a threat to all societies, international trade which will benefit both US and others, global warming which will raise sea level along American coasts as well as those of other countries, easily contamination and spread of infectious diseases by ship or plane and financial instability which will hurt all, can be incorporated into a broad and far-sighted concept of national interest. [33]

As a study shows, many Americans want global values to be incorporated into national interest. Seventy three percent agreed with the poll statement: " I regard myself as a citizen of the world as well as a citizen of the United States, and 44 percent agreed strongly". [34] But the traditionalists bring out a distinction between foreign policy based on values and a foreign policy based on interest. They describe as vital those interests that would directly affect our safety and thus deserve the use of force in their defence-for example, to prevent attacks on the US, to prevent the emergence of hostile hegemonies in Asia or Europe or to prevent hostile powers on our borders or in control of the seas and to ensure the survival of US allies. [35] No doubt national strategic interests are vital and important for survival and need priority. That does not mean humanitarian and global interests are to be sidelined. These are more important and vital to Americans and their foreign policy. What America preaches at its home front in terms of democracy, human rights and justice that provide America a sense of identity and righteousness, should be translated into concrete terms at the global level. This would certainly make America exemplary and righteous before others meriting respect from them. But in practice the dichotomy or disconnect between what it preaches at home and practice abroad questions America how its emphasis on democracy and human rights stands in an unequal world?

Are Americans prepared to over consume in the knowledge that life for their children will be at a lower level? Probably not. Humanity cannot live at the North American level on prevailing technology; it would take many planets to sustain this. In reality, to build a new world order based on values such as democracy, human rights, equity and justice, needs a kind of rethinking of American life style, pattern of development and consumption for which the big question mark is whether American public is prepared to bear the brunt of such a new thinking to form the basis of its foreign policy. In all international forums say, WTO, Environment and Sustainable Development, Climate Change, Convention on Biological Diversity America has not taken any exemplary step by voluntarily bearing the brunt of what-it has done to the planet, rather has successfully tried to reinforce its self defined national interests at the cost of others.

New world order and American strategy: prescriptions

The World order unfolded on American script and command Is not going to usher in any new hope and vision. The post Iraq war stands as a witness to American enthronement in the international system as the world policeman .All euphoria following the end of the cold war about the advent of a New world order dissipated with America in total disregard of UN and other international institutions intervened militarily in various states which started from Bosnia to Iraq. All talks about multilateralism, democratization, and new economic order based on justice and equity remained mere texts. One cannot but argue with what historian Robert Tucker said: America "did not go from unilateralism to multilateralism but from a position of isolation to the unilateralism of a position of undisputed leadership over a global alliance". [36] Nobody will dispute the fact that America is likely to remain the most powerful country well into this century. The focus on unipolarism and hegemony does not mean that the United States is able to get the outcomes it wants in a changing world. There are limits to its power. According to Joseph Nye Jr. power structure in the world is like a three-dimensional chess game. "The top military board is unipolar with the United States far outstripping all other states, but the middle economic board is multipolar, with the United States, Europe and Japan accounting for two thirds of world product and the bottom board of transnational relation that cross borders outside the control of government has widely dispersal structure of power". [37] Too much focus on military overstretches of America blinds it to the limits of power. America is not equally great in economic and transnational dimension. Many transnational and global common issues such as global warming, climate change and AIDS, proliferation of weapons of mass destruction, terrorism, drugs, trade, ecological stability cannot be resolved without cooperation of others. If collective action and cooperation is a necessary part of what the world wants for its survival, then America is bound to share. Many events that may occur outside over which America has no control, are bound to affect America, as seen from September 11 incident, a very poor and remote country can pose a threat to US. For these reasons Americans' concept of world order should go beyond its border and narrow national interest. It is time that America pursue a legitimate national interest that is in any case congruent with the greater good of the entire humanity. It is not the military supremacy but its exemplary lead on various global issues that will bring legitimacy to its role in restructuring the world order. International order is a public good-something everyone can consume without diminishing its availability to others.[38] To define public good in terms of its own narrow self interests, results in self-serving ideology for the powerful, as America does at present. There may not be unanimity about what constitutes the public good. But the need arises to identify first the global or planetary objective needs and accept it as the principal political concept constituting its national interest. If the United States being the largest beneficiary of a public good does not take lead in directing disproportionate resources out of its over consumption towards its provision, the smaller beneficiaries and the deprived, are unlikely to produce the public good. Two things deserve attention by American policy makers.

America should embark on rethinking economy to promote a new international order. Not consumption but criteria of modesty, altruism and other humanitarian concerns should be the basis of economic development. Not fossil fuel based industrialization be the basis of development but alternatives should be worked out to define what constitutes development. Promoting an international economic system and openness of global market is a necessary step that will benefit both America and other poor countries. Bringing down walls of protectionism at home with democratization of world economic organization on the basis of equity and justice is more likely to foster stable and democratic societies in other countries.

Apart from democratizing world economy and rethinking its economy, lifestyle and over consumption, top priority should be given to international development, which is an important public good. Flow of large-scale financial, scientific and technological wherewithal and aid to the poor developing and least developed countries who are simmering in poverty, disease and political instability, will help wipe out the squalor of poverty from the face of the earth. It will be beneficiary to both the United States and other countries receiving the aid, as Harvard economist Jeffery Sachs has argued, "because even remote countries become outposts of disorder for the rest of the world"[39]. But America's record in this case is very dismal. Its foreign aid during these years has plummeted to 0.1 percent of America's GNP, roughly one third of European levels. Protectionist trade measures often hurt poor countries most. The American public opinion favours an increase say 15 to 20 times more on it than America is at present doing. Not only aid, openness of market, strengthening accountable institutions and discouraging corruption are even more important[40] for American policy makers to eke out a new international order- a public good of which every one wants to have a legitimate share.

The image that its soft power has created in other nations through flow of information on Americans ideas on liberty, human rights and values and high educational institutions, prospective job markets, TV and films on various transnational channels and contracts across national borders and boundaries, wants America lead by example. But on some issues, such as the global climate, the US has taken less of a lead than is necessary. Instead of owning the responsibility for its historic emission of greenhouse gases to the atmosphere, and accepting the "polluter pay" the principle, the US has put its narrow economic interests before the global interest. The expectations of a lead role from America on many global issues can easily slip into disappointment and contempt. [41] A democratic global governance of planetary commons, and other issues such as trade, environment weapons of proliferation, human rights, terrorism and other concerns requires America to develop and maintain international regimes of laws and institutions that organize international action and bind national interest on such domains. This, America should do not from a position of one power arrogance but of a new leadership believing in multilateralism mediated through Wilsonian idealism and realism of new planetary ethics of survival and environmental integrity.

The key reason why none of the major powers today is able to form a coalition against the US, whether in the context of Bush's preventive strategy or global trade, development and environmental negotiations, is that they have been closely allied with the US for decades and have derived substantial benefits. They fear that they will have to forgo these benefits if they take on US. India also sits on the same boat hoping to sail through the nuclear energy crisis with the active help of US." The one entity with the capacity to challenge the United States in the near future is the European Union, if it were to become a right federation with major military capabilities and if relations across the Atlantic were allowed to sour".[42] The diminished fungibility of military power in a global information age places European Union in an advantageous position to challenge the US on the economic and transnational fronts. The world is changing so fast that US cannot be able to achieve its objective without consulting and taking into confidence others nations and world public opinion. The French critic Dominique Moisi puts it: "The global age has not changed the fact that nothing in the world can be done without the United States. And the multiplicity of new actors mean that there is very little the United States can achieve alone".[43]

The surge of public opinion in the world rising against the US is suggestive of the fact that US cannot make the whole world play according to its tune. A public opinion poll conducted for the World Economic Forum released in January this year reveals that people are increasingly disenchanted with the direction in which the world is moving. A future challenge will be in ensuring that the public does not just stop short of demanding change, but has the information to define the nature of this change as well. Enlightened global public intervention, coupled with increased democracy in countries across the world so that leaders are held accountable and cannot ignore the will of the people, can play a major role in countering US unilateralism.[44] Nongovernmental organization particulariy those who work in the global arena have not succeeded in raising public debate on the role of US in ensuring global democracy. But there is growing a myriad group of grass root organizations in the US far more outspoken than national NGOs, and responsible for changes in local and state level legislation. Greater engagement of the US public in this issue is crucial. They have to reassert their democracy, in the face of global criticism that US functions like a business plutocracy.

The future world will depend a lot on the foresight of US leaders and the intensity of public opinion to guide its leaders in the direction of rethinking their inordinate profligate life style, and pattern of development, and democratizing world economic institutions and putting implicit faith in multilateralism and UN. Its leaders need to understand that super power status notwithstanding, the country still needs the rest of the world. The US bears a large part of the responsibility for the current strain in global relations. If the country's leaders are indeed interested in global peace and security, they have to lead by example, by first changing domestic policies to match what they have been demanding of the other countries and then strengthening multilateralism. An Austrian analyst may be right in her view that if the United States plays its card well and acts not as a soloist but, as the leader of a concert of nations, the Pax Americana, in terms of its duration might...become more like the Pax Romana than the Pax Britannica.[45] Thus, if a paradigm shift in American foreign policy toward a transformative and enlightened national interest based on the above principles takes place, there will be no difficulty in India to strike a strategic note with America. In the absence of any inkling of such transformation in American foreign policy behaviour, if India is bound up with American strategic partnership marking a shift from its non aligned policy, then, it will cast doubts on India's ability to fight for the cause of the developing South countries. India's quest for a major role in international realm on the indices of power, and alignment with America will appear as more India specific and less visionary than during the years of Nehruvian foreign policy.

References

1. Richard N. Gardner, "The Comeback of Liberal Internationalism", Washington Quarterly, 13 Summer, 1990, p.23.
2. Eugene R. Wittkopf, Faces of Internationchism, Public Opinion and American Foreign Policy (Durham, N.C.: Duke University Press, 1990)
3. Eugene R. Wittkopf, American Foreign Policy Beliefs and Behaviour at the Water's Edge", International Studies Notes, Vol.22, no.3, Fall 1997, p.3
4. Eugene R. Wittkopf, " What Americans Really Think about Foreign Policy", Washington Quarterly, 19, Summer 1996, pp91-106, See also Wittkopf, "Faces of Internationalism in a Transitional Environment", Journal of Conflict Resolution, 38,September 1994,pp.376-401.
5. Wittkopf , American's Foreign Policy, op.cit, p.5
6. Joseph S. Nye, Jr, " U.S. Power and Strategy after Iraq", Foreign Affairs 82, no.4, July-August 2003
7. Peter Trubowitz, Defining the National Interest: Conflict and Change in America Foreign Policy (Chicago: University of Chicago Press, 1998), p.12
8. Joseph S. Nye Jr., "The American national interest and global public goods", International Affairs, Vol.78, November 2, April 2002.
9. William Schneider," The New Isolationism", in Eagle Adrift: "American Foreign Policy at the End of the century, ed. Robert J.Lieber (New York: Longman, 1997), p.30.
10. The Hindu, September 13, 2006

11. Steven Kull, "What the Public knows that Washington does not ", Foreign Policy, Winter 1995-96,p.114.
12. Henry Kissinger, "America at the apex", The National Interest, Summer 2001,p.15.
13. Joseph Joffe, "Who's afraid of Mr. Big", The National Interest, Summer 2001,p.52
14. Kenneth F. Scheve and Matthew J. Slaughter, Globalization and the Perception of American Workers (Washington DC.: Institute for International Economics, 2001)
15. See Charles Krauthammer, "Unilateral? Yes indeed", Washington Post, 14 December 2001, p. A45. See also Richard Perle's comments in Sept.11: a conversation", The National Interest, special issue, Thanks giving 2001, pp.82-95
16. Robert Kagan and William Kristol, "The present danger", The National Interest, Spring 2000, pp.58, 64,67.
17. Robert W.Tucker, "American power- for what? " a symposium, Commentary, 109,January 2000, p.46.
18. Joseph S.Nye Jr., "The American national interest and global public Goods', op.cit.
19. Quoted by Vikas Singh, "Bush's Men-o-War: Ideologues of Neo-Imperialism, Times of India, April 17, 2003.
20. Ibid
21. Vikas Singh, op.cit.
22. Sudha Mahalingam, "US forging a partnership of expediency"? The Hindu, October 25, 2005, p.10
23. Down to Earth, vol.11, no.23, April 30, 2003, p.28
24. Nirupama Subramanian, " Pakistan and U.S.: two together, two apart", The Hindu, 10 June, 2006, p.12
25. Praveen Swami, "American claims and question of fact", The Hindu, 5 August, 2006,p.12
26. John Perkins, " American Empire: Slaver or Saviour", World Affairs, Vol.9, no.1, Spring 2005,p.16
27. Leonard Weiss, "The U.S.-India nuclear agreement is the wrong deal with the wrong energy source", Atomic Scientists, Vol.62, no.3, May/June 2006,p.2
28. Quoted in Down to Earth, op.cit, and p.29.
29. Times of India, 24 March 2003.
30. Praful Bidwai, "Great power delusions", Hindustan Times, 15 June 2003.

31. Sunday Herald (Britain), June 8, 2003.
32. Peter Ludlow, "Wanted: a Global Partner", Washington Quarterly, Summer 2001,p.167
33. Joseph S.Nye Jr., "The American national interest and global public goods", op.cit.
34. Program on International Policy Attitudes, "Americans on globalization; a study of US public attitudes" (University of Maryland, 1999), p.8
35. America's national interests: a report from the Commission on America's National Interests (Co chairs Robert Ellworth, Andrew Good Pasteur and Rita Hauser, 1996), p.13
36. Quoted by Jacques Fomerand , "Has American Multilateralism a Future?", UNU nexions, December 2002, p.1
37. Joseph S.Nye Jr., op.cit.
38. Inge Kaul, Isabelle Grunberg and Marc A. Stern, eds, Global public goods: International cooperation in the 21st century (New York: Oxford University Press, 1999)
39. Jeffrey Sachs, "What is good for the poor is the good for America", The Economist, 14 July 2001, pp.32-33.
40. William Esterly, "The failure of development", Financial Times, 4 July 2001,p.32 ; Dani Rodrik , The new global economy and developing countries : making openness work (Washington DC.: Overseas Development Council,1999)
41. Philip Bowring , "Bush's America is developing an image problem", International Herald Tribune, 31 May 2001, p.8
42. Joseph S.Nye Jr., op.cit.
43. Dominique Moisi, "The real crisis over the Atlantic", Foreign Affairs, July-August 2001,p.153.
44. Down to Earth, op.cit. , P.33
45. Coral Bell, American ascendancy – and the pretense of concert", The National Interest, Fall 1999, p.60.

Bibliography

Books

Ashley J. Tellis and Michael Wills, *Strategic Asia 2004–05: Confronting Terrorism in the Pursuit of Power*, (Seattle, WA: The National Bureau of Asian Research, 2004).

Ashley J. Tellis, *India's Emerging Nuclear Posture: Between Recessed Deterrence and Ready Arsenal*, New Delhi: Oxford University Press, 2001.

Ashok Sharma, *Lobbying in the US Foreign Policy Process: A Study of the US-India Relations*, Ph. D. Thesis , Jawaharlal Nehru University, New Delhi, 2005.

Brahma Chellaney, *Nuclear Proliferation: The US-India Conflict* (New Delhi: Orient Longman, 1993)

C. Raja Mohan, *Crossing the Rubicon: The Shaping of India's New Foreign Policy* (New Delhi: Penguin, 2003)

Chintamani Mahapatra, *Indo-US Relations into the 21st Century* (New Delhi: 1998)

Dennis Kux, *Estranged Democracies: India and the United States, 1941-1991* (New Delhi: 1993)

Frank Carlucci, Robert Hunter, and Zalmay Khalilzad, eds., *Taking Charge: A Bipartisan Report to the President Elect on Foreign Policy and National Security—Papers* (Santa Monica, Calif.: RAND, 2000)

Harold Isaacs, *Scratches on Our Minds* (New York: 1980)

Henry Kissinger, *Does America Need a Foreign Policy*, New York, Simon and Schuster, 2003

J. N. Dixit, *India's Foreign Policy: 1947-2003* (New Delhi: 2003).

Jaswant Singh, *A Call to Honour* (New Delhi: Rupa Publications, 2006).

Jaswant Singh, *Defending India* (London: Macmillan, 1999).

John P. Lewis, *India's Political Economy, Governance and Reform* (Delhi: 1995).

John W. Melior, "Conclusion" in John W. Melior, ed., *India: A Rising Middle Power* (Boulder, Colo.: 1979)

John W. Melior, ed., *India: A Rising Middle Power* (Boulder, Colo.: 1979)

John Young, *Cold War and Detente 1941-1991*(New York: 1993).

Mahesh Kumar Singh, *Inda's Defense Strategy and Tactics: A Geographical Analysis,* 1st Edition (Delhi: 1984),

Myron Weiner, "Critical Choices for India and America", in Donald C. Hellmann, ed.,*Southern Asia: The Politics of Poverty and Peace* (Lanham, Md.: 1976)

Niall Ferguson, *Colossus: The Price of America's Empire*, New York: Penguin, 2004

Norman D. Palmer, *South Asia and United States Policy* (Boston: 1966)

Robert McMohan, *Cold War on the Periphery: The United States, India, and Pakistan* (New York: Columbia University Press, 1994).

Sanjay Gandhi, ed., *The Tilt: The U.S. and the South Asian Crisis of 1971*, National Security Archive Electronic Briefing Book No. 79, December 16, 2002.

Shekhar Gupta, *India Redefines its Role* (Oxford: 1995),

Shivaji Ganguly, *US Policy toward South Asia* (Boulder: Coloumbia, 1990)

Stephen Cohen, *India: Emerging Power* (New Delhi: 2002)

Stephen P. Cohen, *The Pakistan Army* (California: 1984)

Steven P. Cohen, *India: Emerging Power* (New Delhi: 2002)

Strobe Talbott, *Engaging India: Diplomacy, Democracy and the Bomb,* Penguin Group, Brookings Institution Press, 2004.

Sulochana Raghavan Glazer and Nathan Glazer, ed., *Conflicting Images: India and the United States* (Glen Dale, Md.: 1990)

Thomas Perish, *The Cold War Encyclopedia*, 1st Edition (New York: 1996).

Trade Strategy? India Policy Forum, Volume 1, 2004.

Vijay Gupta, ed., *India and Nonalignment* (Delhi: 1983)

William Watts, *The United States and Asia: Changing Attitudes and Policies* (Lanham, Md.: 1982).

Articles/Papers

A. Gopalakrishnan, "Indo-US Nuclear Cooperation: A Non-starter," *Economic and Political Weekly*, July 2, 2005, 4, available at www.epw.org.in.

Adam Wolfe, Yevgeny Bendersky, Federico Bordonaro, India, China, the U.S. and the Balance of Power in the Indian Ocean, *Japan Focus*. Cornell University, 25 July 2005.

Ajai Sahni, "Ends and Beginnings", *Outlook India*, New Delhi, 09 March 2006.

Alexander Evans, Reducing Tension is Not Enough, *The Washington Quarterly*, Spring 2001 (.pdf file).

Alistair McMillan, Attitudes Towards the United States Amongst the Indian Electorate, Posted on the author's website at Nuffield College, Oxford University, November 2001 (.pdf file).

Amit Baruah, "India, Russia May Invite China to Join Fighter Aircraft Project, *The Hindu*, June 27, 2004.

Amit Baruah, "Multilateralism the Best Solution," *The Hindu*, October 11, 2004.

Amit Baruah, "We Are Disappointed: Manmohan," *The Hindu,* March 26, 2005, available at www.hindu.com/2005/03/26/stories/2005032606320100.htm.

Amit Baruah, Unequal Partners?, *The Hindu*, India, 02 March 2006.

Amit Gupta, "After the Bomb: U.S. Policy Towards a Nuclear South Asia," *Mediterranean Quarterly,* Spring 1999, pp.40-63.

Amit Gupta, "Fire in the Sky: The Indian Missile Program," *Defense and Diplomacy*, October 1990.

Amit Gupta, "I Want My M-i-G: How India's Force Structure and Military Doctrine are Determined," *Asian Survey*, Vol. XXXV, No. 5, May 1995, pp. 441-458.

Amit Gupta, "N plus 20? India's Third Tier Nuclear State Dilemma," *Asian Survey*, Vol. XLI, No. 10, November/December 2001.

Amit Gupta, "The Indian Diaspora's Political Efforts in the United States, *ORF Occasional Paper*, September 2004.

Amit Gupta, Partnering the United States: India's Window of Opportunity, *Security Research Review*. *Bharat Rakshak*, India, August 2005.

Amit Gupta, The U.S.-India Relationship: Strategic Partnership or Complementary Interests?, Strategic Studies Institute, U.S. Army War College, February 2005 (.pdf file).

Amit Kumar, Indo-U.S. Cooperation: Next Step in the Indian Ocean, Institute of Peace and Conflict Studies, New Delhi, 19 May 2006.

Andy Mukherjee, "Commentary: A nuclear-powered India would charge up global trade," (*http://www.iht.com/articles/2006/03/02/bloomberg/sxmuk.php*) *International Herald Tribune*, March 2, 2006.

Anil Kakodkar interviewed by T. S. Subramanian, *The Hindu*, August 12, 2005, available at www.thehindu.com/2005/08/12/stories/2005081204521100.htm.

Anil Rane, "First DP world in port controversy and now India uses lobbyists to clinch nuclear deal in US," (*http://www.indiadaily.com/editorial/7401.asp*) *India Daily*, March 13, 2006: "Indian Embassy in Washington had signed up two lobbying firms to 'sell the deal'. ... a $700,000 contract with Barbour, Griffith and Rogers, an outfit led by Robert Blackwill, US ambassador to India from 2001 to 2003, ... [and is] also paying $600,000 to Venable, a firm that 'boasts' of former Democratic Senator Birch Bayh of Indiana as its point man."

Annpurna Nautiyal, Current Trends in India-U.S. Relations: Hopes for a Secure Future, *Strategic Insights*. Center for Contemporary Conflict, U.S. Naval Postgraduate School, April 2006 (.pdf file).

Annpurna Nautiyal, U.S. Policies in the Post-Cold War Era: An Indian Perspective, *Strategic Analysis*. Institute for Defence Studies and Analyses, New Delhi, January-March 2004 (.pdf file).

Anupam Srivastava, "Positive-Sum GameAccruals in US-India Relations," *Bharat Rakshak Monitor*, Vol. 51, July-September, 2002. Available at *http://www.bharat-rakshak.com/MONITOR/ISSUE5-1/anupam.html*.

Anupam Srivastava, Evolving Strategic Ties Between India and the United States, Chapter in "India's National Security: Annual Review 2002," edited by Satish Kumar. Posted on the author's website at the University of Georgia, April 2002.

Anupam Srivastava, Indo-U.S. Strategic Dialogue: From Sound Bytes to Sound Decisions, *Bharat Rakshak Monitor*, January/February 2000.

Anupam Srivastava, Positive-Sum Game Accruals in U.S.-India Relations, *Bharat Rakshak Monitor*, July-September 2002.

Ashley J. Tellis, "The U.S. India Global Partnership How Significant for American Interests: Testimony before the House Committee of International Relations," *Carnegie* (03/18/05)

Ashley J. Tellis, "The Strategic Implications of a Nuclear India," *Orbis*, Vol. 26, No. 1, Winter, 2002.

Ashley J. Tellis, Atoms for War? U.S.-Indian Civilian Nuclear Cooperation and India's Nuclear Arsenal, Carnegie Endowment for International Peace, June 2006 (.pdf file).

Ashley J. Tellis, India as a New Global Power: An Action Agenda for the United States . Carnegie Endowment for International Peace, 14 July 2005 (.pdf file).

Ashley J. Tellis, Seeking Breakthroughs, *Force*, Noida, India, October 2004. Posted on the Carnegie Endowment for International Peace website.

Ashley J. Tellis, The U.S.-India "Global Partnership": How Significant for American Interests?, Testimony before the Committee on International Relations, U.S. House of Representatives, 16 November 2005 (.pdf file).

Ashley Tellis, "Lost Tango in Washington," *The Indian Express*, November 15, 2004.

Ashley Tellis, "Seeking Breakthroughs," *Force*, October 2004.

Ashok Dasgupta, "New thrust to Indo-US ties in civilian nuclear, hi-tech areas," *The Hindu Business Line*, January 14, 2004, at:http://www.blonnet.com/2004/01/14/stories/2004011402650100.htm

Ashok Sharma, *Lobbying in the US Foreign Policy Process: A Study of the US-India Relations*, Ph. D. Thesis , Jawaharlal Nehru University, New Delhi, 2005.

Ashton B. Carter, America's New Strategic Partner?, *Foreign Affairs*, July/August 2006.

Atal Bihari Vajpayee, India-U.S. Relations in the Emerging Global Environment, Speech at the Asia Society, 22 September 2003.

B. Muralidhar Reddy, "Pak. Rejects Sinha's 'Talk of Pre-emption'," *The Hindu*, April 4, 2003.

B. Raman, "Will He Walk the Talk?" *Outlook,* January 14, 2002, available at: www.outlookindia.com.

B. Raman, Indo-U.S. Relations: The Pakistan Factor, South Asia Analysis Group, Noida, India, 14 May 2004.

B.S. Raghavan, "India-US Defence Pact-I: Bonding of Two Unequal Partners", *Hindu Business Line* (New Delhi), July 13, 2005, India-US Defence Pact II: Commerce May Fetter Judgment" *Hindu Business Line* (New Delhi), July 14, 2005

Background Briefing by Administration Officials on U.S.-South Asia Relations, no. 2. C. Uday Bhaskar, "F-16s for Pakistan augur well for India," March 27, 2005, at http://www.idsa-india.org/CUBArticle_UNI5.htm

Barry R. Posen, "Command of the Commons: The Military Foundation of U.S. Hegemony," *International Security*, Vol. 28, No. 1, Summer 2003.

Bhabani Mishra, "Post 1998 Track Two Diplomacy Between India and the USA", *Strategic Analysis,* 28 (1), Jan-Mar 2004, pp. 117-23.

Bhabani Mishra, India-U.S. Relations: A Paradigm Shift, *Strategic Analysis.* Institute for Defence Studies and Analyses, New Delhi, January-March 2005 (.pdf file).

Bharat Karnad, "India's Vision Void", *Indian Express* (New Delhi), July 2, 2005.

Bharat Karnad, Do As the U.S. Would, *Asian Age*, India, February 2006. Posted on the *Frontier India* website.

Binnendijk, Hans and Patrick Clawson, New Strategic Priorities. *The Washington Quarterly.* 1995, 18 (2).

Blackwill, Robert D., The Quality and Durability of the US India Relationship. Kolkata, November 27, 2002.

Brahma Chellaney, "Vaunted U.S.-India nuclear deal begins to fall apart," (*http://www.iht.com/articles/2006/02/13/opinion/edchell.php*) *International Herald Tribune*, February 13, 2006.

Brahma Chellaney, New Delhi's Dilemma, *The Washington Quarterly*, Summer 2000 (.pdf file).

Brajesh Mishra, "India, United States and New World Order: Prospects for Cooperation", Speech to the Council on Foreign Relations", New York, May 7, 2003, available at: http://www.indianembassy.org/indusrel/2003/nsa_cfr_may_7_03.htm

Brig. Arun Sahgal and Parama Sinha Palit, The 'Singh Doctrine', *Armed Forces Journal*, May 2006.

Brinkley, Douglas, Democratic Enlargement: The Clinton Doctrine. *Foreign Policy*. Spring 1997.

Bruce Reidel, New Directions in Indo-U.S. Relations and New Opportunities in U.S.-South Asia Relations, Center of the Advanced Study of India, University of Pennsylvania, 21 February and 09 May 2000 (.pdf file).

Bush II Presidency: Implications for Indo-US Relations, 61 ORF Policy Brief, http://www.observerindia.com/Publications/PolicyBrief/exsummary.htm

Bush Signals End to Clinton Approach in the Middle East. *The Hindustan Times*. February 10, 2001.

C. Christine Fair, Jalil Roshandel, Sunil Dasgupta and P.R. Kumaraswamy, The 'Strategic Partnership' Between India and Iran, Asia Program, Woodrow Wilson International Center for Scholars, April 2005 (.pdf file).

C. Christine Fair, Military Operations on Urban Areas: The Indian Experience, *India Review*, London, January 2003. Posted on the author's website.

C. Christine Fair, The Counterterror Coalitions: Cooperation with Pakistan and India, RAND, 2004 (.pdf file).

C. Christine Fair, U.S.-Indian Army-to-Army Relations: Prospects for Future Coalition Operations, *Asian Security*, U.S., April 2005. Posted on the author's website (.pdf file).

C. Raja Mohan and Gurcharan Das, "Will India Become a Global Power?", *Council on Foreign Relations*, 19 June 2006.

C. Raja Mohan, "India, U.S. in high tech talks", *The Hindu,* September 18, 2003

C. Raja Mohan, "India, U.S. wrapping up talks", *The Hindu*, September 20, 2003

C. Raja Mohan, "Indo-U.S. Dialogue on Pakistan?" *The Hindu*, April 10, 2003.

C. Raja Mohan, "On N-energy for India, US says it's serious, will begin talks," *The Indian Express*, March 30, 2005, at: http://www.indianexpress.com/full_story.php?content_id=67402;

C. Raja Mohan, A Paradigm Shift Toward South Asia?, *The Washington Quarterly*, Winter 2002-03 (.pdf file).

C. Raja Mohan, What If Pakistan Fails? India Isn't Worried ... Yet, *The Washington Quarterly*, Winter 2004-05 (.pdf file).

C. S. Kuppuswamy, India's Look-East Policy: More Aggressive, Better Dividends, South Asia Analysis Group, Noida, India, 03 January 2006.

Carothers, Thomas, Promoting Democracy and Fighting Terror. *Foreign Affairs.* January- February 2003, 82 (1).

Celia W. Dugger, "Group in Pakistan Is Blamed by India for Suicide Raid," *New York Times,* December 15, 2001.

Celia W. Dugger, "Wider Military Ties with India Offer U.S. Diplomatic Leverage," *New York Times*, June 10, 2002.

Celia W. Dugger, Wider Military Ties With India Offer U.S. Diplomatic Leverage, *The New York Times*, 10 June 2002. Posted on the Indian Ministry of External Affairs website.

Chaudhuri, Pramit Pal, Missiles, Nukes, Trade and the New Administration. *Span.* March/April 2001.

Chellaney, Brahma, Lessons from Iraq. *The Hindustan Times.* April 21, 2003.

Chidanand Rajghatta, "U.S. Opens High-tech Tap to India," *Times of India*, February 7, 2003.

Chidanand Rajghatta, "US-India nuclear deal under Iran gun," (*http://timesofindia.indiatimes.com/articleshow/1237146.cms*) *Times of India*, September 20, 2005.

Chidananda Rajghatta, "Rice Good on India's Plate", *The Times of India*, November 16, 2004

Christina Rocca, New Horizons in United States' Relations with South Asia, Center for the Advanced Study of India, University of Pennsylvania, July 2004 (.pdf file).

Christophe Jaffrelot, India, The United States' New Ally In Asia, Centre D'Etudes et de Recherches Internationales, France, July 2005. Posted on the Alliance Program website at Columbia University (.pdf file).

Christopher Van Hoellen, "The Tilt Policy Revisited: Nixon-Kissinger Geopolitics and South Asia", *Asian Survey 20* (April 1980)

Christopher Van Hoellen, *The Tilt Policy Revisited: Nixon-Kissinger Geopolitics and South Asia Asian Survey 20* (April 1980)

Christopher, Warren, America's Leadership, America's Opportunity. *Foreign Policy.* Spring 1995

Christopher, Warren, Principles and Opportunities for American Foreign Policy. US Department of State Despatch. January 23, 1995, 6 (4), pp. 1-45.

Claude Arpi, Indo-U.S. ties: The China factor, *Rediff*, India, 28 February 2006.

Claudio Lilienfeld, "Defense Cooperation: Where Are We Today?" remarks presented at "U.S.-India Bilateral Cooperation: Taking Stock and Moving Forward," a conference hosted by The Sigur Center for Asian Studies of The Elliott School of International Affairs at The George Washington University, Washington, D.C. April 1-2, 2004.

Clinton, William J., A National Strategy of Engagement and Enlargement. The White House; Washington DC. July 1994.

Col. John H. Gill, Dissuasion and Confrontation: U.S. Policy In India-Pakistan Crises, *Strategic Insights*. Center for Contemporary Conflict, U.S. Naval Postgraduate School, October 2004.

Coll, Alberto R., America as the Grand Facilitator. *Foreign Policy*. Summer 1992, 47-89.

Condoleezza Rice, "Promoting the National Interest," *Foreign Affairs*, vol. 79 (January/February 2002), pp. 45–62.

Condoleezza Rice, Interview with *India Today,* March 21, 2005, at http://www.indiatoday.com/itoday/20050328/

Condoleezza Rice, Interview with *The Washington Post,* March 25, 2005, at http://www.washingtonpost.com/wp-dyn/articles/A2015-2005Mar25.html

Conn Hallinan, India, Iran, and The United States, Foreign Policy in Focus, Silver City, NM and Washington, DC, 19 October 2005.

CRS Issue Brief for Congress, "India-US Relations", 4 April, 2006, available at: http://www.fas.org/sgp/crs/row/IB93097.pdf

Daalder Ivo H. and James M. Lindsay, No. 42, 370-7152.

Dafna Linzer, "Bush Officials Defend India Nuclear Deal. Aim Is Not to Reverse Policies, Allies Told," (*http://www.washingtonpost.com/wp-dyn/content/article/2005/07/19/AR2005071901847.html*) *Washington Post*, July 20, 2005.

Daryl G. Kimball, India's Choice, Congress' Responsibility, *Arms Control Today*, Washington, DC, January/February 2006.

David C. Mulford, Advancing U.S.-India Economic Relations, Speech to the Indian Chamber of Commerce/Indo-American Chamber of Commerce Luncheon, Calcutta, 18 August 2005. Posted on the U.S. State Department website.

David C. Mulford, From a Strategic to a Comprehensive Relationship, *The Hindustan Times*, India, 06 June 2004. Posted on the Mumbai U.S. Consulate General website.

David E. Sanger and Kurt Eichenwald, "Citing India Attack, U.S. Aims at Assets of Groups in Pakistan," *New York Times*, December 21, 2001.

David Frum, Our Friends in New Delhi, *National Post*, Canada, 07 March 2006. Posted on the American Enterprise Institute for Public Policy Research website.

David Jackson and Barbara Slavin, "More work ahead for U.S.-India nuclear deal," *http://www.usatoday.com/news/washington/2006-03-02-US-india-nuclear_x.htm?csp=34*) *USA Today*, March 2, 2006.

Deepa Ollapally, U.S.-India Relations: Ties That Bind?, The Sigur Center Asia Papers, George Washington University, 2005 (.pdf file).

Dennis Kux, "A Remarkable Turnaround: U.S.-India Relations," *Foreign Service Journal*, October 2002, pp. 18–23.

Dennis Kux, "India's Fine Balance," *Foreign Affairs*, May/June 2002, Vol. 81, No. 3.

Dennis Kux, India's Fine Balance, *Foreign Affairs*, May/June 2002. Posted on the Fletcher School website at Tufts University (.pdf file).

Department of Atomic Energy, Government of India, *http://www.dae.gov.in/*

Donald L. Berlin, India in the Indian Ocean, *Naval War College Review*. U.S. Naval War College, Spring 2006 (.pdf file).

Eric Lorber and Pramit Mitra, U.S.-India Relations: Convergence of Interests, *South Asia Monitor*. Center for Strategic and International Studies, Washington, DC, 04 July 2005.

Esther Pan, The U.S.-India Nuclear Deal - Q&A, Council on Foreign Relations, 24 February 2006.

Fareed Zakaria, Nixon to China, Bush to India, *Newsweek*, 27 February 2006.

Farhan Bokhari and Edward Luce, "Bombers Kill 33 in Kashmir as US Envoy Visits India," *Financial Times*, May 15, 2002.

Fouad, Ajami, Iraq and the Arab's Future. *Foreign Affairs*. January-February, 2003, 82 (1), pp. 2-18.

Francine R. Frankel, India's Potential Importance for Vital U.S. Geopolitical Objectives in Asia: A Hedge Against a Rising

China? Testimony before the Committee on International Relations, U.S. House of Representatives, 16 November 2005 (pdf file).

Franklin Kramer, "Toward a Mature Defense Relationship: Limits, Possibilities and Lessons," remarks presented at "U.S.-India Bilateral Cooperation: Taking Stock and Moving Forward," a conference hosted by The Sigur Center for Asian Studies of The Elliott School of International Affairs at The George Washington University, Washington, D.C. April 1-2, 2004

Fred Kaplan, The President's Indian Fantasy, *Slate*, 01 March 2006.

G. Balachandran, Indo-U.S. Relations: Perception and Reality, *Strategic Analysis*. Institute for Defence Studies and Analyses, New Delhi, April-June 2005 (.pdf file).

G. Balachandran, Separation is Not Rocket Science, *Indian Express*, New Delhi, 27 January 2006. Posted on the Frontier India website.

G. Parthasarathy, "Pervez, the Proliferator," *India Abroad*, November 1, 2002.

G.M. Hiranandani, Indo-U.S. Naval Cooperation, *Bharat Rakshak Monitor*, May-June 2002.

Gaddis, John Lewis, And Now This: Lessons From the Old Era For the New One. In Strobe Talbot and Nayan Chanda, *Eds. The Age of Terror: America and the World After*. 2001. Basic Books; New York. p. 323.

Galina Yaskina,"Russia-China-India: Prospects for Trilateral Cooperation," *Far Eastern Affairs*, Vol. 31, No. 1, 2003, pp. 16-27.

Gary K. Bertsch and Anupam Srivastava, U.S.-India Strategic Relations: Issues Before the New Administration, *Bharat Rakshak Monitor*, January/February 2001.

Gary Milhollin, Testimony of Gary Milhollin, Testimony before the Committee on Foreign Relations, U.S. Senate, 26 April 2006.

Gary R. Hess, *America Encounters India: 1941-1947*, Baltimore, John Hopkins Press, 1971, p. 2.

Gaurang Bhatt, India America Nuclear Deal - A Strategic Analysis, *India Defence*, New Delhi, 16 January 2006.

Gaurav Kampani, "Nuclear Overview," (*http://www.nti.org/e_research/profiles/India/Nuclear/index.html*) NTI, January 2006.

Gautam Adhikari, U.S. India Relations: Report on AEI'S 2003-04 Roundtable Discussions, American Enterprise Institute for Public Policy Research, 22 June 2005.

George Perkovich, "Bush's Nuclear Delusions," *Foreign Affairs*, vol. 82, no. 2 (March/April 2003).

George Perkovich, A Realist Case for Conditioning the U.S.-India Nuclear Deal, Working paper prepared for a Nonproliferation Policy Education Center seminar, 15 May 2005. Posted on the Carnegie Endowment for International Peace website.

George Perkovich, Faulty Promises: The U.S.-India Nuclear Deal, Carnegie Endowment for International Peace, September 2005 (.pdf file).

George Perkovich, Jessica T. Mathews, Joseph Cirincione, Rose Gottemoeller, and Jon B. Wolfsthal, *Universal Compliance: A Strategy for Nuclear Security* (Washington, D.C.: Carnegie Endowment for International Peace, 2005)

Gholz, Eugene, Deryl G. Press and Harvey M. Sapolsky, Come Home America: The Strategy of Restraint in the Face of Temptation. *International Security*. Spring 1997, 21 (4), pp. 5-48.

Graham Allison, "Tick, Tick, Tick," *The Atlantic Monthly*, Vol. 294, Issue 3, October 2004.

Gulab Hiranandani, The Indian End of the Telescope: India and its Navy, *Naval War College Review*. U.S. Naval War College, Spring 2002.

Hard Bargain, *NewsInsight*, New Delhi, 08 December 2005.

Hari Sud, India and U.S. Relations – Ground Realities, South Asia Analysis Group, Noida, India, 24 December 2004.

Hari Sud, India: The Strategic Partner of USA?, South Asia Analysis Group, Noida, India, 11 June 2003.

Harinder Sekhon, "NSSP – Are We Really Moving Forward?" *ORF Strategic Trends*, Vol. II, No., 43, November 1, 2004.

Harsh V. Pant, The U.S.-India Nuclear Deal, Iran, and India's Future, *ZNet Magazine*, Woods Hole, MA, 31 January 2006.

Harsh V. Pant, U.S. and Iran at Loggerheads: India's Role in Rapprochement, *Security Research Review*. Bharat Rakshak, India, October 2004.

Hass, Richard N., Paradigm Lost. *Foreign Affairs*. January/ February, 1995, 74, pp. 43-58.

Henry J. Hyde, U.S.-India: Global Partnership: How Significant for American Interests?, Opening remarks before the Committee on International Relations, U.S. House of Representatives, 16 November 2005 (.pdf file).

High Level Committee Report on the Indian Diaspora, New Delhi: Government of India, January 8, 2002.

Howard B. Schaffer, Reconsidering the U.S. Role, *The Washington Quarterly*, Spring 2001 (.pdf file).

HTCG Dialogue on Defense Technology, Data Privacy, and Export Licensing", November 18, 2004, Washington, DC, Bureau of Industry and Security, US Department of Commerce, available at: http://www.bis.doc.gov/InternationalPrograms/HTCG_Dialogue.htm

Huntington, Samuel P, The Lonely Superpower. *Foreign Affairs.* March/April, 1997, 38-39.

Huntington, Samuel P., Why International Security Matters. *International Security*. 1993, 17 (4), pp. 82-83.

Hyland, William G., America's New Course: *US Policies in the Post-Cold War Era, Foreign Affairs*. Spring 1990.

Immanuel Wallerstein, The U.S., India, and China, Fernand Braudel Center, Binghamton University, 01 August 2005.

Implementation of the India-United States Joint Statement of July 18, 2005: India's Separation Plan, Full text as approved by Indian Parliament, 07 March 2006. Posted on the *Outlook India* website.

India – U.S. Relations: A General Overview, available at: http://www.indianembassy.org/newsite/induspolAug06.asp

India and weapons of mass destruction," *http://en.wikipedia.org/wiki/India_and_weapons_of_mass_destruction*) *Wikipedia*.

India As A Nuclear Power: 1998-2001," (*http://nuclearweaponarchive.org/India/IndiaNPower.html*) *Nuclear Weapon Archive*, Last changed March 30, 2001.

India, Pakistan and Kashmir: Stabilising a Cold Peace, Asia Briefing #51. International Crisis Group, 15 June 2006 (.pdf file).

India, USA and the World," Remarks by Indian Prime Minister Atal Bihari Vajpayee at the Asia Society, New York, September 28, 1998, available at www.asiasociety.org/speeches/vajpayee.html.

India's Place in the U.S. Strategic Order, *Aspects of India's Economy*. Research Unit for Political Economy, Mumbai, December 2005.

India-U.S. Relations: A Vision for the 21st Century, Joint India-U.S. Statement, during President Bill Clinton's visit to India, 21 March 2000. Posted on the Indian Embassy website.

Indo-U.S. Framework for Maritime Security Cooperation, U.S. Department of Defense, March 2006 (.pdf file).

Indo-U.S. Joint Military Exercises after 2002 – a Partial List, *Aspects of India's Economy*. Research Unit for Political Economy, Mumbai, December 2005.

Indo-U.S. Joint Statement on High Technology Commerce", New Delhi, November 13, 2002, available at: www.mea.gov.in

Intelligence Brief: U.S.-India Nuclear Deal," (*http://www.pinr.com/report.php?ac=view_report&report_id=452&language_id=1*) *PINR*, March 7, 2006.

Interview with Anil Kakodkar by T.S. Subramanian, "Fast Breeder Reactors More Important for India," *The Hindu*, November 24, 2004.

Ivo H. and James M. Lindsay, Bush's Revolution. Current History. November 2003, 102 (667) 375.

Jabin T. Jacob, Indo-U.S. Nuclear Deal: The China Factor, Institute of Peace and Conflict Studies, New Delhi, March 2006 (.pdf file).

James Cetrone, U.S. Acknowledges India as Regional Force: Pledge to Share Civilian Nuclear Technology Follows Military Cooperation, Indian Navy Growth, The Jewish Institute for National Security Affairs, Washington, DC, 04 August 2005.

James Warner Bjorkman, "Public Law 480 and the Policies of Self-Help and Short-Tether: Indo-American Relations, 1965-68," in Lloyd I. Rudolph and Susanne Hoeber Rudolph, ed., *The Regional Imperative: U.S. Foreign Policy towards South Asian States* (New Jersey: 1980)

James Warner Bjorkman, "Public Law 480 and the Policies of Self-Help and Short-Tether: Indo-American Relations, 1965-68," in Lloyd I. Rudolph and Susanne Hoeber Rudolph, ed., *The Regional Imperative: U.S. Foreign Policy towards South Asian States* (New Jersey: 1980)

Jasjit Singh, "A partnership for the Future", *Daily News Analysis*, July 10, 2006, available at: http://www.dnaindia.com/report.asp?NewsID=1040808&CatID=19

Jasjit Singh, "India Wants Nuclear Disarmament, NOT JUST A ban on Test,", *International Herald Tribune*, Jnue 26, 1996.

Jaswant Singh, Against Nuclear Apartheid, *Foreign Affairs*, September/October 1998. Posted on the Indian Embassy website.

Jaswant Singh, India-U.S. Strategic Partnership: Perceptions, Potential, and Problems, Speech delivered at The Brookings Institution, Washington, DC, 31 May 2005 (.pdf file).

Jay Bushkinsky, "Radar System Sale to India Approved," *The Washington Times*, March 1, 2004.

Jefferson E. Turner, What is Driving India's and Pakistan's Interest in Joining the Shanghai Cooperation Organization, *Strategic Insights*. Center for Contemporary Conflict, U.S. Naval Postgraduate School, August 2005.

Jeffrey E. Key, "Beyond Tilting Both Ways: A New Post Cold War South Asia Policy," *Asian Affairs* 25, No.2, Summer 1998, 116.

Jim Lobe, "US Critics Question Nuclear Pact With India," (*http://www.antiwar.com/lobe/?articleid=8660*) *AntiWar.com*, March 4, 2006.

Jim VandeHei and Dafna Linzer, "U.S., India Reach Deal On Nuclear Cooperation. With Fuel Imports Allowed, Arms Program Could Grow," (*http://www.washingtonpost.com/wp-dyn/content/article/2006/03/02/AR2006030200183.html?nav=rss_email/components?nav=slate*) *Washington Post*, March 2, 2006.

Jim Vandehei and John Lancaster, "Bush offers Praise to Pakistani Leader," *The Washington Post*, March 5, 2006, A1; also see Editorial Board, "A Message for Gen. Musharraf," *The Washington Post*, March 2, 2006, A20.

John R. Bolton, "An All-Out War on Proliferation," *The Financial Times*, September 7, 2004, available at: www.acronym.org.uk/docs/0409/doc01.htm.

John W. Garver, The China-India-U.S. Triangle: Strategic Relations in the Post-Cold War Era, The National Bureau of Asian Research, Seattle, WA, October 2002 (.pdf file).

Joint Press Statement: Next Steps in Strategic Partnership between India and the United States", Washington DC, September 17, 2004, available at: http://www.indianembassy.org/press_release/2004/sep/17.htm

Joint Statement Between President George W. Bush and Prime Minister Manmohan Singh, White House, 18 July 2005.

Joint Statement between the United States of America and the Republic of India," November 9, 2001, available at www.whitehouse.gov/news/releases/2001/11/20011109-10.html.

Joint Statement by India-U.S. Defence Policy Group

U.S. India Defense Policy Group, 2003. Posted on the Mt. Holyoke College website.

Joseph Cirincione, "The US's nuclear cave-in," (*http://www.atimes.com/atimes/South_Asia/HC04Df03.html*) *Asia Times*, March 4, 2006.

Josy Joseph, "India, U.S. to Discuss China Formally for First Time," *India Abroad*, October 11, 2002.

Josy Joseph, "India, US Hold Biggest-ever Joint War Exercise at Agra," *India Abroad*, May 24, 2002.

Jyotika Saksena & Suzette Grillot, "The Emergence of Indo-US Defence Cooperation: From Specific to Diffuse Reciprocity", *Engaging India,* edited by Gary K. Bertsch, Seema Gahlaut & Anupam Srivastava, (New York: Routledge, 1999).

Jyotika Saksena & Suzette Grillot, "The Emergence of Indo-US Defence Cooperation: From Specific to Diffuse Reciprocity", *Engaging India*, edited by Gary K. Bertsch, Seema Gahlaut & Anupam Srivastava, (New York: Routledge, 1999).

K. Alan Kronstadt and Kenneth Katzman, India-Iran Relations and U.S. Interests, Congressional Research Service, 02 August 2006 (.pdf file).

K. Alan Kronstadt, "India-U.S. Relations," *CRS Issue Brief for Congress*, July 29, 2004.

K. Alan Kronstadt, India-U.S. Relations, Congressional Research Service, 31 July 2006 (.pdf file).

K. Subrahmanyam, "A Meaningless Treaty," *The Economic Times*, July 6, 1996.

K. Subrahmanyam, "Enduring Failures: US Dancing to Pakistan's Tune," *The Times of India*, July 26, 2002.

K. Subrahmanyam, "Hidden strings and free lunches," *The Indian Express*, May 18, 2005, at http://indianexpress.com/full_story.php?content_id=70543

K. Subrahmanyam, A New Nuclear Age, Reuven Pedhatsur. *Haaretz*, Israel, 08 March 2006.

Kalyan Chaudhuri, "Routes of Promise," *Frontline*, Vol. 20, Issue 14, July 5-18, 2004.

Kanti Bajpai, Add Five 'E's To Make a Partnership
The Washington Quarterly, Summer 2001 (.pdf file).

Karen Yourish Roston and Delano D'Souza, "Despite Khan, Military ties with Pakistan to Grow," *Arms Control Today*, April 2004.

Kaushik Vyas, "High Technology, Dual Use Technology and Critical Economic Issues," roundtable at "U.S.-India Bilateral Cooperation: Taking Stock and Moving Forward," a conference hosted by The Sigur Center for Asian Studies of The Elliott School of International A.airs at The George Washington University, Washington, D.C. April 1-2, 2004.

Kenneth I. Juster, "Cybersecurity: A Key to U.S.-India Trade," keynote address to the India-U.S. Information Security Summit 2004, New Delhi, India, October 12, 2004, available at www.state.gov/p/sa/rls/rm/37039.htm.

Kenneth I. Juster, Cybersecurity: A Key to U.S.-India Trade, Keynote Address at the India-U.S. Information Security Summit, 12 October 2004. Posted on the Bureau of Industry and Security, U.S. Department of Commerce website.

Kenneth Juster, "Widening High-Tech Trade," remarks presented at "U.S.-India Bilateral Cooperation: Taking Stock and Moving Forward," a conference hosted by The Sigur Center for Asian Studies of The Elliott School of International Affairs at The George Washington University, Washington, D.C. April 1-2, 2004.

Khalilzad, Zalmay, Losing the Unipolar Moment. *The Washington Quarterly*. 18 87-107.

Kissinger, Henry A., Does America Need a Foreign Policy? *In* Towards a Diplomacy for the 21st Century. 2001. Simon & Schuster; New York. p. 17

Kristol William and Robert Kagan, "Towards a Neo-Reaganite Foreign Policy". *Foreign Affairs*. July/August 1996, 18-32.

L. Venkateshwaran, Indo-U.S. Military Cooperation: U.S. Perceptions, Institute of Peace and Conflict Studies, New Delhi, 10 June 2006.

Laxman B. Bahroo, India Looks East . *Bharat Rakshak Monitor*, November/December 2000.

Lee Feinstein et al, A New Equation: U.S. Policy Toward India and Pakistan After September 11, Carnegie Endowment for International Peace, May 2002 (.pdf file).

Left Turns Red at Natwar's Iraq Troops Remark," *The Times of India*, June 11, 2004.

Leonard Weiss, Power Points: The U.S.-India Nuclear Agreement is the Wrong Deal with the Wrong Energy Source, *Bulletin of the Atomic Scientists*, May/June 2006.

Letter to Congress, Arms Control Association, 20 June 2006 (.pdf file).

Lloyd I. Rudolph and Susanne Hoeber Rudolph, Why Bush Blinked, *The Times of India*, March 2006.

Lloyd Richardson, Now, Play the India Card, *Policy Review*, Washington, DC, October 2002.

Lora Saalman, Redrawing India's Geostrategic Maps with China and the United States, *ZNet*. Woods Hole, MA, 22 September 2005.

Lora Saalman, The Implications of the U.S.-India Strategic Partnership, Power and Interest News Report, 05 August 2005.

M. S. Kohli, "Down the Memory Lane China's Missile Tests", *India Strategic*, vol. 1 issue 1 July 2006.

Mandavi Mehta and Teresita C. Schaffer, India And The United States: Security Interests, *South Asia Monitor*. Center for Strategic and International Studies, Washington, DC, 01 June 2001 (.pdf file).

Mandelbaum, Michael, The Bush Foreign Policy. *Foreign Affairs*. "America and the World". 1990/91, pp. 5-22.

Mapping the Global Future, Report of the National Intelligence Council's 2020 Project, CIA, December 2004 (.pdf file).

Marshall, Joshua Micah, Remaking the World: Bush and the Neoconservatives. *Foreign Affairs*. November/December 2003, 142-146.

Martin Walker, "India to fight U.S. nuclear deal," (*http://www.upi.com/InternationalIntelligence/view.php?StoryID=20060223-064857-9002r*) UPI, February 23, 2006.

Mary Beth Nikitin and Jon Wolfsthal, The U.S.-India Nuclear Agreement, Center for Strategic and International Studies, Washington, DC, 03 March 2006.

Matthew Cooper, The President's Passage to India, *Time Magazine*, 23 February 2006.

Matthew S. Borman, "NSSP: U.S., India Interests in Action," *The Hindu*, October 2, 2004.

Maynes, Charles William, What the US Must Do to Regain the Respect of the World. P*hiladelphia Inquirer.* April 14, 1995.

Mead, Walter Russell, *Special Providence: American Foreign Policy and How it Changed the World.* 2001. Foundation Books; New York.

Michael A. Levi and Charles D. Ferguson, U.S.-India Nuclear Cooperation: A Strategy for Moving Forward, Council on Foreign Relations, June 2006 (.pdf file).

Michael Forsythe and Veena Trehan, "Friends in high places help India (*http://www.iht.com/articles/2006/07/17/bloomberg/sxrupee.php*)", *International herald Tribune*, July 17, 2006.

Michael Krepon, Betting the Ranch on the U.S.-India Nuclear Deal, The Henry L. Stimson Center, 05 June 2006.

Michael Krepon, The U.S.-India Nuclear Deal: Another Wrong Turn in the War on Terror, The Henry L. Stimson Center, 29 March 2006.

Mira Kamdar, India and the New American Hegemony, *Connecticut Journal of International Law*, Spring 2004. Posted on the author's website.

Mira Kamdar, "India and the New American Hegemony", *Connecticut Journal of International Law,* Vol. 19:3, Spring 2004, Special Issue: The New American Hegemony 154 *Strategic Analysis/Jan-Mar 2004*

Mohammed Ayoob, India Matters, *The Washington Quarterly*, Winter 2000 (.pdf file).

Mohan Malik, China Responds to the U.S.-India Nuclear Deal, China Brief. The Jamestown Foundation, 29 March 2006.

Mohan Malik, The China Factor in the India-Pakistan Conflict, *Parameters*, U.S. Army War College, Spring 2003.

Myron Weiner, "Critical Choices for India and America", in Donald C. Hellmann, ed., *Southern Asia: The Politics of Poverty and Peace* (Lanham, Md.: 1976).

Nacht, Alexander, US Foreign Policy Strategies. *The Washington Quarterly*. Summer 1995, 195-210.

Navnita Chadha Behera, Kashmir: Redefining the U.S. Role, Policy Brief #110, Brookings Institution, November 2002 (.pdf file).

N-Deal: Boon for India, US, World . *Rediff*, India, 09 March 2006.

New Framework for the U.S.-India Defense Relationship, Signed by Indian Defense Minister Pranab Mukherjee and U.S. Defense Secretary Donald Rumsfeld, Washington, DC, 28 June 2005. (Note: Will open as a Word document).

Noorani, A. G., Manufacturing Consent. *The Hindustan Times*. November 26, 2002.

Norman Palmer, "Indo-American Relations: The Politics of Encounter", *South Asia and US Policy,* 23, Summer, 1979, pp. 403-19.

Nuclear Deal with India Breaks with Past U.S. Policy," (*http://www.npr.org/templates/story/story.php?storyId=5243419*) NPR, March 3, 2006.

Nuclear Issues in India and Pakistan: Selected Internet Resources," (*http://www.lib.berkeley.edu/SSEAL/SouthAsia/nuclear.html*) University of California Berkeley.

Nuclear Power Corporation of India Limited, (*http://www.npcil.nic.in*).

Nuclear Power in India and Pakistan," (*http://www.world-nuclear.org/info/inf53.htm*) World Nuclear Association, February 2006.

Nuclear Weapons, Energy and Nonproliferation: Pressures on the Global Community, 41st Conference on the United Nations of the Next Decade, sponsored by The Stanley Foundation, Sedona, AZ, 16-21 June 2006 (.pdf file).

Nuclear Weapons, India (*http://www.fas.org/nuke/guide/india/nuke*), Federation of American Scientists, Last Updated November 8, 2002.

Nye, Joseph S. Jr., Redefining the National Interest. *Foreign Affairs*. July/August 1999.

P. Chari, "High on Hype: Indo-U.S. Tech Transfer Deal is Meaningless," *The Times of India*, October 11, 2004.

P.R. Chari, Parsing the Separation PLan: The Indo-U.S. Subsidiary Deal,

Institute of Peace and Conflict Studies, New Delhi, March 2006 (.pdf file).

Pact sends inspectors, U.S. expertise to India's nuclear programs," (*http://www.cnn.com/2006/WORLD/asiapcf/03/02/bush.india.visit/index.html*) CNN, March 3, 2006.

Pankaj Mishra, "Kashmir: One Cheer for Democracy," *New York Review of Books*, February 27, 2003.

Pankaj Mishra, The Myth of the New India, *The New York Times*, 06 July 2006.

Parag Khanna and C. Raja Mohan, Getting India Right, *Policy Review*, Washington, DC, February/March 2006.

Patrick E. Tyler and Celia W. Dugger, "Powell's Message: America's Courting of Pakistan Will Not Come at India's Expense," *New York Times,* October 18, 2001.

Paul D. Taylor, India and Pakistan: Thinking About the Unthinkable, *Naval War College Review*. U.S. Naval War College, Summer 2001.

Paul Richter, In Deal with India, Bush Has Eye on China, *Los Angeles Times*, 04 March 2006. Posted on the Global Policy Forum website.

People, Progress and Partnership: The Transformation of US-India Relations, Embassy of the United States of America, New Delhi.

Perkovich, George, Bush's Nuclear Revolution. *Foreign Affairs.* March/April 2003, 82 (2), pp. 2-8.

Peter Dougherty, "High Technology, Dual Use Technology and Critical Economic Issues," roundtable at "U.S.-India Bilateral Cooperation: Taking Stock *U.S.-India Relations: Ties That Bind? The Sigur Center Asia Papers* and Moving Forward," a conference hosted by The Sigur Center for Asian Studies of The Elliott School of International Affairs at The George Washington University, Washington, D.C. April 1-2, 2004.

Peter Wallsten, "Bush Brokers Landmark Nuclear Deal With India," (*http://www.latimes.com/news/nationworld/world/la-030206bush_lat,0,3005734.story?coll=la-home-headlines*) *Los Angeles Times*, March 2, 2006.

Praful Bidwai, India Moves Toward a New Compact with the United States, Foreign Policy in Focus, Silver City, NM and Washington, DC, 14 July 2005.

Praful Bidwai, Indo-U.S. Ties After the Bush Visit, *Rediff*, India, 06 March 2006.

Praful Bidwai, U.S. and India: Unequal Allies, Uneasy Partners, Antiwar.com, U.S., 06 October 2004.

Pramit Mitra and Vibhuti Hate, India-Iran Relations: Changing the Tone?, *South Asia Monitor*. Center for Strategic and International Studies, Washington, DC, 08 March 2006 (.pdf file).

Pramit Mitra, India's International Oil Ties Risk U.S. Displeasure, *International Herald Tribune*, 07 April 2005. Posted on the Center for Strategic and International Studies website (.pdf file).

Pratap Bhanu Mehta, Uncharted Waters, *Outlook India*, New Delhi, 07 March 2006.

President Bush's Visit to India (2006) Reviewed, Subhash Kapila. South Asia Analysis Group, Noida, India, 03 March 2006.

Public Opinion in India and America, World Public Opinion. Program on International Policy Attitudes, University of Maryland, 26 February 2006.

R. Nicholas Burns, Daniel Markey, Jessica Tuchman Mathews, George Perkovich, Ashley J. Tellis and Albert Thibault, "U.S.-India Relations: The Global Partnership",

panels sponsored by the Carnegie Endowment for International Peace, 16 May 2006. (.mp3 audio files).

R. Nicholas Burns, India and Pakistan: On the Heels of President Bush's Visit, Remarks to the Heritage Foundation, Washington, DC, 06 March 2006. Posted on the Mt. Holyoke College website.

R. Nicholas Burns, The U.S. and India: The New Strategic Partnership, Speech at the Asia Society, New York, 18 October 2005.

R. Ramachandran, "India, U.S. & Trade in Technology, *The Hindu*, September 27, 2004.

R. Ramachandran, "India, U.S. and Trade in Technology," *The Hindu*, September 27, 2004. For a direct response to this article, see Mathew Borman, "NSSP: U.S., India Interests in Action," *The Hindu*, October 2, 2004. See also P.R.

R. Ramachandran, "India, US and trade in technology", *The Hindu* (New Delhi), September 27, 2004

Rahman, Sabeel, Another New World Order. *Harvard International Review.* Winter 2002, pp. 40-44.

Rahul Bedi, "A New Doctrine for the Navy," *Frontline*, Vol. 21, Issue 14, July 3-16, 2004.

Rahul Bedi, "Strategic realignments," *Frontline*, Vol. 20, Issue 13, June 21-July 4, 2003.

Raja Menon, Off-Key Techno Notes: Indo-U.S. Technology Relations, Despite Go-Aheads From Top, Remain Rudderless, *Outlook India*, New Delhi, 19 April 2004.

Raja Mohan, C., "US and the World Since September 11". *World Focus,* August 2002, 23 (7&8).

Rajat Pandit, "Nixon badmouthed India", *The Times of India,* 17 June 2005.

Rajat Pandit, "Nixon badmouthed India", *Times of India,* 17 June 2005.

Rajesh Kumar Mishra, Indo-U.S. Nuclear Deal and Non-Proliferation, *Strategic Analysis.* Institute for Defence Studies and Analyses, New Delhi, October-December 2005 (.pdf file).

Rajesh Kumar Mishra, Indo-U.S. Relation and the China Factor: Realities and Compulsions . South Asia Analysis Group, Noida, India, 25 September 2000.

Rajesh Kumar Mishra, South Asian Quagmire: U.S.-India Relations after December 13, South Asia Analysis Group, Noida, India, 21 December 2001.

Raju G. C. Thomas, "U.S. Transfers of "Dual-Use" Technologies to India," *Asian Survey*, Vol. XXX, No. 9, September 1990.

Ram Narayanan, "Is a Solid and a Comprehensive US-India Strategic Partnership Inevitable?", www.usindiafriendship.net

Ram Narayanan, Is a Solid and Comprehensive U.S.-India Strategic Partnership Inevitable?, Presentation made to Security and Political Risk Analysis at the India International Center, New Delhi, 17 January 2005. Posted on the U.S.-India Friendship website.

Ram Narayanan, The U.S., India and China, *United Press International*, 09 February 2005.

Randeep Ramesh, Spinning a Web for India, *The Guardian*, UK, 03 March 2006.

Ranjit Bhushan, "Shock Therapy," *Outlook India*, December 24, 2001.

Rapid India-U.S. Military Links Stagger Officials, *NewsInsight*, New Delhi, 02 February 2002.

Remarks by Foreign Secretary Shri Shyam Saran at the Opening Session of Fourth India-US High-Technology Cooperation Group Meeting, available at http://www.mea.gov.in/

Reshmi Kazi, "Proliferation Security Initiative and India," *Peace and Conflict*, Vol. 7, No. 7, October 2004;

Rice, Condoleezza, quoted by Michael O Hanlon, Come Partly Home America. How to Downsize US Deployment Abroad. *Foreign Affairs.* March/April, 2001.

Richard N. Haass, The United States and India: A Transformed Relationship, Remarks to the Confederation of Indian Industry, Hyderabad, 07 January 2003.

Richard Speier, U.S. Space Aid to India: On a "Glide Path" to ICBM Trouble?, *Arms Control Today*, Washington, DC, March 2006.

Richard T. Cupitt and Seema Gahlaut, "Non—Proliferation Export Controls: US and Indian Perspectives," in *Engaging India: US Strategic Relations with the World's Largest Democracy*, ed. Gary K. Bertsch, Seema Gahlaut, and Anupam Srivastava (New York: Routledge, 1999)

Richard Ullman, "The Covert French Connection," *Foreign Policy* 75 (Summer 1989)

Rielly, John E., America and the World: A Survey at Century's End. *Foreign Policy.* Spring 1999, 97-114.

Rober D. Blackwill, The Quality and Durability of the U.S.-India Relationship, Speech delivered in Kolkata, India, 27 November 2002. Posted on the Mt. Holyoke College website.

Robert D. Blackwill, "A New Deal for New Delhi," *The Wall Street Journal,* March 21, 2005

Robert D. Blackwill, The India Imperative, *The National Interest*, Washington, DC, Summer 2005.

Robert D. Blackwill, The United States, India and Asian Security, Presented to the 5th Asia Security Conference sponsored by the Institute for Defense Analyses, New Delhi, 27 January 2003. Posted on the Mt. Holyoke College website.

Robert D. Blackwill, US Ambassador to India, "The Quality and Durability of the US-India Relationship," Kolkata, India,

November 27, 2002; available at http://www.mtholyoke.edu/acad/intrel/bush/blackwill.htm

Robert Hathaway, "Unfinished Passage: India, Indian Americans, and the U.S. Congress," *The Washington Quarterly*, Vol. 24, No. 2, Spring 2001, available at: *http://www.state.gov/t/np/rls/rm/32293.htm*.

Robert J. Einhorn, The U.S.-India Nuclear Deal, Testimony before the House International Relations Committee, 26 October 2005. Posted on the Center for Strategic and International Studies website (.pdf file).

Robert M. Hathaway, "Coming of Age: Indian-Americans and the US Congress", no. 9, *India-US Relations: A Paradigm Shift*.

Robert O. Blake, Jr., "U.S. Foreign Policy Challenges," Address given at the Observer Research Foundation, New Delhi, January 23, 2004, at http://newdelhi.usembassy.gov/wwwhpr12304a.html

Robert O. Blake, U.S.-India Relations: The Making of a Comprehensive Relationship, Speech delivered in Indore, India, 23 August 2004. Posted on the Mt. Holyoke College website.

Robert S. Norris and Hans M. Kristensen, "India's nuclear forces, 2005" *http://www.thebulletin.org/article _ nn. php? art_of n=so05 norris*) Federation of American Scientists, September/October 2005.

Robert Z. Lawrence and Rajesh Chada, "Should a U.S.-India FTA Be Part of India's Trade Strategy?" in Suman Bery, Barry Bosworth, and Arvind Panagariya, eds., *India Policy Forum* 2004, Volume 1 (Washington, D.C., and New Delhi)

Rollie Lal and Rajesh Rajagopalan, U.S.-India Strategic Dialogue, RAND, 2005 (.pdf file).

Ron Hutcheson and Jonathan S. Landay, "Nuclear Pact between U.S., India Draws Fire," (*http://www.commondreams.org/headlines06/0303-06.htm*) Knight Ridder (*Common Dreams*), March 3, 2006.

Ronen Sen, Indo-U.S. Relations: Where Are They Headed?, Text of lecture sponsored by the Center for the Advanced Study of India, University of Pennsylvania, 26 October 2005 (.pdf file).

S. D. Muni, "India and the Post-Cold War: Opportunities and Challenges," *Asian Survey* (September 1991), pp. 862–74.

S. Enders Wimbush, Tech That, and That: Not Ideology, But a Convergence of Interests is Shaping the New Indo-U.S. Ties, *Outlook India*, New Delhi, 01 August 2005.

S. Raghavan, India-U.S. Defence Pact - II: Commitments May Fetter Judgment, *The Hindu Business Line*, India, 14 July 2005.

Sameer Suryakant Patil, India-U.S. Civilian Nuclear Deal: Impact on Asian Balance of Power, Institute of Peace and Conflict Studies, New Delhi, 17 March 2006.

Sandeep Dikshit, "Decoding India-US defence tie-up", *The Hindu* (New Delhi), July 5, 2005

Sapolsky, Harvey M., Eugene Gholz, and Allen Kaufmann, Security Lessons from the Cold War. *Foreign Affairs*. July-August 1999, pp. 77-89.

Satu P. Limaye, Hearing on 'The U.S.-India 'Global Partnership': How Significant for American Interests?', Testimony before the Committee on International Relations, U.S. House of Representatives, 16 November 2005 (.pdf file).

Satu P. Limaye, Mediating Kashmir: A Bridge Too Far, *The Washington Quarterly*, Winter 2002-03 (.pdf file).

Schlesinger, Arthur, *New York Review of Books*. October 23, 2003.

Schlesinger, James, Quest for a Post-Cold War Foreign Policy. *Foreign Affairs*. 1992/93, 72 America and the World, 17—28.

Seal Scorpene Deal Fast: Navy Chief," *The Times of India*, August 12, 2004.

Secretary of State Condoleezza Rice, "Interview with Shirvaj Prasad of NDTV," New Delhi, India, March 16, 2005, available at www.state.gov/secretary/rm/2005/43511.htm.

Secretary of State Condoleezza Rice, "Remarks at Sophia University," Tokyo, March 19, 2005, available at www.state.gov/secretary/rm/2005/43655.htm.

Secretary of State Condoleezza Rice, "Remarks with Indian Minister of External Affairs Natwar Singh Following Meeting," Department of State, Washington, D.C., April 14, 2005, available at: www.state.gov/secretary/rm/2005/44662.htm.

Secretary of State Condoleezza Rice, Interview With Raj Chengappa of *India Today,* New Delhi, India, March 16, 2005,available at: www.state.gov/secretary/rm/2005/43626.htm.

Secretary of State Condoleezza Rice, Remarks with Indian Foreign Minister Natwar Singh, Hyderabad House, New Delhi,India, March 16, 2005, available at www.state.gov/secretary/rm/2005/43490.htm.

Seeking Breakthroughs: The Meandering U.S.-India Relationship Needs A Fresh Impetus, Ashley J. Tellis, *Force* (October 2004).

Seema Gahlaut, "Misfiring at the India Nuclear Deal," available at: *http://www.foreignpolicy.com/story/cms.php?story_id=3404*) *Foreign Policy*, February 27, 2006.

Selig Harrison, How to Regulate Nuclear Weapons: The U.S. Deal With India Could Be a Good Starting Point, *Washington Post*, 23 April 2006. Posted on the Center for International Policy website.

Selig S. Harrison, "A nuclear partnership with India," *http://www.boston.com/news/world/asia/articles/2006/03/02/a_nuclear_partnership_with_india/*) *Boston Globe*, March 2, 2006.

Senator Kennedy's Remarks at United States-India Conference, May 20, 1959, available at: *http://www.jfklink.com/speeches/jfk/congress/jfk200559_usindiaconference.html*

Sergounin, Alexander A., An Age of Uncertainty: Building a Post-Cold War US Security Strategy for East and South East Asia. *Journal of North East Asian Studies.* Summer 1997, 15 (2).

Seventh Meeting of the India-US Defence Policy Group, Press Release, November21-23, Washington D.C. available at: http://www.indianembassy.org/press_release/2005/Nov/37.htm

Sharon Squassoni, India's Nuclear Separation Plan: Issues and Views, Congressional Research Service, 03 March 2006 (.pdf file).

Sharon Squassoni, U.S. Nuclear Cooperation with India: Issues for Congress, Congressional Research Service, 29 July 2005 (.pdf file).

Shehzad Nadeem, The Regional Implications of the U.S.-India Nuclear Agreement, Foreign Policy in Focus, 29 April 2006.

Shekhar Gupta, *India Redefines its Role* (Oxford: 1995)

Shyam Saran, Transforming India-U.S. Relations: Building a Strategic Partnership, Speech at the Carnegie Endowment for International Peace, 21 December 2005 (.pdf file).

Siddharth Srivastava, "Now Indians Cry Foul Over Iraq,"*Asia Times Online*, May 8, 2004.

Siddharth Varadarajan, "F-16s for Pakistan Will Fuel Arms Race," *The Hindu,* March 27, 2005, available at www.hindu.com/2005/03/27/stories/2005032707050100.htm.

Siddharth Varadarajan, America, India and the Outsourcing of Imperial Overreach, *The Hindu*, India, 13 July 2005. Posted on the author's blog.

Siddharth Varadarajan, Defence Pact with the U.S.: India Entering Risky Territory, *The Hindu*, India, 01 July 2005. Posted on the author's blog.

Siddharth Varadarajan, Indo-U.S. Nuclear Deal: Safeguards for Breeder Reactors a Key Obstacle, *The Hindu*, India, 21 January 2006. Posted on the Global Research website.

Siddharth Varadarajan, The Piper's Price: India and the U.S. After Kargil, *The Times of India*, 17 July 1999. Posted on the author's blog.

Siddharth Varadarajan, The Truth Behind the Indo-U.S. Nuclear Deal, *The Hindu*, India, 29 July 2005.

Simes, Dimitri K., America's Imperial Dilemma. *Foreign Affairs.* November- December, 2003, 82 (6).

Sisir Gupta, "The Indian Dilemma," in Alastair Buchan, ed., *A World of Nuclear Powers?* Englewood Cliffs, NJ: Prentice Hall, 1966.

Sitakanta Mishra, "Making America More Indian", *Mainstream*, 22-28 October 2006.

Sixth and Seventh Reviews Under the Three Year Arrangement Under the Poverty Reduction and Growth Facility and Request for Waiver of Performance Criteria," *IMF Country Report,* No. 03/338, Washington: IMF Publications Services, October 2003

Snehalata Panda, Sino-Indian Relations in a New Perspective, *Strategic Analysis*. Institute for Defence Studies and Analyses, New Delhi, January-March 2005 (.pdf file).

Sonia Trikha, "We have questions about Pakistan: Armitage", Indian Express (New Delhi), May 12, 2001.

Sridhar Krishnaswami, "U.S. to Ease Curbs on Space, N-facilities," *The Hindu*, September 20, 2004.

Stephen Cohen, The United States and South Asia: Core Interests and Policies and Their Impact on Regional Countries,

Presented at the Conference on Major Powers and South Asia, 11-13 August 2003. Posted on The Brookings Institution website on 01 October 2003 (.pdf file).

Stephen J. Blank, Natural Allies? Regional Security in Asia and Prospects for Indo-American Strategic Cooperation, available at: http://www.strategicstudiesinstitute.army.mil/pdffiles/PUB626.pdf

Stephen J. Blank, Natural Allies? Regional Security in Asia and Prospects for Indo-American Strategic Cooperation, Strategic Studies Institute, U.S. Army War College, September 2005 (.pdf file).

Stephen P. Cohen, India and America: An Emerging Relationship, Paper presented to the Conference on The Nation-State System and Transnational Forces in South Asia, Kyoto, Japan, 08-10 December 2000. Posted on The Brookings Institution website (.pdf file).

Stephen P. Cohen, Moving Forward in South Asia, The Brookings Institution, May 2001 (.pdf file).

Stephen Philip Cohen, India and the Middle East, Testimony before the Committee on International Relations, U.S. House of Representatives, 16 November 2005 (.pdf file).

Stephen Zunes, Bush Administration Stokes Dangerous Arms Race on Indian Subcontinent, Foreign Policy in Focus, Silver City, NM and Washington, DC, 20 July 2005.

Steven Mufson, "One Man's Long Battle To Get U.S. to Kick Oil (*http://www.washingtonpost.com/wp-dyn/content/article/2006/07/24/AR2006072400976.html*)", *Washington Post*, July 25, 2006.

Strobe Talbott, "Dealing with the bomb in South Asia," *Foreign Affairs*, Vol. 78, No. 2, March 1999, p. 120.

Strobe Talbott, "The Changing Nature of U.S.-India Relations: The Clinton, Bush Eras and Beyond" remarks presented at "U.S.-India Bilateral Cooperation: Taking Stock and Moving Forward" conference hosted by The Sigur Center for Asian Studies of The Elliott School of International Affairs at The George Washington University, Washington, D.C. April 1-2, 2004.

Strobe Talbott, Dealing with the Bomb in South Asia, *Foreign Affairs*, March/April 1999. Posted on the Fletcher School website at Tufts University (.pdf file).

Strobe Talbott, From Estrangement to Engagement: U.S.-India Relations Since May 1998, Text of lecture sponsored by the Center for the Advanced Study of India, University of Pennsylvania, 13 October 2004 (.pdf file).

Strobe Talbott, Good Day for India, Bad Day for Non-Proliferation . *International Herald Tribune*, 21 July 2005. Posted on The Brookings Institution website.

Strobe Talbott, U.S. Department of State Deputy Secretary Talbott Address at India International Center, Address at the India International Center, New Delhi, 30 January 1999. Posted on the Mt. Holyoke College website.

Subhash Kapila, India-USA Strategic Partnership: The Advent of the Inevitable, South Asia Analysis Group, Noida, India, 22 April 2000.

Subhash Kapila, South Asia Security- Divergence in United States and India's Perceptions: An Analysis, South Asia Analysis Group, Noida, India, 22 January 2002.

Subhash Kapila, United States and the Agra Summit, South Asia Analysis Group, Noida, India, 10 August 2001.

Subhash Kapila, United States-India Civil Nuclear Deal Reviewed, South Asia Analysis Group, Noida, India, 10 January 2006.

Subhash Kapila, United States-India Defense Relationship Agreement (June 2005) Analysed, South Asia Analysis Group, Noida, India, 06 July 2005.

Sudha Ramachandran, "India, Iran, Russia Map Out Trade Route," *Asia Times*, June 29, 2002.

Sulochana Raghavan Glazer and Nathan Glazer, "Introduction" in Sulochana Raghaven Glazer and Nathan Glazer,ed., *Conflicting Images: India and the United States* (Glen Dale, Md.: 1990)

Sultan Shahin, "India and Pakistan in nuclear dead heat," *http://www.atimes.com/atimes/South_Asia/FJ16Df05.html*) *Asia Times*, October 16, 2004.

Sultan Shahin, India Doubting Its U.S. 'Strategic Partnership', *Asia Times*, Hong Kong, 27 March 2004.

Suman Bery, "Needed: A U.S.-India FTA," *Rediff.com,* Business, November 9, 2004, available at: http://us.rediff.com/money/2004/nov/09guest1.htm.

Sumit Ganguly and Andrew Scobell, India and the United States: Forging a Security Partnership?, *World Policy Journal*, New York, Summer 2005.

Sumit Ganguly, "Giving India a Pass," *Foreign Affairs*, August 17, 2005.

Sumit Ganguly, The Start of a Beautiful Friendship? The United States and India, *World Policy Journal*, New York, Spring 2003.

Surjit Mansingh, *India's Search for Power,* New Delhi: Sage Publications, 1984, p. 71.

Swaminathan S. Anklesaria Aiyar, U.S. and India: Partners, Not Allies, *The Times of India*, 26 February 2006.

T. Jayaraman, "India's Bush Backers," *The Hindu*, November 23, 2004.

T.V. Paul, "The Systemic Bases of India's Challenge to the Global Nuclear Order", *The Non-proliferation Review,* Fall 1998, pp. 1-11.

Tara Shankar Sahay, "India Hands Over List of 20 Wanted Terrorists to Pakistan," *India Abroad*, January 11, 2002.

Teresita C. Schaffer and Mandavi Mehta, Rising India and U.S. Policy Options in Asia, *South Asia Monitor*. Center for Strategic and International Studies, Washington, DC, 01 December 2001 (.pdf file).

Teresita C. Schaffer and Pramit Mitra, India as a Global Power, Deutsche Bank Research, 16 December 2005. Posted on the Center for Strategic and International Studies website (.pdf file).

Teresita C. Schaffer, Building a New Partnership with India, *The Washington Quarterly*, Spring 2002 (.pdf file).

Teresita Schaffer, India and the United States: Turning A Corner, *South Asia Monitor*. Center for Strategic and International Studies, Washington, DC, 01 August 2005 (.pdf file).

Text of Ambassador Robert Blackwill's speech" at the Confederation of Indian Industry, New Delhi, July 17, 2003; available at http://www.rediff.com/news/2003/jul/17black1.htm?zcc=rl.

Text of the "India-US Energy Dialogue Joint Statement", Washington DC, May 31, 2005, available at: http://www.indianembassy.org/press_release/2005/May/5.htm

Text of the India-US Joint Statement on the occasion of the official working visit of Prime Minister Atal Bihari Vajpayee to Washington DC" November 9, 2001, available at: www.mea.gov.in

The American Vision of U.S.-India Economic Cooperation ,16 September,2004, *Press Release,* by US Embassy, *http://chennai.usconsulate.gov/wwwhprind.html*

The Carnegie Endowment for U.S. Strategy: Assisting Pakistan's Transformation, Ashley J. Tellis,*The Washington Quarterly* (Winter 2004–2005).

The Credibility Question, *NewsInsight*, New Delhi, 28 February 2006.

The documents declassified and available at the U.S. National Archives and the Presidential Library system detail how United States policy, directed by Richard Nixon and Henry Kissinger, followed a course that became infamously known as "The Tilt." Sanjay Gandhi, ed., *The Tilt: The U.S. and the South Asian Crisis of 1971*, National Security Archive Electronic Briefing Book No. 79, December 16, 2002.

The Eternal India-Pakistan-US Triangle, Husain Haqqani, *Gulf News* (April 6, 2005).

The Great Indian Hope Trick, *The Economist*, 23 February 2006.

The India-China Relationship: What the United States Needs To Know

Conference Report. Asia Society and the Woodrow Wilson International Center for Scholars, Washington, DC, 30 November 2001 (.pdf file).

The Seventh Flight of the Brahmos," *Frontline*, Vol. 21, Issue 13, June 19-July 2, 2004.

The Times of India, August 7, 2004. While the FTA may make economic sense, there are serious political hurdles to be overcome. For an excellent discussion on the political economy of a U.S.-India FTA, see Robert Lawrence and Rajesh Chadha, "Should a U.S.-India FTA be Part of India's

The U.S. role in getting Pakistan's troops to withdraw from Kargil is described in Bruce Riedel, "American Diplomacy and the 1999 Kargil Summit at Blair House," Center for the Advanced Study of India, Policy Paper Series 2002, available at: *http://www.sas.upenn.edu/casi/reports/RiedelPaper051302.htm.*

The U.S.-India Nuclear Cooperation Agreement: Issues for the Nuclear Suppliers Group, Summary of conference sponsored by The Stanley Foundation, in New York, 24 April 2006 (.pdf file).

The U.S.-India Nuclear Cooperation Deal, Arms Control Association Page Resource Page, 24 July 2006.

The U.S.-India Nuclear Deal: The End Game Begins," (*http:// www.pinr.com report.php? ac= view_report& report_id=428 & language_id=1*) *PINR*, January 27, 2006.

The White House, A National Security Strategy for a New Century and The White House, Washington DC. October 1998.

Thomas Glardon, Balancing U.S. Interests Amidst the India and Pakistan Conflict, Strategic Studies Institute, U.S. Army War College, 18 March 2005 (.pdf file).

Thomas L. Friedman, "Vote France Off the Island," *New York Times*, February 9, 2003.

Thomas Pickering, "U.S. Policy in South Asia: The Road Ahead", Address to the Foreign Policy Institute, Johns Hopkins University, Washington DC, April 27, 2000, *Washington File* (New Delhi), April 28, 2000.

Thomas R. Pickering, "U.S. Policy in South Asia: The Road Ahead," address to the Foreign Policy Institute, South Asia Program, Paul H. Nitze School of Advanced International Studies, Johns Hopkins University, Washington, D.C., April 27, 2000, available at www.fas.org/news/pakistan/2000/ 000427_pickering_sa.htm.

U.S. Congress, House Committee on Foreign Affairs, *Subcommittee on the Near East and South Asia, The United States and South Asia,* 93rd Congress, 1st session, 25 May 1973.

U.S. Department of State, "Background Briefing by Administration Officials on U.S.-South Asia Relations," March 25,2005, available at www.state.gov/r/pa/prs/ps/2005/43853.htm.

U.S. Department of State, *South Asia, Office of the Historian,* FRUS, Vol. XIX, 1961-1963

U.S. Nuclear Cooperation With India: Issues for Congress" prepared by Sharon Squassoni, Specialist in National Defense, Foreign Affairs, Defense, and Trade Division, Congressional Research Service, Updated January

12, 2006, available at: *http://fpc.state.gov/documents/organization/59365.pdf*

U.S., India Announce Progress in Strategic Trade Talks, US Embassy in India, *Press Releases*, 17 September 2004.

U.S.-India Defense Relationship, U.S. Department of Defense fact sheet, March 2006 (.pdf file).

U.S.-India Joint Statement during President George W. Bush's Visit to India

White House, 02 March 2006.

US and India seal nuclear accord," (*http://news.bbc.co.uk/1/hi/world/south_asia/4764826.stm*) BBC, March 2, 2006. Transcript: US-India agreement, *http://news.bbc.co.uk/1/hi/world/south_asia/4766256.stm*), March 2, 2006.

US-India Nuclear Accord 2006

US-India Partnership: Cooperation and Trust, New York, September 21, 2004, available at: http://www.indianembassy.org/press_release/2004/sep/21.htm

US-India Relations: The Making of a Comprehensive Relationship Remarks by Robert O. Blake, Jr., Chargé d'Affaires, US Embassy in India, *Press Release*, 23 August 2004.

Vijay Sakhuja, Iran Stirs India-U.S. Waters, Institute of Peace and Conflict Studies, New Delhi, 10 April 2006.

Walker, Martin, A New American Isolationism. *International Journal*. Summer 1997.

We Facilitated Indo-Pak talks: US. *The Hindustan Times*. February 19, 2004.

William C. Potter, India and The New Look of U.S. Nonproliferation Policy, Center for Nonproliferation Studies, Monterey, CA, 25 August 2005.

Wills Garry, Bully of the Free World. *Foreign Affairs*. March/April, 1999, pp. 50-59.

World Nuclear Association, "Thorium," Information and Issue Briefs, November 2004, available at: www.world-nuclear.org/info/inf62.htm.

Y. K. Malik and Ashok Kapur, "India and America: Engaging Each Other in a Changing World", in Ashok Kapur, Y. K. Malik, Harold Gould, Arthur G. Rubinoff (*Eds.*), *India and The United States In A Changing World,* New Delhi: Sage Publications, 2002, pp. 1-39.

Zakaria Fareed, "Nixon to China, Bush to India; Thirty years of lectures on nonproliferation and sanctions have done nothing to stop, slow down or make India's nuclear program safer,"*Newsweek,* February 27, 2006, 45.

Zalmay Khalilzad, David Orletsky, Jonathan Pollack, Kevin Pollpeter, Angel Rabasa, David Shlapak, Abram Shulsky, and Ashley J. Tellis, *The United States and Asia: Toward a New U.S. Strategy and Force Posture* (Santa Monica, Calif.: RAND, 2001)

Zhang Guihong, U.S. Security Policy Toward South Asia After September 11th and Its Implications for China: A Chinese Perspective, Henry L. Stimson Center, January 2003 (.pdf file).

Zhang Guihong, U.S-India Security Relations: Implications for China, *Faultlines.* Institute for Conflict Management, New Delhi, 2003.

Zia Mian, The United States, China, and India: A Story of Leaders, Partners, and Clients, *Foreign Policy in Focus*, Silver City, NM and Washington, DC, 27 September 2005.

Index

D

O

P

R